THE NEW ENCYCLOPEDIA OF
AMERICAN
ANIMALS

THE NEW ENCYCLOPEDIA OF
AMERICAN ANIMALS

TOM JACKSON

CONSULTANT: MICHAEL CHINERY

HERMES
HOUSE

This edition is published by Hermes House
an imprint of Anness Publishing Ltd
Hermes House
88–89 Blackfriars Road
London SE1 8HA
tel. 020 7401 2077
fax 020 7633 9499

www.hermeshouse.com; www.annesspublishing.com

If you like the images in this book and would like to investigate using
them for publishing, promotions or advertising, please visit our website
www.practicalpictures.com for more information.

Publisher: Joanna Lorenz
Senior Managing Editor: Conor Kilgallon
Project Editor: Felicity Forster
Copy Editor: Steve Setford
Designer: Nigel Partridge
Map Illustrator: Anthony Duke

Illustrators: Jim Channell, Julius Csotonyi,
John Francis, Stuart Jackson-Carter, Paul Jones,
Martin Knowelden, Stephen Lings,
Richard Orr, Mike Saunders, Sarah Smith,
Ildikó Szegszárdy
Production Manager: Steve Lang

ETHICAL TRADING POLICY

At Anness Publishing we believe that business should be conducted in an ethical and ecologically sustainable way, with
respect for the environment and a proper regard to the replacement of the natural resources we employ. As a publisher,
we use a lot of wood pulp to make high-quality paper for printing, and that wood commonly comes from spruce trees.
We are therefore currently growing more than 500,000 trees in two Scottish forest plantations near Aberdeen –
Berrymoss (130 hectares/320 acres) and West Touxhill (125 hectares/305 acres). The forests we manage contain twice
the number of trees employed each year in paper-making for our books. Because of this ongoing ecological investment
programme, you, as our customer, can have the pleasure and reassurance of knowing that a tree is being cultivated on
your behalf to naturally replace the materials used to make the book you are holding. Our forestry programme is run in
accordance with the UK Woodland Assurance Scheme (UKWAS) and will be certified by the internationally recognized
Forest Stewardship Council (FSC). The FSC is a non-government organization dedicated to promoting responsible
management of the world's forests. Certification ensures forests are managed in an environmentally sustainable and
socially responsible basis. For further information about this scheme, go to www.annesspublishing.com/trees.

A CIP catalogue record for this book
is available from the British Library.

1 3 5 7 9 10 8 6 4 2

PAGE 1: *Guanaco.* PAGE 2: *Grizzly bear and cub.* PAGE 3: *Moose.* PAGE 4: *Kinkajou; California tiger salamander.*
PAGE 5: *Green anole; prairie dogs; cougar; Amazon squirrel monkey.*

CONTENTS

INTRODUCTION

North and South America stretch from the barren ice fields of the Arctic to the stormy coast of Cape Horn, which twists into the Southern Ocean. A huge number of different animals make their home in the Americas because the continents support a wide range of habitats. These include the humid forests of the Amazon – the world's largest jungle; the searing Atacama Desert – the world's driest place; and the rolling plains of the American wild west. The Americas are also home to many of the world's record-breaking animals. The world's largest deer, the moose, is a common resident of the coniferous forests of Canada and the northern United States. The largest land carnivore, the Kodiak bear, is found on Alaska's Kodiak Island. The world's largest rodent, the capybara, lives in the Amazon rainforest, and the largest snake in the world, the green anaconda, is found in the wetlands across tropical South America.

This book examines the amphibians, reptiles and mammals of the Americas, but can only scratch the surface of the fantastic range of life forms packed into the United States, Canada, Central and South America. Within these geographical areas, the diversity of life is mind-boggling. A blue whale can reach lengths of up to 30m (100ft), with weights of up to

Below: Snakes are a large group of legless reptiles. Most, like this emerald boa, live in hotter parts of the world, such as rainforests. Many snakes have a venomous bite, while others squeeze the breath out of their prey with their muscular, coiled bodies.

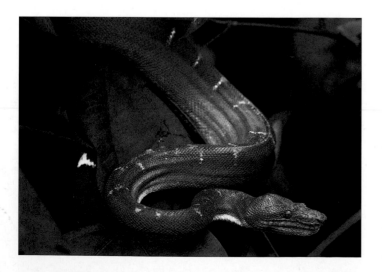

Above: The American bison, a member of the wild cattle family, was once very common across the grasslands and among the woodlands of North America. Following indiscriminate hunting to clear the prairies for domestic cattle, the bison was pushed to the brink of extinction. It has now recovered thanks to conservation programmes.

160 tonnes (352,000lb), while the smallest salamander is less than 3cm (1.25in) long. The rest appear in every shape and size in between.

The introductory section of the book opens with the question "what is an animal?" From very simple organisms such as jellyfish and corals through to complex creatures such as birds and mammals, see how animal bodies are organized, how they have evolved over time, and how their current forms survive and reproduce. Next, the section focuses on the lives of amphibians, reptiles, placental mammals and marsupials, as well as providing information about migration and hibernation, introduced and endangered species, and how ecologists are working to conserve wildlife. Finally, this first section looks at the principal life zones, or biomes, in which animals live – oceans, fresh water, tropical forests, temperate forests, boreal forests, grasslands, polar regions, deserts, mountains and human settlements – and how animals survive in such varied environments.

The directory section of the book explores in detail the many animals that populate the varied habitats of America. Animals are displayed in related groups,

Above: Many reptiles, such as this double-crested basilisk, are well suited to the tropical climate of Central America, being excellent climbers with a diet that includes insects, fruit, flowers and baby birds. The basilisk can even run across water to escape from predators.

Above: Not all mammals are furry and four-legged. Although dolphins have a few bristly hairs and are related to the land mammals, they never leave the water. Like whales and other sea mammals, a dolphin's limbs look more like a fish's fins than the legs of a land animal.

focusing in turn on amphibians, reptiles and mammals: there are salamanders, frogs and toads, turtles and tortoises, lizards, crocodilians, snakes, cats, dogs, bears, small carnivores, raccoons, rodents, rabbits, bats, armadillos, marsupials, insectivores, New World monkeys, marmosets and tamarins, hoofed animals, seals, dolphins and whales.

In North America, noteworthy animals include the brown bear, which lives alone but occasionally gathers together in groups to catch schools of salmon beneath waterfalls, and the American alligator, which inhabits freshwater swamps and rivers, and travels long

Below: The American black bear is smaller than the brown and polar bears that also live in North America. This species is found further south than the other two bears and unlike them, American black bears can climb trees. Zoologists think that they evolved to do this to avoid being attacked by hungry brown bears.

distances to find food, sometimes finding shelter in swimming pools along the way. The lush, steamy climate of Central America favours tropical species such as the strawberry poison-dart frog, which produces a toxic chemical that kills its predators, and the ocelot, a small cat that sleeps in shady thickets or on leafy branches by day and hunts by night. South America is home to many of the world's largest species, including the giant green anaconda that lives in the shallow waters of swamps and stream banks, and also some of the smallest, such as the pygmy marmoset that lives in family groups among the treetops of the Amazon rainforest.

Throughout the directory section, there are fact boxes containing distribution maps and summarized information about each animal's habitat, food, size, maturity, breeding, lifespan and conservation status, as well as lists of related animals and their main characteristics and behaviour.

Right: Amphibians were the first vertebrate land animals, and have kept their close links to water, where their ancestors originated. Therefore amphibians such as this treefrog are most common in warm and damp places, such as rainforests, where they can easily keep their bodies moist.

UNDERSTANDING ANIMALS

Animals can be defined in terms of their body organization, their place in evolution and their anatomy and key features, and this first part of the book examines how they see, hear, smell and taste, how they find food, how they defend their territories, and how they find mates and care for their offspring. It then examines amphibians, reptiles, placental mammals and marsupials, describing and illustrating each type's body features and some of their behaviours. There are also discussions about migration and hibernation, introduced species, endangered species and conserving wildlife. The section then looks at America's principal life zones or biomes – oceans, fresh water, tropical forests, temperate forests, boreal forests, grasslands, polar regions, deserts and mountains – and how animals have adapted to life there. For example, desert-dwelling animals are frequently only active at night when temperatures are cooler, and many of them do not need to drink liquid because they get all the moisture they need from plants. In contrast, animals from mountainous regions are often specially adapted for climbing and surviving windswept conditions, with sturdy legs and dense coats. The section concludes with an examination of the fastest growing habitat in the world – human settlements – with examples of the opportunistic animals that have learned to thrive in our cities.

Left: The cougar – also known as the puma, panther or mountain lion – is the second largest cat in the Americas, second only to the jaguar. It lives alone, patrolling large territories and hunting mule deer and moose. It is extremely agile, being able to leap over 5m (16.5ft) into the air. Cougar cubs are able to eat meat at 3 months old, usually hunting with their mother during their first winter.

WHAT IS AN ANIMAL?

More than two million animal species have been described by scientists, and there are probably millions more waiting to be discovered. They live in all corners of the world, and come in a huge range of shapes and sizes. The largest weighs over a hundred tonnes, while the smallest is just a fraction of a millimetre long.

Active feeders

The living world is divided into five kingdoms: animals, plants, fungi, protists and monerans, which include bacteria. The protists and monerans are micro-organisms. Each individual is just a single cell, and although they often form large masses or colonies – for example, yoghurt is actually a colony of bacteria – the micro-organisms do not form bodies. The plants, fungi and animals do grow bodies, which are made from millions of cells, all of which work together. These three types of macro-organism, as they are called, tackle the problems of life in different ways.

Plants are the basis of life on Earth, and without them animals would not exist. This is because plants get the energy they need from sunlight (because they do not have to feed actively they are called autotrophs, meaning self-feeders). The green pigments in the plants' leaves trap the energy found in light and convert carbon dioxide and water into glucose, a simple sugar, in a process of food production called photosynthesis. Its by-product is oxygen, which gradually drifts into the atmosphere.

Below: Anemones are members of the group of cnidarians, like jellyfish. Starfish belong to the group of echinoderms.

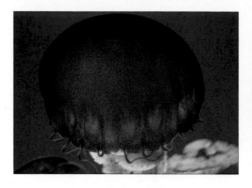

Above: Jellyfish are very simple animals, related to corals and sea anemones. They catch food by spearing prey with tiny cells called nematocysts.

Above: Crabs, such as this hermit crab, are crustaceans. Other crustaceans include lobsters, prawns and krill. Their forelegs are armed with strong pincers.

Above: Snails belong to a large group of invertebrates called molluscs. Most live in water, but many snails, such as this giant land snail, survive on land.

Above: Spiders, scorpions and mites are arachnids. Many spiders build a sticky silk web to trap prey; others lie hidden and pounce on passing victims.

Fungi are largely invisible organisms that live in large masses of tiny fibres which run through the soil. They only pop up above the surface in the form of mushrooms and toadstools when they are ready to reproduce. Fungi do not photosynthesize, but they are valuable as decomposers. They grow over the dead bodies of other organisms, such as trees which have fallen to the ground, secreting digestive enzymes that break down the dead body from the outside. They thereby release valuable carbon, nitrogen, phosphorus and other elements which each tree locks up in itself over its lifetime.

Animals, on the other hand, could not be more different. They are active feeders (called heterotrophs or "other-eaters") which collect food from their surroundings. Unlike plants and fungi, animals have bodies that can swim, walk, burrow or fly during at least the early part of their lives.

Body organization

With the exception of primitive forms, such as sponges, all animal bodies are organized along the same the lines. They process their food in a gut, a tube which passes through the body. In most cases the food enters the gut through an opening in the head, that is, the mouth. Once inside the body, the food is broken down into its constituent parts. The useful parts, such as proteins, fats and sugars – made by plants during photosynthesis – are absorbed into the body. The left-over waste material passes out of the gut through the anus, a hole at the other end of the body.

The useful substances absorbed from the food then need to be transported around the body to where they are needed. This job is done by the animal's circulatory system. The insides of many animals are simply bathed in a liquid containing everything required by the body. However, larger animals, including reptiles, amphibians and mammals, need to pump the useful substances around the body in the blood. The pump is the heart, a strong muscle that keeps the blood circulating through a system of vessels.

The blood carries food for the body and also oxygen, which reacts with the sugar from the food, releasing the energy that is essential for all living things to survive. Animals get their oxygen in a number of ways. Some simply absorb it through their skin, many that live in water extract it using gills, and those that live in air breathe it into their lungs.

Compared with other organisms, animals are more aware of their surroundings and certainly more responsive to them. This is because they have a nervous system which uses sensors to detect what is happening in their environment, such as changes in temperature, the amount of light and various sounds. This information is then transmitted by means of nerves to what could be called the central control. This might just be a dense cluster of nerves, of which the animal might possess several, or it may be a single controlling brain. The brain or nerve cluster then passes the information from the senses to the muscles so that the body can respond appropriately, for example either by running away to avoid being eaten or by attacking its prey.

Mammals, reptiles and amphibians share a similar body plan, having four limbs. They are members of the larger group of tetrapods, to which birds also belong. Almost all possess a visible tail. The brain and most of the sensors are positioned at the front of the body in the head. The vital organs, such as the heart and lungs (or gills), are located in the central thorax (chest area), while the gut and sex organs are found mainly in the abdomen at the rear of the body.

Left: Apart from bats, birds, such as this bee-eater, are the only flying vertebrates. Their forelimbs have evolved into wings that allow them to perform amazing feats of flight. Feathers are better than hair for keeping the body streamlined for flight.

Above: Fish live in all corners of the world's oceans. They also live in fresh water, where they are found everywhere from submerged caves to mountain lakes.

Above: Frogs are the most familiar of the amphibians. Others include salamanders and newts. This frog spends its life in trees, using suckers on its feet to cling to the branches.

Above: While a few other lizards can alter the shade of their scales slightly, chameleons can change colour completely. This may help them hide from predators or it may reflect their mood.

Above: Mammals, such as this ground squirrel, are the most widespread of vertebrates. They can survive in just about any habitat on Earth.

EVOLUTION

Animals and other forms of life did not just suddenly appear on the Earth. They evolved over billions of years into countless different forms. The mechanism by which they evolved is called natural selection. The process of natural selection was first proposed by British naturalist Charles Darwin.

Many biologists estimate that there are approximately 30 million species on Earth, but to date only about two million have been discovered and recorded by scientists. So where are the rest? They live in a staggering array of habitats – from the waters of the deep oceans, where sperm whales live, to the deserts of Mexico, inhabited by poisonous gila monster lizards. The problems faced by animals in these and other habitats on Earth are very different, and so life has evolved in great variety. Each animal needs a body that can cope with its own environment.

Past evidence

At the turn of the 19th century, geologists began to realize that the world was extremely old. They studied animal fossils – usually the hard remains, such as shells and bones, which are preserved in stone – and measured the age of the exposed layers of rock found in cliffs and canyons. Today we accept that the Earth is about 4.5 billion years old, but in the early 1800s the idea that the world was unimaginably old began to change people's ideas about the origins of life completely.

In addition, naturalists had always known that there was a fantastic variety of animals, but now they realized that many could be grouped into families, as if they were related. By the middle of 19th century, two British biologists had independently formulated an idea that would change the way that people saw themselves and the natural world forever. Charles Darwin and Alfred Wallace thought that the world's different animal species had gradually evolved from extinct relatives, like the ones preserved as fossils.

Darwin was the first to publish his ideas, in 1859. He had formulated them while touring South America where he studied the differences between varieties of finches and giant tortoises on the Galápagos Islands in the Pacific Ocean. Wallace came up with similar ideas about the same time, when studying different animals on the islands of South-east Asia and New Guinea.

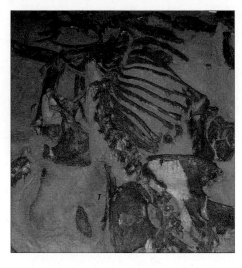

Above: Scientists know about extinct animals from studying fossils such as these mammoth bones. Fossils are the remains of dead plants or animals that have been turned to stone by natural processes over millions of years.

Survival of the fittest

Both came up with the same idea – natural selection. As breeders had known for generations, animals pass on their characteristics to their young. Darwin and Wallace suggested that wild animal species gradually evolved through natural selection, a similar system to the artificial selection that people were using to breed prize cattle, sheep and pedigree dogs.

The theory of natural selection is often described as the survival of the fittest. This is because animals must compete with each other for limited resources including food, water, shelter and mates. But they are not all equal or exactly similar, and some members of a population of animals will have characteristics which make them "fitter" – better suited to the environment at that time.

The fitter animals will therefore be more successful at finding food and avoiding predators. Consequently, they will probably produce more offspring, many of which will also have the same characteristics as their fit parents.

Jumping animals

Most animals can leap into the air, but thanks to natural selection this simple ability has been harnessed by different animals in different ways. For example, click beetles jump in somersaults to frighten off attackers, while blood-sucking fleas can leap enormous heights to move from host to host.

Above: The flying frog uses flaps of skin between its toes to glide. This allows these tree-living frogs to leap huge distances between branches.

Above: The bobcat is an agile mammal with powerful legs that allow it to leap over 3.6m (12ft) into the air to pounce on its prey, such as hares, porcupines, birds and even deer.

Because of this, the next generation will contain more individuals with the "fit" trait. And after many generations, it is possible that the whole population will carry the fit trait, since those without it die out.

Variation and time

The environment is not fixed, and does not stay the same for long. Volcanoes, diseases and gradual climate changes, for example, alter the conditions which animals have to confront. Natural selection relies on the way in which different individual animals cope with these changes. Those individuals that were once fit may later die out, as others that have a different set of characteristics become more successful in the changed environment.

Darwin did not know it, but parents pass their features on to their young through their genes. During sexual reproduction, the genes of both parents are jumbled up to produce a new individual with unique characteristics. Every so often the genes mutate into a new form, and these mutations are the source of all new variations.

As the process of natural selection continues for millions of years, so groups of animals can change radically, giving rise to a new species. Life is thought to have been evolving for 3.5 billion years. In that time natural selection has produced a staggering number of species, with everything from oak trees to otters and coral to cobras.

A species is a group of organisms that can produce offspring with each other. A new species occurs once animals have changed so much that they are unable to breed with their ancestral relatives. And if the latter no longer exist, then they have become extinct.

New species may gradually arise out of a single group of animals. In fact the original species may be replaced by one or more new species. This can happen when two separate groups of one species are kept apart by an impassable geographical feature, such as an ocean or mountain range. Kept isolated from each other, both groups then evolve in different ways and end up becoming new species.

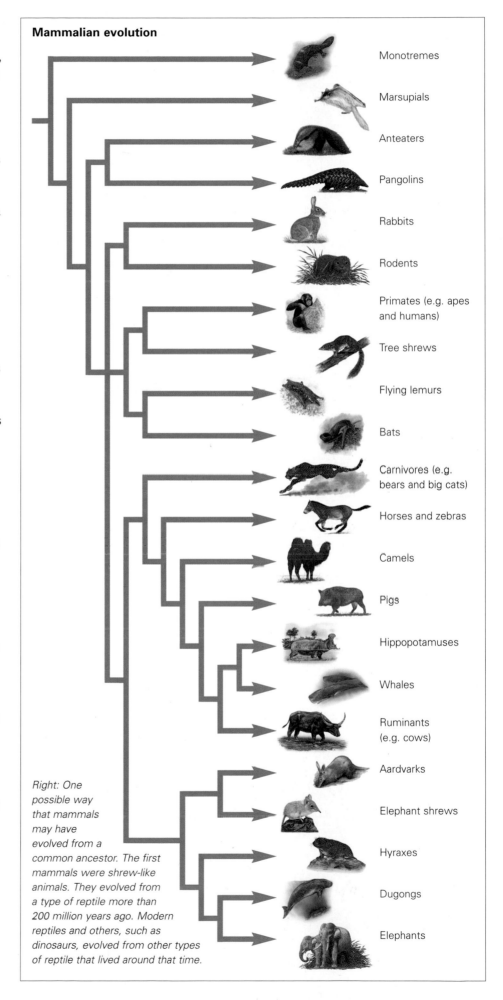

Mammalian evolution

Monotremes

Marsupials

Anteaters

Pangolins

Rabbits

Rodents

Primates (e.g. apes and humans)

Tree shrews

Flying lemurs

Bats

Carnivores (e.g. bears and big cats)

Horses and zebras

Camels

Pigs

Hippopotamuses

Whales

Ruminants (e.g. cows)

Aardvarks

Elephant shrews

Hyraxes

Dugongs

Elephants

Right: One possible way that mammals may have evolved from a common ancestor. The first mammals were shrew-like animals. They evolved from a type of reptile more than 200 million years ago. Modern reptiles and others, such as dinosaurs, evolved from other types of reptile that lived around that time.

ANATOMY

Mammals, reptiles and amphibians (which are vertebrates, as are fish and birds), come in a mind-boggling array of shapes and sizes. However all of them, from whales to bats and frogs to snakes, share a basic body plan, both inside and out.

Vertebrates are animals with a spine, generally made of bone. Bone, the hard tissues of which contain chalky substances, is also the main component of the rest of the vertebrate skeleton. The bones of the skeleton link together to form a rigid frame to protect organs and give the body its shape, while also allowing it to move. Cartilage, a softer, more flexible but tough tissue is found, for example, at the ends of bones in mobile joints, in the ears and the nose (forming the sides and the partition between the two nostrils). Some fish, including sharks and rays, have skeletons that consist entirely of cartilage.

Nerves and muscles

Vertebrates also have a spinal cord, a thick bundle of nerves extending from the brain through the spine, and down into the tail. The nerves in the spinal cord are used to control walking and other reflex movements by coordinating blocks of muscle that work together. A vertebrate's skeleton is on the inside, in contrast to many invertebrates, which have an outer skeleton or exoskeleton. The vertebrate skeleton provides a solid structure which the body's muscles pull against. Muscles are blocks of protein that can contract and relax when they get an electrical impulse from a nerve.

Invertebrates

The majority of animals are invertebrates. They are a much more varied group than the vertebrates and include creatures as varied as shrimps, slugs, butterflies and starfish. Although some squid are thought to reach the size of a small whale, and while octopuses are at least as intelligent as cats and dogs, most invertebrates are much smaller and simpler animals than the vertebrates.

Below: The most successful invertebrates are the insects, including ants. This soldier army ant is defending workers as they collect food.

Reptile bodies

Reptiles have an internal skeleton made from bone and cartilage. Their skin is covered in scales, which are often toughened by a waxy protein called keratin. Turtles are quite different from other reptiles. They have a simpler skull and a shell that is joined to the animal's internal skeleton.

Below: Crocodiles have a very strong body, designed for life in and around shallow water.

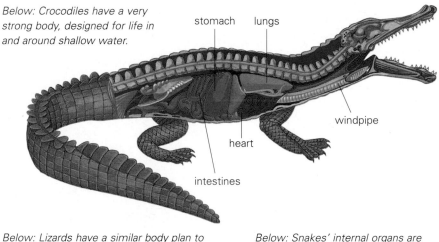

stomach · lungs · windpipe · heart · intestines

Below: Lizards have a similar body plan to crocodiles, although they are actually not very closely related.

Below: Snakes' internal organs are elongated so that they fit into their long, thin body. One of a pair of organs, such as the lungs, is often very small or missing.

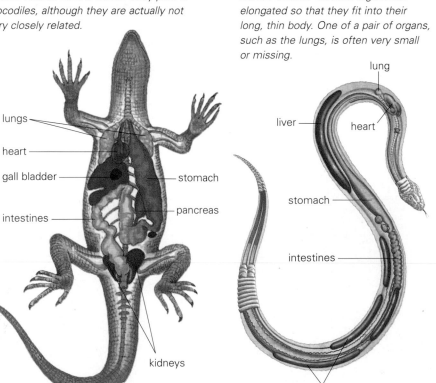

lungs · heart · gall bladder · intestines · stomach · pancreas · kidneys

lung · liver · heart · stomach · intestines · kidneys

When on the move, the vertebrate body works like a system of pulleys, pivots and levers. The muscles are the engines of the body, and are attached to bones – the levers – by strong cables called tendons. The joint between two bones forms a pivot, and the muscles work in pairs to move a bone. For example, when an arm is bent at the elbow to raise the forearm, the bicep muscle on the front of the upper arm has to contract. This pulls the forearm up, while the tricep muscle attached to the back of the upper arm remains relaxed. To straighten the arm again, the tricep contracts and the bicep relaxes. If both muscles contract at the same time, they pull against each other, and the arm remains locked in whatever position it is in.

Vital organs

Muscles are not only attached to the skeleton. The gut – including the stomach and intestines – is surrounded by muscles. These muscles contract in rhythmic waves to push food and waste products through the body. The heart is a muscular organ made of a very strong muscle which keeps on contracting and relaxing, pumping blood around the body. The heart and other vital organs are found in the thorax, that part of the body which lies between the forelimbs. In reptiles and mammals the thorax is kept well protected, the rib cage surrounding the heart, lungs, liver and kidneys.

Vertebrates have a single liver consisting of a number of lobes. The liver has a varied role, making chemicals required by the body and storing food. Most vertebrates also have two kidneys. Their role is to clean the blood of any impurities and toxins, and to remove excess water. The main toxins that have to be removed are compounds containing nitrogen, the by-products of eating protein. Mammal and amphibian kidneys dissolve these toxins in water to make urine. However, since many reptiles live in very dry habitats, they cannot afford to use water to remove waste, and they instead get rid of it as a solid waste similar to bird excrement.

Mammalian bodies

Most mammals are four-limbed (exceptions being sea mammals such as whales). All have some hair on their bodies, and females produce milk.

They live in a wide range of habitats and their bodies are adapted to survive. Their internal organs vary depending on where they live and what they eat.

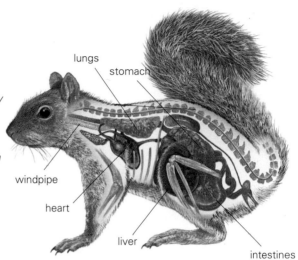

Right: Squirrels have very lightweight bodies, so they are able to climb the thinnest of tree branches. They have a long, slender shape which ensures that their weight is spread evenly across tree limbs. They extend their tail for balance when jumping, and keep it curved over their back when sitting. Their forelimbs have strong muscles and thick, sharp claws for gripping branches, and their strong leg muscles and large hind feet help to propel them forward when leaping.

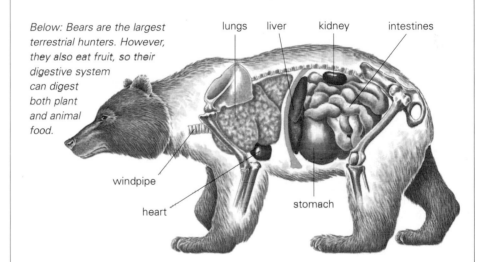

Below: Bears are the largest terrestrial hunters. However, they also eat fruit, so their digestive system can digest both plant and animal food.

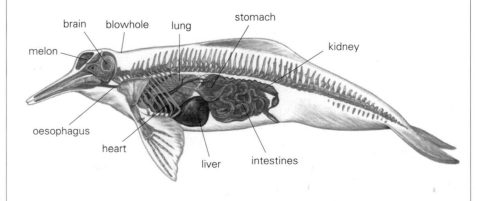

Below: River dolphins are streamlined, torpedo-shaped aquatic mammals, spending their entire lives in water. They breathe air into lungs like other animals, but through a single nostril, or blowhole, *on the top of their head. They also have a fatty "melon" inside their domed skull, which is used to focus sonar beams to locate (and possibly stun) their prey. Their muscular tails are used for propulsion.*

SENSES

To stay alive, animals must find food and shelter, and defend themselves against predators. To achieve these things, they are equipped with an array of senses for monitoring their surroundings. Different species have senses adapted to nocturnal or diurnal (day-active) life.

An animal's senses are its early-warning system. They alert it to changes in its surroundings – changes which may signal an opportunity to feed or mate, or the need to escape imminent danger. The ability to act quickly and appropriately is made possible because the senses are linked to the brain by a network of nerves which send messages as electric pulses. When the brain receives the information from the senses it coordinates its response.

In many cases, generally in response to something touching the body, the signal from the sensor does not reach the brain before action is taken. Instead, it produces a reflex response which is "hardwired" into the nervous system. For example, when you touch a very hot object, your hand automatically recoils; you don't need to think about it.

All animals have to be sensitive to their environment to survive. Even the simplest animals, such as jellyfish and roundworms, react to changes in their surroundings. Simple animals, however, have only a limited ability to move or defend themselves, and therefore generally have limited senses. Larger animals, such as vertebrates,

have a much more complex array of sense organs. Most vertebrates can hear, see, smell, taste and touch.

Vision

Invertebrates' eyes are generally designed to detect motion. Vertebrates' eyes, however, are better at forming clear images, often in colour. Vertebrates' eyes are balls of clear jelly which have an inner lining of light-sensitive cells. This lining, called the retina, is made up of one or two types of cell. The rod cells – named after their shape – are very sensitive to all types of light, but are only capable of forming black and white images. Animals which are active at night generally have (and need) only rods in their eyes.

Colour vision is important for just a few animals, such as monkeys, which need, for example, to see the brightest and therefore ripest fruits. Colour images are made by the cone cells – so named because of their shape – in the retina. There are three types of cone, each of which is sensitive to a particular wavelength of light. Low wavelengths appear as reds, high wavelengths as blues, with green colours being detected in between.

Above: Frogs have large eyes positioned on the upper side of the head so that the animals can lie mainly submerged in water with just their eyes poking out.

The light is focused on the retina by a lens to produce a clear image. Muscles change the shape of the lens so that it can focus the light arriving from different distances. While invertebrates may have several eyes, all vertebrates have just two, and they are always positioned on the head. Animals such as rabbits, which are constantly looking out for danger, have eyes on the side of the head to give a wide field of vision. But while they can see in almost all directions, rabbits have difficulty judging distances and speeds. Animals that have eyes pointing forward are better at doing this because each eye's field of vision overlaps with the other. This binocular vision helps hunting animals and others, such as tree-living primates, to judge distances more accurately.

Eyes can also detect radiation in a small band of wavelengths, and some animals detect radiation that is invisible to our eyes. Flying insects and birds can see ultraviolet light, which extends the range of their colour vision. At the other end of the spectrum many snakes can detect radiation with a lower wavelength. They sense infrared, or heat, through pits on the face which enables them to track their warm-blooded prey in pitch darkness.

Below: The raccoon is a nocturnal animal with excellent night vision, and eyes that glow bright yellow in the dark. These animals have a distinctive black mask across their eyes.

Below: Like other hunters, a seal has eyes positioned on the front of its head. Forward-looking eyes are useful for judging distances, making it easier to chase down prey.

Hearing

An animal's brain interprets waves of pressure travelling through the air, and detected by the ears, as sound. Many animals do not hear these waves with ears but detect them in other ways instead. For example, although snakes can hear, they are much more sensitive to vibrations travelling through the ground, which they detect with their lower jaw. Long facial whiskers sported by many mammals, from cats to dugongs, are very sensitive touch receptors. They can be so sensitive that they will even respond to currents in the air.

In many ways, hearing is a sensitive extension of the sense of touch. The ears of amphibians, lizards and mammals have an eardrum which is sensitive to tiny changes in pressure. An eardrum is a thin membrane of skin which vibrates as the air waves hit it. A tiny bone (or in the case of mammals, three bones) attached to the drum transmits the vibrations to a shell-shaped structure called a cochlea. The cochlea is filled with a liquid which picks up the vibrations. As the liquid moves inside the cochlea, tiny hair-like structures lining it wave back and forth. Nerves stimulated by this wave motion send the information to the brain, which interprets it as sound.

A mammal's ear is divided into three sections. The cochlea forms the inner ear and the middle ear consists of the bones between the cochlea and eardrum. The outer ear is the tube joining the outside world and the

Below: Hares have very large outer ears which they use like satellite dishes to pick up sound waves. They can rotate each ear separately to detect sound from all directions.

auricle – the fleshy structure on the side of the head that collects the sound waves – to the middle ear. Amphibians and reptiles do not possess auricles. Instead, their eardrums are either on the side of the head – easily visible on many frogs and lizards – or under the skin, as in snakes.

Smell and taste

Smell and taste are so closely related as to form a single sense. Snakes and lizards, for example, taste the air with their forked tongues. However, it is perhaps the most complex sense. Noses, tongues and other smelling

Below: Lizards do not have outer ears at all. Their hearing organs are contained inside the head and joined to the outside world through an eardrum membrane.

Above: Snakes have a forked tongue that they use to taste the air. The tips of the fork are slotted into an organ in the roof of the mouth. This organ is linked to the nose, and chemicals picked up by the tongue are identified with great sensitivity.

organs are lined with sensitive cells which can analyze a huge range of chemicals that float in the air or exist in food. Animals such as dogs, which rely on their sense of smell, have long noses packed with odour-sensitive cells. Monkeys, of the other hand, are less reliant on a sense of smell, and consequently have short noses capable only of detecting stronger odours.

Below: Wolves have an excellent sense of smell and taste. They communicate with pack members and rival packs by smell, as part of a complex set of social behaviours.

SURVIVAL

In order to stay alive, animals must not only find enough food, but also avoid becoming a predator's meal. To achieve this, animals have evolved many strategies to feed on a wide range of foods, and an array of weapons and defensive tactics to keep safe.

An animal must keep feeding in order to replace the energy used in staying alive. Substances in the food, such as sugars, are burned by the body, and the subsequent release of energy is used to heat the body and power its movements. Food is also essential for growth. Although most growth takes place during the early period of an animal's life, it never really stops because injuries need to heal and worn-out tissues need replacing. Some animals continue growing throughout life. Proteins in the food are the main building blocks of living bodies.

Plant food
Some animals will eat just about anything, while others are much more fussy. As a group, vertebrates get their energy from a wide range of sources – everything from shellfish and wood to honey and blood. Animals are often classified according to how they feed, forming several large groups filled with many otherwise unrelated animals.

Animals that eat plants are generally grouped together as herbivores. But this term is not very descriptive because there is such a wide range of plant foods. Animals that eat grass are known as grazers. However, this term can also apply to any animal which

Above: Bison are grazers. They eat grass and plants that grow close to the ground. Because their food is all around them, grazers spend a long time out in the open. They feed together in large herds, since there is safety in numbers.

eats any plant that covers the ground in large amounts, such as seaweed or sedge. Typical grazers include bison but some, such as the marine iguana, are not so typical. Animals such as deer, which pick off the tastiest leaves, buds and fruit from bushes and trees, are called browsers. Other browsing animals include many monkeys, but some monkeys eat only leaves (the folivores) or fruit (the frugivores).

Many monkeys have a much broader diet, eating everything from shellfish to the sap which seeps out from the bark of tropical trees. Animals that eat both plant and animal foods are called omnivores. Bears are omnivorous, as are humans, but the most catholic of tastes belong to scavenging animals, such as rats and other rodents, which eat anything they can get their teeth into. Omnivores in general, and scavengers in particular, are very curious animals. They will investigate anything that looks or smells like food, and if it also tastes like food, then it probably is.

A taste for flesh
The term carnivore is often applied to any animal that eats flesh, but it is more correctly used to refer to an order of mammals which includes cats, dogs, bears and many smaller animals, such as weasels and racoons. These animals are the kings of killing, armed with razor-sharp claws and powerful jaws crammed full of dagger-like teeth. They use their strength and speed to overpower their prey, either by running them down or taking them by surprise with an ambush.

Below: Amazon squirrel monkeys feed on small insects, soft fruits and the nectar from flowers. Their highly dexterous fingers are ideally suited to searching for this kind of food.

Below: Grizzly bears are omnivores, eating both vegetation and animals. When salmon are abundant, they congregate in groups to share this protein-rich resource.

Above: Wolverines are primarily meat-eaters, capable of bringing down prey that are five times bigger than themselves. Their diet includes beavers, squirrels, marmots, rabbits, deer, moose, wild sheep and carrion.

However, land-dwelling carnivores are not the only expert killers. One of the largest meat-eaters is the orca, or killer whale, which is at least three times the size of the brown bear, the largest killer on land.

While snakes are much smaller in comparison, they are just as deadly, if not more so. They kill in one of two ways, either suffocating their prey by wrapping their coils tightly around them, or by injecting them with a poison through their fangs.

Arms race

Ironically, the same weapons used by predators are often used by their prey to defend themselves. For example, several species of frog, toad and salamander secrete poisons on to their skin. In some cases, such as the poison-dart frog, this poison is enough to kill any predator that tries to eat it, thus making sure that the killer won't repeat its performance. More often, though, a predator finds that its meal tastes horrible and remembers not to eat another one again. To remind the predators to keep away, many poisonous amphibians are brightly coloured, which ensures that they are easily recognized.

Many predators rely on stealth to catch their prey, and staying hidden is part of the plan. A camouflaged coat, such as a jaguar's spots, helps animals blend into their surroundings. Many species also use this technique to ensure that they do not get eaten.

Other animals avoid being attacked by advertising their presence. For example coral snakes let predators know that they will suffer a bite filled with deadly venom by being brightly coloured. Many non-venomous snakes, including harmless milksnakes and corn snakes, have evolved to look the same as venomous snakes so that they, too, are left alone.

Plant-eating animals that live in the open cannot hide from predators that are armed with sharp teeth and claws. And the plant-eaters cannot rely on similar weapons to defend themselves. They are outgunned because they do not possess sharp, pointed teeth

Right: This small and brightly coloured frog has enough poison in its skin to kill anything, or anyone, that eats it. The species is called the yellow-banded poison-dart frog, one of several poison-dart frogs that contain neurotoxins – poisons that attack the nervous system. The frogs earn their name because Amazonian hunters used the frogs' skins to make a paralyzing liquid, which they then dipped their blowpipe darts into.

Filter-feeders

Some animals filter their food from water. The giant baleen whales do this, sieving tiny shrimp-like animals called krill out of great gulps of sea water. Some tadpoles and larval salamanders filter-feed as well, extracting tiny plant-like animals which float in fresh water. However, after becoming adults, all amphibians become hunters and eat other animals. All snakes and most lizards are meat-eaters, or carnivores, as well.

Below: The largest animals of all, baleen whales, are filter-feeders. They do not have teeth. Instead, their gums are lined with a thick curtain of baleen that filters out tiny shrimp-like krill from sea water.

but flattened ones to grind up their plant food. The best chance they have of avoiding danger is to run away. Animals such as deer consequently have long, hoofed feet that lengthen their legs considerably; they are, in fact, standing on their toenails. These long legs allow them to run faster and leap high into the air to escape an attacker's jaws.

Animals that do not flee must stand and fight. Most large herbivores are armed with horns or antlers. Although used chiefly for display, the horns are the last line of defence when cornered.

REPRODUCTION

All animals share the urge to produce offspring which will survive after the parents die. The process of heredity is determined by genes, through which characteristics are passed from parents to offspring. Reproduction presents several problems, and animals have adopted different strategies for tackling them.

Animals have two main goals: to find food and a mate. To achieve these goals, they must survive everything that the environment throws at them, from extremes of the weather, such as floods and droughts, to hungry predators. They have to find sufficient supplies of food, and on top of that locate a mate before their competitors. If they find sufficient food but fail to produce any offspring, their struggle for survival will have been wasted.

One parent or two?

There are two ways in which an animal can reproduce, asexually or sexually. Animals that are produced by asexual reproduction, or parthenogenesis, have only one parent, a mother. The offspring are identical to their mother and to each other. Sexual reproduction involves two parents of the opposite sex. The offspring are hybrids of the two parents, with a mixture of their parents' characteristics.

The offspring inherit their parents' traits through their genes. Genes can be defined in various ways. One simple definition is that they are the units of inheritance – single inherited

Below: Crocodiles bury their eggs in a nest. The temperature of the nest determines the sex of the young reptiles. Hot nests produce more males than cool ones. Crocodile mothers are very gentle when it comes to raising young.

Above: Many male frogs croak by pumping air into an expandable throat sac. The croak is intended to attract females. The deeper the croak, the more attractive it is. However, some males lurk silently and mate with females as they approach the croaking males.

Above: In deer and many other grazing animals, the males fight each other for the right to mate with the females in the herd. The deer with the largest antlers often wins without fighting, and real fights only break out if two males appear equally well endowed.

characteristics which cannot be subdivided any further. Genes are also segments of DNA (deoxyribonucleic acid), a complex chemical that forms long chains. It is found at the heart of every living cell. Each link in the DNA chain forms part of a code that controls how an animal's body develops and survives. And every cell in the body contains a full set of DNA which could be used to build a whole new body.

Animals produced through sexual reproduction receive half their DNA, or half their genes, from each parent. The male parent provides half the supply of genes, contained in a sperm. Each sperm's only role is to find its

way to, and fertilize, an egg, its female equivalent. Besides containing the other half of the DNA, the egg also holds a supply of food for the offspring as it develops into a new individual. Animals created through parthenogenesis get all their genes from their mother, and all of them are therefore the same sex – female.

Pros and cons

All mammals reproduce sexually, as do most reptiles and amphibians. However, there are a substantial number of reptiles and amphibians, especially lizards, which reproduce by parthenogenesis. There are benefits and disadvantages to both types of reproduction. Parthenogenesis is quick and convenient. The mother does not need to find a mate, and can devote all of her energy to producing huge numbers of young. This strategy is ideal for populating as yet unexploited territory. However, being identical, these animals are very vulnerable to attack. If, for example, one is killed by a disease or outwitted by a predator, it is very likely that they will all suffer the same fate. Consequently, whole communities of animals produced through parthenogenesis can be wiped out.

Sexual animals, on the other hand, are much more varied. Each one is unique, formed by a mixture of genes from both parents. This variation means that a group of animals produced by sexual reproduction is more likely to triumph over adversity than a group of asexual ones. However, sexual reproduction takes up a great deal of time and effort.

Attracting mates

Since females produce only a limited number of eggs, they are keen to make sure that they are fertilized by a male with good genes. If a male is fit and healthy, this is a sign that he has good genes. Good genes will ensure that the offspring will be able to compete with other animals for food and mates of their own. Because the females have the final say in agreeing to mate, the

Above: Prairie dogs usually have one litter of four to six young per year. The young are born hairless and helpless, with their eyes closed. They remain underground for the first six weeks of life, then emerge from their dens.

Below: An Argentine grey zorro vixen suckles her fox cubs. The milk contains a mixture of fats and proteins, and also includes antibodies, so that they will have resistance to diseases.

Above: Grizzly bear cubs are blind and helpless at birth. Their mother's milk is rich in fat and calories, so the cubs develop quickly. Mothers are fiercely protective of their young, defending them against wolves and cougars. Cubs stay with their mothers for up to three years.

males have to put a lot of effort into getting noticed. Many are brightly coloured, make loud noises, and they are often larger than the females. In many species the males even compete with each other for the right to display to the females. Winning that right is a good sign that they have the best genes.

Parental care

The amount of care that the offspring receive from their parents varies considerably. There is a necessary trade-off between the amount of useful care parents can give to each offspring, the number of offspring they can produce and how regularly they can breed. Mammals invest heavily in parental care, suckling their young after giving birth, while most young amphibians or reptiles never meet their parents at all.

By suckling, mammals ensure that their young grow to a size where they can look after themselves. Generally, the young stay with the mother until it is time for her to give birth to the next litter – at least one or two months. However, in many species, including humans, the young stay with their parents for many years.

Other types of animal pursue the opposite strategy, producing large numbers of young that are left to fend for themselves. The vast majority in each batch of eggs – consisting of hundreds or even thousands – die before reaching adulthood, and many never even hatch. The survival rates, for example of frogs, are very low.

Animals that live in complicated societies, such as monkeys and humans, tend to produce a single offspring every few years. The parents direct their energies into protecting and rearing the young, giving them a good chance of survival. Animals which live for a only a short time, such as mice, rabbits, and reptiles and amphibians in general, need to reproduce quickly to make the most of their short lives. They produce high numbers of young, and do not waste time on anything more than the bare minimum of parental care. If successful, these animals can reproduce at an alarming pace.

CLASSIFICATION

Scientists classify all living things into categories. Members of each category share features with each other – traits that set them apart from other animals. Over the years, a tree of categories and subcategories has been pieced together, showing how all living things seem to be related to each other.

Taxonomy, the scientific discipline of categorizing organisms, aims to classify and order the millions of animals on Earth so that we can better understand them and their relationship to each other. The Greek philosopher Aristotle was among the first people to do this for animals in the 4th century BC. In the 18th century, Swedish naturalist Carolus Linnaeus formulated the system that we use today.

By the end of the 17th century, naturalists had noticed that many animals seemed to have several close relatives that resembled one another. For example lions, lynxes and domestic cats all seemed more similar to each other than they did to dogs or horses. However, all of these animals shared common features that they did not share with frogs, slugs or wasps.

Linnaeus devised a way of classifying these observations. The system he set up – known as the Linnaean system – orders animals in a hierarchy of divisions. From the largest division to the smallest, this system is as follows: kingdom, phylum, class, order, family, genus, species.

Each species is given a two-word scientific name, derived from Latin and Greek. For example, *Panthera leo* is the scientific name of the lion. The first word is the genus name, while the second is the species name. Therefore *Panthera leo* means the "*leo*" species in the genus "*Panthera*". This system of two-word classification is known as binomial nomenclature.

Lions, lynxes and other genera of cats belong to the *Felidae* family. The *Felidae* are included in the order *Carnivora*, along with dogs and other

Above: The bats form the order of mammals called the Chiroptera, *which means "hand wings". Vampire bats belong to the major subgroup of bats called microchiropterans, which use sonar to orientate themselves in the dark of night. The other subgroup of bats are the megachiropterans, or flying foxes, which fly during the day and orientate themselves by sight.*

Below: Despite resembling a number of animals, including small hippos and pigs, capybaras are rodents, and thus are more closely related to rats, squirrels and beavers. Capybaras belong to a subgroup of rodents that also contains chinchillas, guinea pigs and many other South American species.

similar predators. The *Carnivora*, in turn, belong to the class *Mammalia*, which also includes horses and all other mammals.

Mammals belong to the phylum *Chordata*, the major group which contains all vertebrates, including reptiles, amphibians, birds, fish and some other small animals called tunicates and lancelets. In their turn, *Chordata* belong to the kingdom *Animalia*, comprising around 31 living phyla, including *Mollusca*, which contains the slugs, and *Arthropoda*, which contains wasps and other insects.

Although we still use Linnaean grouping, modern taxonomy is worked out in very different ways from the ones Linnaeus used. Linnaeus and others after him classified animals by their outward appearance. Although they were generally correct when it

Close relations

Cheetahs, caracals and ocelots all belong to the cat family *Felidae*, which also includes lions, tigers, wildcats, lynxes and jaguars. Within this family there are two groups: big and small cats. These can generally be distinguished by their size, with a few exceptions.

For example, the cheetah is often classed as a big cat, but it is actually smaller than the cougar, a small cat. One of the main differences between the two groups is that big cats can roar but not purr continuously, while small cats are able to purr but not roar.

Above: The jaguar (Panthera onca) *belongs to the genus* Panthera, *the big cats, to which lions and tigers also belong. All cats are members of the order* Carnivora (carnivores) *within the class of* Mammalia *(mammals).*

Above: The cougar may look like a big cat, being larger than some of the Panthera *genus. However, this hunter belongs to the* Felis *genus, so despite appearances it is more closely related to small, domestic cats than jaguars.*

Above: The ocelot (Felis pardalis) *is a medium-sized member of the* Felis *or small cat genus. Like many cats, this species has evolved a spotted coat to provide camouflage – unfortunately attractive to fashion designers.*

Distant relations

All vertebrates (backboned animals) including birds, reptiles and mammals such as seals and dolphins, are thought to have evolved from common fish ancestors that swam in the oceans some 400 million years ago. Later, one group of fish developed

limb-like organs and came on to the land, where they slowly evolved into amphibians and later reptiles, which in turn gave rise to mammals. Later, seals and dolphins returned to the oceans and their limbs evolved into paddle-like flippers.

Above: Fish are an ancient group of aquatic animals that mainly propel themselves by thrashing their vertically aligned caudal fin, or tail, and steer using their fins.

Above: In seals, the four limbs have evolved into flippers that make highly effective paddles in water but are less useful on land, where seals are ungainly in their movements.

Above: Whales and dolphins never come on land, and their hind limbs have all but disappeared. They resemble fish but the tail is horizontally – not vertically – aligned.

came to the large divisions, this method was not foolproof. For example, some early scientists believed that whales and dolphins, with their fins and streamlined bodies, were types of fish and not mammals at all. Today, accurate classification of the various genera is achieved through a field of study called cladistics. This uses genetic analysis to check how animals are related by evolutionary change. So animals are grouped according to how they evolved, with each division sharing a common ancestor somewhere in the past. As the classification of living organisms improves, so does our understanding of the evolution of life on Earth and our place within this process.

AMPHIBIANS

Amphibians are the link between fish and land animals. One in eight of all vertebrate animals are amphibians. This group includes frogs, toads and newts as well as rarer types, such as giant sirens, hellbenders and worm-like caecilians. Amphibians are equally at home in water and on land.

Amphibians live on every continent except for Antarctica. None can survive in salt water, although a few species live close to the sea in the brackish water at river mouths. Being cold-blooded – their body temperature is always about the same as the temperature of their surroundings – most amphibians are found in the warmer regions of the world.

Unlike other land vertebrates, most amphibians spend the early part of their lives in a different form from that of the adults. As they grow, the young gradually metamorphose into the adult body. Having a larval form means that the adults and their offspring live and feed in different places. In general the larvae are aquatic, while the adults spend most of their time on land.

The adults are hunters, feeding on other animals, while the young are generally plant eaters, filtering tiny plants from the water or grazing on aquatic plants which line the bottom of ponds and rivers.

Below: Amphibians must lay their eggs near a source of water. In most cases, such as this frog spawn, the eggs are laid straight into a pond or swamp. The tadpoles develop inside the jelly-like egg and then hatch out after the food supply in the egg's yolk runs out.

Life changing
Most amphibians hatch from eggs laid in water or, in a few cases, in moist soil or nests made of hardened mucus. Once hatched, the young amphibians, or larvae, nearly all live as completely aquatic animals. Those born on land wriggle to the nearest pool of water or drop from their nest into a river.

The larvae of frogs and toads are called tadpoles. Like the young of salamanders – a group that includes all other amphibians except caecilians – tadpoles do not have any legs at first. They swim using a long tail that has a fish-like fin extending along its length. As they grow, the larvae sprout legs.

In general the back legs begin to grow first, followed by the front pair. Adult frogs do not have tails, and after the first few months a tadpole's tail begins to be reabsorbed into the body – it does not just fall away.

All adult salamanders keep their tails, and those species that spend their entire lives in water often retain the fin along the tail, as well as other parts, including external gills, a feature that is more commonly seen in the larval stage.

Above: Amphibians begin life looking very different from the adult form. Most of the time these larval forms, such as this frog tadpole, live in water as they slowly develop into the adult form, growing legs and lungs so that they can survive on land.

Body form
Amphibian larvae hatch with external gills but, as they grow, many (including all frogs and the many salamanders which live on land) develop internal gills. In most land-living species these internal gills are eventually replaced by lungs. Amphibians are also able to absorb oxygen directly through the skin, especially through the thin and moist tissues inside the mouth. A large number of land-living salamanders get all their oxygen in this way because they do not have lungs.

All adult frogs and toads return to the water to breed and lay their eggs, which are often deposited in a jelly-like mass called frog spawn. Several types of salamander do not lay eggs; instead, the females keep the fertilized eggs within their bodies. The larvae develop inside the eggs, fed by a supply of rich yolk, and do not hatch until they have reached adult form.

Above: After the first few weeks, a tadpole acquires tiny back legs. As the legs grow, the long tail is gradually reabsorbed into the body. The front legs appear after the back ones have formed.

Adult form

Most adult amphibians have four limbs, with four digits on the front pair and five on the rear. Unlike other land-living animals, such as reptiles or mammals, their skin is naked and soft. Frogs' skin is smooth and moist, while toads generally have a warty appearance.

The skins of many salamanders are brightly coloured, with patterns that often change throughout the year. Colour change prior to the mating season signals the salamander's readiness to mate. Many frogs also have bright skin colours. Although their skin shades can change considerably in different light levels, these colours are generally not mating signals to fellow frogs. Instead, they are warnings to predators that the frog's skin is laced with deadly poison. While toads tend to be drab in colour, many also secrete toxic chemicals to keep predators away. These substances are often stored in swollen warts which burst when the toad is attacked.

Below: Adult frogs may live in water or on land. Aquatic ones have webbed feet, while those on land have powerful legs for jumping and climbing. All frogs must return to a source of water to mate.

Forever young

Salamanders which have changed into adults, but which have not yet reached adult size, are called efts. The time it takes for an amphibian to grow from a newly hatched larva to an adult varies considerably, and the chief factor is the temperature of the water in which it is developing. Most frogs and toads develop in shallow waters, warmed by the summer sun, and they generally reach adulthood within three to four months. However, salamanders, especially the largest ones, can take much longer, and at the northern and southern limits of their geographical spread some salamanders stay as larvae for many years. It appears that the trigger for the change into adult form is linked to the temperature, and in cold climates this change happens only every few years. In fact it may not happen during a salamander's lifetime, and consequently several species have evolved the ability to develop sexual organs even when they still look like larvae.

Below: Marbled salamanders are unusual in that the females lay their eggs on dry land and coil themselves around them to keep them as moist as possible. They stay like this until the seasonal rains fall. The water stimulates the eggs to hatch.

REPTILES

Reptiles include lizards, snakes, alligators, crocodiles, turtles and tortoises, as well as now-extinct creatures such as dinosaurs and the ancestors of birds. Crocodiles have roamed the Earth for 200 million years and are still highly successful hunters.

Reptiles are a large and diverse group of animals containing about 6,500 species. Many of these animals look very different from each other and live in a large number of habitats, from the deep ocean to the scorching desert. Despite their great diversity, all reptiles share certain characteristics.

Most reptiles lay eggs, but these are different from those of an amphibian because they have a hard, thin shell rather than a soft, jelly-like one. This protects the developing young inside and, more importantly, stops them from drying out. Shelled eggs were an evolutionary breakthrough because they meant that adult reptiles did not have to return to the water to breed. Their waterproof eggs could be laid anywhere, even in the driest places. Reptiles were also the first group of land-living animals to develop into an adult form inside the egg. They did not emerge as under-developed larvae like the young of most amphibians.

Below: Alligators and other crocodilians are an ancient group of reptiles that have no close living relatives. They are archosaurs, a group of reptiles that included the dinosaurs. Other living reptiles belong to a different group.

Released from their ties to water, the reptiles developed unique ways of retaining moisture. Their skins are covered by hardened plates or scales to stop water being lost. The scales are also coated with the protein keratin, the same substance used to make fingernails and hair.

All reptiles breathe using lungs; if they were to absorb air through the skin it would involve too much water loss. Like amphibians, reptiles are cold-blooded and cannot heat their bodies from within as mammals can. Consequently, reptiles are most commonly found in warm climates.

Ancient killers

Being such a diverse group, reptiles share few defining characteristics besides their shelled eggs, scaly skin and lungs. They broadly divide into four orders. The first contains the crocodiles, alligators and caimans; these are contemporaries of the dinosaurs, both groups being related to a common ancestor.

In fact today's crocodiles have changed little since the age when dinosaurs ruled the world over 200

Above: Turtles and their relatives, such as these giant tortoises, are unusual reptiles. Not only do they have bony shells fused around their bodies, but they also have skulls that are quite different from other reptiles. Turtles are also unusual because many of them live in the ocean, while most reptiles live on land.

million years ago. Unlike the dinosaurs, which disappeared 65 million years ago, the crocodiles are still going strong. Technically speaking, the dinosaurs never actually died out; their direct descendants, the birds, are still thriving. Although birds are now grouped separately from reptiles, scientists know that they all evolved from ancestors which lived about 400 million years ago. Mammals, on the other hand, broke away from this group about 300 million years ago.

Above: Most reptiles, including this tree boa, lay eggs. The young hatch looking like small versions of the adults. However, several snakes and lizards give birth to live young, which emerge from their mother fully formed.

Distant relatives

The second reptile order includes turtles, terrapins and tortoises. These are only distantly related to other reptiles, and it shows. Turtles are also the oldest group of reptiles, evolving their bony shells and clumsy bodies before crocodiles, dinosaurs or any other living reptile group existed. Although turtles evolved on land, many have since returned to water. However, they still breathe air, and all must return to land to lay their eggs.

The third group of reptiles is the largest. Collectively called the squamates, this group includes snakes and lizards. Snakes, with their legless bodies and formidable reputations, are perhaps the most familiar reptiles. They evolved from animals that did have legs, and many retain tiny vestiges of legs. The squamates include other legless members such as the amphisbaenians (or worm lizards). These are more closely related to lizards than snakes, despite looking more like the latter. Lizards are not a simple group of reptiles, and many biologists refer to them as several different groups, including the skinks, monitors, geckos and iguanas.

Below: Lizards, such as this iguana, are the largest group of reptiles. Most are hunters that live in hot parts of the world, and they are especially successful in dry areas where other types of animal are not so common.

The squamates are so diverse in their lifestyles and body forms that it is hard to find factors which they have in common. One feature not found in other reptile orders is the Jacobson's organ. It is positioned in the roof of the mouth and is closely associated with the nose. All snakes and most lizards use this organ to "taste" the air and detect prey. The long forked tongue of most of these animals flicks out into the air, picking up tiny particles on its moist surface. Once back inside the mouth, each fork slots into the Jacobson's organ which then analyzes the substances.

Amphisbaenians

Often confused with burrowing worms or small blind snakes, amphisbaenians or worm lizards are perhaps the least-known form of reptile. They are rarely seen by people because they spend most of their lives burrowing through soil. Most worm lizards are small, and live in the shallow soils and leaf litter of tropical forests. Several species live in the forests of South and Central America, but only a few species live in other parts of the Americas.

The reptiles' name comes from Amphisbaena, a mythical serpent that had a head at both ends. This is an apt description because the head is small and blunt to help the animal wriggle through loose earth, and it is hard to differentiate it from the tail at first glance. On closer inspection the head can by identified most easily by feeling for the hard skull. The tail end is considerably softer.

The skin of the worm lizard is only loosely attached to the tiny skeleton beneath, so it can be stretched and squeezed as the animal moves through the soil in an accordion fashion.

Below: The Florida worm lizard is the only species of amphisbaenian to live in the United States. It is found in the soils of northern and central Florida and in the extreme south of Georgia. It can reach 28cm (11in) long and smaller individuals are sometimes confused with earthworms.

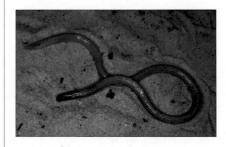

PLACENTAL MAMMALS

Mammals are the most familiar of all vertebrates. This is because not only are human beings mammals, but also most domestic animals and pets belong in this category. Placental mammals are also more widespread than other types of animal, being found in all parts of the Americas.

Mammals are grouped together because they share a number of characteristics. However, these common features do not come close to describing the huge diversity within the mammal class. For example, the largest animal that has ever existed on Earth – the blue whale – is a mammal, and so this monster of the deep shares several crucial traits with even the smallest mammals, such as the tiniest of shrews. Other mammals include elephants and moles, monkeys and hippopotamuses, and bats and camels. To add to this great diversity, mammals live in more places on Earth than any other group of animals, from the frozen ice fields of the Arctic to the humid treetops of the Amazon rainforest, and even under the sandy soil of African deserts.

Mammal bodies

The most obvious mammalian feature is hair. All mammals have hair made of keratin protein and, in most cases, it forms a thick coat of fur, though many

Below: Although they are often mistaken for fish, dolphins are mammals: they breathe air and suckle their young. However, life under water requires flippers and fins, not legs.

mammals are relatively naked, not least humans. Unlike reptiles and amphibians, all mammals are warm-blooded, which means that they can keep their body temperature at a constant level. While this requires quite a lot of energy, it means that mammals are not totally dependent on the temperature of their surroundings. In places where other vertebrates would be frozen solid, mammals can survive by seeking out food and keeping themselves warm. Many mammals,

Above: With their thick brown fur and powerful clawed paws, bears are very well adapted to life at the top of the food chain. All bears have a similar basic body plan, which is what makes them such successful terrestrial hunters.

including humans, can also cool their bodies using sweat. The water secreted on the skin cools the body efficiently, but it does mean that these animals need to drink more replacement water than do other groups.

Incidentally, the name mammal comes from the mammary glands. These glands are the means by which all female mammals provide milk (or liquid food) to their developing young. The young suck the milk through teats or nipples for the first few weeks or months of life.

Reproduction

Mammals reproduce in a number of ways. Monotremes, such as the duck-billed platypus, lay eggs, but all other mammals give birth to their young. Marsupials, a relatively small group of animals which includes opossums, give birth to very undeveloped young which then continue to grow inside a fold or pouch on the mother's skin.

Above: Polar bears sleep for long periods during the winter and give birth in the spring. They produce fat-enriched milk and their cubs stay with them for two years.

Above: Plenty of mammals can glide, but only bats join birds and insects in true flight. A bat wing is made from skin that is stretched between long finger bones.

The majority of mammals, called the placental mammals or eutherians, do not give birth to their young until they are fully formed and resemble the adults. The developing young, or foetuses, grow inside a womb or uterus where they are fed by the mother through a placenta. This large organ allows the young to stay inside the mother for a lot longer than in most other animals. It forms the interface between the mother's blood supply and that of the developing foetus, where oxygen and food pass from the parent to her offspring. The foetus is attached to the placenta by means of an umbilical cord which withers and drops off soon after the birth.

Widespread range

Mammals are found in a wider variety of habitats than any other group of animals. While mammals all breathe air with their lungs, this has not prevented many from making their homes in water.

In many ways the streamlined bodies of whales and dolphins, for example, resemble those of sharks and other fish. However, they are very much mammals, breathing air through a large blowhole in the top of the head, but their body hair has been reduced to just a few thick bristles around the mouth.

At the other end of the spectrum, some mammals even fly. Bats darting through the gloom of a summer evening may appear to be small birds, but they too are mammals with furry bodies and wings made from stretched skin instead of feathers. Although most other mammals have a more conventional body plan, with four legs and tail, they too have evolved to survive in a startling range of habitats. They have achieved this not just by adapting their bodies but by changing their behaviour. In general, mammals have larger brains than reptiles and amphibians, and this allows them to understand their environment more fully. Many mammals, such as monkeys and dogs, survive by living in complex social groups in which individuals cooperate with each other when hunting for food, protecting the group from danger and even finding mates.

Right: One factor that makes mammals unique is that the females have mammary glands. These glands produce milk for the young animals to drink, as this fallow deer fawn is doing. The milk is a mixture of fat, protein and sugars.

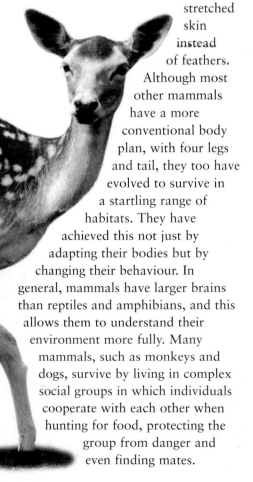

MARSUPIALS AND MONOTREMES

Not all mammals begin their lives as foetuses growing inside a uterus within their mother. Marsupials (and the very rare monotremes) develop in other ways. Marsupials raise their young inside a pouch on the outside of their body. Monotremes lay eggs.

Life in a pouch

With just 270 species the marsupials are a much smaller group than the 4,000 or so species of placental mammals that inhabit every corner of the world. Marsupials are found mainly in Australia and the islands of New Guinea, but a few species live in both North and South America.

Biologists believe that marsupials evolved first in the Americas and then spread to Australia via Antarctica, in the days when the three continents were joined together. Once Australia became an island, its marsupials remained the dominant mammals, while placental mammals began to take over from them elsewhere in the world, including in the Americas. The only American marsupials to survive the arrival of placental mammals were the opossums. These are generalist feeders that can adapt to a range of habitats.

The placental mammals have a single uterus connected to both ovaries by oviducts, while marsupials have two much smaller chambers, each

Above: A young Virginia opossum rides on its mother's back. This species is the most common marsupial in North America. It is an opportunistic animal that eats a wide range of foods. Consequently, it does well in suburban areas, where household rubbish provides a good supply of food. Virginia opossums are good climbers and have a semi-prehensile tail that provides extra support.

Below: Woolly opossums live in the tropical forests of Central America and the northern region of South America. The are omnivores and eat whatever they can find. Like other American marsupials they are good climbers. They have an opposable halux (thumb), a little like that of many primates, which allows them to grasp branches and hold food.

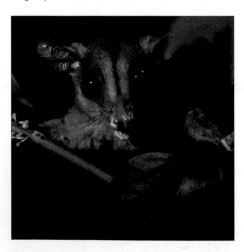

connected to a single ovary. The uterus of a placental mammal can swell up as the foetus grows. However, those of a marsupial cannot, which means that the young have to be born much earlier.

Like a newly hatched monotreme, the tiny marsupial baby is hairless and blind, and has stubby forelegs. After two or three weeks in the uterus, the baby makes its way out through a birth canal that grows especially for this journey. Once outside, the baby battles through its mother's fur to her nipples.

Many marsupials have their nipples inside a pouch or marsupium. Once inside, the baby latches on to the nipple, which swells inside its mouth to create a very firm connection.

Egg-laying mammals

As the most primitive form of mammal, monotremes form the link between more common mammals and reptiles. They differ from other mammals because they still lay their young inside eggs. There just three monotreme species. There are two species of echidna, short and long-nosed (also called spiny anteaters), and the odd-looking duck-billed platypus. These animals are found only in Australia and New Guinea today. None of these mammals now lives in the Americas, but fossil evidence shows that echidnas once lived in South

Below: The southern opossum is a close relative of the Virginia opossum, but as its name suggests, it is found further south, from central Mexico all the way to northern Argentina. Like its northern cousin, it does well in most habitats.

Above: A grey four-eyed opossum with its young. So-called for the white marks above each eye, this species suckles its young in the pouch for about 90 days. During this time, the young increase in weight by a factor of ten. Females become sexually mature at about 6 months and reproduce throughout the year.

America. It is possible that they evolved here and spread around the world before dying away to their current range.

Although monotremes are hairy and feed their young with milk, they are distant relatives of other mammals. Monotremes lay very tiny spherical eggs which have a much softer shell than those of birds or many reptiles. And unlike other mammals, monotremes do not have a birth canal. Instead, their eggs travel through the same body opening as the urine and faeces. A single multi-purpose body opening like this is called a cloaca (Latin for drain), and it is a feature that monotremes share with birds and reptiles. In fact, the name monotreme means one-holed animal.

The young of monotremes stay in the egg for only a matter of days before hatching out, and then they continue their development while being nursed by their mother. Nursing echidnas keep their young in a pouch on their underside, while platypus young spend their early days in an underground nest. While all other mammals have teats or nipples for delivering milk, the monotremes do not possess this adaptation. Instead, the mother secretes the fatty liquid on her fur and the young then lap it up.

Monotremes hatch out in a very undeveloped state. They are hairless, blind, barely 1cm (0.25in) long and have just blunt buds for limbs. The young are dependent on their mother's milk for a long time – six months in the case of echidnas. Although

Right: The white-eared opossum is found throughout South America. Its sharp teeth allow it to eat a wide range of foods, and its agile body allows it to move through an equally wide range of habitats in search of food.

they are a tiny group compared to other mammal orders, the monotremes are highly adapted to their habitats and are quite amazing mammals. One other feature makes monotremes unique. All males and some females in the echidna species have spurs on their hind feet. These are connected to venom sacs. When the spur scratches another animal it leaves a little weak venom in the cut, which irritates it and prevents it from healing properly. This makes the monotremes the only venomous mammals.

ECOLOGY

Ecology is the study of how groups of organisms interact with members of their own species, other organisms and the environment. All types of animals live in a community of interdependent organisms called an ecosystem, in which they have their own particular role.

The natural world is filled with a wealth of opportunities for animals to feed and breed. Every animal species has evolved to take advantage of a certain set of these opportunities, called a niche. A niche is not just a physical place but also a lifestyle exploited by that single species. For example, even though they live in the same rainforest habitat, sloths and tapirs occupy very different niches.

To understand how different organisms interrelate, ecologists combine all the niches in an area into a community, called an ecosystem. Ecosystems do not really exist because it is impossible to know where one ends and another begins, but the concept is a useful tool when learning more about the natural world.

Food chains

One way of understanding how an ecosystem works is to follow the food chains within it. A food chain is made up of a series of organisms that prey on each other. Each habitat is filled with them, and since they often merge into and diverge from each other, they are often combined into food webs.

Below: Nature creates some incredible alliances. The American badger, for example, goes on hunting trips with a coyote. The coyote sniffs out the prey, and the badger digs it out of its burrow for both of them to eat.

Ecologists use food chains to see how energy and nutrients flow through natural communities. Food chains always begin with plants. Plants are the only organisms on Earth that do not need to feed. They derive their energy from sunlight, whereas all other organisms, including animals, get theirs from food. At the next level up the food chain come the plant-eaters. They eat the plants, and extract the sugar and other useful substances made by them. And, like the plants, they use these substances to power their bodies and stay alive. The predators occupy the next level up, and they eat the bodies of the plant-eating animals.

At each stage of the food chain, energy is lost, mainly as heat given out by the animals' bodies. Because of this, less energy is available at each level up the food chain. This means that in a healthy ecosystem there are always fewer predators than prey, and always more plants than plant-eaters.

Nutrient cycles

A very simple food chain would be as follows: grass, mule deer and wolf. However, the reality of most ecosystems is much more complex, with many more layers, including certain animals that eat both plants and animals. Every food chain ends with a top predator, in our example, the wolf. Nothing preys on a wolf, at least when it is alive, but once it dies the food chain continues as insects, fungi and other decomposers feed on the carcass. Eventually nothing is left of the wolf's body. All the energy stored in it is removed by the decomposers, and the chemicals which made up its body return to the environment as carbon dioxide gas, water and minerals in the soil. And these are the very same substances needed by a growing plant. The cycle is complete.

Above: Nothing is wasted in nature. The dung beetle uses the droppings of larger grazing animals as a supply of food for its developing young. Since the beetles clear away all the dung, the soil is not damaged by it, the grass continues to grow, and the grazers have plenty of food.

Living together

As food chains show, the lives of different animals in an ecosystem are closely related. If all the plants died for some reason, it would not just be the plant-eaters that would go hungry. As all of them began to die, the predators would starve too. Only the decomposers might appear to benefit. Put another way, the other species living alongside an animal are just as integral to that animal's environment as the weather and landscape. This is yet another way of saying that animal species have not evolved isolated from each another.

The result is that as predators have evolved new ways of catching their prey, the prey has had to evolve new ways of escaping. On many occasions this process of co-evolution has created symbiotic relationships between two different species. For example, coyotes guide badgers to ground squirrel burrows.

Some niches are very simple, and the animals that occupy them live simple, solitary lives. Others, especially those occupied by mammals, are much more complex, and require members of a species to live closely together. These aggregations of animals may be simple herds or more structured social groups.

Food chain

Food chains show how the energy needed for life passes through an ecosystem. The energy originates in the sun. This makes plants grow, which are then eaten by animals. The plant-eating animals then become meals themselves.

Below: This food chain shows what animals eat in a temperate country, such as Britain. Herbivores eat only plants, while carnivores eat mainly other animals. Animals that eat both plants and animals are omnivores – for example, humans.

bird of prey (carnivore)

human (omnivore)

fox (carnivore)

thrush (omnivore)

hedgehog (carnivore)

rabbit (herbivore)

mouse (herbivore)

grasshopper (herbivore)

deer (herbivore)

sheep (herbivore)

cow (herbivore)

snail (herbivore)

Group living

A herd, flock or shoal is a group of animals which gathers together for safety. Each member operates as an individual, but is physically safest in the centre of the group, the danger of attack being greatest on the edge. Herd members do not actively communicate dangers to each other. When one is startled by something and bolts, the rest will probably follow. Members of a social group, on the other hand, work together to find food, raise their young and defend themselves.

Many mammals, for example monkeys, dogs and dolphins, form social groups, and these groups exist in many forms. At one end of the spectrum are highly ordered societies, such as wolf packs, which are often controlled by a dominant male-female pair, the other members having their own ranking in a strict hierarchical structure. At the other end of the spectrum are leaderless gangs of animals, such as squirrel monkeys, which merge and split with no real guiding purpose.

There are many advantages of living in social groups, with members finding more food and being warned of danger, for example. However, in many societies only a handful of high-ranking members are allowed to breed. In these cases, the groups are held together by a complex fusion of family ties in which brothers and sisters help to raise nephews and nieces. Politics also plays its cohesive part, with members forming and breaking alliances in order to rise to the top.

Below: Bison have poor eyesight but good hearing and sense of smell. Living in vast herds gives them a better chance of detecting wolves. If attacked, bulls often form a defensive circle around their females and young.

MIGRATION AND HIBERNATION

Everywhere across the Americas, the climate changes throughout the year with the cycle of seasons. In some places these changes are hardly noticeable from month to month, while in others each new season brings extremes of weather, from blistering summers to freezing winters, or torrential rains followed by drought.

Change of lifestyle

In temperate regions, such as New England, the year is generally divided into four seasons. By contrast, in the far north, the change between the short summer and long winter is so quick that, in effect, there are only two seasons. Other regions experience a different annual cycle of changes. For example, tropical regions do not really have fluctuating temperatures, but many areas do experience periods of relative dryness and at least one period of heavier rains each year.

Animals must, of course, react to these changes if they are to survive the harshest weather and make the most of clement conditions. Monkeys, for example, build up a mental map of their patch of forest so that they know where the fresh leaves will be after the rains, and where to find the hardier forest fruits during a drought. Wolves living in chilly northern forests hunt

together in packs during the cold winter, cooperating to kill animals which are much larger than they are. However, when the summer arrives they tend to forage alone, picking off the many smaller animals, such as rodents and rabbits, which appear when the snow melts.

Hibernation

The reason the wolves find these smaller animals in the summer is that they suddenly emerge having passed the winter in cosy burrows or nests. This behaviour is commonly called hibernating, but there is a distinction between true hibernation and simply being inactive over winter.

Animals such as bears and tree squirrels are not true hibernators. Although they generally sleep for long periods during the coldest parts of winter, hunkered down in a den or drey, they do not enter the deep, unconscious state of hibernation. Unable to feed while asleep, these animals rely on their bodily reserves of fat to stay alive. However, they often wake up during breaks in the harshest weather and venture outside to urinate

Above: Reptiles that live in cooler parts of the world – rattlesnakes, for example – spend a long time lying dormant. They do not hibernate like mammals, but because they are cold-blooded and do not need lots of energy to function, they can go for long periods without food.

or snatch a meal. Because tree squirrels have smaller fat reserves than bears, they frequently visit caches (stores) of food which they filled in the autumn.

On the other hand, the true hibernators, such as woodchucks, do not stir at all over winter. They rely completely on their reserves of fat to stay alive, and to save energy their metabolism slows to a fraction of its normal pace.

Only warm-blooded animals hibernate because they are the main types of animals which can survive in places where hibernation is necessary. However, rattlesnakes often pass the winter in rocky crevices and burrows in a dormant state. Reptiles and amphibians that live in very hot and dry places have a similar response to inhospitable weather. They become dormant when their habitat becomes too dry. Most bury themselves in moist sand or under rocks, only becoming

Hibernating heart rate

The hibernating animal's heart rate slows to just a few beats per minute. It breathes more slowly and its body temperature drops to just a few degrees above the surrounding air temperature.

Below: Bears may be out of sight for most of the winter, but they do not become completely dormant and their temperature does not fall drastically. The bodies of true hibernators, such as the dormouse, shut down almost completely during hibernation.

active again when rain brings the habitat back to life. Some aestivating frogs (those which are dormant in the summer) even grow a skin cocoon which traps water and keeps their bodies moist while they wait for the rains to return.

Migration

Another way of coping with bad conditions is to migrate. Migrations are not just random wanderings, but involve following a set route each year. In general they are two-way trips, with animals returning to where they started once conditions back home become favourable again.

All sorts of animals migrate, from insects to whales, and there are many reasons for doing so. Most migrators are looking for supplies of food, or for a safe place to rear their young. For example, once their home territory becomes too crowded, young lemmings stampede over wide areas looking for new places to live, sometimes dying in the process. Herds of caribou leave the barren tundra as winter approaches, and head for the relative warmth of the forest. Mountain goats act in a similar way: having spent the summer grazing in high alpine meadows, they descend below the treeline when winter snow begins to cover their pastures.

Other migrations are on a much grander scale, and in some cases an animal's whole life can be a continual migration. Among the greatest migrants are the giant whales, which travel thousands of miles from their

Above: Whales make the longest migrations of all mammals. They move from their warm breeding grounds near the equator to feeding areas in cooler waters near the poles.

breeding grounds in the tropics to their feeding grounds near the poles. The cool waters around the poles teem with plankton food, while the warmer tropical waters are a better place for giving birth.

Day length

How do animals know that it is time to hibernate or migrate? The answer lies in the changing number of hours of daylight as the seasons change. All animals are sensitive to daylight, and use it to set their body clocks or circadian rhythms. These rhythms affect all bodily processes, including the build-up to the breeding season. The hibernators begin to put on weight

Above: Bats spend long periods hibernating. They mate before winter, and the females store the sperm inside their body, only releasing it on the eggs as spring approaches.

or store food as the days shorten, and many migrants start to get restless before setting off on their journey. However, not all migrations are controlled by the number of hours of daylight. Some migrators, such as wildebeest and lemmings, move because of other environmental factors, such as the lack of food caused by drought or overcrowding.

Below: Moose move across wide regions of mountains, rivers and even roads, migrating south each winter. They are known to migrate up to 196km (122 miles) from Alaska to northern Canada. The trigger for this migration is the arrival of large accumulations of snow in their feeding grounds, leading them to search for warmer browsing land.

INTRODUCED SPECIES

Centuries ago, as people started exploring and conquering new lands, many animals travelled with them. In fact, that's the only way many animals could travel such long distances, often crossing seas. Many introduced species then thrived in their new habitats, often at the expense of the native wildlife.

Perhaps one of the first animals introduced to the Americas was the dog. The ancestors of the Native Americans arrived with a domesticated hunting and guard dog. These dogs were probably descended from grey wolves, many years before. Genetic research suggests that wolves were first tamed in southern Asia and the Middle East.

Horses are closely associated with the image of the American West. However, these are also introduced animals. They arrived with the Spanish conquistadors 500 years ago. Domestic horses proved essential for exploring the New World and they carried settlers to their new homes. Horses were also quickly adopted by Native Americans, especially those tribes that were uprooted from their traditional

Below: The coypu is a native of South America. Its soft fur was once used to make clothing and the coypu was transported across the world to be raised in fur farms. The fur and often the animals themselves are sometimes called nutria. As fur clothing went out of fashion, many of these coypus were released and now live wild in wetland areas. They are especially common in the Mississippi Delta area.

lands and were forced to make new lives on the open prairies. For example, they used horses for hunting American bison. Groups of the introduced horses escaped from captivity and began to live wild. The feral American horses were called mustangs.

Domestic animals

Looking around the prairies of North America (and the pampas of South America) today, you would be forgiven for thinking that cows, sheep and other farm animals are naturally occurring species. In fact, all come from distant parts of the world. Over the centuries, livestock animals have been selectively bred to develop desirable characteristics, such as lean meat or high milk production. Despite this, they can be traced back to ancestral species. For example, goats are a domestic breed of an Asian ibex. Sheep are descended from an Asian hoofed animal called a mouflon.

Rodent invaders

While many animals were introduced to new areas on purpose as livestock or pets, other animals hitched a lift.

Cows and sheep

European cows are believed to be descendants of a now-extinct species of oxen called the auroch, while modern sheep are descended from the mouflon. From their beginnings in the Middle East, new breeds were introduced to all corners of the world, where they had a huge effect on the native animals and wildlife.

Above: Cattle have been bred to look and behave very differently from their wild ancestors. Few breeds have horns, and they are generally docile animals. Some breeds produce a good supply of milk, while others are bred for their meat.

Below: Sheep were among the first domestic animals. They are kept for their meat and sometimes milk, which is used for cheese. The thick coat or fleece that kept their ancestors warm on mountain slopes is now used to make woollen garments.

Above: While the ancestors of domestic horses have become extinct, horses have become wild in several parts of the world. Perhaps the most celebrated of these feral horses are the mustangs, which run free in the wild American West, after escaping from early European settlers.

For example, some animals were more or less stowaways on ships, but only those that could fend for themselves at their new destination were successfully introduced. These animals tended to be generalist feeders, and the most successful were rodents, especially mice and rats. In fact the house mouse is the second most widespread mammal of all, after humans. It lives almost everywhere that people do, except in the icy polar regions, although it is very likely that rodents did reach these places but then failed to thrive in the cold.

The black rat – also known as the ship rat – has spread right around the world from Asia over the last 2,000 years. On several occasions it has brought diseases with it, including bubonic plague, or the Black Death, which has killed millions of people.

Another prolific travelling rodent is the brown rat, which is thought to have spread from Europe, and which now exists across the Americas and everywhere else except the poles.

There are two main reasons why rodents are so successful. The first is that they will eat almost anything, including all the types of food that are typically discarded by humans. The second reason is that they can

reproduce at a prolific rate, with females producing up to 56 offspring per year. These two characteristics have meant that mice and rats have become pests wherever they breed.

Below: With their sharp and ever-growing teeth, rodents are very adaptable animals. Mice and rats have spread alongside humans, and wherever people go, these little gnawing beasts soon become established, breeding very quickly and spreading into new areas.

ENDANGERED SPECIES

Many animals are threatened with extinction because they cannot survive in a world which is constantly being changed by human intervention. Many species have already become extinct, and if people do nothing to save them, a great many more will follow.

Surprising though it may sound, there is nothing unusual in extinctions, for they are an important part of the natural world. As the climate and landscape have changed in a given area over millions of years, the animals that live there have also changed. And as a new species evolves, so another is forced out of its habitat and becomes extinct. All that remains, if we are lucky, are a few fossilized bones – a record in stone.

Mass extinction?

Biologists estimate that there are at least several million species alive today, and possibly as many as 30 million. Whatever the figure, there are probably more species on Earth right now than at any other time. Therefore, because of the habitat destruction caused by people, more species are becoming extinct or are being threatened with extinction than ever before.

Geologists and biologists know that every now and then there are mass extinctions, in which great numbers of the world's animals die out forever. For example, it is widely believed that the dinosaurs and many other reptiles were wiped out after a meteorite smashed into Mexico 65 million years ago. But the questions that geologists and biologists are now asking include: are we witnessing the natural world's latest mass extinction? And are humans the cause?

Most of the world's animal species are actually insects – especially beetles – and other invertebrates. It is likely that many of these species, especially those living in tropical forests, are becoming extinct. However, since scientists may never have had a chance to describe many of them, it is difficult to estimate the true number that are being lost.

Below: The pronghorn is a unique hoofed grazer. Before Europeans arrived there were 35 million pronghorns in North America. Their numbers plummeted after the prairies were cleared for grazing cattle, and today only half a million survive in the United States and Canada. They are now extinct in Mexico.

Above: Leatherback turtles are the largest turtles in the world – even larger than the better-known giant tortoises. They are becoming rare because of the decline in untouched beaches on which to lay their eggs. Fewer leatherbacks are being born, and even fewer reach adulthood.

Life list

With vertebrate animals, it is a different story. Because there are only a few thousand species of animals with backbones, most of which have been recognized for hundreds of years, we know a great deal more about the plight of each species. Many species, for example mice, dogs and horses, thrive in a world dominated by people. However, a great many more species have suffered as people have destroyed their habitats, either deliberately or by upsetting the balance of nature by introducing species from other parts of the world.

The International Union for the Conservation of Nature and Natural Resources (IUCN) produces a Red List of animals which are in danger of extinction. There are currently about 5,500 animals listed in a number of categories, including extinct in the wild, endangered and vulnerable. Nearly one-quarter of all mammals

are included on the list, and about four percent of reptiles and three of amphibians.

However, while the status of all mammals has been assessed by the IUCN, only a fraction of reptiles and amphibians has been as thoroughly checked, and it is very likely that many more species are much closer to extinction than was previously thought.

Below: Golden lion tamarins have been saved from extinction by extensive captive breeding programmes in zoos around the world. An area of the monkey's forest habitat in Brazil is now being protected, and captive-bred monkeys are being reintroduced to the wild.

Above: Woolly spider monkeys, or muriquis, are among the most endangered of any animal. There are only 500 left in the wild. This large monkey has suffered because the rainforests of Brazil have been broken up into areas that are too small for large groups to live in.

Wiped out

People have been clearing forests for thousands of years. Europe and China for example, used to be thickly forested, but were gradually cleared by farmers and turned to the fields and grasslands that we see today. As people migrated to the Americas, a similar process took place, although on a huge scale and at a much faster rate. The

Above: Spectacled bears are the only bears to live in South America. They live in forests that grow on the slopes of the Andes. This forest habitat has been severely damaged by people and only 2,000 spectacled bears now survive in the wild.

major habitat being destroyed was, and still is, the tropical rainforest of South America. The number of species living in these tropical areas is much higher than elsewhere, and a large proportion of animals are finding it increasingly difficult to survive while their habitats are shrinking so rapidly.

Although few animals on the Red List have actually become extinct, the situation is becoming graver for most species. The monkeys and apes of the tropical rainforests are among the worst affected, with nearly one in four species being very close to extinction. This is because rainforests are complicated places, and many primate species there have evolved a specialized lifestyle, for example feeding on fruit in the tallest trees. These species are usually very badly affected by sudden changes in their environment, for example when a logging team cuts down all the tall trees leaving just the shorter ones behind. Without their preferred food, survival is precarious.

CONSERVING WILDLIFE

With so many species facing extinction, conservationists have their work cut out. Conservationists try to protect habitats and provide safe places for threatened animals to thrive, but the activities of ordinary people can often also have an adverse effect on the future of natural habitats.

People give many reasons why wildlife should be conserved. Some argue that if all the forests were cleared and the oceans polluted, the delicate balance of nature would be so ruined that Earth would not be able to support any life, including humans. Others suggest that if vulnerable species were allowed to die, the natural world would not be sufficiently diverse to cope with future changes in the environment. Another reason to save diversity is that we have not yet fully recorded it. Also, there are undoubtedly many as yet unknown species – especially of plants – which could be useful to humankind, for example in the field of medicine. But perhaps the strongest argument for the conservation of wildlife is that it would be totally irresponsible to let it disappear.

Habitat protection

Whatever the reasons, the best way to protect species in danger of being wiped out is to protect their habitats so that the complex communities of plants and animals can continue to live. However, with the human population growing so rapidly, people are often forced to choose between promoting their own interests and protecting wildlife. Of course, people invariably put themselves first, which means that the conservationists have to employ a range of techniques in order to save wildlife.

In many countries it has now become illegal to hunt certain endangered animals, or to trade in any products made from their bodies. Whales, gorillas and elephants are protected in this way. Many governments and charitable organisations have also set up wildlife

Below: One of the main causes of deforestation is people clearing the trees and burning them to make way for farmland. The ash makes good soil for a few years, but eventually the nutrients needed by the crops run out and so the farmers often begin to clear more forest.

Above: If logging is done properly, it can make enough money to pay to protect the rest of the rainforest. Only selected trees are cut down and they are removed without damaging younger growth. Forests can be used to grow crops, such as coffee and nuts, without cutting down all the trees.

reserves, where the animals stand a good chance of thriving. The oldest protected areas are in the United States, where it is illegal to ruin areas of forest wilderness and wetland. Consequently, these places have become wildlife havens. Other protected areas include semi-natural landscapes which double as beauty spots and tourist attractions. Although these areas often have to be extensively altered and managed to meet the needs of the visitors, most still support wildlife communities.

Reintroduction

Large areas of tropical forests are now protected in American countries such as Brazil and Costa Rica, but often conservation efforts come too late because many animals have either become rare or are completely absent after years of human damage. However, several conservation programmes have reintroduced animals bred in zoos into the wild.

Zoo animals

Once zoos were places where exotic animals were merely put on display. Such establishments were increasingly regarded as cruel. Today, the world's best zoos are an integral part of conservation. Several animals, which are classified as extinct in the wild, can only be found in zoos where they are being bred. These breeding programmes are heavily controlled to make sure that closely related animals do not breed with each other. Later, individual animals may be sent around the world to mate in different zoos to avoid in-breeding.

Below: Many of the world's rarest species are kept in zoos, partly so that people can see them, since they are too rare to be spotted in the wild. Bears do well in zoos when they are provided with an enriched environment that includes food puzzles.

To reintroduce a group of zoo-bred animals successfully into the wild, conservationists need to know how the animal fits into the habitat and interacts with the other animals living there. In addition, for example when trying to reintroduce golden lion tamarins to the forests of Brazil, the animals had to learn how to live among the moving branches of trees.

Below: Breeding centres are an important way of increasing the number of rare animals. Most, such as this giant panda centre in China, are in the natural habitat. If the animals kept there are treated properly, they should be able to fend for themselves when released back into the wild.

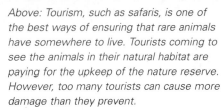

Above: Tourism, such as safaris, is one of the best ways of ensuring that rare animals have somewhere to live. Tourists coming to see the animals in their natural habitat are paying for the upkeep of the nature reserve. However, too many tourists can cause more damage than they prevent.

Understanding habitats

A full understanding of how animals live in the wild is also vitally important when conservationists are working in a habitat that has been damaged by human activity. For example, in areas of rainforest which are being heavily logged, the trees are often divided into isolated islands of growth surrounded by cleared ground. This altered habitat is no good for monkeys, which need large areas of forest to swing through throughout the year. The solution is to plant strips of forest to connect the islands of untouched habitat, creating a continuous mass again.

Another example of beneficial human intervention involves protecting rare frogs in the process of migrating to a breeding pond. If their migration necessitates crossing a busy road, it is likely that many of them will be run over. Conservationists now dig little tunnels under the roads so that the frogs can travel in safety. Similar protection schemes have been set up for hedgehogs and ducks, to allow them safe passageways.

BIOMES

The Earth is not a uniform place but has a complex patchwork of habitats covering its surface from the equator to the poles. Biologists have simplified this patchwork by dividing it into zones called biomes, each of which has a particular climate and a distinct community of animals.

The places where animal communities live can be radically different. So, for example, vipers slither along the tops of sand dunes in the middle of the Sahara Desert while sperm whales live hundreds of metres down in the gloomy, ice-cold depths of the ocean. The environmental conditions determine what kind of animals and plants are able to survive there.

Climate control

The world's habitats are generally divided into 11 biomes: oceans, fresh-water rivers and wetlands, tropical forests, temperate forests, boreal forests, tropical grasslands or savannahs, temperate grasslands or prairies, tundra, polar ice caps, deserts and mountains.

The overriding factor that determines whether a piece of land belongs to one biome or another is its climate – chiefly the rainfall and temperature. Understanding the climate of a place is a complicated business because the factors involved – including rainfall, temperature and light levels – vary from day to night and throughout the year. The latitude is probably the best place to start. In general terms, regions close to the equator, at a latitude of 0°, are hot. The coldest places are the poles, with a latitude of 90°. The territory in between generally cools as you travel to higher latitudes.

However, other factors also affect climate. For example, during the hot days of summer, the land at certain latitudes warms up more quickly than the ocean. Six months later, in the depths of winter, the land cools down more quickly than the ocean. This means that the oceans and the areas of land bordering them tend to enjoy a mild climate with smaller fluctuations of temperature each year, while the interiors of large continental landmasses experience very hot summers and extremely chilly winters.

Animal communities

Other geographical factors – ocean currents, mountains and depressions in the Earth's surface – also have a major influence on climate and biomes. The climate defines which plants can grow in any particular spot and how quickly. And since the plants form the basis of all food webs and ecosystems, each biome has a particular community of animals which have evolved to exploit the plant life.

Below: This map shows how the world can be divided into biomes. The climate of a region has the greatest effect on the sorts of plants and animals that can survive there. Some animals may live across an entire biome, while others are found only in particular habitats.

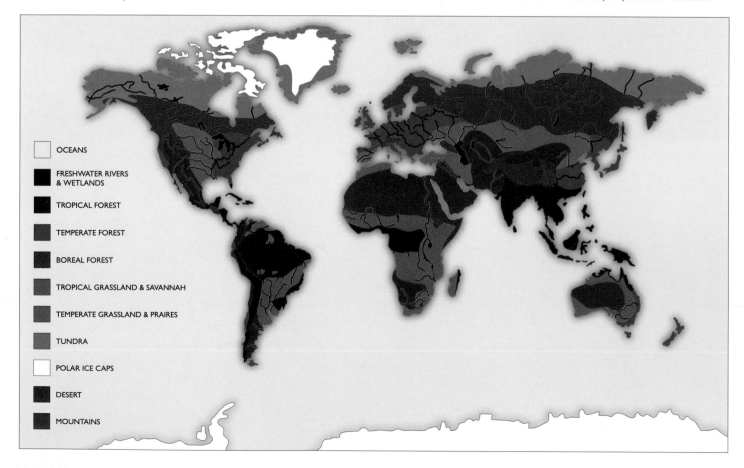

- OCEANS
- FRESHWATER RIVERS & WETLANDS
- TROPICAL FOREST
- TEMPERATE FOREST
- BOREAL FOREST
- TROPICAL GRASSLAND & SAVANNAH
- TEMPERATE GRASSLAND & PRAIRES
- TUNDRA
- POLAR ICE CAPS
- DESERT
- MOUNTAINS

Biomes and size

Closely related animals that live in different biomes are different sizes, and this is linked to the conditions in which they must survive. For example, moose live in cold forest areas and they are huge – in fact, the largest deer in the world. White-tailed deer live in the eastern United States, a temperate zone with relatively mild weather all year round, and they are average-sized deer. In contrast, pudus live in the thick, consistently warm tropical jungles of South America, and they are the smallest deer in the world. Animals that live in warm areas tend to be small, while those that live in cold areas tend to be large. The reason for this is the relationship between the surface area and weight of an animal. Large animals lose body heat more slowly than smaller ones, so being large in a cold climate is better than being small. However, being large in hot conditions makes it hard for the animal to lose excess body heat, so these animals tend to be smaller.

Moose

White-tailed deer

Southern pudu

Rainfall has a major influence on biomes. It is generally heaviest in tropical regions, resulting in lush rainforests. In colder regions, rainfall may be almost as high but it results in a different type of forest. In areas with less rain, deserts or grasslands appear.

The animals in different biomes face the same challenges: finding enough food and water, and finding a mate to raise offspring. However, the different conditions in each biome mean that the animals have to meet these challenges in very different ways.

In all biomes, the animal communities have a similar structure. Grazers and other plant-eating animals survive by eating any plants which have evolved to make the most of the climatic conditions. These grazers are, in turn, preyed upon by a series of hunters. In the most productive biomes, such as forests, many of these hunting animals might be hunted in turn by larger, fiercer predators.

However, the plant-eaters of grasslands, such as bison and antelopes, live a very different life from their counterparts in tropical forests, such as monkeys and tapirs. Similarly, ocean hunters, such as mighty orcas (killer whales), have a body adapted to swimming at great speed through the water; the predators in a boreal forest, such as wolves, have very different bodies for covering long distances quickly and bringing down animals more than twice their size. One of the main purposes of biology is to understand how communities of plants and animals have evolved to survive in the world's different biomes.

Grassland animals

Grasslands are unusual habitats because food is everywhere. While animals that live in other biomes must seek out and defend a source of food, grazing animals are surrounded by it, and no single animal can control it. Instead of competing for food, they compete for mates, and many grazers are tough fighters. Grass and other plant foods are not very nutritious, so animals have to eat a lot of them. Since they have plenty of food, many grassland animals, such as bison, are big. Smaller animals cannot defend themselves. Many of them, such as prairie dogs, live in burrows, which protect them from attack. Coyotes are small hunters that prey on ground-living rodents, such as prairie dogs.

Bison

Prairie dogs

Coyote

OCEANS

The oceans cover nearly three-quarters of the Earth's surface and create by far the largest and most complex biome. They contain the world's smallest and largest animals, from tiny zooplankton to the mighty blue whale. Between these two extremes, the oceans contain an incredible wealth of life.

The oceans are not a simple biome because they consist of countless habitats, including everything from colourful coral reefs to mysterious, deep-sea hydrothermal vents. The depth of the ocean obviously has a marked effect on the conditions. Depth can range from just a few centimetres along the coast to about 11km (6.75 miles), the deepest ocean point in the Mariana Trench, near the Pacific island of Guam. The first few 100m (330ft) or so below the surface is called the photic zone, where the water is bathed in sunlight during the day. This upper layer is the limit of plant growth in the ocean because below this depth the light fades, unable to penetrate any deeper, and plants rely on light to make their food.

As on land, many ocean animals graze on plants, which means that they have to live in the photic zone. Ocean plants tend to be simple algae, known as phytoplankton, which float in the current. These plants do not have complicated body structures, and many

Marine iguanas can be found along rocky coastlines. They can stay underwater for over an hour.

Sea otters do not need land to survive. When sleeping, they wrap themselves in kelp.

Common seals have large, sensitive eyes which help them to see underwater.

Harp seals are able to survive in the open sea, but they give birth on ice floes.

are just single cells. Consequently, many of the ocean plant-eaters are also tiny floating organisms, known collectively as zooplankton. Zooplankton – largely shrimp-like crustaceans – is a very important part of the ocean food chain, being the main food for toothless baleen whales. These ocean giants filter out the zooplankton from gulps of sea water.

Deeper down, in the dark depths, life continues without plants. Despite conditions being too dark for plants, most deep-sea animals still get their energy from them indirectly by feeding on marine "snow". This consists of the waste products and dead bodies of the organisms higher up.

These food chains provide the basis of animal life in the ocean, feeding many types of larger vertebrate animals including fish, turtles and sea mammals.

While fish evolved in the sea, the sea-living reptiles, such as turtles and sea snakes, and the sea mammals, such as seals and whales, actually evolved from animals which once lived on land. A great deal of this evolution must have taken place in shallow coastal waters, and while whales and dolphins have become completely independent of land, other sea mammals and most reptiles must return to land at some point during the year to breed.

Seals and sea lions make their homes in coastal waters where the ocean meets the land. These shallow waters are very different from the dark abyss of the deep ocean. Coral reefs, sometimes described as the rainforests of the ocean because they support so much life, are a feature of coastal waters in the tropics. In shallow seas, tall kelps and other kinds of seaweed can grow into thick underwater forests, providing habitats for a whole range of animals, such as sea otters.

White-beaked dolphins live in coastal waters. They are famed for leaping and somersaulting.

Orcas, also known as killer whales, live throughout the world's oceans. They are expert hunters.

In autumn, northern right whales migrate from cold northern waters to warmer areas in the south.

Humpback whales live in deep waters, spending the summer in cold waters near the poles.

FRESH WATER

Only three percent of the world's water is fresh, but experts estimate that this covers a total of over 100,000sq km (38,610sq miles), including the polar icecaps. Freshwater rivers, lakes and wetlands are some of the best places to see wildlife. But where does fresh water come from?

The Earth's atmosphere is a huge water pump that transfers water from the oceans to the land. The heat from the sun makes water evaporate from the surface of the ocean, and the water vapour produced becomes part of the atmosphere. The warm water vapour in the air may then cool down for various reasons. As it cools, the vapour begins to turn back into a liquid, forming tiny droplets on the surface of dust particles carried in the wind. These moist particles of dust gather together to form the clouds that often obscure clear skies. If the air cools even more, the amount of water condensing in a cloud becomes too much for it to hold, and the water falls to the surface as rain.

Since most of the Earth's surface is covered by oceans, most of the rain falls back into the sea. However, some falls on to land where it forms rivers, lakes and waterlogged ground, such as swamps and marshes, known collectively as wetlands. Mountain ranges receive high rainfall because they force the moist air to rise up over

Water opossums, or yapoks, live beside freshwater streams and lakes in tropical forests.

Amazon river dolphins inhabit slow-moving river waters. They use sounds to find their prey.

Black caimans are found in rivers and flooded forests. At night they may hunt on land.

Green anacondas spend much of their time in shallow water, waiting for their prey to drink.

them and cool. The rain then flows down the mountainsides in torrents and waterfalls. Down in the lowlands, these fast-flowing streams join together to make larger, deeper rivers which move more slowly across the landscape. Nearly all the fresh water falling on land eventually makes its way back to the oceans via rivers. Some fresh water does seep into rocks under the ground, but it reappears as springs which feed yet more rivers.

All the rivers in the world combined contain just a fraction of the Earth's water, though some of them form huge freshwater systems. The largest river system is in the Amazon Basin. This South American network of rivers contains more water than the Nile, Mississippi and Yangtze rivers together, and hosts many thousands of animal and plant species.

Rain water and other forms of precipitation provide fresh water. When water evaporates from the oceans, the salt is left behind and only the water molecules rise into the atmosphere. Although fresh water acquires small amounts of dissolved salts as it flows over rocks on its journey to the sea, it is much less salty than sea water, and this has a marked effect on the animals that live in it. While sea water is saltier than the body fluids of animals, fresh water is less salty, which means that water tends to flow into the animal from outside. If the animal does not frequently get rid of some moisture, it will become swollen, and its body fluids will be too diluted to work efficiently.

Freshwater fish and amphibians tackle this problem by urinating all their excess water. Semi-aquatic animals, such as otters and anacondas, rely on their skin to act as a barrier to the influx of water.

Surinam toads spend their lives in the muddy waters at the bottom of turbid streams and ponds.

Alligator snapping turtles live on the beds of lakes and slow-flowing rivers, waiting for approaching fish.

Capybaras live in herds on the banks of rivers and in swampy areas, using water as a refuge.

Muskrats are largely nocturnal, living in large family groups along riverbanks and in marshes.

TROPICAL FORESTS

Tropical forests are the oldest and most complex forests on Earth. They contain a greater variety of animal species than anywhere else, from the great apes, such as gorillas and orang-utans, and big cats, such as tigers and leopards, to tiny frogs and pencil-thin snakes.

The lush, steamy jungles of tropical forest grow in a band around the Earth's equator. These forests are packed with wildlife, more so than any other biome. The total number of animal species living in tropical forests is unknown because most have never been identified, but it probably adds up to several million. The majority of these species are insects, such as beetles and bugs, but tropical forests also contain the greatest diversity of vertebrate animals. Unfortunately, large tracts of these forests are now under threat from human activities such as logging.

Tropical forests are among the wettest places on Earth. Most receive about 2.5m (8.25ft) of rain every year, while forests that grow on ocean islands often receive over 6m (19.75ft). The tropics receive so much rain because near the equator the sun is always high in the sky, keeping temperatures elevated. Consequently, a great deal of water evaporates from the oceans and rises into the sky here. The water vapour cools as it rises and

Strawberry poison-dart frogs live mostly on the ground, although females lay their eggs in trees.

Ocelots are agile climbers, often hunting in trees. They sleep in shady thickets and hunt at night.

Brazilian tapirs live in woodland habitats with a source of water. They are excellent swimmers.

Southern pudus live alone in the humid forests of the southern Andes mountains.

condenses into vast rain clouds. Generally towards the end of the day, these clouds release their load of water on to the lush forests beneath.

Rainfall defines the two main types of tropical forest – rainforest and monsoon forest. Rainforests grow in places where rainfall is heavy all year round, although there are often drier spells throughout the year. The main areas of American rainforest are in the Amazon Basin and in Central America. Monsoon forests grow in tropical areas where most rain falls during an annual wet season. The largest monsoon forests are along the coast of Brazil.

With so much water and warmth, plants grow larger than just about anywhere else on land. Most trees reach at least 50m (165ft) tall and form a dense network of branches, or canopy, high above the ground. The canopy is so thick in places that underneath it is very gloomy and humid. Taller trees poke their crowns out above the canopy. The tallest of these emergent trees grow over 100m (330ft) high.

Tropical forest plants grow more thickly than elsewhere, too. Some plants, known as air plants or epiphytes, do not grow in the ground but attach themselves to the trunks or branches of larger plants. Within this complex framework of plant life, there are countless places for all types of animal to thrive. For example, amphibians need to live in water during the early stages of their life. And with so much rain falling, tropical forests are rarely short of water. Some epiphytes have bowl-shaped leaves to catch the rain, and several amphibian species use these aerial ponds as breeding sites. Down on the ground some frogs and salamanders just lay their eggs in damp soil, which is wet enough for their young to develop in.

Jaguars take refuge in secluded spots by day and stalk by night, pouncing on their prey from trees.

Emerald tree boas have leaf-green camouflage which helps keep them safe from birds of prey.

Three-toed sloths hang upside down in trees, only coming down when moving to new trees.

Brown capuchins are highly adaptable, living in dense jungle trees and also in towns and cities.

TEMPERATE FORESTS

Before the rise of agriculture, temperate forests covered most of North America. Today, however, nearly all of these wild woodlands have been replaced by meadows and farmland. After tropical forests, temperate forests contain the greatest diversity of animal life.

Temperate forests grow in mild regions that receive a lot of rain but do not get too hot or cold. The largest temperate forests are in the northern hemisphere, in a belt north of subtropical regions.

The main difference between the temperate forests and other forest biomes is that most temperate trees are deciduous, dropping their leaves in the autumn, and growing new ones in spring. Although there are a few deciduous trees, such as paper birch, growing in the southern zones of northern boreal forests, there are many more evergreen conifers.

The reason why temperate forests lose their leaves is to save energy during the winter. Because it is rarely very bright over winter, the leaves would not be able to photosynthesize food from sunlight. And because the cold and frosts would damage the redundant leaves during winter, it is best that they are dropped. As autumn progresses, the leaves' valuable green pigments, which trap the sun's energy, withdraw back into the tree. Then, as

American martens move with ease in trees. They have large eyes to help them see in low light.

Five-lined skinks prefer damp areas. They bask on rocky outcrops and tree stumps.

White-tailed deer hide in grasses, raising their white tail as a warning when they spot predators.

Porcupines rest in hollow trees by day and spend the night looking for food, using their sensitive nose.

the green disappears, so the less important red and brown pigments are revealed, giving the forest its beautiful autumn colours.

As with a few other land biomes, temperate forests are poorly represented in the southern hemisphere, with almost none growing in South America. The temperate forests that grow in slightly warmer and drier regions, such as California, are not deciduous. They are populated with evergreen trees with toughened leaves that keep the moisture in with a coating of oily resin. Perhaps the most spectacular forests in this biome are the temperate rainforests found on the coast of British Columbia, Canada. Due to the unusual climate, the forests receive more rain than most tropical rainforests, which is one reason why the redwood, the world's tallest tree, flourishes here.

Although temperate forests do not grow as densely as tropical forests, they still contain many places for animals to thrive. Tree-dwellers scamper from tree to tree collecting seeds and fruit, and snatching insects to eat. Down on the ground, the forests are populated by larger animals such as wild boar and deer and, in a few places, wood bison – the even rarer woodland relative of the plains bison.

During winter, with the leaves fallen and growth almost stopped completely, temperate forests become desolate places with little food available.

Larger animals may migrate to warmer, more productive areas to spend the winter, or scratch out a living while depending on their body fat reserves. Smaller animals, such as ground squirrels, hibernate to save energy until the spring, while others, such as most tree-living squirrels, rely on food caches that they built up in the autumn.

Corn snakes hunt on the ground and in trees. Their wide underside helps them grip vertical surfaces.

Striped skunks forage under thick vegetation at night. They produce a foul spray when threatened.

Virginia opossums prefer forested areas with plenty of rain. They use their tail to cling to branches.

Black bears share the forest with grizzly bears, foraging for fruit, nuts, insects, fish and rodents.

BOREAL FORESTS

Boreal forest, or taiga as it is also known, grows in the icy conditions of the far north. This biome is dominated by conifers, which are almost the only trees that can survive the harsh conditions. Boreal forests form the largest swathes of continuous forest and cover about ten percent of the Earth's land.

Boreal forest gets its name from the Greek god of the north wind, Boreas. The name is apt because this type of forest only grows in the northern hemisphere – not because the climatic conditions for boreal forest do not exist in the southern hemisphere, but because there is little land down there where such forests can grow. The alternative name, taiga, is a Russian word meaning marshy pine forest. This name is also apt because boreal forests often grow around moss-filled bogs, the actual bogs being too wet for tree growth.

Boreal forests grow in huge unbroken swathes in Canada and Alaska. These parts of the far north enjoy a short summer with very long days and a long, cold winter when the sun only rises for a few hours. Winter temperatures regularly plunge to –25°C (–13°F).

Compared to other forests, boreal ones are very simple because they contain far fewer species; in fact, almost all the trees in these forests are conifers.

American red squirrels live high up in trees. In winter they are able to survive on caches of food.

Wolverines prefer remote areas, far away from humans. Females give birth in rocky dens.

Grey wolves live in conifer forests, in packs with strict hierarchies. They hunt by scent and hearing.

Alaska marmots occupy the spaces formed under rocks, hibernating during the winter.

Because of the cold and dark, boreal forests appear frozen in time for much of the year as the wildlife endures the cold, waiting for the intense activity of the short summer growing season. Even the summer is too cold for nearly all cold-blooded animals, such as amphibians and reptiles. Rattlesnakes do survive in the southern fringes of the Canadian forest, but amphibians are uncommon on land and only a few survive in the often-frozen water. Mammals such as marmots and bears, and also the rattlesnakes, hibernate or become inactive during the coldest months of the year. Incredibly, wood frogs endure the winter frozen inside river ice, becoming active again after the thaw.

Mammals that do not hibernate often adopt a very different lifestyle to survive the winter months. For example, herds of reindeer migrate into the forests, only heading back to the barren tundra in summer. Small rodents, such as mice or shrews, construct tunnels in the snow during winter, and moose survive by eating strips of bark.

Because their growth is so slow and intermittent, boreal forests are relatively free of animals compared to other forests. However, many of the animals that do live there are much larger than their relatives living farther south. For example, the moose is the world's largest deer. Wolverines are much larger than most mustelids, and the grizzly bears of Canada and Alaska are much larger than bears found farther south.

The reason for this is that larger animals need to eat less food per unit of weight than smaller ones. They lose heat more slowly, and do not have to burn food at a such a high rate. Scientists have noticed that even animals of the same species tend to be bigger if they are living further north.

Brown bears live a solitary life in the forest but may gather in groups when hunting for salmon.

Moose plod through forests and marshes, browsing on a variety of leaves, mosses and lichens.

Snowshoe hares shelter in shallow depressions called forms, which they dig out of soil or snow.

Western heather voles make nests in underground burrows, lining them with moss, lichens and twigs.

GRASSLANDS

Although a lot of wild countryside is covered in different grasses – not to mention the many acres of garden lawns – little of it is true grassland. If left alone, these habitats would eventually become thick woodland. True grasslands, from prairies to the savannah, have very few trees but contain many creatures.

Grasslands appear in areas where there is some rain, but not enough to support the growth of large numbers of trees. They come in many forms, growing in both tropical and more temperate regions. The temperate grasslands of North America are called prairies, whereas in South America they are known as the pampas. The tropical grasslands of South America are called savannahs, and a similar scrubland is called *chaco*.

North America's largest temperate grasslands tend to be located in so-called rain shadows. For example, the North American prairies are in the rain shadow of the Rocky Mountains. A rain shadow is an area which rarely gets rain because the wind bringing it must first travel over mountains. As the wind rises up, it cools and releases the rainwater on the windward side. The wind then whistles down the leeward side carrying much less water. If the wind is very dry, then that area becomes a desert. However, the wind often carries enough moisture to let grasses grow.

Black-tailed prairie dogs live in grassland burrows, a collection of which is called a town.

Gopher tortoises are excellent diggers. They build long tunnels, each with a chamber at the end.

Western diamondback rattlesnakes live among grass and rocks, preying upon mice, rats and rabbits.

American bison move about the grassland continuously, eating a range of grasses and rushes.

The main plant food in grasslands is, of course, grass. Grass is an unusual type of plant because its growing points are near to the ground rather than at the tip of the stem, as with most other plants. This means that it can keep growing despite having its juicy blades eaten by grazing animals.

Grazing animals are commonly found in grasslands, as are the browsers which pick the leaves and fruit of small shrubs which often grow in the area. With few places to hide in the wide-open spaces, grazing animals group together into herds for safety. Fortunately, grass and other plant foods are virtually omnipresent, which means that members of these herds only need to compete when it comes to choosing a mate. This has led them, especially the males, to evolve elaborate weapons and display structures, such as horns or tusks.

Without trees to hide in, smaller animals, such as ground squirrels and marmots, take refuge under the ground in burrow complexes. Many, such as moles and mole rats, have adapted to a totally subterranean lifestyle.

Many of the world's temperate grasslands have been turned into farmland for growing cereal crops and raising livestock. Cereals, such as wheat and rye, are actually domestic breeds of grass which would naturally grow in these regions anyway.

Most of the animals once found on grasslands have suffered because of the rise of agriculture. Prairies used to contain huge herds of bison, but now these are very rare, having been slaughtered by hunters. Similarly, pampas deer were once common but have now been pushed out by cattle and other livestock. Meanwhile, burrowing animals, such as prairie dogs, have been persecuted by cattle ranchers because the holes they make injure grazing cattle.

Maras prefer grassland or dry scrub, grazing the young shoots of grasses and herbs.

Meadow jumping mice move unnoticed in thick undergrowth, following voles' runways.

Giant anteaters break open ant and termite nests and lick up the insects with their sticky tongues.

Pronghorns live in large herds in grasslands, and are the fastest land mammals in America.

POLAR REGIONS

Despite being freezing cold and largely covered with ice, polar regions can be characterized as deserts. Although there is solid water almost everywhere, the few plants and animals which do live there often have great difficulty in obtaining liquid water, just like the wildlife in scorching deserts.

The polar regions – the Arctic in the north and Antarctic in the south – begin at 66° North and 66° South. These positions on the globe are marked as the Arctic and Antarctic Circles. Within these imaginary circles, something very strange happens on at least one day every summer: the sun does not set. Similarly, for at least a single 24 hours in winter, it does not rise. The wildlife of the Arctic is not similar to that around the Antarctic. This is not just because they are at opposite ends of the world, but also because the geography of the two areas is very different. The Antarctic is dominated by Antarctica, a mountainous landmass which is a significantly sized continent, larger than Australia. Meanwhile the Arctic has the Arctic Ocean – the world's smallest ocean – at its centre.

The wildernesses of ice and rock in the Antarctic are the coldest places on Earth, and are too inhospitable for any completely terrestrial animals. Antarctic animals, such as seals,

Polar bears cover vast distances in search of food, swimming across water and coming far inland.

Southern elephant seals come ashore on to flat beaches to breed in the spring.

Walruses spend most of their life in water. They have a thick coat of blubber to help keep them warm.

Leopard seals rest on the ice that covers the ocean in winter. They hunt other seals and penguins.

penguins and whales, rely on the sea for their survival. No reptiles or amphibians survive there, and even warm-blooded animals leave in winter, with the exception of the hardy emperor penguin.

In the Arctic, seals, whales and other sea life also thrive, while the lands and islands of the Arctic Ocean provide a home for many animals dependent on land, such as musk ox and reindeer. Animals such as polar bears spend their time on the thick shelves of sea ice which extend from the frozen coastlines for much of the year.

While Antarctica is almost entirely covered in snow and ice, the ground in lands around the Arctic circle is mainly ice-free during the summer and so has periods of frenzied growth and breeding. North of the boreal forests it is too cold and dark for trees to grow, and treeless tundra takes over. Plants – mainly tough grass and sedges, mosses and lichens (not actually plants but a symbiotic relationship between fungi and tiny algae) must be able to survive the long and desolate winters. When the summer – which generally lasts little more than six weeks – arrives, they must be ready to reproduce.

While the summer sun thaws the snow and ice, it never heats the soil for more than a few centimetres below the surface. The deep layer of soil remains frozen and is called permafrost. It forms a solid barrier which prevents the melt waters from seeping away. The trapped water forms shallow pools and bogs, which are a haven for insects.

Billions of insects, which spent the winter underground as inactive pupae, emerge from hiding in the spring. They swarm across the tundra, mating and laying eggs in the water as they race against time to produce the next generation before winter arrives again.

Arctic hares make their homes in areas of broken ground, where rocks provide some shelter.

Lemmings construct tunnel systems under the snow. This protects them from predators.

Muskoxen survive by eating hardy grasses, mosses and sedges within the Arctic Circle.

Caribou have large hooves that help them to walk on the deep snow of the tundra.

DESERTS

Deserts make up the largest terrestrial biome, covering about one-fifth of the world's dry land. The popular image of a desert is a parched wilderness with towering sand dunes and no sign of life. However, deserts can also be very cold places and most contain a surprising amount of wildlife.

A desert forms wherever less than 25cm (10in) of rain falls in a year. Areas that get less than about 40cm (16in) of rain per year are semi-deserts. The largest and hottest desert in the Americas is the Sonoran Desert that spreads from northern Mexico to Arizona and south California. The Sonoran Desert includes regions such as the Mojave. The Great Basin Desert around Utah, Nevada and Idaho is another large American desert. However, although dry, this region is also very cold. The driest place in North America is Death Valley in California. The driest desert in South America – indeed the world – is the Atacama desert in Peru and Chile.

Desert life is tough. The wildlife has to contend with lack of water and also survive extremes of temperature. With little or no cloud cover for most of the year, land temperatures rocket during the day to over 40°C (104°F) but can plunge to near freezing at night. Plants are the basis for all life in this biome, being the food for grazing animals.

Gila monsters are active at night. During the day they shelter in rocky crevices or burrows.

Chuckwallas live near rocks and boulders, eating the hardy plants that survive in desert conditions.

Desert horned lizards prefer hot, sandy environments. They have spiky bodies to help them blend in.

Kingsnakes live among clumps of vegetation and under rocks. They hibernate during cold periods.

Deserts are not completely dry, of course, because rain does eventually arrive. True to the extremes of a desert, rainstorms are so violent that they often cause devastating flash floods which gush down temporary rivers, known as wadis or arroyos. Then the desert plants bloom and breed for a few short weeks before withering and waiting for the next supply of water.

Many desert animals, such as blind snakes and several types of frog, follow a similar pattern. They only come to the surface during and after the rains, preferring to stay moist underground during the hot and dry parts of the year. Desert frogs prevent themselves from drying out by growing a thin, fluid-filled skin bag around their bodies.

Even the more active desert animals remain hidden during the day, sheltering from the scorching sun among rocks or in burrows. When night falls, plant-eaters, such as the addax and ass, begin to pick at the dried leaves, fruit and twigs of scrawny desert plants, while smaller jerboas and ground squirrels collect seeds and insects. Other insect-eaters include geckoes and other lizards. Many have wide, webbed feet to help them walk across the loose sand and burrow into it when danger approaches. Larger meat-eaters include vipers, which patrol in search of small rodents, and coyotes, which scavenge for the carcasses of dead animals.

Most of these animals never drink liquid water, getting all the moisture they need from their food. They have to hold on to every last drop, though. In a similar way to how camels store food in their humps, gila monsters and other American lizards store fat in their tails, while many desert rodents build up food stores in their burrows to survive long periods of drought.

Coachwhips inhabit both rocky and sandy ground, taking refuge in burrows or under vegetation.

Desert cottontails feed at dawn and dusk, spending the hottest part of each day under cover.

Desert kangaroo rats live where there are wind-blown sand-dunes. They never drink water.

White-tailed antelope squirrels burrow into loose soil to avoid the most intense heat of the day.

MOUNTAINS

Mountains form an unusual biome because they encapsulate a number of climate zones within a small geographical area. This variation defines the lives of the inhabitants. Some animals are highly evolved for mountain life; others have extended their lowland ranges into high altitudes.

A mountainside is like several biomes stacked on top of one another. As the mountain rises out of the surrounding lowlands, the air temperature, wind speed, light levels, water supply and, on the highest peaks, even the amount of oxygen begin to change. The largest mountain ranges in North America, the Rockies and Appalachians, rise out of temperate or boreal biomes. Therefore the foothills of these ranges are generally covered in temperate forest or woodland. As the altitude increases, the weather conditions become colder and harsher and the trees of the temperate forest find it increasingly hard to grow. They eventually become smaller and more gnarled, and then conifer trees take over. Like their relatives in boreal forests, mountain conifers are better at surviving in colder conditions than broad-leaved trees.

As the journey up the mountain continues, the conditions get worse. Rain that falls on the mountain runs through or over the surface before

Mountain goats have strong, sturdy legs and hooves to allow them to negotiate steep slopes.

Bighorn sheep are excellent climbers, seeking refuge in areas where predators cannot reach.

Vicuñas have specialized blood cells with a high oxygen affinity, allowing them to live at altitude.

Chinchillas have very dense coats, enabling them to survive on bleak, windswept mountain slopes.

joining a torrential mountain stream and being carried swiftly down. With all the water sluicing rapidly down the mountain, territory nearer the top has less water for the plants to draw on, and eventually there is not enough moisture in the soil for trees to grow. The point where conditions become just too tough for even conifer trees to grow is called the treeline (timberline).

Above the timberline, small, hardy alpine plants grow in regions which resemble a cold desert. Alpine plants share features with desert species because they, too, must hang on to any water they can get before it is evaporated by the strong mountain wind. At even higher altitudes, as in the polar regions, plant life eventually gives way to snow and ice at the snowline. From here upwards very little plant life survives and animals are infrequent visitors, except for the birds of prey soaring on the thermals of warmer air high above the peaks.

The story is different in tropical regions. Most of the Andes range in South America is located in the tropics. Here the mountain slopes are clothed in so-called cloud forests. These are similar to other tropical forests, but with shorter trees and a thinner canopy. In the humid tropics, these mountain forests are often shrouded in cloud, and this extra moisture makes them ideal places for epiphytes (plants which grow on other plants rather than in the ground). Cloud forests sometimes look as if they are dripping with plant life.

In Chile at the southern end of the Andes, where the climate is colder, unique conifer forests grow on the mountain slopes. In tropical regions, conifer forests do not really take hold on the higher slopes. Instead alpine shrublands form, which then give way to high alpine meadows.

Pikas collect piles of grass and leaves, which dry to make alpine hay. They shelter in areas of scree.

Cougars ambush their prey from high vantage points. At night they shelter in caves and thickets.

Mule deer spend the summer in the mountains, coming down to warmer areas for the winter.

Spectacled bears have very long claws that enable them to climb trees with ease.

HUMAN SETTLEMENTS

The fastest growing habitats are those made by humans, which are generally expanding at the expense of natural ones. Fortunately, many animals (as well as pets) do thrive with people. Animals that feed on a wide range of foods are the most successful species in human settlements.

Human beings have a huge effect on their environment. Since the dawn of agriculture, people have been clearing natural landscapes to make way for their livestock and crops. Agriculture began in the Americas about 7,000 years ago. This agriculture produced maize, squashes and eventually potatoes. The Incas bred llamas and alpacas for milk, meat and wool. With the arrival of Europeans, domestic grasses such as wheat were also introduced, and the incomers also brought domestic animals such as cattle and sheep. Within a few centuries the continents' natural grasslands were converted to huge farms and temperate forests had been cleared for fields. More recently, tropical and boreal forests have also been cut back to make room for agriculture. In evolutionary terms, this change has been very fast, and the

natural world is reeling in shock, unable to respond to the changes quickly enough.

Building cities

Several thousand years ago, people began to learn how to farm more efficiently, and farmers began to produce more than they could consume themselves. With a surplus of food, farmers began to trade it for other items. Uniquely among mammals, some members of these large human communities did not find any of their own food. Instead, they bought what they needed with other products. The first American cities were in Mexico and Peru, where the Mayan, Aztec and Inca civilizations were based.

But while agriculture creates a habitat that mirrors the grassland in some ways, cities were a brand new

Above: Red foxes are very adaptable animals. They have become very common in suburban and more built-up areas, where they make their homes in gardens and wasteland, and feed on rubbish.

Below: Polar bears were once known as the only bears to hunt for every meal – other bears also eat plants and scavenge for food. However, as human settlements in the polar bears' icy range grow, the bears have learned to find food in rubbish dumps. Here a bear feeds at a tip in Churchill, Manitoba.

Above: Raccoons are generalist feeders that have found rich pickings in human settlements. They use their climbing and digging abilities to get at food wherever it may be. For this reason, farmers consider them to be pests.

type of habitat. In 1700, the population of North and South America was perhaps three million. Only 300 years later, this figure had increased more than 200-fold, topping 700 million. Huge sprawling urban centres, such as Mexico City, now contain more than 25 million people each – and, of course, also millions of animals.

Below: The domestic cat is a very popular pet. Like most wild cats, domestic ones are solitary animals and spend their time patrolling their territory looking for mates and rivals.

Opportunists

Although changes to the environment caused by humans are happening at a lightning pace, many animals have made the most of the opportunity presented. The destruction of natural habitats has had a terrible effect on those animals which live in particular places. For example, leaf-eating monkeys cannot survive without trees bearing plentiful leaves. However, animals which make the most of any feeding opportunity can survive anywhere, including cities. These so-called generalist feeders have thrived

Below: Domestic guinea pigs, or cavies, are related to wild forms that live in South America. Selective breeding has resulted in individuals that have long, colourful fur.

alongside humans for many thousands of years. The most familiar generalists are rodents such as mice and rats. They are typical generalist feeders because they will investigate anything for its food potential and are not fussy about what they eat. Other generalists are monkeys, such as capuchins, which are a common sight in many tropical cities. Suburban areas packed with gardens are the perfect environment for many other adaptable animals, such as squirrels, raccoons and foxes.

Although some people enjoy sharing their cities with wildlife, others regard wild creatures in cities as dirty and dangerous. Several diseases, such as typhus and plague, are associated with rats and other city animals. These animals are so successful that their populations have to be controlled. On the whole, however, as cities mature, their wildlife communities stabilize into a sustainable ecosystem.

Prized pets

Another group of animals live in our cities – pets. People have kept pets for thousands of years. Typical pets, such as cats and dogs, are not generalist feeders and rely on their owners to provide food and shelter. Unlike scavenging city animals, pets live in partnership with people and have done well out of this relationship in which almost every facet of their lives is often controlled. Without their human masters, many of these species would now be close to extinction.

Below: Perhaps the most popular pet reptiles are tortoises, which can live for many years if properly looked after. Trade in tortoises is heavily controlled to protect wild populations.

DIRECTORY
OF ANIMALS

The Americas, stretching from the top of the Arctic Circle to the southernmost tip of South America, support an enormous range of animals. This section of the book focuses on the most significant amphibians, reptiles and mammals that live in these continents. The animal species are organized into a number of related groups: salamanders, frogs and toads, turtles and tortoises, lizards, crocodilians, non-venomous snakes, venomous snakes, cats, dogs, bears, small carnivores, raccoons, rodents, rabbits, bats, armadillos, marsupials, insectivores, New World monkeys, marmosets and tamarins, hoofed animals, seals, dolphins, toothed whales and other whales. Each entry is accompanied by a fact box containing a map that shows where the animal lives, and details about the animal's distribution, habitat, food, size, maturity, breeding, life span and conservation status. This last category gives a broad indication of each species' population size, as recorded by the International Union for the Conservation of Nature and Natural Resources (IUCN). At one end of the scale a species might be described as common or lower risk, then vulnerable, threatened, endangered or critically endangered. In addition to the main animal entries, the directory also contains lists of related animals, with short summaries indicating their distribution, main characteristics and behaviour.

Left: The caribou – also known as the reindeer – is the only species of deer in which both males and females have antlers. When fighting, they lower their heads, charge and lock antlers, trying to push each other away. There are over three million caribou living in North America, and each year they migrate very large distances in pursuit of food.

SALAMANDERS

Salamanders and newts are amphibians with tails. All of them have legs, although a few species have lost a pair or have vestigial limbs. Like all amphibians, salamanders need a certain amount of water to reproduce. Some species are completely aquatic, while others live entirely on land. Many species are truly amphibious, spending the early part of their lives in water and living both on land and in water as adults.

Hellbender

Cryptobranchus alleganiensis

Hellbenders are among the largest salamanders in the Americas and one of three giant salamanders in the world. These monstrous and heavy set amphibians spend their entire lives on the beds of rivers and streams.

Hellbenders are nocturnal and spend the day sheltering under rocks. At night the animals become more active, but generally lurk in crevices while waiting for prey. Giant salamanders lose their gills as they change from larvae into adults. They absorb most of their oxygen through their wrinkly skin but will sometimes rise to the surface to take gulps of air into their small lungs.

Hellbenders breed in late summer. A male digs a hole under a rock and will only allow females that are still carrying eggs into his hole. Several females may lay their eggs in a single male's hole before he fertilizes them with a cloud of sperm. The male guards them for three months until the young hatch out.

Hellbenders have a dark, wrinkled skin that secretes toxic slime. These salamanders do not have gills, and the wrinkles in their skin increase the surface area of their bodies so that they can absorb more oxygen directly from the water.

Distribution: Eastern North America.
Habitat: Rivers and streams.
Food: Crayfishes, worms, insects, fish and snails.
Size: 30–74cm (12–29in).
Maturity: 2–3 years.
Breeding: 450 eggs laid in late summer.
Life span: 50 years.
Status: Unknown.

Greater siren

Siren lacertina

The greater siren lives in the mud on the bottom of slow-flowing creeks and in swamps. Most salamanders change considerably as they mature into adults, but the adult body of a siren, with its external gills, long tail and single pair of legs, is very similar to the larval form. Greater sirens spend the day resting on the bottom. At night they drag themselves through the mud with their small legs or swim, with an S-shaped motion, through the murky water. These salamanders do not have teeth, but suck their prey through tough, horny lips.

Greater sirens sometimes live in seasonal pools, which dry up in the summer. The salamanders survive these droughts by burying themselves in the moist sediment and coating their bodies with slimy mucus. Breeding takes place at night, under mud. It is thought that females lay single eggs on water plants and males follow the females around, fertilizing each egg soon after it is laid.

The greater siren has a very long body with feathery gills behind its head and a single pair of legs. The body is mottled to help the salamander hide on the river bed. The greater siren propels itself through the water, twisting its body into S-shaped curves.

Distribution: Eastern parts of the United States.
Habitat: Swamps, streams and lakes.
Food: Crayfishes, worms and snails.
Size: 50–90cm (19.5–36in).
Maturity: Unknown.
Breeding: Eggs laid in spring.
Life span: 25 years.
Status: Not known.

Mudpuppy

Necturus maculosus

Distribution: Eastern United States.
Habitat: Muddy ponds, lakes and streams.
Food: Aquatic insects, crayfishes and fish.
Size: 29–49cm (11.5–19in).
Maturity: 4–6 years.
Breeding: Mating occurs in autumn; eggs laid in spring.
Life span: Unknown.
Status: Common.

Mudpuppies and waterdogs, their close relatives, get their names from the myth that they bark like dogs when handled.

Mudpuppies spend their whole lives underwater. They do not change a great deal when they metamorphose from larvae into adults, retaining their gills for breathing and their long tail for swimming. The gills vary in size depending on how much oxygen there is dissolved in the water. They are very large in stagnant pools, where there is not very much oxygen available, and smaller in faster-running streams.

Mudpuppies mate in the late autumn or early winter. The eggs are fertilized inside the female's body, but they are not laid until spring. Before laying, the female makes a nest in a hollow under a rock or log on the bed of a shallow stream. The eggs have a gelatinous coating and stick together in layers.

Mudpuppies have a long, mottled body with two pairs of legs and a laterally flattened tail. There is a pair of feathery gills behind the head, but mudpuppies also have small lungs.

Cave salamander (*Eurycea lucifuga*): 8–16cm (3–6in)
Cave salamanders are pale orange with black spots on their back. They live in the mouths of caves in the Midwest region of the United States. Cave salamanders have a long, grasping tail, which they use for clinging to the rocky cave walls. Lacking lungs, they absorb oxygen from the air through their skin and through the lining of their mouth. Their skin must be kept moist for oxygen-absorption to occur, so they can only live in damp areas while on land, and have long periods of inactivity when conditions are unfavourable.

Olympic torrent salamander
(*Rhyacotriton olympicus*): 9–12cm (3.5–4.75in)
The Olympic torrent salamander is one of four salamanders found in the rocky watercourses of the Pacific North-west in North America. This species lives in crystal-clear streams that tumble down mountainsides. The water is so rich in oxygen that the adult salamanders have only tiny lungs because they can easily get enough oxygen through their skins.

Coastal giant salamander (*Dicamptodon tenebrosus*): 17–34cm (6.5–13.5in)
Coastal giant salamanders are the largest land-living salamanders in the world. They have brown skin, mottled with black, which helps them to blend in with the floor of their woodland homes. They secrete foul-tasting chemicals through their skin as a defence when attacked by predators.

Three-toed amphiuma

Amphiuma tridactylum

With their slimy, cylindrical bodies, amphiumas are also called Congo eels. This is misleading because they are amphibians, not eels (which are fish), and they live in North America, not the African Congo.

Three-toed amphiumas are the longest salamanders in the Americas, although large hellbenders are probably heavier. Adult amphiumas have neither lungs nor gills. They have to take in oxygen directly through their skin. Three-toed amphiumas spend most of their lives in water, foraging at night and sheltering in streambed burrows during the day. However, during periods of heavy rainfall, the salamanders may make brief trips across areas of damp ground.

Three-toed amphiumas begin to mate in late winter. The females rub their snouts on males they want to attract. During mating males and females wrap around each other, while sperm is transferred into the female's body. The females guard their strings of eggs by coiling their bodies around them until they hatch, about 20 weeks later. By then, the water level may have dropped, so the larvae often have to wriggle over land to reach the water.

Distribution: Southern United States.
Habitat: Swamps and ponds.
Food: Worms and crayfishes.
Size: 0.5–1.1m (1.5–3.5ft).
Maturity: Not known.
Breeding: 200 eggs laid in spring.
Life span: Not known.
Status: Common.

Three-toed amphiumas have a very long, cylindrical body with a laterally flattened tail. They have two pairs of tiny legs, each with three toes. The legs are too small to be of use for locomotion.

Tiger salamander

Ambystoma tigrinum

Tiger salamanders are found in grassland, forest and marshy habitats. The adults spend much of the year underground. They usually dig their own burrows, sometimes down to a depth of more than 60cm (24in). The burrows not only provide them with the humidity levels they need, but also shelter them from the extremes of temperature on the surface. Tiger salamanders start life in pools of water. While larvae, they have external gills and a fin down the middle of their tails. They feed on aquatic insects and even on other tiger salamander larvae. The larvae may stay in the water for several years before metamorphosing into the adult body form. The gills are then absorbed into the body, the tail fin is lost, and the skin becomes tougher and more resistant to desiccation. Metamorphosis is thought to be catalyzed by the warming of the water during summer. Warm water can absorb more oxygen than cold water, which may trigger the change. However, the warming of the water may also suggest to the animal that the pool is in danger of drying up, indicating that it ought to leave.

The metamorphosed salamander now looks like an adult, but it is still smaller than the mature animal. This subadult form is called an eft. The eft crawls out of the water and begins to forage on the leaf-strewn floor. It catches insects and other animals with flicks of its sticky tongue, and then shakes them to death before chewing them up. After hibernating in burrows, mature adults make mass migrations in springtime to pools and mate over a period of two or three days.

Tiger salamanders may be dark green or grey with black markings, or yellow with black markings. Some specimens have yellow and black stripes, which make them even more reminiscent of their namesake.

Distribution: Central and south-eastern North America.
Habitat: Woodland.
Food: Worms and insects.
Size: 18–30cm (7–12in).
Maturity: Unknown.
Breeding: Migrate to breeding pools in spring.
Life span: 20 years.
Status: Common.

Axolotl

Ambystoma mexicanum

Axolotls are related to tiger salamanders and other species that spend their adult lives on land. However, axolotls never go through the change from the aquatic larval stage to the more robust, terrestrial adult form. Consequently, they spend their whole lives in water.

Adult axolotls look almost identical to the larval stage. They have four legs – which are too small for walking on land – feathery gills behind their head and a long, finned tail used for swimming. Like the larvae, the adults feed on aquatic insects and other invertebrates, such as worms. The only major difference between the two forms is that the adults have sexual organs, enabling sperm to be transferred from male to female during mating.

Axolotls do not metamorphose because their thyroid glands cannot produce the hormone necessary to bring about the change. When biologists injected captive axolotls with this hormone they found that the animals changed into a land-living form similar to that seen in other species. Because they cannot naturally get out of the water, axolotls are confined to their aquatic habitat. They live in a single lake system in Mexico and are therefore vulnerable to pollution and exploitation, and are becoming increasingly rare.

Distribution: Lake Xochimilco, Mexico.
Habitat: Water.
Food: Aquatic insects.
Size: 10–20cm (4–8in).
Maturity: Unknown.
Breeding: Unknown.
Life span: 25 years.
Status: Vulnerable.

In the wild, most axolotls are black, but several colour variants have been bred in captivity. In fact, there are more axolotls in captivity around the world than in the wild.

Long-toed salamander
(*Ambystoma macrodactylum croceum*): 10–17cm (4–6.5in)
The long-toed salamander is found in the Pacific North-west, from northern Canada to British Columbia. It is a member of the mole salamander group, which includes tiger salamanders and axolotls. These amphibians are called mole salamanders because many, such as the long-toed salamander, live in burrows below damp ground. In spring, they breed in ponds.

Cayenne caecilian (*Typhlonectes compressicauda*): 30–60cm (12–24in)
The Cayenne caecilian lives in the tributaries and lakes of the Amazon River basin system. Its long, dark body resembles that of an eel at first glance, but, like other caecilians, it has well-defined rings around its body. This species is completely aquatic: its tail is flattened into a paddle shape, and a small fin runs along the top of the body. Female Cayenne caecilians carry their developing eggs inside their bodies. Then they give birth to live young, which look like miniature adults.

Red-spotted newt

Notophthalmus viridescens

Red-spotted newts, also known as eastern newts, have a very complex life cycle. Their lives begin in water, where they hatch out from eggs as aquatic larvae. The larvae then develop into land-living juveniles called efts. The eft stage has the body form of a normal adult salamander, with four legs and a long, grasping tail. However, it is unable to breed.

The eft spends up to four years living out of water in damp woodland and grassland. Red-spotted newts must return to ponds and streams to become mature. When they return to water, the maturing red-spotted newts actually redevelop many larval features, such as a deep tail – ideal for swimming – and a thinner skin, used for absorbing oxygen directly from the water.

The adults breed during spring and early summer in bodies of fresh water. They then leave the water and return to a life on land. Many newts return to the same ponds to breed each year. They may navigate by storing maps of their surroundings in their memory, or by using either the Earth's magnetic field or polarized light from the Sun.

Distribution: Eastern United States.
Habitat: Damp land and fresh water.
Food: Tadpoles, insects, slugs, worms and other small invertebrates.
Size: 6.5–11.5cm (2.5–4.5in).
Maturity: 1–4 years.
Breeding: In water in spring.
Life span: Unknown.
Status: Common.

Red-spotted newts are named after the red and black markings along their back. During the juvenile or eft stage, the newts are bright orange, but when they eventually reach maturity, they turn green with yellow undersides.

Ringed caecilian

Siphonops annulatus

Caecilians are amphibians, but they belong to a separate group entirely from salamanders, newts, frogs and toads. All caecilians lack legs and resemble large worms. The ringed caecilian burrows through the soil of steamy tropical forests, wriggling its body in waves to push its way forward. It breathes using only one properly developed lung.

Ringed caecilians eat anything they come across while on the move, providing it is small enough. They use their head like a trowel to probe areas of soil, and use their tentacles to pick up the scent of prey. The tentacles are closely linked to the nose, and detect chemicals in the soil. They can also detect the movements and faint electric currents produced by the muscles of prey animals.

Distribution: North-eastern South America.
Habitat: Tropical forest.
Food: Worms and insects.
Size: 20–40cm (8–15.5in).
Maturity: Unknown.
Breeding: Rainy season.
Life span: 10 years.
Status: Common.

Ringed caecilians have blue, scaly bands around the body. Like all caecilians, ringed caecilians have a retractable tentacle on each side of the head, near to their nostrils.

Ringed caecilians mate when the soil is at its most damp, during the rainy seasons. The female's eggs are fertilized by the male when they are still inside her body. She lays the eggs in the soil. Unlike many species of caecilian, which have an aquatic larval stage, young ringed caecilians hatch looking like miniature adults.

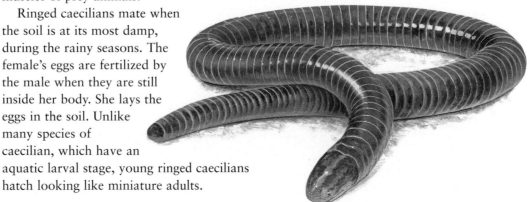

California newt

Taricha torosa

These newts are found only in the state of California. There are two main populations. The larger group lives in the coastal region, ranging from San Diego in the south to Mendocino County north of San Francisco. The second population lives on the western slopes of the Sierra Nevada mountains in the north-west of the state. California newts are mostly found in slow-flowing streams, lakes and ponds surrounded by forests of oak or evergreen conifers. Those in the Sierra Nevada occupy more swiftly flowing waterways.

The females lay their eggs between December and May. The eggs are deposited on aquatic plants or among leaf litter that has settled on the bottom of a waterway. The larvae, which are just 1cm (0.4in) long, live underwater until at least the autumn, or until the following spring in colder areas. Once the larvae reach the right size, they transform into the land-living adult form. These terrestrial newts return to water to breed.

This species has warty skin that that is reddish-brown on the upper side and dark yellow underneath. The eyes are larger than those of most newts. Breeding males develop smooth skin and become fatter.

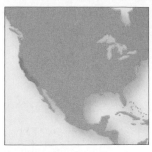

Distribution: Coastal region of California and Sierra Nevada mountains.
Habitat: Streams, lakes and ponds in hill and mountain forests, grasslands and chaparral.
Food: Invertebrates.
Size: 12.5–20cm (5–8in).
Maturity: 1–2 years.
Breeding: 20 eggs laid underwater in spherical masses in winter or spring
Life span: Unknown.
Status: Common.

Amazon climbing salamander

Bolitoglossa altamazonica

Amazon climbing salamanders live in the shrubs and bushes that carpet the floor of lowland rainforests in the northern Amazon Basin of Brazil. These amphibians spend their whole lives off the ground. They are most often seen on the wide leaves of low-growing bushes, and also on the long leaves of large epiphytes, including bromeliads. (Epiphytes are plants that grow perched on trees and other larger plants.) The salamanders are rarely seen higher than 2m (6.5ft) above the forest floor.

Amazon climbing salamanders are nocturnal animals. They forage for small insects that move up into the trees when night falls. During the daytime, these small salamanders curl up underneath a large leaf, or in leaf debris trapped amid the branches.

Comparatively little is documented about the breeding habits of this species, although it is known to reproduce all year round. The females lay small clutches of large eggs in moist nooks and crannies at the base of leaves or among branches. The young do not hatch as aquatic larvae, since there is no standing water for them to live in. Instead, the young salamanders emerge in the full adult form.

Distribution: Northern Amazon Basin.
Habitat: Bushes.
Food: Insects.
Size: 7.5–9cm (3–3.5in).
Maturity: 1 year.
Breeding: No larval stage.
Life span: Unknown.
Status: Common.

These climbing salamanders have grey-brown skin, webbed feet and a constriction at the base of their tail. The tail is a little longer than the combined head and body length. Bolitoglossa salamanders wave their tail and arch their back when threatened.

Arboreal salamander

Aneides lugubris

Distribution: Coastal mountains of California and Baja California.
Habitat: Woodlands.
Food: Insects.
Size: 11–18.5cm (4.25–7.25in).
Maturity: 1 year.
Breeding: 10–30 eggs laid in summer; hatching is in autumn.
Life span: Unknown.
Status: Common.

As their name suggests, arboreal salamanders live in trees, especially yellow pines and black oaks. While climbing through the branches, they grip with wide pads on the tips of their toes. Their long prehensile tail can be wrapped around branches to give extra stability.

Arboreal salamanders are lungless salamanders. Lacking lungs, they breathe through their skin, especially the thin and moist areas inside the mouth. As a result, these salamanders are only able to get a limited amount of oxygen into their bodies, restricting the size to which they can grow. This is one of the larger species.

Female arboreal salamanders lay their eggs on rotting wood or in moist leaf litter. There is no larval stage, and the young emerge as miniature, fully formed salamanders about three months later.

Like most lungless salamanders, this climbing species spends its whole life on land. However, its grey-brown skin must be kept moist because, being a lungless salamander, this is where oxygen passes from the air into the amphibian's blood.

Bassler's slender caecilian (*Oscaecilia bassleri*): 90cm (36in)
With its narrow, grey body this amphibian is often mistaken for a giant earthworm. It does not burrow into soil, but moves through thick leaf litter on the floor of its rainforest habitat. Bassler's slender caecilian lives in the north-west of the Amazon Basin in Ecuador, Peru and Colombia. The head can be differentiated from the tail because it is slightly paler than the rest of the body. It has a shovel-shaped snout with white nostrils. The eyes are covered in bone and are not visible. Little is known about this species' reproductive behaviour. It does not seem to have an aquatic phase in its life cycle, and it probably gives birth to live young rather than laying eggs.

Desert slender salamander (*Batrachoseps aridus*): 5.5–9.5cm (2.25–3.75in)
This rare, thin-bodied lungless salamander is only found in two canyons in the Mojave Desert, California. It survives the arid desert conditions by making use of water that seeps from the canyons' limestone. It shelters from the heat under loose limestone rocks.

Green salamander (*Aneides aeneus*): 8–14cm (3–5.5in)
This lungless species is closely related to black and arboreal salamanders. It is native to the Appalachian Mountains in the eastern United States, where it inhabits damp woodlands. The upper body is black with green patches. The green salamander spends the daytime in moist crevices, emerging at night to climb tree trunks in search of ants, beetles and other insect prey.

Black salamander

Aneides flavipunctatus

Black salamanders are lungless salamanders that live almost exclusively in California, although a few are found in the far south of Oregon. Their range encompasses the low Coastal Range mountains of the West Coast, but they rarely occur above 600m (2,000ft).

In southern parts of their range, black salamanders are most common in moist areas of evergreen or deciduous forest, while in the north, they inhabit open grassy environments. Along the California and Oregon border, these salamanders are usually found in moss-covered rock slides.

Grasslands are drier than woodlands, so grassland-dwelling salamanders aestivate in summer to protect themselves against heat and drought. Aestivation is a similar dormant state to hibernation. A black salamander may aestivate in an burrow for six or seven months.

Distribution: United States, from Northern California to southern edge of Oregon.
Habitat: Forests and prairies.
Food: Insects.
Size: 10–16.5cm (4–6.5in).
Maturity: Unknown.
Breeding: Eggs laid in summer; hatching is in autumn.
Life span: Unknown.
Status: Common.

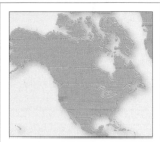

This species is black all over, with a frosted colouring on its upper surface and a paler underside. Black salamanders are buck-toothed, with their upper teeth sticking out over their lower jaw.

Dusky salamander

Desmognathus fuscus

The brownish back of the adult dusky salamander is covered in darker blotches, which sometimes join to form ragged stripes. The young salamanders have yellow or red spots on the back. The hind legs of this species are sturdier than the front legs, and the tail is laterally compressed.

This species is the most common of the dusky salamanders. Its range covers much of the eastern United States, from New England and the eastern Great Lakes to the Mississippi Delta. It does not live along the southern Atlantic coast, and is almost unheard of in Florida, where its place is taken by the southern dusky salamander, a close relative.

In the northern parts of its range, the dusky salamander inhabits creeks and rocky pools. In more southerly parts, it is usually found in swampy areas. Being largely nocturnal, this salamander spends daylight hours under debris or in a burrow. It feeds on a variety of invertebrates, and may occasionally eat other salamanders and their larvae.

The female lays her eggs between June and September, depositing a single cluster of up to 40 eggs in a moist location near water, perhaps under a rock or in a hole in the bank of a stream. The aquatic larvae hatch about two to three months later. The rate at which the eggs and larvae develop depends on temperature, and takes longer in colder regions.

Distribution: Eastern United States, from New Brunswick to Louisiana.
Habitat: Rocky creeks running through woodlands.
Food: Insect larvae, woodlice and worms.
Size: 6.5–14cm (2.5–5.5in).
Maturity: 3–4 years.
Breeding: Up to 40 eggs laid in mid- to late summer; hatching takes 6–13 weeks.
Life span: Unknown.
Status: Common.

Seal salamander

Desmognathus monticola

This average-sized salamander has a laterally compressed tail and a stout body. It is light brown or grey on the upper surface, often with dark blotches surrounded by pale borders. The underside is paler, and there is an obvious transition between the two. Juveniles have a similar background coloration, but with four pairs of orange-brown spots along the back.

This salamander always remains close to water, and as it rests beside a stream it resembles a seal basking on a rocky shore. A shy, nocturnal animal, the seal salamander scurries beneath rocks or dives into stream-side burrows when disturbed. Most of the time it stays under cover, lying in wait for passing insect prey, particularly ants and beetles. When an insect wanders within range, the salamander pounces. It may also eat other salamanders. This species is one of the lungless salamanders, in which respiration occurs through the skin and the lining of the mouth.

In the breeding season, males will attack and bite rivals that try to interrupt their courtship of the females. A female seal salamander lays her eggs between June and October. Each egg is attached individually to the underside of a submerged rock or in a cavity in a rotten log. The salamander always lays in a damp area where water seeps out of the soil or runs off the ground into streams after rain storms. The female guards the eggs until they hatch in the autumn, and the larvae live in the stream water. They are about 2cm (0.8in) long when they emerge from the egg. Once they reach a length of 4–5cm (1.5–2in), the larvae transform into juveniles. The larval stage of this species usually last for nine to ten months.

Distribution: United States, in Appalachian Mountains and uplands of Pennsylvania and Alabama.
Habitat: Mountain streams.
Food: Insects, especially ants and beetles; occasionally other salamanders.
Size: 7.5–15cm (3–6in).
Maturity: 1–2 years
Breeding: 10–40 eggs laid in mid- to late summer; hatching is in autumn
Life span: Unknown.
Status: Common.

Ensatina

Ensatina eschscholtzii

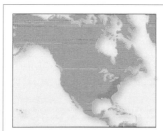

Distribution: West coast of North America, from British Columbia to Baja California.
Habitat: Woodland, mountain forest and scrubland.
Food: Spiders, grasshoppers and springtails.
Size: 7.5–15cm (3–6in).
Maturity: 2–4 years.
Breeding: Eggs laid in late spring hatch 4–5 months later.
Life span: 15 years.
Status: Common.

This lungless species is found along the Pacific coast of North America, in a variety of habitats and climate types. In the north of the range, which experiences high rainfall, ensatinas occupy fir and maple forests. Along the coast, between the ocean and the Coastal Range mountains, the salamanders live in forests of redwoods and oaks, and, in the south, dry areas of bush known as chaparral. There is also a population in the cedar forests that grow on the slopes of the Sierra Nevada mountains in central California.

The ensatina is most often seen after rains. At the height of summer, it retreats to a damp burrow or log crevice to avoid the heat and dry conditions. It does the same in winter to avoid the cold weather. When threatened, this salamander becomes stiff and arches its tail and head toward each other. If a predator takes hold of the tail, the salamander can shed the grasped portion and make its escape. It has no tadpole stage.

The ensatina is the only five-toed salamander possessing a tail with a constricted base. In males, the tail is longer than the body. This species has a variety of colours on its upper surface, from red-brown to yellow and black. There are also spots and blobs in cream, yellow or orange. The belly is white or pink.

Pygmy salamander (*Desmognathus wrighti*): 3.5–5cm (1.5–2in)
This small, nocturnal salamander spends the day under rocks or in leaf litter. It lives in fir and spruce forests at the southern end of the Appalachian Mountains in eastern North America. Pygmy salamanders are most active after rain, when they emerge to forage for insects. They may also climb up tree trunks in search of food. In spring and autumn, a small clutch of eggs is laid at the end of a single stalk and left dangling from a rock over running water. The female guards the eggs. There is no aquatic larval stage, and the young hatch in miniature adult form.

Mountain dusky salamander (*Desmognathus ochrophaeus*): 7–11cm (2.75–4.25in)
The mountain dusky salamander is found in the north-eastern United States, west of the Hudson River and south to the northern tip of Georgia. Much of its range is mountainous. It is found in large numbers close to springs, especially at lower altitudes. Higher up, where it is cooler and damper, this species is less dependent on standing water, and often inhabits conifer forests. Its diet consists of flies, beetles and mites.

Imitator salamander (*Desmognathus imitator*): 7–10cm (2.75–4in)
This rare salamander lives in the Great Smoky Mountains along the Tennessee–North Carolina border. It has the same coloration as either the mountain dusky salamander or the Appalachian woodland salamander. It is such a good mimic that only laboratory analysis of its DNA could prove that it was in fact a separate species.

Long-tailed salamander

Eurycea longicauda

The long-tailed salamander lives in damp environments close to streams and flooded areas. It is found throughout most of the eastern United States, from the Arkansas Valley (a major western tributary of the mighty Mississippi River) to the Atlantic Coast. Like many species in this part of the world, it does not spread into Florida, where the climate and habitat are very different to conditions in the rest of eastern North America.

Long-tailed salamanders are nocturnal animals. They are most active on damp nights, when they patrol the forest floor looking for invertebrates such as insects and springtails. Eggs are laid in crevices close to pools and streams. The larvae hatch about two months later. After living in water for three to seven months, they transform into the juvenile form, which resembles the adult.

Distribution: New York state to northern Florida and western Mississippi Valley.
Habitat: Streams and swamps.
Food: Small insects.
Size: 10–20cm (4–8in)
Maturity: 2 years.
Breeding: Eggs are laid between late autumn and spring.
Life span: Unknown
Status: Common.

Only a handful of other lungless salamanders grow to a larger size than this species, and none of them is as widespread. Despite being long, this salamander's tail rarely measures more than the combined length of its head and body.

Slimy salamander

Plethodon glutinosus

Slimy salamanders live in ravines and flooded woodlands (bayous) in the southern part of their range. Much of their habitat is filled with mountains, and this species is found from sea level to 1,700m (5,600ft). The slimy salamander gets its name from the fact that it secretes a sticky substance on to its shiny black skin. If this salamander is touched, the slime is extremely difficult to remove from the fingers.

Slimy salamanders are nocturnal and spend the day hidden under flat rocks and rotting logs. They emerge on most nights to search for insects on the forest floor. In the south of their range, it is warm and wet enough for this species to be active all year round. In the north, the salamanders spend the coldest part of the winter and the driest periods of summer under cover. These territorial salamanders can become aggressive to competitors from both their own and other species. Breeding takes place in spring and autumn in the north, when it is wet enough. In the south of the range, the salamanders lay their eggs in summer. The male develops breeding colours, with his chin, feet and spots turning first pink and then red. Prior to mating, he performs an elaborate courtship dance. About 25 eggs are laid in a nest under leaves or a log and guarded by the female. There is no aquatic larval stage, and the young that emerge from the eggs a few months later are miniature versions of the adults.

The slimy salamander has black skin, covered by a liberal sprinkling of silver-white or brass-coloured specks, or both. The underside is generally lighter than the back.

Distribution: Eastern United States, from New York south through much of the eastern seaboard to northern Florida and the Gulf coast, and west to parts of Oklahoma and Texas.
Habitat: Swamps and stream sides.
Food: Insects, especially ants and beetles, and earthworms and other invertebrates.
Size: 11.5–20.5cm (4.5–8in).
Maturity: 3 years.
Breeding: 25 eggs laid; hatching takes 3 months.
Life span: Unknown.
Status: Common.

Mud salamander

Pseudotriton montanus

This North American amphibian is aptly named, since the adults are found in mud and swampy ground. Although relatively common in such habitats, these secretive salamanders are rarely seen, since they burrow into the mud and may hide in moist places such as under sphagnum moss, rocks or logs. They may even retreat into crayfish holes to escape predators. Their diet consists mainly of invertebrates, although they have been known to eat other salamanders. Mud salamanders are native to the United States, occurring at sea level on the coastal plain between the Appalachian Mountains and the Atlantic Ocean.

Breeding takes place in autumn or early winter, when the female lays about 100 eggs. The aquatic larvae that hatch in late winter breathe underwater using gills. The larvae live in the silt or plant debris that builds up on the bottom of streams. After a year or two in the water, the larvae transform into a lungless, air-breathing form which then goes on to develop the adult coloration. In males this takes about a year, while females continue to mature for two or three years after leaving the water.

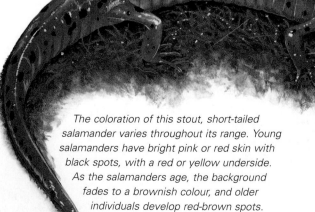

The coloration of this stout, short-tailed salamander varies throughout its range. Young salamanders have bright pink or red skin with black spots, with a red or yellow underside. As the salamanders age, the background fades to a brownish colour, and older individuals develop red-brown spots.

Distribution: Eastern United States, from the Appalachian Mountains to the Atlantic coast.
Habitat: Muddy streams and swamps.
Food: Beetles, spiders, mites and other small invertebrates.
Size: 7.5–19.5cm (3–7.75in).
Maturity: 3–5 years.
Breeding: Eggs are laid in autumn or early winter and attached to the substrate or to submerged objects such as roots or leaves; hatching is in late winter.
Life span: Unknown.
Status: Common.

Zigzag salamander (*Plethodon dorsalis*): 6.5–11cm (2.5–4.25in)
Named after the jagged stripe running from its neck to its tail, this small, slender lungless salamander lives in two populations: the smallest is found in the Ozark hills of Arkansas; the larger group extends from central Indiana to northern Alabama and Georgia. This species occurs in rocky areas such as ravines, scree and caves. The eggs are laid in spring and lie dormant over the dry summer in an underground retreat, before hatching into efts during autumn. As with most lungless species, there is no aquatic phase.

Red salamander (*Pseudotriton ruber*): 10–18cm (4–7in)
This robust lungless species is red when young, but turns orange or purple with age. It lives near springs in the eastern United States, from the western slopes of the Appalachians to the coast of New Jersey and the Gulf of Mexico. It does not reach the southern Atlantic coast. Females lay up to 100 eggs in an underground nest in autumn. The larvae hatch in early winter and make their way to the water. They change into adults after after about two or three years.

Four-toed salamander (*Hemidactylium scutatum*): 5–10cm (2–4in)
This species has four toes on its hind feet and a constriction at the base of its tail. It occurs right across the Mississippi Basin, from the Great Lakes to the Gulf coast. Adults live under stones in boggy areas within forests. Like many salamanders, this species will break off its tail when attacked. The lost tail quickly grows back.

California tiger salamander
Ambystoma californiense

The California tiger salamander is a mole salamander, so-called because many of them are burrowers. Their stout bodies, strong legs and blunt heads allow them to dig efficiently. Mole salamanders also have lungs in their adult form, which makes it easier for them to breathe in the confines of an underground burrow.

This species lives on the slopes of the Coastal Range mountains in south California, where it can be found under plant debris or in soft soil near to ponds in grasslands and woodlands. It feeds on worms, insects and other invertebrates.

Breeding takes place in puddles and temporary bodies of water in January and early February, when heavy rains reach California. The jelly-covered eggs are laid singly on plants, and the aquatic larvae hatch out soon after and burrow into wet ground. The larvae breathe using gills, and feed on various invertebrates such as water snails and tadpoles. They transform into the adult form after four months.

Distribution: West of the Sierra Nevada in south California.
Habitat: Burrows near streams and ponds.
Food: Invertebrates.
Size: 15–21.5cm (6–8.5in).
Maturity: 1–2 years.
Breeding: Eggs laid in rainy season during January.
Life span: Unknown.
Status: Common.

Despite their names, few of the tiger salamanders have stripes. The upper body of this species is black, with a few cream or yellow spots. The belly is grey and also often spotted. The snout is rounded and the eyes are relatively small.

Blue-spotted salamander

Ambystoma laterale

This species is found around the Great Lakes and north through Quebec to the south of Hudson Bay. The range also follows the St Lawrence River valley to the Atlantic coast and the Canadian Maritime provinces. Blue-spotted salamanders are also found in New England and as far south as New Jersey. They inhabit deciduous forests. The adults stay under cover in winter to avoid the freezing temperatures. As a mole salamander, this species is a skilled burrower.

In spring, the salamanders gather at breeding ponds and mate in the water. The eggs are laid singly or in small masses at the bottom of the pond. The larvae change into adult form in late summer.

When alarmed, a blue-spotted salamander holds its tail over its body. If a predator attacks this part of the body, it gets a mouthful of a noxious fluid released by glands on the tail.

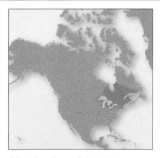

Distribution: Great Lakes region, St Lawrence River Valley and New England.
Habitat: Forest.
Food: Invertebrates.
Size: 7.5–13cm (3–5in).
Maturity: Unknown.
Breeding: Up to 200 eggs laid underwater between March and April.
Life span: Unknown.
Status: Common.

Blue-spotted salamanders have been interbred with Jefferson salamanders, which live in a similar habitat to the south. These crosses produce new female-only species. Blue-spotted males can mate with these female hybrids; their sperm does not result in fertilization, but it stimulates egg development.

Small-mouthed salamander

Ambystoma texanum

Small-mouthed salamanders live in much of the Mississippi Basin, from Ohio in the north to Louisiana on the Gulf of Mexico. To the west, the salamanders range into Texas and Kansas. This species is often found alongside marbled and spotted salamanders. They live in pine woodlands and low-lying deciduous forests, generally near to streams and springs. In the west of their range, they are found in drier prairies, where they make use of temporary ponds.

Being a mole salamander, this species spends a lot of its time hiding in burrows. Breeding takes place during late winter and spring in flooded ditches and other bodies of standing water. The females lay about 700 eggs close to the water's edge. They are laid in small clusters attached to sticks, blades of grass on under rocks. The larvae are 1.3cm (0.5in) when they hatch. They spend a few months living in water before transforming into an air-breathing form when they are about 4cm (1.5in).

Distribution: Ohio to Texas.
Habitat: Forests and prairies near ponds and streams.
Food: Invertebrates.
Size: 11.5–18cm (4.5–7in).
Maturity: 1 year.
Breeding: 700 eggs laid in late winter and spring.
Life span: Unknown.
Status: Common.

The small-mouthed salamander has a very small head and a correspondingly small mouth. It is dark brown or black on its back, with grey-blue or yellow mottled patches, although on some individuals these patches are absent. The belly is black and covered with tiny flecks.

Marbled salamander

Ambystoma opacum

Distribution: Eastern United States, except Florida and New England.
Habitat: Woodland.
Food: Invertebrates.
Size: 9–12.5cm (3.5–5in).
Maturity: 1–2 years.
Breeding: 50–200 eggs laid in autumn or winter.
Life span: Unknown.
Status: Common.

Marbled salamanders occupy a large range that covers most of the eastern United States. They are found from Massachusetts and the shore of Lake Erie in the north to the Florida panhandle and the Gulf of Mexico in the south. They live in woodlands and are especially common in lowland swamps, but they also live at higher altitudes, where the ground is drier and better drained.

The only time that marbled salamanders come together is during the breeding season. The breeding strategy relies on the rains that arrive in autumn and winter. In the north of their range, breeding occurs during the autumn to avoid the freezing winter conditions. In the south, the eggs are laid in early winter, which is wet but not too cold. The female lays up to 200 eggs in a nest made inside a small hollow. She wraps her body around the eggs and waits for the rains. After heavy rain, the hollow fills with water, allowing the eggs to hatch.

This species is so-named because the silvery-white bands that cross the black skin on its back look like seams of marble or quartz. Young marbled salamanders have brown or grey skin.

Dwarf waterdog (*Necturus punctatus*): 11.5–19cm (4.5–7.5in)
The smallest of the waterdogs, this species has narrow gills behind the head, and a short tail that is used for swimming. Waterdogs and their close relative the mudpuppy remain in the aquatic larval form throughout their lives, retaining their gills and paddle-like bodies even after reaching sexual maturity. Dwarf waterdogs live on the coastal plain of the eastern United Sates, between Virginia and Georgia. They are found in muddy streams with slow-moving water, and are also common in irrigation ditches.

One-toed amphiuma (*Amphiuma pholeter*): 21–33cm (8.25–13in)
This rarely seen, eel-like salamander has four tiny, largely functionless legs, each possessing just a single toe. The one-toed amphiuma lives in the Florida panhandle, from the Gulf coast to southern Georgia. It spends almost all of its time at the bottom of muddy ponds and streams, where the long body is ideal for squirming through the soft sediment.

Lesser siren (*Siren intermedia*): 18–70cm (7–27.5in)
The lesser siren occurs from the Atlantic coast coast of Virginia to eastern Texas and northern Mexico, and northward up the Mississippi Valley to Michigan. It is found in swamps, ponds and other shallow bodies of water. The diet of the lesser siren is made up of invertebrates and the tadpoles of other amphibians. Like other sirens, this species has two forelegs but no hind legs. It makes clicking noises and yelps when captured.

Ringed salamander

Ambystoma annulatum

Distribution: Central
Missouri to western Arkansas
and eastern Oklahoma.
Habitat: Damp forests.
Food: Invertebrates such as
insects, worms and snails.
Size: 14–23.5cm
(5.5–9.25in).
Maturity: 1–2 years.
Breeding: Over 100 eggs laid
underwater in clusters of
10–20 during autumn.
Life span: Unknown.
Status: Common.

Ringed salamanders live on the Ozark Plateau and in the
Ouachita Mountains, the only significant highlands in
North America between the Rockies and Appalachians.
They are found in the damp forests and clearings of this
region. Apart from during the breeding season, ringed
salamanders are solitary and rarely seen above ground. They
are most active during wet weather. Their diet probably
consists of insects and other invertebrates that move through
the leaf litter on the forest floor.

The autumn rainfall in the area is high, and
numerous temporary pools form in the forests.
Ringed salamanders breed in the water, after
which the females lay small clusters of
eggs on submerged plants. The
larvae hatch in October and
spend the winter in the water,
where they feed on insect
larvae and other small
invertebrates. They change
into the air-breathing form
and emerge from the water
during early summer.

*This very long mole salamander
has a slender body and a small
head. It has a brown or black
upper body and a grey belly. The
body and tail of the salamander
are circled by yellow bands –
hence its common name.*

Pacific giant salamander

Dicamptodon ensatus

Distribution: Coast of
southern British Columbia to
central California and the
Rockies of Idaho and
Montana.
Habitat: Rivers, streams,
lakes and ponds, and
surrounding forests.
Food: Large insects, mice,
amphibians and small snakes.
Size: 18–30cm (7–12in).
Maturity: 2–3 years.
Breeding: Both terrestrial
and aquatic forms can breed.
Females lay 85–200 eggs
underwater singly and in
clumps.
Life span: Unknown.
Status: Rare.

The Pacific giant salamander inhabits the many rivers that
flow into the Pacific ocean along the US and Canadian
coasts. In central California, in the south of its range, the
rivers are smaller and more seasonal. Further north, a wetter
climate along the coastal mountains makes the rivers larger.
Pacific giant salamanders are found in the lower reaches
of the huge Columbia River and its tributaries, including
the Willamette of western Oregon. A smaller population
survives far from the ocean, in the mountain streams of
the Rockies in Idaho.

Giant Pacific salamanders spend more time in water than
most mole salamanders. They lay their eggs on submerged
wood or rocks. In colder places, the weather may not get
warm enough to stimulate the change from aquatic
larvae to air-breathing, land-living adults,
even though they become sexually
mature. Their offspring,
however, may transform
into land-living
adults if
the conditions
are suitable.
Transformed
animals forage on
the forest floor
on rainy nights.

*The Pacific giant salamander, one
of the world's largest land-living
salamanders, has large eyes and
a laterally compressed tail. The
salamander's coloration typically
consists of dark marbling on a
brown background. In some parts
of this species' range – generally
the cooler regions – the
salamanders never
transform into land-
living adults but retain
their larval features,
including the gills.*

FROGS AND TOADS

Frogs and toads form the largest group of amphibians, called Anura. Toads are better adapted to terrestrial habitats with thicker, warty skin to avoid desiccation, while frogs have thin, smooth skin that needs to be kept moist. Most species follow similar life cycles. Tailed larvae called tadpoles hatch from eggs called spawn and develop in water before sprouting legs, losing their tails and emerging on to land.

Surinam toad

Pipa pipa

Surinam toads spend their whole lives in water. The toads' fingers have a star of highly sensitive tentacles at their tips, which they use to feel for prey on the muddy bottoms of turbid ponds streams and ponds. They also have sense organs along their sides that can detect water movements caused by other animals. The eyes are located on the top of the head so the toads can spot danger approaching from above the surface.

These toads mate during the wettest time of the year. A male grabs a female around the waist and the couple spin around in the water several times. The female releases her eggs and the male uses his hind feet to sweep them into the space between her back and his belly. His sperm fertilizes the eggs, which then embed themselves on the mother's back. The eggs develop into tiny toadlets after three or four months.

Surinam toads have flattened bodies with triangular heads and large, webbed hind feet. Their forefeet have sensitive fingers for feeling around in murky waters. A female may carry up to 100 fertilized eggs on her back.

Distribution: Amazon Basin and northern South America.
Habitat: Muddy water.
Food: Small fish and aquatic invertebrates.
Size: 5–20cm (2–8in).
Maturity: Unknown.
Breeding: Rainy season.
Life span: Unknown.
Status: Common.

Darwin's frog

Rhinoderma darwinii

Darwin's frogs have small, slender bodies with pointed snouts and long fingers. The upper body is green or brown, the underside dark brown or black. The long digits on the hind feet are webbed. There are spur-like skin extensions on the rear legs – hence the alternative name of cowboy frog.

Darwin's frogs live in the steamy mountain forests of the Andes in Chile and Argentina. Despite their natural habitat being damp and lush, Darwin's frogs do not have the aquatic stage that typifies the amphibian life cycle. Most frogs, toads and other amphibians spend at least part of their lives – generally the larval stage – living in water, but Darwin's frogs do not need this truly aquatic form because of their unusual breeding system. The frogs breed at all times of the year. The male first attracts the female with a bell-like call. The female lays around 20 eggs in a suitably moist spot, and the male fertilizes the eggs and guards them for about 25 days until they hatch into tadpoles. He then scoops the tadpoles into his mouth. Males of a species related to Darwin's frogs carry the tadpoles to the nearest body of water, but male Darwin's frogs keep the tadpoles in their mouths until they develop into froglets. The tadpoles develop in their father's vocal pouch for another 50 days before climbing out and becoming independent.

Distribution: Southern Andes, in southern Chile and Argentina.
Habitat: Shallow cold streams in mountain forests.
Food: Insects.
Size: 2.5–3cm (1–1.25in).
Maturity: Unknown.
Breeding: All year.
Life span: Unknown.
Status: Common.

South American bullfrog

Leptodactylus pentadactylus

Distribution: Central and northern South America, from Costa Rica to Brazil.
Habitat: Tropical forest near water.
Food: Insects and other invertebrates.
Size: 8–22cm (3.25–8.5in).
Maturity: Unknown.
Breeding: Rainy season.
Life span: Unknown.
Status: Common, although these frogs are hunted by humans in some areas and their hind legs eaten.

South American bullfrogs are not closely related to the bullfrogs of North America. They all have powerful bodies and large external eardrums, but the similarity ends there. The South American bullfrog is, in fact, more closely related to the horned frogs, which have pointed protuberances of skin above their eyes.

The South American bullfrog is mainly nocturnal. It shelters under logs or in burrows by day and during periods when it is too dry to move around. The bullfrog reportedly lets out a piercing scream when picked up. This is probably intended to startle predators so that they drop the frog in fright, giving it a chance to make its escape.

South American bullfrogs breed in the wet season when the forest streams and ponds are swelled by the rains. The males whip up mucus into a blob of foam, using their hind legs, and attach it to a branch over a body of water. The females then choose a male's foam nest in which to lay their eggs. The tadpoles hatch out and fall into the water below.

The South American bullfrog is a large, robust, aggressive animal with long limbs and widely spaced toes without webbing. Male South American bullfrogs defend territories at the edges of ponds. They have a sharp, black spine on each forethumb. During the mating season, they use these spines as weapons in fights with rival males over females.

Greenhouse frog (*Eleutherodactylus planirostris*): 2–4cm (0.75–1.5in)
One of the world's smallest frogs, this nocturnal species lives in Florida and on several Caribbean islands, including Cuba. It inhabits damp forests and woodland, where it uses suction discs on its fingers and toes to cling to smooth bark, large leaves or, on occasion, greenhouse glass. It prefers wet weather, and is often seen foraging on lawns that are watered by sprinkler systems.

Amazon harlequin toad (*Atelopus pulcher*): 4cm (1.5in)
There are 65 species of harlequin toad in South America, most of them outside of the Amazon Basin. The Amazon harlequin has been found in the rainforests of Peru, but it is unclear whether its range spreads across the rest of the basin. This species has orange areas on its inner thighs and the soles its feet, which are exposed when the toad stretches its limbs. They are probably flashed to startle would-be predators.

Mexican treefrog (*Smilisca baudinii*): 5.1–9cm (2–3.5in)
This large frog of eastern Mexico and southern Texas occurs in a variety of colours, from light green to grey and yellow. Like other treefrogs, it has sucker-like toe-pads to give it a firm grip as it moves over branches or leaves. Unusually for a treefrog, this species is found in canyons and other dry environments in the north of its range. Further south, it lives in humid forests.

Four-eyed frog

Physalaemus nattereri

Four-eyed, or false-eyed, frogs inhabit tropical forests near the Atlantic coast of South America. The adults spend their lives foraging on land. They breed after heavy rains have created ponds and puddles for the tadpoles to develop in. The male four-eyed frog, like his South American bullfrog counterpart, whips up a nest of foamy mucus near to water. The female's eggs hatch into tadpoles, which wriggle or drop the short distance into the water.

While most frogs rely on poisons or alarm calls to ward off predators, four-eyed frogs have a different strategy. When threatened, they inflate their bodies so that they appear to be much larger. They then turn around and point their rump at the attacker. The eyespots on the rump convince the attacker that it is looking at the face of a much larger, and potentially dangerous, animal. The frogs also secrete a foul-smelling fluid from a gland in their groin.

Four-eyed frogs are so-named because of the two black eyespots on their rumps.

Distribution: Southern Brazil and northern Argentina.
Habitat: Coastal forest.
Food: Insects.
Size: 3–4cm (1.25–1.5in).
Maturity: Not known.
Breeding: Rainy season.
Life span: Unknown.
Status: Unknown.

Marine toad

Bufo marinus

Marine toads are the largest toads in the world. They have several other common names, including giant toads and cane toads, their Australian name. Marine toads occur naturally from the southern United States through Mexico to Chile. They were introduced to Queensland, Australia, in the 1930s to help control the pest beetles that were infesting sugar cane crops. However, the toads did not like living amongst the cane plants because there were few places to shelter during the day. Consequently, the toads spread out over the countryside, where they ate not beetle pests but small reptiles and mammals, some of which are now rare because of their predation. Today the toads are a serious pest in Australia.

Marine toads are extremely adaptable. They live a wide range of habitats, eating just about anything they can get into their mouths, from small rodents, reptiles and birds to invertebrates such as snails, centipedes, cockroaches, grasshoppers, ants and beetles. They protect themselves against attack using the toxin glands on their backs, which ooze a fluid that can kill many animals that ingest it. In small amounts, the toxin causes humans to hallucinate.

Female cane toads produce several thousand eggs each year. They lay them in long strings, wrapped around water plants. The eggs are then fertilized by the males.

Female marine toads are larger than the males. Both sexes have warty glands on their backs that squirt a milky toxin when squeezed.

Distribution: Southern North America and Central and South America, from Texas to Chile; now introduced to other areas, including eastern Australia.
Habitat: Most land habitats, often near pools and swamps.
Food: Insects (particuarly beetles), snakes, lizards and small mammals.
Size: 5–23cm (2–9in).
Maturity: 1 year.
Breeding: 2 clutches of between 8,000 and 35,000 eggs produced each year. Eggs hatch into tadpoles that become adult in 45–55 days.
Life span: 40 years.
Status: Common.

Red-eyed tree frog

Agalychnis callidryas

Red-eyed tree frogs have long toes with rounded suction discs at their tips. Their bodies have a bright green upper side. These colourful frogs have blue and white stripes on their flanks and yellow and red legs. The family of tree frogs, about 600 species strong, is found on all the continents except Antarctica.

Red-eyed tree frogs live in the rainforests of Central America. Their long legs allow them to reach for branches and spread their body weight over a wide area when climbing through flimsy foliage. The discs on the tips of each toe act as suction cups, so the frogs can cling to flat surfaces, such as leaves.

Red-eyed tree frogs are nocturnal. Their large eyes gather as much light as possible so the frogs can see even on the darkest nights. During the day, the frogs rest on leaves. They tuck their brightly coloured legs under their bodies so only their camouflaged, leaf-green upper sides are showing.

At breeding time, males gather on a branch above a pond and call to the females with clicking sounds. When a female arrives, a male climbs on to her back and she carries him down to the water. She takes in water and climbs back to the branch again, where she lays eggs on a leaf. The male fertilizes the eggs and they are then abandoned. After hatching, the tadpoles fall into the water below.

Distribution: From north-eastern Mexico along the Caribbean coast of Central America to Panama.
Habitat: Tropical forests in the vicinity of streams.
Food: Insects, including flies crickets, grasshoppers and moths; sometimes small frogs.
Size: 4–7cm (1.5–2.75in).
Maturity: Unknown.
Breeding: Eggs laid in summer.
Life span: Unknown.
Status: Common.

Strawberry poison-dart frog

Dendrobates pumilio

Distribution: Southern Central America.
Habitat: Tropical forest.
Food: Ants, termites, beetles and other small leaf-litter arthropods.
Size: 2–2.5cm (0.75–1in).
Maturity: Unknown.
Breeding: Rainy season; clutches of 3–5 eggs laid in a jelly-like mass that keeps them moist.
Life span: Unknown.
Status: Common.

Many frogs and toads secrete toxic chemicals on to their skins. Most are harmless to humans, but many make predators sick after they eat the frogs. However, the strawberry poison-dart frog and other closely related species have much more potent toxins. A single lick is enough to kill most predators.

The frogs earn their name from the fact that their skins are used by forest people to make poison for hunting darts. The toxins of some frogs are so strong that a single skin can produce enough poison to tip 50 darts. Hunters use them to kill monkeys and other forest animals.

The strawberry poison-dart frog is not always red. During the breeding season, males often change colour to brown, blue or green. Although these frogs rarely climb trees when foraging, the females will scale tree trunks to lay their eggs in holes filled with water. The males then fertilize the eggs.

Strawberry poison-dart frogs have bright red bodies with blue on their hind legs. These bright colours serve as a warning to predators that their skins are covered in a poison so deadly that just one lick is generally fatal. The family contains around 120 species.

Reticulated glass frog (*Centrolenella valerioi*): 2–5cm (0.75–2in)
This species of glass frog lives in mountain rainforests in South and Central America. It lives in the trees and is an expert climber, having slender legs with suction discs on its toes for clinging to the flat surfaces of leaves. Glass frogs get their common name from their translucent skin, through which the major bones and blood vessels are visible.

Blue poison-dart frog (*Dendrobates azureus*): 4.5cm (1.75in)
This arboreal frog, one of the larger poison-dart species, has a bright blue body with black spots and bars on its back. The potency of the poison in the skin, which gives this and similar frogs their common name, depends on the frog's diet. This species eats ants. Red ants contain formic acid, which the frog uses to make powerful toxins.

Pasco poison-dart frog (*Dendrobates lamasi*): 1.5cm (0.5in)
The tiny Pasco poison-dart frog of eastern Peru divides its time between the rainforest floor and moss-covered tree trunks and branches. This species has five green or yellow stripes along its black back. Females lay their eggs in the small pools that form among the leaves of bromeliad plants, which grow on trees and other plants, often high above the ground. The tadpoles develop into frogs while swimming in these suspended pools.

Paradoxical frog

Pseudis paradoxa

The paradoxical frog is aptly named. Most other frogs are considerably larger than their tadpoles. However, adult paradoxical frogs are smaller than their fully grown tadpoles, hence the paradox. Young paradoxical frogs stay in their larval tadpole stage for much longer than other species. They grow to 25cm (10in) long – four or five times the size of an adult. As they metamorphose into adults, the frogs therefore shrink in size, mainly by absorbing their tails back into their bodies.

Adult paradoxical frogs have bodies that are well adapted to a life in water. Their powerful hind limbs are webbed and are used as the main means of propulsion. Like many other aquatic frogs, this species has long fingers that are good for delving into the muddy beds of lakes and ponds. They stir up the mud to disturb prey animals and catch them in their mouths. The female lays her eggs in a floating foam nest, before the male fertilizes them.

Paradoxical frogs have slimy bodies and a dark green and brown coloration. They have very long hind legs with webbed feet. Their forefeet have two long toes.

Distribution: Central and eastern South America.
Habitat: Fresh water.
Food: Aquatic invertebrates.
Size: 5–7cm (2–2.75in).
Maturity: Unknown.
Breeding: Rainy season.
Life span: Unknown.
Status: Common.

Tailed frog

Ascaphus truei

Tailed frogs live in the clear mountain streams of the Cascade Range in the north-western United States and southern Canada. These frogs often stray from the water into damp forests, and are especially common on land during periods of damp weather.

Tailed frogs have a head with rounded a snout. The males have a short, tail-like extension, which is actually a flexible organ used to deliver sperm to a female's eggs while they are still inside her body. This is an adaptation to ensure fertilization, where releasing sperm and eggs into the fast-flowing water would be unlikely to succeed.

After mating, the females lay short strings of eggs on the downstream side of rocks. The tadpoles develop into adults slowly, taking up to four years in colder parts of their range. They use their mouth as a sucker to cling on to rocks so that they are not swept away by the current. Tailed frogs will attempt to eat anything solid that comes within reach. Their diet generally consists of plant matter and the aquatic larvae of insects and other invertebrates. They will bite into human flesh given the opportunity.

The "tail" seen on the males contains the anus and sexual opening. This is used during mating, which takes place during the summer.

Distribution: Pacific coast of North America, from southern British Columbia in Canada to northern California in the United States and the northern Great Basin.
Habitat: Cold mountain streams up to the treeline.
Food: Algae and aquatic invertebrates.
Size: 4cm (1.5in).
Maturity: 3 years.
Breeding: Strings of eggs laid in fast-flowing streams between May and September.
Life span: Unknown.
Status: Common.

Golden toad

Bufo periglenes

The golden toad is probably extinct in the wild – its tiny population is thought to have been wiped out by drought. It was last reported in 1991, although there continue to be unverified sightings, so it is possible that a small number of golden toads still survive and may one day repopulate their range. Golden toads have always been very rare. They were known to live only in a small area of cloud forest in the mountains of Costa Rica. Their habitat was protected until 1991, and is still being preserved in case the toads make a recovery.

Golden toads are explosive breeders, meaning they reproduce in huge numbers when conditions are right. The toads gather in huge crowds around temporary pools of water that form during the rains. The male to female ratio is about 8:1, and several males may cluster around each female, forming "toad balls." Competition between males is fierce, and males will try to interrupt mating pairs. Mating itself can be prolonged: one pair was recorded locked in an embrace for 25 hours. The females deposit between 200 and 400 large eggs at a time, and the tadpoles take five weeks to metamorphose into adults.

Distribution: Northern Costa Rica.
Habitat: Cloud forest.
Food: Invertebrates.
Size: 4–5cm (1.5–2in).
Maturity: 5 weeks.
Breeding: Eggs laid between April and June.
Life span: Unknown.
Status: Extinct in the wild.

Only the male golden toads are in fact bright gold or orange in colour. Females, which are slightly larger, are black with scarlet blotches edged with yellow. Developing toads do not display this sexual colour difference. It is only possible to distinguish their sex when the toads reach maturity.

American toad

Bufo americanus

American toads are found in most parts of eastern North America, from Hudson Bay to the Carolinas. Some American toads survive in irrigated areas of the western United States, where it is too dry for them to live naturally. They are also widespread from California to Washington.

This species is similar to its European cousin, the common toad, in that it has a brownish, wart-covered body. American toads are most active at night, especially in warm and humid weather. They eat mainly insects, slugs and worms. The toads catch their prey by flicking out their sticky tongue, which grabs food and drags it back into the mouth. The tadpoles graze on water plants.

American toads breed in spring, when the days lengthen and the temperature rises. These normally solitary animals congregate in large numbers to mate. The females lay thousands of eggs in the water, forming a huge string of eggs up 20m (66ft) long.

Distribution: United States and eastern Canada.
Habitat: Ponds.
Food: Insects and slugs.
Size: 5–9cm (2–3.5in).
Maturity: 2 years.
Breeding: Eggs laid in spring.
Life span: 10 years.
Status: Common.

This toad has relatively short legs compared to its stout body. Like many toads, it has warts on its head and back. The warts squirt a toxic milky liquid into the mouth of any attacker that tries to bite the toad.

Oak toad (*Bufo quercicus*): 1.9–3.3cm (0.75–1.25in)
This is the smallest toad in North America. It is found in the extreme south-east of the United States. Its range covers the whole of Florida, including the Keys, and extends up the east coast to southern Virginia, as well as along the Gulf coast to Louisiana and eastern Texas. It occupies oak woodlands that grow on sandy soils, where it hunts for insects during the day. Oak toads have a white stripe down their back, and the males have a dark throat. The males produce a high-pitched whistle to attract mates. Breeding takes place in summer after thunderstorms. The storms swell streams and produce temporary pools in which the toads lay their eggs.

Canadian toad (*Bufo hemiophrys*): 5–8.5cm (2–3.25in)
This large species has crests on its head that connect between the eyes to form a ridge. The body is greenish-brown with hints of red. The warts, which are characteristic of toads, are pale brown. This species lives in the Great Plains region of North America, specifically the southern Canadian provinces of Alberta, Manitoba and Saskatchewan. A small population exists in North Dakota and Montana. The range does not extend to the extreme north of the plains region, where it is too cold for the toads, nor to the extreme south, where conditions are too dry. Canadian toads are nocturnal. When threatened, they seek refuge in water; if that is not available, they dig into soft soil using spade-like appendages on their hind feet.

Crested forest toad

Bufo margaritifer

This species occurs in most forest habitats across northern South America. Crested forest toads live in both primary and secondary forests. A primary forest is a pristine habitat that has been undisturbed for many years. Increasingly, however, the forests of South America are becoming secondary forests, where the communities of trees and other large plants are disturbed regularly, mainly by human activities. Such disturbance increases the amount of small, fast-growing shrubs in the forest.

Crested forest toads are most commonly seen at night, often in clearings and gaps between trees, as they perch on a wide leaf or flimsy branch a few feet off the ground. Breeding occurs all year around, with males calling to females from the banks of watercourses. The females lay large egg clutches in quiet streams and pools.

Distribution: Northern South America.
Habitat: Forest.
Food: Insects and other invertebrates.
Size: 7cm (2.75in).
Maturity: Unknown.
Breeding: Up to 2,000 eggs laid in forest pools.
Life span: Unknown.
Status: Common.

This species has two large crests on either side of its head. The crests vary in size across what many scientist believe is a number of separate, but as yet undescribed, species.

North American bullfrog

Rana catesbeiana

The North American bullfrog is the largest frog in North America. It is found from Nova Scotia on the Atlantic coast of Canada south to central Florida and into Mexico. From the east coast it ranges west as far as the Great Plains and Rocky Mountains. It seldom strays far from a pond or other source of water. North American bullfrogs have also been introduced to areas west of the Rockies, such as California and Colorado. Here, they generally survive in cultivated areas that are irrigated by rivers and groundwater.

The North American bullfrog has a reputation for having a large appetite, and will consume almost any animal that it can overpower. It lives in lakes, ponds and slow-flowing streams. During the summer breeding season, the males defend their territories by wrestling with their rivals. They attract females by voicing deep croaks. The female bullfrog deposits a foaming mass of eggs in water, and the eggs are then fertilized by one or more males.

This large green frog is perhaps most recognizable from the large external eardrums on either side of its head, which in the males are bigger than the eyes. At dusk and during summer, American bullfrogs give a deep call that sounds like "jugoram."

Distribution: Atlantic coast of North America west to Rocky Mountains and south to Mexico.
Habitat: Ponds and lakes.
Food: Snakes, worms, fish, insects, crayfish, tadpoles, turtles, frogs and small mammals.
Size: 9–20cm (3.5–8in).
Maturity: 3 years.
Breeding: Up to 20,000 eggs laid in early summer; hatching occurs after about 4 days.
Life span: 16 years.
Status: Common.

Mexican burrowing toad

Rhinophrynus dorsalis

The Mexican burrowing toad has a unique, egg-shaped body – ideal for wriggling through soft soil – and a small, pointed head with a calloused snout. The body is dark brown to near black, with a mid-dorsal red to dark orange stripe and similar coloured patterning on the flanks. Females of this species tend to be substantially larger than males.

Mexican burrowing toads are found from southern Texas to Costa Rica, in areas with soft, sandy soils that are easy to burrow into. The frogs have smooth, moist skin with a red or yellow line running along their back.

Mexican burrowing toads eat insects and other invertebrates. They are especially fond of termites, which they lick up with their tongues. These toads spend most of their time underground to avoid drying out, and only coming to the surface after heavy rain. The smooth skin and pointed body makes it easier for the toads to shimmy through the soil, propelled by the powerful rear legs. The hind feet have a thick arc of skin supported by very long toes, making them very effective digging tools. To deter predators, a threatened toad swells its body by swallowing air. In this inflated state, the toad is difficult to extract from its burrow.

These toads breed in the temporary pools that form after heavy rains at the start of the wet season. The tadpoles are filter-feeders, straining tiny, floating plants and animals from the water. They take up to three months to transform into adults.

Distribution: Extreme southern Texas and Mexico through Central America as far south as Costa Rica.
Habitat: Soil in savannah and seasonally dry forests.
Food: Termites and other insects.
Size: 6–8cm (2.5–3.25in).
Maturity: 3 months.
Breeding: Several thousand eggs laid in the rainy season, either individually or in small groups; the fertilized eggs sink to the bottom and hatch within a few days.
Life span: Unknown.
Status: Common.

Eastern spadefoot toad

Scaphiopus holbrookii

Distribution: Eastern United States.
Habitat: Areas of loose soil in a range of habitats.
Food: Worms and insects.
Size: 4.4–8.25cm (1.75–3.25in).
Maturity: 8 weeks.
Breeding: Eggs laid in summer.
Life span: Unknown.
Status: Common.

Eastern spadefoot toads live in two main populations in eastern North America. The smaller population lives in eastern Texas and the western Mississippi Valley, and extends to north-eastern Mexico. The larger population lives to the east of the Mississippi and covers most of the south-eastern United States, reaching as far north as Ohio and Massachusetts. The toads are absent from the higher areas of the Appalachian Mountains, which cut through their range.

Both populations of these toads prefer areas with loose, sandy soil. These toads are found in a range of habitats, from forests to dry scrublands. Eastern spadefoot toads are nocturnal. By day, they remain hidden in burrows. They emerge on damp nights to hunt for worms and insects. Breeding takes place when heavy summer rainfall creates temporary pools. Females are attracted to the pools by the grunting calls of the males. After mating, the females lay their eggs on underwater vegetation.

Eastern spadefoot toads are so named for the spade-shaped structure on each hind foot with which they dig burrows in loose, sandy soil.

Plains spadefoot toad (*Scaphiopus bombifrons*): 3.8–6.3cm (1.5–2.5in)
The plains spadefoot toad lives to the north of Couch's spadefoot. It is found from northern Mexico to the southern edge of Canada, including the prairies and semi-deserts of the Great Plains region in western North America. This nocturnal toad is rarely seen above ground when it is not raining. It hunts for beetles, ants, earthworms and other invertebrates. When startled, the toad burrows backwards into the soil with its spade-like feet. As a defence, the warts on its back can secrete an unpleasant liquid that smells of garlic.

Plains leopard frog (*Rana blairi*): 5.1–11.1cm (2–4.25in)
This is another species that survives on the arid grasslands of the Great Plains, where it inhabits the region's few streams and ponds. It is most common on the eastern plains of Indiana and Nebraska, where rainfall is higher. The frog's skin is greenish-brown, with dark spots on yellow ridges across the back. Plains leopard frogs hunt at night for insects along the water's edge.

Colombian horned frog (*Ceratophrys calcarata*): 6.5cm (2.5in)
Occupying a range of habitats in northern South America, this frog is found from Colombia and Venezuela to northern Peru. Females are brown with pale patches; males are similar but smaller, and they have horn-like projections on their upper eyelids. Like other horned frogs, this species has a huge head. Colombian horned frogs feed on insects and small lizards. They have a powerful bite, which is often used against rivals.

Couch's spadefoot toad

Scaphiopus couchii

This toad occurs in the extreme south of California, Arizona and New Mexico, as well as in much of western Texas and northern Mexico. Like other spadefoot toads, this species lives in burrows dug in soft soil. Couch's spadefoot toad is most commonly found in dry grassland and areas covered by mesquite shrubs.

Couch's spadefoot toads use their burrows to avoid the high temperatures of their arid habitat. In the warmest part of the year, the toads dig a deep burrow and stay dormant until rainy weather arrives, spending up to 10 months underground. During the rainy season, the toads emerge on the surface on cool nights to hunt for insects. Males attract females by calling from temporary pools of rainwater. A male will grab hold of a receptive female and fertilize her eggs as she lays them in the water.

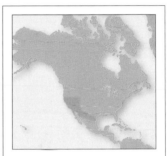

Distribution: South-western United States, California and northern Mexico.
Habitat: Soil of grasslands.
Food: Insects.
Size: 5.6–8.8cm (2.25–3.5in).
Maturity: 40 days.
Breeding: Eggs laid in summer.
Life span: Unknown.
Status: Common.

Like other spadefoot toads, this species digs burrows using the spade-like structures on the underside of its hind feet. The toad's skin is covered in tiny tubercles.

Crawfish frog

Rana areolata

Distribution: South-eastern United States, from coast of Carolinas to Gulf of Mexico and river valleys farther west.
Habitat: Meadows and woodlands.
Food: Insects, crayfish, amphibians and reptiles.
Size: 5.7–11.4cm (2.25–4.5in).
Maturity: 3 years.
Breeding: Up to 7,000 eggs laid in spring; hatching takes about 12 days.
Life span: Unknown.

This species is found in areas of North America with large floodplains and many wetlands, where it feeds on crayfish (crawfish), insects, reptiles and other frogs. There are two separate populations. One follows the upper Mississippi Valley from south of the confluence with the Arkansas River up the Mississippi to Iowa, from where it extends west to the Missouri River. The range also reaches into the watershed of the Ohio and Tennessee Rivers. The second population ranges from the Atlantic coastal plain of the Carolinas to the coast of the Gulf of Mexico.

Crawfish frogs may spend much of the year underground, waiting for the right conditions for breeding. They do not dig their own burrows, but occupy tunnels abandoned by other animals, including those of crayfish and small mammals. During the spring rains, crawfish frogs emerge from their tunnels and arrive beside the swelling waterways in large numbers. The males attract mates with their snore-like calls.

This frog has a stout body and short, strong legs. On the back and sides it is brownish or greyish in colour with darker spots, while the belly is white and the undersides of the legs and groin are yellowish. These frogs can move swiftly on land, but in the water they tend to be rather slow swimmers.

Green frog

Rana clamitans

This frog is found in the marshes of the maritime provinces of Canada in the north and east. From here, it ranges south to the swamps of northern Florida and the mountain lakes of Oklahoma. Older adults lead relatively sedentary lives, but younger frogs often disperse through damp woodlands and meadows during periods of heavy rain. If a young frog is caught away from water as a dry period approaches, it may survive if it buries itself in moist soil until the rains return. Those that reach suitable bodies of standing water spend the summer feeding on insects and other invertebrates, both in the water and along the banks. In periods of cold weather, the frogs submerge themselves in the leaf litter and sediment at the bottom of a pond or stream. Like leopard frogs and bullfrogs, startled green frogs often emit a loud, high-pitched yelp as they leap away.

Breeding occurs in late spring, when males attract females with their twanging calls. Some males, however, stay silent and mate with females as they approach calling males. Each female lays up to 7,000 eggs, which float on the water's surface or hang from aquatic plants. The eggs hatch in about a week, and the tadpoles are usually green and speckled with black, often with a yellow belly. Some tadpoles change into adults before winter, but many hibernate and delay the transformation until spring. In fact, it can take up to 22 months for metamorphosis to occur.

Distribution: Eastern North America to Oklahoma, Florida and Eastern Canada.
Habitat: Swamps, ponds, lakes and rivers.
Food: Insects, slugs and crayfish.
Size: 5.4–12.5cm (2.25–4.75in).
Maturity: 2 years.
Breeding: Eggs laid in late spring.
Life span: 10 years.
Status: Common.

Although most members of this species are green or brown, a few rare individuals are blue. Males also have a bright yellow patch on the throat.

Amazonian rain frog (*Eleutherodactylus altamazonicus*): 3cm (1.25in)
Amazonian rain frogs live in the shrubs and large herbaceous plants that grow on rainforest floors. These tiny frogs are found in Ecuador and Peru in the west and across the Amazon Basin to southern Brazil. This species is largely brown with white speckles. It is most active at night, when it feeds on tiny insects. The males, which are slightly larger than the females, attract mates with a soft clicking call.

Forest chirping frog (*Adenomera hylaedactyla*): 2.5cm (1in)
The forest chirping frog has a sharp nose and a plump-looking fawn body with a dark V or X between the eyes. It inhabits the rainforests of Peru, Ecuador, Colombia and Brazil, where it is found in the thick leaf litter on forest floor. The diet comprises insects, spiders, millipedes and other small invertebrates. This frog is named for the chirping calls the males use to attract mates. Females lay eggs in a foam nest. The tadpoles only emerge from the nest once they have lost their tail and grown into miniature froglets.

Sharp-nosed jungle frog (*Leptodactylus bolivianus*): 10cm (4in)
This species has long hind legs and a pointed nose, giving it an elongated look. Sharp-nosed jungle frogs live in open areas beside ponds or in forest clearings, often near human settlements. They live in the upper Amazon in Peru and Bolivia. Males attract females with a single "whop" call. The female encloses the eggs in a floating foam nest. Each nest contains several hundred eggs.

Red-legged frog

Rana aurora

This species inhabits the ponds and streams of the coastal mountains that run along the west coast of North America. The northern tip of the range is Vancouver Island in British Columbia. The range then extends south all the way to Mexico's Baja California. Red-legged frogs are seldom found far from water, preferring deep and slow-moving stretches with thick vegetation. They may wander into damp forests in search of food such as insects and, occasionally, small mammals and frogs.

Red-legged frogs live alone. They are generally most active during the day, although those in California are primarily nocturnal. This may reflect the fact that the California frogs have different predators, including wading birds, which are a threat during daylight.

Female red-legged frogs grow to a larger size than males. Only the hind legs are red. Male red-legged frogs in the south of the range have a pair of vocal sacs, which swell when the frogs croak. Males in the north lack these sacs.

Distribution: West coast of the United States.
Habitat: Rivers and ponds.
Food: Small mammals, invertebrates and other amphibians.
Size: 5.1–13.6cm (2–5.25in).
Maturity: 4 years.
Breeding: Eggs laid in spring.
Life span: 15 years.
Status: Threatened.

Pig frog

Rana grylio

This frog is often called a bullfrog by people in southern US states, due to the large external eardrum on either side of its head. Females continue growing after the males have stopped, and may eventually reach a larger size.

The highly aquatic pig frog prefers to live in streams and ponds with thick vegetation, especially bladderworts, water lilies and saw grass. Pig frogs occur throughout Florida and as far north as the swamplands of southern Georgia. The range also extends west along the Gulf of Mexico to the Mississippi Delta and the barrier islands of the Texas coast.

Pig frogs are named after their mating call, which sounds like the grunt of a pig. During the breeding season, choruses of males create a roaring barrage of sound as they float in the water. After mating, the female attaches several thousand eggs to the stems of pickerel weed and other plants. Pig frogs hunt at night. They feed on insect larvae and small crustaceans that live underwater.

Distribution: South-eastern United States.
Habitat: Rivers and lakes.
Food: Insects and crustaceans.
Size: 8–16.2cm (3.25–6.5in).
Maturity: 2 years.
Breeding: Eggs laid in summer.
Life span: Unknown.
Status: Common.

Eastern narrow-mouthed toad

Gastrophryne carolinensis

Distribution: South-eastern United States, from eastern Texas to the Florida peninsula (including the Keys) and north to Oklahoma and Maryland.
Habitat: Ponds and ditches.
Food: Ants, termites, beetles and other insects.
Size: 2.2–3.8cm (1–1.5in).
Maturity: 30 days to metamorphosis.
Breeding: Mating, which is brought on by the rains, occurs between March and September. Up to 800 eggs are laid in floating clusters.
Life span: Unknown.
Status: Common.

The eastern narrow-mouthed toad lives in a variety of different habitats across the south-east of the United States. The toad is most commonly seen in areas with plenty of moisture and places to hide. This species is a good burrower – its narrow shoulders enable it to wriggle easily into soft earth. The toad will also seek refuge under logs and amongst leaf litter.

Eastern narrow-mouthed toads are nocturnal hunters. They prey on beetles, termites, ants and other ground-dwelling insects. They are especially fond of ants, and several toads may be seen feeding at a single anthill. Since these toads do not have teeth, the ants are licked up by the tongue. The toads have a flap of skin running behind each eye. These fold forward when the toad is feeding to protect the eyes from attack by their insect prey.

Narrow-mouthed toads have a small shoulder girdle, which makes their head look pointed. The skin is very smooth, without the warts and bumps seen on most toads. Although a good burrower, this species is a relatively weak jumper, moving with a series of short, rapid hops.

Johnson's casque-headed treefrog

Hemiphractus johnsoni

Although Johnson's casque-headed treefrog is rarely seen and is known only from about 20 specimens, it has been recorded across a huge swathe of South America. It is possible that within this range the frog exists in severely fragmented populations. Some experts believe that Johnson's casque-headed treefrog is actually a number of closely related species, particularly those populations in Brazil. The main habitat of this frog is the dense rainforest that covers the low-lying Amazon Basin, but it also survives at altitudes of up to 2,000m (6,500ft) in forests on the slopes of the Andes in Colombia, Ecuador, Peru and northern Bolivia. The frog is thought to divide its time between the branches and the forest floor.

This species does not lay eggs in water or enclose them in a nest. Instead, the female holds about a dozen eggs in a pouch on her back. The eggs develop through the tadpole phase inside the pouch, and then emerge as fully formed froglets.

Johnson's casque-headed frog hunts for insects and other invertebrates, plus smaller frogs and the occasional lizard. When disturbed, the frog attempts to ward off attackers by gaping its large mouth as wide as possible and snapping at anything that comes near.

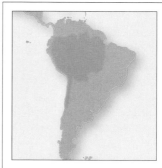

Distribution: Western Andes and Amazon Basin.
Habitat: Rainforest.
Food: Insects.
Size: 5.3–7.7cm (2–3in).
Maturity: Unknown.
Breeding: Eggs develop in dorsal pouch.
Life span: Unknown.
Status: Unknown.

When seen from above, this frog's head is triangular, due to two pointed sections, or casques, behind each eye. The females of this species tend to be larger than the males.

Northern cricket frog

Acris crepitans

The northern cricket frog is found across much of the United States. Its most northerly extent is to Michigan south of the Great Lakes. The range extends west to Nebraska and south to Texas. In the east, the range covers the Deep South (except most of Florida) and extends northward along the Atlantic coastal plain to southern New England. Northern cricket frogs live close to ponds and streams where plenty of cover is provided by aquatic plants. They are often seen basking on sunny banks to raise their body temperature. These frogs cannot climb, but they can make large leaps of up to 1m (3ft). They are diurnal (day-active) hunters, seeking out mosquitos and other damp-loving insects.

Large numbers of northern cricket frogs gather at ponds in the breeding season. However, many of these frogs do not survive long enough to become sexually mature, and the species is now classed as vulnerable due to the loss of its habitat. The frog's range covers some of the most intensively farmed land on Earth, and much of the standing water that the frogs need to survive is channelled and collected to drain and irrigate fields.

Distribution: Eastern and central north America.
Habitat: Ponds and streams.
Food: Insects.
Size: 1.6–3.8cm (0.5–1.5in).
Maturity: 1 year.
Breeding: Eggs laid in summer.
Life span: 1 year.
Status: Vulnerable.

This species is closely related to treefrogs, although it lives on the ground. It has webbed hind feet rather than long, suckered toes like the treefrogs. There is a dark triangular mark on the head.

Southern cricket frog (*Acris gryllus*): 1.6–3.2cm (0.5–1.25in)
This treefrog lives in swamps, marshes and streams. Its range covers the south of the United States and overlaps with that of the northern cricket frog, but only this species occurs in the Florida peninsula. Cricket frogs are strong jumpers – hence the comparison to crickets and grasshoppers. During the day they feed on insect prey, hiding in waterside vegetation and ambushing victims as they pass.

Lowland burrowing treefrog (*Pternohyla fodiens*): 2.5–6cm (1–2.5in)
Although it is related to frogs that live in trees, this species makes its home underground in the deserts of western Mexico and southern Arizona. The frog shelters from the daytime heat in burrows, where conditions are cooler and more humid than the surface. It only emerges on cool nights. Like many burrowing frogs, this species has a spade-like tubercle (projection) on its hind feet. It may use its large, bony head to plug the burrow entrance, preventing predators from entering and making it difficult for them to pull the frog out.

Spring peeper (*Hyla crucifer*): 2–3.5cm (0.75–1.25in)
This insect-eating species ranges from southern Canada and New England to Texas; it is absent from the swamplands of southern Georgia and Florida. Spring peepers are related to treefrogs and can climb well, although they are most often seen on river banks or in damp leaf litter. They are named after the high-pitched whistling calls that the males make to attract females in spring.

Striped chorus frog

Pseudacris triseriata

This species, sometimes simply called the chorus frog, is another "treefrog" that does not live in trees. Chorus frogs live further north than most American frogs, with a range that extends into the far north of Canada, reaching the Great Bear Lake and the often icy upper reaches of the Mackenzie River. Their range also encompasses much of central North America, as well as the Deep South of the United States, where the climate is much warmer and more humid.

Chorus frogs feed on a range of invertebrates, depending on their location. They are nocturnal and spend the day hiding under logs or in the burrows of larger animals. In the north of their range, they hibernate in these hideaways for several months of the year. However, on rare occasions they may emerge and begin to call before all the winter snow has melted.

Distribution: Central North America.
Habitat: Marshes and meadows.
Food: Insects and spiders.
Size: 1.9–3.8cm (0.75–1.5in).
Maturity: 1 year.
Breeding: Eggs laid in early summer.
Life span: 5 years.
Status: Common.

The three pale stripes running down the back of this frog are the source of its common name. Males have a yellow vocal sac that expands as the animal makes its calls.

Pacific treefrog

Hyla regilla

This variably coloured species has a dark stripe that runs from the nostril to the shoulder. The frog's rough skin can change colour. Such changes are triggered by the prevailing temperature and humidity, rather than being actively controlled by the frog itself. Female Pacific treefrogs are slightly larger than males.

The Pacific treefrog occurs in the Pacific North-west region of North America. The northern limit of its range is southern British Columbia and Vancouver Island. From here, the frogs range along the Pacific coast and through the coastal mountains to Mexico's Baja California. They are found inland as far as Montana and Nevada.

Pacific treefrogs usually live on the ground. They occupy a wide range of habitats, and are most often found near ponds, springs and streams. They prefer rocky areas, where there are plenty of damp nooks and crannies in which to hide.

Pacific treefrogs are generally solitary, but they may assemble in large numbers during the breeding season. At night, the males repeat their two-toned "kreck-ek" mating call to attract females and tell other males to stay out of their territory.

As tadpoles, the frogs eat aquatic plant material such as algae. The adult frogs are carnivores. They catch flying insects with their tongue, which they flick out at high speed. The tongue is coated with a sticky substance that helps the frogs to grab prey.

Distribution: Western North America, from southern Canada and United States to Baja California, Mexico.
Habitat: Close to water.
Food: Insects.
Size: 1.9–5cm (0.75–2in).
Maturity: 1 year.
Breeding: Mating season in spring. Female lays a mass of 10–70 eggs, which either floats or is attached to vegetation; eggs hatch within 3–4 weeks.
Life span: Unknown.
Status: Common.

Green treefrog

Hyla cinerea

This species has rough, bright green skin and a dark spot under each eye. There are bright yellow patches on the inner thighs. The skin becomes greyer during cold weather, and males turn yellow during the breeding season. The long legs and large, adhesive pads at the end of the toes are adaptations to an arboreal existence. These small frogs can leap about 3m (10ft), and they are able to hang on to leaves and other surfaces by just one toe.

Green treefrogs live along the edges of swampy ponds and in marshes. They are often found at ground level, but also climb into the tall shrubs and trees that grow beside the water. This species is found across south-eastern North America, from Delaware to Florida and Texas. The range also extends north up the Mississippi River Valley to the southern tip of Indiana.

Green treefrogs spend the day lurking under the cover of plants. They may give away their presence by their clanking, bell-like calls. During periods of high humidity, many frogs may call together, creating a loud chorus. The rise in humidity is often a prelude to rain, and consequently to mating. The green treefrog is often nicknamed the "rain frog", since it begins to call just before wet weather arrives.

However, not all the males call in these mating choruses. Some "satellite" males remain silent and attempt to intercept and mate with females attracted by the bellowing choruses.

By night, the frogs hunt for insects. They are often seen near houses, where they feed on insects attracted by the light.

Distribution: Eastern United States.
Habitat: Swamps and river banks.
Food: Insects.
Size: 3.2–6.4cm (1.25–2.5in).
Maturity: Unknown.
Breeding: Mating season is between March and September, but later in the Deep South. The female lays up to 400 eggs in small packets or films in shallow water at or near the surface, attached to floating vegetation; hatching occurs within a week.
Life span: Unknown.
Status: Common.

Bird-voiced treefrog

Hyla avivoca

Distribution: Southern Mississippi Valley, south-eastern United States.
Habitat: Swamps.
Food: Insects.
Size: 2.8–5.1cm (1–2in).
Maturity: Unknown.
Breeding: A total of about 500 eggs laid in late summer.
Life span: Unknown.
Status: Common.

The bird-voiced treefrog has one of the most melodic calls of any American frog. The males produce whistles while perched on waterside shrubs. Bird-voiced treefrogs live in the wooded swamps that are common along the coasts of the Gulf of Mexico. The range extends north following the wetlands created by the seasonal flooding of the Mississippi.

Bird-voiced treefrogs hunt at night. They prey on spiders and small insects that live in trees and shrubs. These treefrogs only come down to the ground during the breeding season, which begins in June. The males climb to a prominent perch, perhaps up to 1.5m (5ft) above the ground, to make their mating calls. They then clamber down to mate with the females that approach. The females lay packets of 6–15 eggs in shallow water. The eggs hatch after a few days, and the tadpoles transform into frogs in about a month.

Like many treefrogs, this species has bright patches on the inner surfaces of its long legs. When the frog is resting, these patches are hidden, but they flash into view when the frog stretches. It is thought that they are used to startle predators.

Barking treefrog (*Hyla gratiosa*): 5–7cm (2–2.75in)
This plump frog is found in the south-east of the United States, along the coastal plain from Virginia to the Gulf coast of Louisiana and the northern half of Florida. This treefrog rarely comes down to the ground. Like other treefrogs, it has sucker-like toe pads to help it grip smooth surfaces. In the summer breeding season, males gather beside permanent bodies of water and give loud, bell-like calls to attract females.

Clown treefrog/giraffe treefrog (*Hyla leucophyllata*): 3cm (1.25in)
This species lives in forests in the Amazon Basin. It has two common names because it exists in two colour phases, possibly more. At all times the frog has orange fingers and toes, which are also webbed. During the "clown" phase, the back is purplish-brown, with golden patterns on the snout. The "giraffe" phase is characterized by reticulations like those of a giraffe. These frogs lay their eggs on leaves overhanging water, and the tadpoles fall into the water when they hatch.

Flat-headed bromeliad treefrog (*Osteocephalus planiceps*): 5cm (2in)
Bromeliad treefrogs are a group of small frogs, some of which breed in the tiny ponds that form when rain water collects amid the leaves of bromeliads. These epiphyte plants often grow on trees many metres above the ground. This particular species of bromeliad frog, which is found across the Amazon, is flat in appearance. It sometimes lays its eggs in bromeliad ponds, but also uses standing water on the ground.

Gladiator treefrog

Hyla boans

Gladiators are among the largest treefrogs. They live across the Amazon Basin, where they are most often found along the banks of the many small rivers and streams that flow through the dense rainforests. Gladiator treefrogs are named after their impressive physique and because males often wrestle with each other to protect their nesting sites.

Reproductive activity is most common during periods of low atmospheric pressure, which herald heavy rains. The males call for mates with a hollow booming note while perching in riverside trees. They use the spurs on their heels to dig a nest in a muddy riverbank. The nest hollow is positioned just below the surface of the water, so that it is kept filled with a pool of water by the rain-swelled waterway. The female deposits her eggs in the nest. After hatching, the gladiator tadpoles disperse into the main waterway.

Distribution: South America, throughout the Amazon Basin.
Habitat: River banks.
Food: Insects.
Size: 12.5 (5in).
Maturity: 1 year.
Breeding: Up to 3,000 eggs laid in rainy season.
Life span: Not known.
Status: Common.

This large treefrog has olive skin with dark blotches. During periods of inactivity, the frog becomes darker. This is a swimming treefrog, so the feet have suction discs on their toes for gripping branches, and webs between the toes to help them swim.

TURTLES AND TORTOISES

Turtles and tortoises have lived on Earth for over 200 million years. They belong to a group of reptiles that have existed since the dinosaurs roamed the Earth. Their soft bodies are protected by shells called carapaces. There is no major difference between turtles and tortoises, however turtles (and terrapins) live in water, while tortoises tend to live on land.

Matamata

Chelus fimbriatus

Distribution: Amazon Basin and northern South America; also on Trinidad.
Habitat: Beds of rivers and streams.
Food: Fish.
Size: 30–45cm (12–17.5in).
Maturity: Not known.
Breeding: 20–30 eggs laid.
Life span: 40 years.
Status: Common.

Matamatas live on the bottom of tropical lakes and rivers. They take breaths by poking their long snouts out of the water, so they can remain hidden below the water at all times. Their knobbly shells are often turned green and red by algae growing on them, helping them blend with rocky river beds. Matamatas wait in ambush for prey to swim near. They have small eyes, set on the sides of their flattened heads, which are useless for hunting in the murky waters, but the turtles are sensitive to the water currents created by prey close by. The flaps of skin on their long necks aid their camouflage, and may also act as lures to attract fish. When the fish come within range matamatas strike with great speed. They suck the unsuspecting fish into their wide mouths. The suction is caused by a rapid opening of the mouth, creating an area of low pressure inside. Matamatas have also been observed walking along river beds, herding fish into shallow water where they can be sucked up more easily.

Matamatas are unusual-looking turtles. They have triangular heads with long flexible snouts, which are used as snorkels to breathe air from above the surface.

Alligator snapping turtle

Macroclemys temminckii

The alligator snapping turtle is the largest freshwater turtle. During the day it is mainly an ambush hunter, lying half-buried in mud on the river bed. While waiting for prey to approach, this turtle holds its large mouth open. The turtle's tongue has a small projection on it, which becomes pink when engorged with blood. The turtle wiggles this fleshy protuberance as a lure to attract prey. Fish and other animals investigate the lure, assuming it is a worm in the mud. As the prey swims into a turtle's mouth, the jaws snap shut. Small prey are swallowed whole, while the sharp, horny beak makes light work of larger prey, which may even be another species of turtle. The largest prey are held in the jaws, while the alligator snapping turtle uses its forefeet to tear it apart.

Male alligator snapping turtles spend their whole lives in muddy rivers and lakes. Females, however, climb on to land in spring to lay eggs in holes dug into mud or sand.

Distribution: South-eastern United States, in the lower Mississippi River Valley.
Habitat: Beds of lakes and slow-flowing rivers.
Food: Fish and turtles.
Size: 40–80cm (15.5–31.5in).
Maturity: Not known.
Breeding: 10–50 eggs buried in mud.
Life span: 70 years.
Status: Vulnerable.

Alligator snapping turtles have a tough carapace covered in pointed, triangular knobbles. They have a large head with a sharp, horny beak.

Galápagos tortoise

Geochelone elephantopus

Distribution: Galápagos Islands in the eastern Pacific.
Habitat: Varied, depending on the island, from moist forest to arid land.
Food: Plants.
Size: 1–1.4m (3.25–4.5ft).
Maturity: Unknown.
Breeding: Several large eggs.
Life span: Over 100 years.
Status: Vulnerable in general; some subspecies are endangered.

Galápagos tortoises are the largest of all the testudines (tortoises and turtles). They are found only on the islands of the Galápagos Archipelago in the equatorial Pacific, off the coast of Ecuador. In general, the shell folds around the body like a saddle. However, the different subspecies located on various islands in the group have varying shell shapes. The general saddle shape allows the forefeet and neck to move more freely than in most tortoises.

Galápagos tortoises are plant-eaters. They use their long necks to reach up to bushes and shrubs, foraging for leaves with their toothless jaws. They also eat grass and even cacti. Their giant size is probably due to this diet. The Galápagos Islands are arid places and plants are not widely available. Plant food contains only small amounts of energy, and larger animals use energy more efficiently than small ones.

For most of the year, the tortoises live in small herds. During the breeding season, however, males defend territories. The dominant males are the ones that can lift their heads higher than the other males. They hector passing females into mating with them. The females dig nest chambers and lay large, spherical eggs.

These giant tortoises have different shell shapes depending on the island they live on in the Galápagos Archipelago. Charles Darwin cited these shell differences to support his theory of natural selection.

Green turtle (*Chelonia mydas*): 1–1.2m (3.25–4ft)
This rare, endangered species has flipper-like legs and a smooth carapace. Green turtles only visit land to lay their eggs. They gather to mate off deserted, sandy beaches across the world, including the Americas. The females then emerge to lay their eggs in holes dug in the sand with their flippers. Green turtles eat sponges, jellyfish, sponges and molluscs.

Hawksbill turtle (*Eretmochelys imbricata*): 87cm (34.25in)
Hawksbills are found in the warm, tropical waters of the Atlantic and the Pacific. They lay eggs on beaches on North America's eastern coast. Adults live in fairly shallow, rocky waters or near reefs, diving down up to 20m (60ft) to feed on crustaceans, molluscs, and sponges. The young remain near the surface and eat floating seaweed. This species is endangered.

Loggerhead turtle (*Caretta caretta*): 0.7–2.1m (2.3–7ft)
Loggerheads are found in all the world's oceans, except the coldest polar waters. The large, chunky head houses powerful jaws capable of crushing hard-shelled prey such as crabs and lobsters. Loggerheads breed every second year, laying their eggs on sandy beaches. They are vulnerable.

Stinkpot

Sternotherus odoratus

Stinkpots are so-named because they release a nasty smelling musk from glands beneath their shells. This smell is meant to ward off predators, but the stinkpot will also give a painful bite if the musk does not do its job.

Stinkpots spend their lives in slow-flowing, shallow streams and muddy ponds and lakes. Their shells often have mats of microscopic algae growing on them. Stinkpots feed both during the day and at night. They use the barbels on their chins to sense the movements of prey buried in the muddy stream beds. Like many other musk turtles, stinkpots have a toughened "shelf" attached to their upper jaws. The turtles uses this shelf to crush the shells of water snails and other prey.

Female stinkpots leave the water to lay their elongated eggs. They make nests under mats of decaying plant matter or under the stumps of trees. Stinkpots lay the smallest eggs of all turtles – only 1.5 × 2.5cm (0.5 × 1in).

Stinkpots have smooth, streamlined shells suitable for living in running water. They have sensitive fleshy projections, called barbels, on their chins.

Distribution: South-eastern United States.
Habitat: Shallow, muddy water.
Food: Insects, molluscs, plants and carrion.
Size: 8–13cm (3.25–5in).
Maturity: Unknown.
Breeding: Eggs laid under tree stumps.
Life span: 54 years.
Status: Common.

Snapping turtle

Chelydra serpentina

The snapping turtle lives in the rivers and swamps of eastern North America. It prefers fresh-water habitats, but it also occurs in brackish environments, where salt water mixes with fresh water in estuaries and coastal marshes.

Snapping turtles are almost completely aquatic, although they will move across land in search of a new place to live should their home range become too crowded. These highly solitary turtles ensure that no other turtle encroaches into their feeding territory. They ambush their prey, burying themselves in mud on the river bottom and then cutting the heads off their victims using their sharp beaks. They also eat plants and carrion.

The only time a snapper will tolerate another individual's presence is during the mating season, between April and November. The male positions himself on the female's back during mating, clinging to her shell with his claws. Between 20 and 30 eggs are laid in a hole in sandy soil, hatching between 9 and 18 weeks later in autumn or winter.

The shells of snapping turtles range in colour from light brown to black. The tail has a serrated keel, while the legs and neck are covered in points called tubercles.

Distribution: Central and eastern North America, from southern Alberta and Nova Scotia in Canada to Texas and the Gulf of Mexico.
Habitat: Rivers and tidal swamps.
Food: Fish, birds, amphibians and small mammals.
Size: 20–45cm (7.75–17.75in).
Maturity: Not known.
Breeding: 20–30 eggs laid in a hole in spring.
Life span: 30 years.
Status: Lower risk.

Central American river turtle

Dermatemys mawii

This large, drab-coloured species is the sole surviving member of a turtle family that dates back more than 65 million years to the Cretaceous Period. Central American river turtles (also known as Mesoamerican river turtles) live in a range of habitats throughout northern Central America. They thrive wherever there is sufficient food, which is primarily aquatic plants such as river grass. They feed below the waterline, and often eat fruits that have fallen into the water. Among the most aquatic of all turtles, they spend much of their time submerged, only occasionally rising to the surface to breathe. Consequently, they move rather awkwardly on land. When submerged, oxygen from the water is absorbed through the thin skin of the throat.

Among the most aquatic of all turtles, Central American river turtles live in all types of water, from deep and clear streams to shallow, muddy marshes. They are most common in lakes and large rivers. They are sometimes also found with barnacles on their shells, which suggests that this species is also able to survive in salty water, perhaps in the tidal region of a river mouth.

The female turtle lays up to 20 eggs just above the water level in a muddy river bank during the flood season. Unlike their plant-eating parents, the young turtles are carnivores, eating molluscs and crustaceans, and perhaps also fish.

Distribution: Southern Mexico (excluding the Yucatan Peninsula) to Guatemala and Honduras.
Habitat: Lakes and swamps.
Food: River grass.
Size: 65cm (25.5in).
Maturity: Not known.
Breeding: 6–20 eggs laid during rainy season.
Life span: 30 years.
Status: Endangered.

Adult Mesoamerican river turtles have broad, smooth, streamlined shells that sometimes resemble leather. Younger turtles have a ridge along the centre line above the spine, but this gradually disappears as they get older.

Painted turtle

Chrysemys picta

Distribution: Central North America, from southern Canada to Mexico.
Habitat: Muddy freshwater.
Food: Plants, fish, insects and crustaceans.
Size: 15–25cm (6–9.75in).
Maturity: 3–10 years.
Breeding: Eggs laid in late spring and early summer.
Life span: 40 years.
Status: Common.

Painted turtles live in fresh water from British Columbia and much of southern Canada to Georgia and northern Mexico. The turtles sleep on muddy river beds at night, and during the daytime feed on leaves, fruits and a range of animal prey. Between feeding periods, large numbers of painted turtles can be seen basking in the sun, often perched on logs. The sun helps to keep parasites such as leeches at bay. If disturbed, the turtles dive into the water and take refuge in the mud or under a submerged object.

Males mature much earlier than female painted turtles. Mating takes place in late spring and early summer after the turtles emerge from hibernation. Eggs are buried in sandy soil in an open area that is exposed to a lot of sun. Each female lays about ten soft-shelled eggs. The young turtles are independent as soon as they hatch.

Painted turtles are so-called because of their smooth, brightly coloured shells. They have black, olive or brown shells with red, black and yellow markings along the edges. Female painted turtles tend to be larger than the males.

Pond slider (*Chrysemys scripta*): 12.5–29cm (5–11.5in)
This large pond turtle is found in lowland areas of south-eastern North America, from south of the Great Lakes to West Virginia and south to the Gulf coast, Texas and New Mexico. Pond sliders live in quiet habitats such as slow-flowing streams with plenty of mud and basking sites. If disturbed, they quickly slide into the water. Young turtles eat small animals such as snails, tadpoles, and crayfish; adults mainly browse on duckweed and water lilies. During courtship, the male rattles his claws on the female's head. If she is receptive, she sinks to the bottom, where mating takes place.

Big-headed river turtle (*Peltocephalus dumerilianus*): 63cm (24.75in)
This species has a large head, a sharply pointed nose and a high-domed shell with a keel along the spine. The head holds powerful jaws, which are used to catch and kill fish and other prey. The turtle lives in the western Amazon Basin, in black-water regions. These are areas of permanently flooded forest where the water is clear but dyed dark brown by tannins leached from submerged leaves.

Amazon mud turtle (*Kinosternon scorpioides*): 9–27cm (3.75–10.5in)
Amazon (or scorpion) mud turtles inhabit shallow water from Mexico to Paraguay. In rainy conditions, when the rivers rise considerably, Amazon mud turtles leave the water and roam through the forest. They often take up residence in a new area when the waters recede. Those stranded far from water as a period of dry weather begins bury themselves until the rains return.

Wood turtle

Clemmys insculpta

Wood turtles have a fragmented range across eastern North America. They live in running water, from small streams to the mighty St Lawrence River. Although they prefer watercourses with rocky bottoms, they are also found in woodlands and meadows far from water. (Females seem to be less water dependent than males.)

Wood turtles feed both in the water and on land. Being omnivores, they eat a range of foods, from leaves and fallen fruits to slugs, tadpoles and fungi. They cannot catch fast-moving, warm-blooded animals, such as small birds and mammals, but they will eat carrion if the chance arises. The turtles drive earthworms, a favourite food, to the surface by thumping their plastron (lower shell) on the ground. Taking the thumping to be vibrations caused by heavy rain, the worms rise to the surface to avoid drowning – only to be eaten by the turtles.

The shells of wood turtles have a low keel along the spine. The scutes, or plates, that make up the shell have well-defined "growth rings".

Distribution: From eastern Canada to New England and the Midwest in the United States.
Habitat: Running water.
Food: Plants, fruits, fungi, snails, slugs, tadpoles and worms.
Size: 14–25cm (5.5–7.5in)
Maturity: 14–20 years
Breeding: Eggs laid in nests in May and June.
Life span: Not known.
Status: Vulnerable.

Giant river turtle

Podocnemis expansa

The giant river turtle is found in large rivers throughout the Amazon Basin, where it is often seen floating near the surface. The adult females are significantly larger than the males, often twice as large. Like many reptiles, this species never stops growing, although the growth rate slows considerably after the onset of maturity, which is triggered by size. The speed at which the young turtles develop is influenced by the amount food available and other conditions, including temperature. As a result, maturity occurs at different ages, depending on how long the turtles take to reach the required size.

Breeding takes place at the start of the dry season, with the turtles crowding into the narrow river channels as the waters recede. After mating in the water, the females spend several weeks basking for up to six hours per day, presumably to hasten egg development. They then lay between 50 and 180 eggs at night in a hole dug in the shore or on an exposed sandbar. These turtles often nest in groups, and nesting sites may become so overcrowded that several females may use the same nesting hole. Incubation of the eggs takes 45–65 days, but the baby turtles may remain longer in the nest, until the rains begin, when they emerge and begin to move down toward the flooded river.

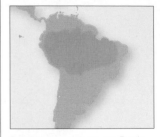

Distribution: Amazon Basin.
Habitat: Large rivers.
Food: Plants, fish, insects and crustaceans.
Size: 61–107cm (24–42in).
Maturity: Females 61cm (24in); males 20cm (7.75in).
Breeding: Up to 180 eggs laid in holes in dry season.
Life span: Not known.
Status: Endangered.

This is the largest turtle species in the Amazon Basin, capable of weighing more than 90kg (200lb). The giant river turtle has a smooth, gently domed shell that is grey-brown. This species has facial markings when young, but these fade with age.

Bog turtle

Clemmys muhlenbergii

Bog turtles are distributed patchily across the eastern United States. A northern population lives from New York and Massachusetts to northern Maryland, while a southern population can be found in the mountains of Virginia and North Carolina. There are also smaller populations in western Pennsylvania and along the southern shore of Lake Ontario.

The bog turtle's distribution is limited because it is restricted to a very specific habitat – shallow wetlands with water that is slow-flowing yet not choked by aquatic vegetation. Habitats like this tend to support dozens of different water-plant species. Human interference often reduces the number of plants in the habitat, or introduces new species that become rampant and make the area unsuitable for bog turtles. As a result, bog turtles are increasingly endangered. Bog turtles are popular as pets, but collecting wild bog turtles is now banned. Individuals bred in captivity fetch high prices, and this continues to fuel illegal collecting. Bog turtles are only active during the warmer parts of the day. They emerge from their nocturnal shelters and bask for a while before foraging. These turtles hibernate through winter, and they may also aestivate during the driest months of the year (July and August).

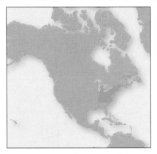

Distribution: Eastern United States.
Habitat: Wetlands.
Food: Invertebrates, seeds, fruits and leaves.
Size: 7.9–11.4cm (3–5in).
Maturity: 10 years.
Breeding: Up to 6 eggs laid yearly in shallow nests in June.
Life span: 40 years.
Status: Endangered.

This species is the smallest of the pond turtles. Younger individuals have obvious growth rings, or annuli, on their scutes. By the time a turtle reaches maturity, these marks have been smoothed away.

Blanding's turtle

Emydoidea blandingii

Distribution: Primarily Great Lakes region of North America.
Habitat: Shallow ponds and marshes.
Food: Crustaceans, frogs, fish, plants, snails and insects.
Size: 15–27.5cm (6–10.75in).
Maturity: 14–20 years.
Breeding: 6–21 eggs laid in June.
Life span: 40 years.
Status: Lower risk.

Blanding's turtle has a fragmented range, with the main population being found around the Great Lakes, from southern Ontario across to Minnesota and Illinois. It is also found as far west as Nebraska, and a third population exists to the east in New Hampshire, Massachusetts and south-eastern New York.

Blanding's turtles prefer shallow and slow-flowing watercourses that are filled with weeds and have a muddy bottom. They lie in wait for prey, such as crustaceans, fish, frogs and even leeches, and lunge forward by extending their long neck and grabbing the food in their mouths.

These turtles hibernate on the bottom between October and April. However, they can sometimes be seen moving around during this time, even under ice. During the breeding season, females may travel up to 1.2km (0.75 mile) away from their wetland homes to lay their eggs in sandy soil, usually at night. The hatchlings emerge 55–75 days later.

The notch on the upper jaw of Blanding's turtle makes it look as if it has a permanent smile on its face. Somewhat similar to a box turtle, this species also has hinge on its plastron (lower shell). Blanding's turtles often bask in the sun on sandbanks or logs.

Common toad-headed turtle (*Phrynops nasutus*): 30cm (11.75in)
The common toad-headed turtle is a large, highly aquatic turtle that inhabits the cochas (oxbows) and swamps of Amazonian Brazil, Ecuador and Colombia. The turtle's body is a uniform green-grey colour, perhaps a little lighter on the plastron. This long-necked, meat-eating species hunts for water snails and small fish.

Western twist-necked turtle (*Platemys platycephala*): 15cm (6in)
The western is the only twist-necked turtle to live in the Amazon. Its name comes from the way the neck folds as the turtle pulls its head under its shell. Unlike other similar species, this turtle is often found far from water during the rainy season. Western twist-necked turtles are mainly carnivorous, but they also eat some plant matter.

Cooter (*Chrysemys floridana*): 19–40cm (7.5–15.75in)
Cooters live in the coastal plain of eastern North America, from the Gulf of Mexico in the south, across Florida and north to Virginia. The shell is brown with yellow stripes, bars and doughnut shapes. Males have longer claws than females, especially on the the forefeet, which they use to stroke females during courtship rituals. Cooters live in large ponds, lakes, sluggish rivers and canals, where they can be seen basking in huge numbers, often alongside their close relatives river cooters and Florida red-bellied turtles. Breeding takes place in late May and early July. Female cooters lay two or more clutches of eggs in small holes.

Common map turtle

Graptemys geographica

Common map turtles occur from southern Quebec and Vermont past the Great Lakes to Wisconsin. The range extends south over the Appalachians to Alabama and west to the plains of Kansas and Arkansas. These turtles live at the bottom of large bodies of water with abundant aquatic vegetation. They prefer environments with plenty of partially submerged debris, such as logs and fallen trees, on which they can bask.

Map turtles hibernate in much of their range, hiding away under submerged logs during the coldest weather. However, some map turtles move across land to new locations in winter. When warmer weather returns, the turtles hunt both day and night. On sunny days they can be seek basking, but they slide into the safety of the water when danger approaches.

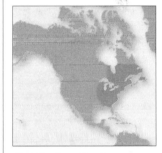

Distribution: Southern Canada to Georgia.
Habitat: Ponds, rivers and lakes.
Food: Snails, clams, crayfish and plants.
Size: 9–26cm; (3.5–10.25in).
Maturity: Not known.
Breeding: Up to 20 eggs laid in nests during early summer.
Life span: Not known.
Status: Common.

The turtle's shell has markings resembling contour lines or a map of a river system. There is a yellow spot behind each eye, and yellow stripes on the turtle's neck, head and legs.

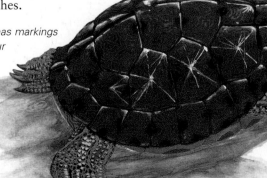

Diamondback terrapin

Malaclemys terrapin

Diamondback terrapins are named after the pattern of growth rings that appear on the pyramidal scutes (plates) that make up the carapace. They use their ridged, beak-like jaws to crush the bodies of their prey. Males may only be half the size of females.

Diamondback terrapins range from southern Texas and the Gulf of Mexico, where they are most common, around Florida and up to southern New England. They inhabit the brackish water of the salt-marshes, estuaries and tidal lagoons that form behind barrier islands, being most abundant in heavily reeded areas. While these terrapins can cope with saline conditions, they still need access to fresh drinking water.

Diamondbacks feed on a range of animal life in the tidal zone, including marine snails, clams and crabs. When not feeding, the terrapins may be seen basking on exposed sandbars or walking across mudflats between feeding sites. They avoid danger by running into water, where they are much more agile and better able to hide than on land.

Distribution: Eastern coast of United States.
Habitat: Estuaries and lagoons.
Food: Snails, crustaceans, fish and insects.
Size: 14–23cm (5.5–9in).
Maturity: 7 years.
Breeding: About 10 eggs (maximum 18) laid in sand during late spring and early summer.
Life span: Not known.
Status: Common.

Eastern box turtle

Terrapene carolina

The keeled, high-domed shell of this species has variable markings throughout its range. As in other box turtles, the lower shell (plastron) is hinged, enabling the turtle to close the shell almost completely when its head, tail and legs are withdrawn inside. Shut in a near-impregnable "box" of horny plates, the turtle is safe from most predators. Male eastern box turtles tend to be slightly larger than the females.

The Eastern box turtle occurs only in North America, where it ranges from Texas in the south to Michigan in the north, and across the Appalachians to the Atlantic coast. (A western box turtle species lives in the central United States.)

Eastern box turtles are seldom found far from streams and ponds, but often forage in woodland and damp meadows. The diet of these omnivorous reptiles includes several plants and mushrooms that are poisonous to humans, and many people have died after eating poisoned box turtle meat. The turtles' feeding behaviour is influenced by temperature. In midsummer, box turtles are most active in the morning and afternoons. During the hottest part of the day they crawl under logs or into burrows to keep cool. In the spring and autumn, the weather is mild enough for the turtles to feed all day long. In the northern part of their range, box turtles hibernate in burrows in the river bed during winter.

Many eastern box turtle populations have been reduced by the destruction of their habitat for urban development or agriculture. Collection of wild turtles for the pet trade also threatens their future.

Distribution: Eastern United States, from Texas in the south to Michigan in the north, and eastward across the Appalachians to the Atlantic coast.
Habitat: Woodlands, meadows and marshes.
Food: Snails, insects, worms, roots, amphibians, snakes, birds' eggs and fruit; turtles become more herbivorous with age.
Size: 10–21.5cm (4–8.5in).
Maturity: 5–7 years.
Breeding: Usually 4–5 eggs (maximum 11) laid from May to July in sandy or loamy soil; 2–3 (maximum 6) clutches may be laid per year.
Life span: 100 years.
Status: Lower risk.

Flattened musk turtle

Sternotherus depressus

Distribution: Black Warrior River in Alabama.
Habitat: Rocky river bed.
Food: Snails and mussels.
Size: 7.5–10cm (3–4in).
Maturity: 4–6 years.
Breeding: Normally 2 eggs laid in a riverbank hole twice a year.
Life span: Not known.
Status: Vulnerable.

The flattened musk turtle is a very rare species, restricted to a single river system in northern Alabama. It is now limited to the upper reaches of the river by a dam. It lives in the clear shallow streams that feed the main river. Avoiding muddy areas, it prefers to move around on rocky or sandy bottoms.

The flattened musk turtle feeds on invertebrates such as clams, snails, insects, crayfish and arachnids. There appears to be a correlation between light levels, feeding behaviour and the age of turtles: the adult turtles tend to feed at night, juveniles feed in twilight and hatchlings hunt during the daytime.

This species is thought to hibernate during the winter, but it is not known how it does this. Like other musk turtles, it probably buries itself in sand or hides under logs and rocks to avoid the coldest weather.

In common with all musk turtles, this species has two glands under the edge of its shell that produce a bad-smelling liquid to deter predators. It has a wider and more flattened carapace than other species in the musk turtle group, which enables it to squeeze between rocks on the river bed.

Red-footed tortoise (*Chelonoides carbonaria*): 45cm (17.75in)
The red-footed tortoise has a black, highly domed shell with the centre of each scute in orange. The head and the front of the forelegs have orange or red scales. Red-footed tortoises live on the edges of rain forests, where trees give way to grassland. This habitat type is found across South America. Most of the tortoise's diet is made up of plant material, but it will occasionally eat insects and other small animals. Breeding takes place all year round. The males attract a mate by making a clucking noise. The females produce a clutch of about 10 eggs that hatch after four months.

Desert tortoise (*Gopherus agassizii*): 15–36cm (6–14.25in)
Found in the deserts of the western United States, from southern Utah to California and northern Mexico, this species is most abundant in California, where there are about 80 individuals per square kilometre (200 per square mile). Like other land-living turtles, it has unwebbed feet. The flattened forelegs are used for digging burrows, while the sturdy, rounded hind legs push the body forward through soft earth. Desert tortoises eat low-growing grasses and herbs. They are slow moving, and are most commonly seen out of their burrows in the early morning. In the hottest part of the year, they spend the daytime below ground, emerging at night to feed. To initiate mating, the male hisses and butts the female. The eggs are laid in a deep hole. The shells of desert tortoises stay soft for the first few years. This species has been collected in large numbers for the pet trade, and is now endangered.

Gopher tortoise

Gopherus polyphemus

This tortoise occurs in the southern United States, including Florida. It lives in sandy areas where the water table never reaches the surface but still supports scrub and woodland. Longleaf pine forests are its preferred habitat.

Gopher tortoises are skilled diggers. They make a long burrow ending in a chamber, up to 3m (10ft) beneath the surface, where temperature and humidity are fairly constant. The tunnel leading to it can be about 12m (40ft) long. The tortoises retreat to their burrows during hot, dry periods. They may share their burrows with small mammals, snakes, toads and even burrowing owls.

On cool days, gopher tortoises bask at the entrance to their burrows to warm up before heading off to feed on grasses and herbs. They mate in spring and nest in early summer, laying their eggs in a shallow pit.

Distribution: Southeastern United States.
Habitat: Sand dunes.
Food: Grasses and herbs, occasionally berries.
Size: 10–24cm (4–15in)
Maturity: 16 to 21 years.
Breeding: Several clutches of 2–7 eggs laid in early summer.
Life span: 40–100 years.
Status: Vulnerable.

Gopher tortoises use their short, flattened forelegs for burrowing. The hind feet are smaller than the forefeet.

LIZARDS

Lizards are reptiles, belonging to the same group as snakes. They are found all over the world except for Antarctica, especially in places that are too hot or dry for mammals to thrive. The main group of American lizards are the iguanas, which include the basilisks and anoles. More widespread lizards, such as geckos and skinks, are also found in the Americas, especially South America.

Rhinoceros iguana

Cyclura cornuta

The rhinoceros iguana gets its name from the toughened scales on its snout that resemble small horns. Males have larger "horns" than females.

Distribution: Island of Hispaniola and other Caribbean islands.
Habitat: Forest.
Food: Leaves and fruit.
Size: 1–1.2m (3.25–4ft).
Maturity: Not known.
Breeding: 2–20 eggs laid in a burrow.
Life span: Unknown.
Status: Vulnerable.

These large grey iguanas live on the island of Hispaniola – divided into the countries of Haiti and the Dominican Republic – as well as a few smaller islands in the Caribbean Sea. They are most active during the day and often bask in the sun to warm up their bodies. They walk slowly through the forest, browsing on leaves and fruit. Their teeth are very sharp and are ideal for cutting through tough leaves and other plant materials.

When threatened, rhinoceros iguanas will run away at high speed. They can only achieve these speeds over short distances. If cornered, they will give a painful bite and thrash their tails, which are armoured with spiky scales.

Male rhinoceros iguanas maintain a hierarchy based on the size of their throat flaps, or dewlaps. The males frequently contest this social structure during the short summer breeding season. The top-ranked males control access to females. They attract females with elaborate displays involving bobs of their heads, press-ups and showing off their dewlaps. Females lay up to 20 eggs in burrows and guard them until they hatch three months later.

Gila monster

Heloderma suspectum

Gila monsters are one of only two poisonous lizards in the world. They produce venom in salivary glands in their lower jaws. The venom flows by capillary action along grooves in their teeth, giving the lizard a poisonous bite. The venom acts on the prey animal's nervous system, preventing the heart and lungs from working. For a healthy human, a bite from a gila monster will be very painful but not life-threatening.

Gila monsters are most active at night. They shelter from the heat of the day in rocky crevices or burrows abandoned by mammals. However, in northern parts of their range, the lizards are completely inactive for several months during the winter. Inactive individuals rely on fat stored in their tails to keep them alive when they cannot feed.

Distribution: South-west United States and northern Mexico.
Habitat: Desert.
Food: Small mammals and eggs.
Size: 35–50cm (14–19.5in).
Maturity: Unknown.
Breeding: Eggs laid in summer.
Life span: 20 years.
Status: Vulnerable.

Gila monsters mate in springtime, and their copulation can last for over an hour. The eggs develop inside the females for about ten weeks. They then bury the eggs in areas that are often bathed in sunlight. The eggs incubate for up to ten months.

Gila monsters have long, robust bodies with short legs. Their bodies are covered in rounded, bead-like scales. Most of them are dark but some have blotches of pink, yellow or orange.

Green basilisk

Basiliscus plumifrons

Distribution: Central America.
Habitat: Forest.
Food: Insects, small mammals, smaller lizards, plus fruits and some flowers.
Size: 60–75cm (23.5–29.5in).
Maturity: Unknown.
Breeding: 20 eggs per year.
Life span: 10 years.
Status: Common.

Green basilisks spend most of their time in trees. They have long fingers and toes that help them grasp branches as they scuttle about looking for food. However, they prefer to stay in trees that are close to water. When threatened by predators, such as birds of prey, the lizards dive into the water below. The crests on their backs and tails are used to propel the reptiles through the water to safety. Basilisks will also shimmy into soft sand to avoid a predator. They can close their nostrils to keep sand out. On land, they run at high speed on their hind legs. They do not have to stop running when they reach water, because their hind feet have scaly fringes that spread their bodyweight, enabling them to sprint over the water's surface. This adaptive ability has earned them (along with other related species) the nickname of "Jesus Christ lizards".

Male basilisks control their territories very aggressively, chasing any other males away. A successful male will control an area that contains a number of females. He has sole mating rights to this harem.

Green basilisks are also known as plumed basilisks because they have crests on the backs of their heads, down their back and along their long tails.

Giant amphisbaenian
(*Amphisbaena alba*): 75cm (29.5in)
This is one of the world's largest amphisbaenians, or worm lizards. These are legless, burrowing reptiles lacking obvious eyes. They form a distinct group from snakes and legless lizards, such as slow worms and glass snakes. The giant amphisbaenian is found throughout the Amazon Basin, typically among the roots of trees, where it preys on earthworms and insect larvae, such as beetle grubs. The body is pale brown, with little patterning on it. The scales form distinct rings around the body.

Florida worm lizard (*Rhineura floridana*): 18–40cm (7–15.5in)
Most American amphisbaenians live in the soils of tropical Central and South America. The Florida worm lizard is the only one to occur north of Mexico, being found in central Florida, where it lives in the sandy soils of pine woodlands. Florida worm lizards are pink with rings of scales, and resemble large earthworms. In fact, this reptile species hunts for earthworms as well termites and other subterranean prey. Florida worm lizards sometimes come to the surface after heavy rains, when the sandy soil is saturated.

Green anole

Anolis carolinensis

Green anoles live in trees. Their long, thin legs are well adapted for leaping from branch to branch and perching on all but the flimsiest of branches. Thanks to the pads on the tips of their fingers and toes, anoles can grip on to just about any surface, including the fronds of palm trees.

Green anoles rest in dense cover at night. When not foraging in daylight, the lizards bask in the sun, generally on vertical surfaces, such as tree trunks or walls. Anoles can change their body colour, although not to the same extent as chameleons. For example, they may darken their normally bright skin when resting in the shade so as not to attract attention.

Although both sexes have dewlaps, only the males use them for communication. They extend them to signal to rival males and mates. A male begins courtship by bobbing his head and displaying his dewlap to a female. He then walks towards her with his legs straightened. If she is receptive to his advances, she allows him to position his body next to hers. He then grasps the back of her neck with his mouth and holds her tail with his hind legs as they copulate. The female lays one egg at a time under moist leaf litter.

Distribution: South-eastern United States.
Habitat: Woodland and shrubbery.
Food: Insects.
Size: 12–20cm (4.75–8in).
Maturity: Unknown.
Breeding: Single eggs laid throughout breeding season.
Life span: Unknown.
Status: Common.

Both male and female green anoles have pink dewlaps – fans of skin beneath their throats. The lizards have very long tails – nearly twice the length of the rest of their bodies – and their elongated fingers and toes are tipped with pads.

Desert horned lizard

Phrynosoma platyrhinos

These small reptiles are sometimes referred to as horned toads, because of their rounded bodies. Despite living in dry areas, much of the desert horned lizard's range can get cold, especially at night. Its round body helps it to warm up quickly in the morning sunshine. The lizard can eat huge quantities of ants, which it licks up with its long tongue.

The many spikes on this lizard's body serve two functions. They help to break up the profile of the lizard so that it can blend in with the rocky terrain, and if the lizard is spotted by a sharp-eyed predator, the tough spikes make it a difficult and potentially painful meal to swallow. Armed with these weapons, a horned lizard will not run when danger approaches. Instead, it will freeze to avoid giving its position away and rely on its camouflage to hide it. If this defensive strategy fails and it is scooped into the mouth of a predator, such as a coyote, the reptile has one final weapon. The horned lizard can ooze blood from membranes that haemorrhage around its eyeballs. The blood mixes with a foul-tasting chemical, causing the predator to release its grip on the lizard.

Distribution: South-western United States.
Habitat: Rocky desert.
Food: Ants.
Size: 7.5–13.5cm (3–5.25in).
Maturity: Unknown.
Breeding: Eggs laid in spring.
Life span: Unknown.
Status: Common.

The desert horned lizard has three pointed scales that form horns pointing backwards from the rear of its head. There are smaller spikes on its back and along the tail.

Chuckwalla

Sauromalus obesus

Chuckwallas live in the Mojave Desert, one of the driest and hottest places in North America. Like all other living reptiles, chuckwallas are cold-blooded or exothermic. Their bodies do not make any heat of their own apart from that generated by muscle movement. The lizards rely on sunlight and the temperature of the air around them to warm up enough for daily activity. Chuckwallas only become fully active when their body temperature exceeds 38°C (100°F). The temperature of the Mojave Desert regularly exceeds this, but in other areas of their range, chuckwallas remain inside their rocky dens until the weather gets warm enough.

Chuckwallas are herbivores. They search through the rock-strewn desert for hardy plants that can survive the scorching conditions. With only a limited food supply, female chuckwallas may not be able to reproduce every year. Some females save energy by skipping a breeding season.

Chuckwallas have an unusual defence strategy. When they are under attack by a bird of prey or coyote, they scuttle into a tight crevice between rocks and inflate their lungs. These reptiles have loose folds of skin around their throats and flanks which allow their bodies to swell up to a considerable size. This makes it difficult for a predator to extract the lizard from its hiding place.

Distribution: California, Arizona and northern Mexico.
Habitat: Desert.
Food: Fruit, leaves and flowers.
Size: 28–42cm (11–16.5in).
Maturity: Unknown.
Breeding: Females breed every 1–2 years.
Life span: Unknown.
Status: Common.

Chuckwallas have powerful limbs and thick tails. The males have completely black heads, while the females have yellow and orange patches on black.

Black and white tegu

Tupinambis merianae

The black and white tegu is the only tegu to be common outside the Amazon and similar jungle habitats. It is larger than its forest-living relatives and lives in the tall grasses of the pampas and open woodlands. Tegus hunt on the ground during the day. They patrol on four legs, but may rise up on to their hind feet to scare off threats or sprint away from predators. Adults have powerful jaws which are used for crushing prey. The large jaw muscles are especially noticeable in the males, where they appear as jowels. As with other tegu species, these lizards supplement their meat diet with plant food.

Tegus spend cold nights in burrows. During the winter, they stay in these burrows for many days, and breeding takes place after the rains. Females create an intricate nest constructed of two chambers, the lower one containing between 10 and 30 eggs, which are surrounded by dried leaves. The heat produced by the leaves as they compost keeps the eggs warm. The female then builds a chamber above the eggs, where she sits guard for about 70 days.

Black and white tegus vary in colour depending on their habitat. Tegus that live in drier grasslands are paler than those that live in damper woodlands.

Distribution: Southern Brazil to eastern Argentina.
Habitat: Open woodlands and pampas.
Food: Insects, rodents, snails, lizards and fruits.
Size: 1.2m (4ft).
Maturity: 2 years.
Breeding: 30 eggs each year.
Life span: Unknown.
Status: Common.

Pink tailed skink (*Eumeces lagunensis*): 16–20cm (6.25–8in)
This skink lives in Baja California. When young, the lizard's long tail is bright pink, but it fades with age. The bright tail probably serves as a diversion to predators, which are more likely to strike at the brightly coloured tail than the camouflaged head. Many lizards can live without their tails, and skinks have special bones in their tails that are designed to break when the tail is attacked. In most cases, a lost tail will grow back again in a matter of weeks.

Middle American night lizard
(*Lepidophyma flavimaculatum*): 7–12cm (2.75–4.75in)
Female Middle American night lizards produce young without having to mate – parthenogenetically. Some populations of these lizards contain no males at all. The lizards do not lay eggs, but keep them inside their bodies until they hatch. The young are then born live from the mother.

Crocodile skink (*Tribolonotus gracilis*): 15–20cm (6–8in)
This armoured lizard lives on the island of Hispaniola in the Caribbean. Its triangular head is protected by a bony shield and it has four rows of scaly spines running along its back and tail, making it look somewhat like a crocodile. Crocodile skinks live in pairs or threesomes, consisting of a male and one or two females. The females lay single eggs in leaf litter.

Ajolote

Bipes biporus

Despite their appearance, ajolotes are not snakes or lizards, but members of a small group of reptiles called amphisbaenians, or worm lizards. These reptiles spend their whole lives burrowing through soft soil, feeding on subterranean prey.

The ajolote is also called the mole lizard or "little lizard with ears". Early observers must have mistaken the ajolote's tiny but powerful forelimbs for ears. This is an easy mistake to make, since the forelegs are very close to the head. Ajolotes use their clawed forefeet to dig tunnels. They also wriggle through the soil, using their blunt heads to push earth aside.

Unlike other amphisbaenians, ajolotes sometimes come to the surface, generally after heavy rains. Above ground they are ambush hunters, lying in wait for lizards and other small animals. They use their forelimbs to haul their long bodies across the ground to grab their prey, which they generally drag underground to be eaten in safety.

Distribution: Baja California.
Habitat: Burrows.
Food: Worms and insects.
Size: 17–24cm (6.75–9.5in).
Maturity: Unknown.
Breeding: Lays eggs.
Life span: 1–2 years.
Status: Common.

Ajolotes have long bodies with scales arranged in rings. They are unique among worm lizards because they still have forelimbs.

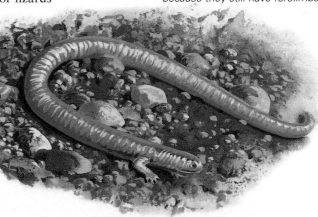

Marine iguana

Amblyrhynchus cristatus

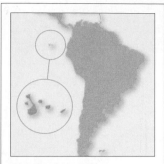

Marine iguanas live on the coastline of the Galápagos Islands in the Pacific Ocean. These volcanic islands, which were made famous by Charles Darwin's use of their fauna to explain his theory of evolution, have never been attached to the mainland. Along with the Galápagos land iguana and the famous giant tortoises, the marine iguanas are the only four-legged land animals on the islands. The iguanas are thought to have floated to the islands on fallen trees.

Marine iguanas dive into the ocean to feed on the seaweed that grows on submerged rocks. Large adults can stay underwater for over an hour at a time. They spend the rest of the day basking in the sun on the rocky shoreline. They need to keep warm when on land because they rapidly lose heat when they enter the water, since the islands are surrounded by cold ocean currents. Marine iguanas may gather in crowds containing thousands of individuals. When they bask, they expel excess salt from their bodies through glands in the nose. As a result, the faces of marine iguanas are often covered in a spray of white salt crystals.

Although there is some variation in skin colour between marine iguanas that live on different Galápagos islands, they are generally black when wet and greyer after basking in the sun. A ridge of triangular scales runs down the back. Young marine iguanas have a pale stripe along their back.

Distribution: Galápagos Islands.
Habitat: Rocky shores.
Food: Seaweed.
Size: 50–100cm (19.5–39.5in).
Maturity: Unknown.
Breeding: 2–3 eggs laid in autumn in holes in the sand.
Life span: Unknown.
Status: Endangered.

Knight anole

Anolis equestris

Knight anoles are found at the top of large trees in Cuba. They have been introduced to southern Florida, where they are common in the Miami-Dade and Palm Beach areas.

This diurnal species searches for beetle grubs and adult insects such as grasshoppers, cockroaches and moths. It also eats spiders and smaller lizards. When the lizard spots a predatory tree snake, it adopts a defensive stance, turning to the side and extending the throat fan, while raising the crest of spines along the back. The lizard then gapes its mouth at the predator.

Rival males display a similar behaviour when confronting one another, except that the throat fan is pulled in and out several times, and the anole stands tall on its four legs. The scales also turn a brighter green. If fighting commences, the males rush forward with gaping mouths and bite at their opponent's limbs or mouth.

Distribution: Cuba.
Habitat: Trees.
Food: Grubs, grasshoppers, moths and spiders.
Size: 32–50cm (12.5–19.5in).
Maturity: Unknown.
Breeding: Eggs laid during summer.
Life span: Unknown.
Status: Common.

The knight anole is the largest of the anole lizards. The tail is compressed and the head is wedge-shaped. The body is covered by small scales that can change from bright green to grey-brown. The males have a pink throat fan that extends when they become excited.

Brown basilisk (*Basiliscus vittatus*): 60cm (24in)
Basilisks are often called Jesus Christ lizards, because of their habit of running over the surface of water to escape predators. Brown basilisks live in Central America and northern Colombia, and are now wild in Florida after escaping from captivity. They are most common in Guatemala, where they are found beside almost all bodies of standing water. These lizards are largely brown, with yellow stripes along their sides. Males have a crest projecting from the back of the head, and another along the back. Females have a hood around the back of the head, as well as a crest on the back, which is smaller than that of the males. Brown basilisks live in thick vegetation beside water. They feed on insects and fruits.

Land iguana (*Conolophus subcristatus*): 120cm (48in)
A close relative of the marine iguana, this large lizard occurs only on the Galápagos Islands. Biologists believe that this species diverged from the common ancestor of marine iguanas about 10 million years ago. Marine iguanas use the ocean to keep cool, but land iguanas seek refuge from the midday sun in burrows. They eat the cacti that grow on the arid volcanic islands.

Forest dragon (*Enyalioides laticeps*): 30cm (12in)
This species lives in the Amazon Basin. Forest dragons are largely arboreal, but they rarely climb far above the ground. Like many lizards, they gape when confronting a threat. It is believed that exposing the bright pink lining of the mouth helps the lizard to startle or scare off predators.

Green iguana

Iguana iguana

The common green iguana occurs throughout Central and South America, from central Mexico to Paraguay. It also lives on many of the Caribbean islands and some islands off the Pacific coast of South America. This species has been introduced to Hawaii and Florida, where it has escaped from captivity and now lives wild.

Green iguanas live high up in trees. Older iguanas tend to live higher up than younger ones. This may be because the young cannot compete with the older iguanas for good basking sites near the top of the canopy, and so are forced to look for patches of sunlight that break through the tree cover lower down. These iguanas prefer to be close to water. They are good swimmers and will leap into the water to escape danger.

Green iguanas eat leaves and some insects. Like all vertebrates, the lizards do not have the correct digestive juices to break down tough plant food. Instead, they have a soupy mixture of bacteria in their colon that digests the plant fibres for them.

Although adult members of this species are largely green, young green iguanas often also have brown bands. The colour of the lizard changes with temperature and humidity. The skin becomes darker during cold weather to absorb more heat. In hot periods, the skin turns paler to reflect the heat. The crest and dewlap are better developed in males than females. The long, whip-like tail is not only used for swimming, but also acts as a defensive weapon that can lash out at adversaries. These lizards will also bite when cornered, although they prefer to flee rather than fight.

Distribution: Central and South America.
Habitat: Trees.
Food: Plants.
Size: 1.75m (5.75ft).
Maturity: 4 years.
Breeding: About 50 eggs laid in dry season.
Life span: 20 years.
Status: Common.

Ctenosaur

Ctenosaura similis

Distribution: Mexico and Central America.
Habitat: Rocky areas.
Food: Plants and small animals.
Size: 91cm (36in).
Maturity: 4 years.
Breeding: Up to 25 eggs laid in a burrow.
Life span: 60.
Status: Common.

A male ctenosaur has a spiny crest along the back and a dewlap. When the animal becomes excited, these are raised to make it look larger, with the aim of deterring rivals and other threats.

Ctenosaurs are found throughout Central America, from northern Mexico to Panama, and also on some of the small islands off the Panamanian coast. Ctenosaurs live in rocky areas, where they spend a lot of the time basking in the sun or digging hollows and burrows to escape the extreme heat. Their skin is dark so that they can absorb the sun's heat quickly to warm up their bodies in the morning.

Ctenosaurs live in large colonies, and individuals spend a lot of time defending territories from their neighbours. The male's crest and dewlap are used for this purpose as well as for attracting females during the breeding season. The dewlap can be extended by a bone in the throat. The ctenosaurs can also change the colour of their scales to ward off rivals, but fights are still common. These involve bites and scratches. Large males secure larger territories encompassing the areas of a number of females; consequently, they breed more. Courtship displays are complex. The male initiates the courtship, but it only proceeds if the female responds in the correct way. After mating, the female digs a burrow and lays her eggs inside. She guards the burrow for a while to stop other females nesting in the same place. When the young ctenosaurs hatch they spend about a week digging their way out of the nest.

Collared lizard

Crotaphytus collaris

This medium-sized iguana is found across the central region of North America, from the western banks of the Mississippi River in Arkansas and Missouri to northern Mexico and Nevada. It lives in rocky areas with only a thin covering of vegetation. Such places tend to be quite dry and hot.

Collared lizards are often seen during the hottest parts of the day. They bask on boulders to warm their bodies in the sunlight. When warmed up, they forage on the ground for insects and other small invertebrates, as well as any smaller lizards they come across. Collared lizards will eat plant material, including flowers and berries, if they cannot find other sources of food.

At night and during cold periods, collared lizards retreat to the relative warmth of a burrow dug under a large rock. They lay their eggs in similar holes.

The adults can be aggressive when threatened, and if cornered they will sometimes bite opponents much larger than themselves. However, escape is always preferred to combat, and the lizards usually run off at high speed on their hind legs, using their tails as a counterbalance.

This species is named after the black-and-white collar around its neck. The rest of the body is generally olive green, with pale yellow spots and stripes, although colour and pattern can vary markedly. The adult males have blue throats. The collard lizard is stocky-bodied, with a chunky head and large eyes and powerful jaws. The strong hind legs make the lizard a good climber and a fast runner. The long tail aids balance when moving through branches or swiftly across ground.

Distribution: Central North America.
Habitat: Rocky areas.
Food: Insects and smaller lizards.
Size: 35cm (14in).
Maturity: Unknown.
Breeding: About 5 eggs laid in summer.
Life span: Unknown.
Status: Common.

Greater earless lizard

Cophosaurus texanus

The greater earless lizard is a desert species. It inhabits the dry rock fields of northern Mexico and parts of Texas, New Mexico and Arizona. This lizard lives and hunts on the ground, but may climb up cliffs in some parts of its range. In such places, the young lizards are often found higher up than their older counterparts.

Like other lizards and reptiles, greater earless lizards are cold-blooded, or more correctly ectothermic. This means that their body temperature is controlled using an external source of heat – in this case, sunlight. Before they can hunt, the lizards must spend the early part of the day basking in sunshine to warm up their muscles. They search for prey in the warmest part of the day, running across rocks and along the ground in pursuit of insects. On cloudy days, the lizards do not get warm enough to hunt and are very lethargic.

Although the ears of many lizards are not easy to see, most species have small ear openings on the sides of their heads. This species, as its name suggests, lacks such openings, although the lizard can still hear using its inner ear.

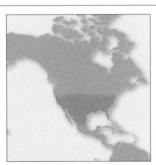

Distribution: Northern Mexico and the southern United States.
Habitat: Deserts and other rocky areas.
Food: Insects, especially beetles and grasshoppers.
Size: 7–18cm (2.75–7in).
Maturity: 1 year.
Breeding: Clutches of about 5 eggs laid monthly from March to August, up to a total of about 25.
Life span: 2 years.
Status: Common.

Keel-scaled earless lizard

Holbrookia propinqua

These unusual lizards live in southern Texas and along the north-eastern coast of Mexico. They live in sand dunes and on the region's long beaches. Keel-scaled earless lizards are well adapted to life both on and under the sand. They have very long legs for their size, allowing them to run quickly across exposed areas of dune and so avoid predators. Their blotchy scales give them further protection, making the lizards hard to spot among the knotted dune grasses. Lacking external ears, they can burrow easily into the loose sand, which they do at night in order to stay warm. During the day, these earless lizards bask in the sun before hunting down sand-dwelling insects. They are largely solitary animals and avoid other lizards, which they ward off with displays of aggression that resemble press-ups.

The tiny scales of this earless lizard have ridges, or keels, along them. The lizard has up to six dark spots or streaks along the belly. Females carrying eggs turn yellow-green.

Distribution: Texas and Mexico.
Habitat: Dry areas.
Food: Insects.
Size: 11–15cm (4.5–6in).
Maturity: Unknown.
Breeding: Eggs laid in early summer.
Life span: Unknown.
Status: Common.

Texas horned lizard (*Phrynosoma cornutum*): 7cm (2.75in)
This species ranges from Kansas to northern Mexico. It lives in barren sandy areas that are too dry for most plants to grow. The Texas horned lizard is a diurnal hunter. It must spend the early part of the day basking to get its body warm enough to forage. As the cool of night approaches, the lizard retreats to the relative warmth of a burrow. It does not dig its own burrow, but takes over one that has been abandoned by another animal. Texas horned lizards are often based close to a nest of harvester ants, their preferred food. They have broad but flattened bodies, which gives them a passing resemblance to a large toad or frog (hence their nickname, the Texas horned toad). The "horns" are spines on the back of the head. Similar spines skirt the body.

Common monkey lizard (*Polychrus marmoratus*): 35cm (14in)
This large lizard has a very long, slender tail, which may be twice as long as its body. The lizard often wraps the tip of this long appendage around a branch, just like many New World monkeys do with their flexible, prehensile tails. The monkey lizard lives in the western Amazon. It is generally olive brown, but may take on a bright green colour.

Amazon thornytail (*Tropidurus flaviceps*): 19cm (7.5in)
This arboreal lizard, which lives in the north-western Amazon, gets its name from the large ridges, or keels, on its tail. Other thornytails in the Amazon are green, but this species is predominantly grey, with a white collar around the neck. This large lizard feeds on ants.

Florida scrub lizard

Sceloporus woodi

This species has rough, overlapping scales. Males are slightly smaller than the females, with a blue patch on each side of the throat.

This member of the iguana family occurs in four small ranges in central and southern Florida. The largest population lives among the sand dunes of Florida's eastern coast. Elsewhere, the lizard is found inland in pine forests that grow in sandy soils.

Florida scrub lizards lie in wait for prey such as ants, beetles and spiders to walk past, then strike with a rapid lunge. Scrub lizards spend a long time basking at the edges of woodlands or in other exposed areas. They often crowd together into basking sites, which results in frequent conflicts between males. As they warm up, the males bob their heads up and down at an increasing rate. Larger, dominant males bob their heads at smaller males, which then flee the area. A more evenly matched rival will turn sideways and compress his body so that he looks larger. This also has the effect of showing off the blue patch on the throat. Males also bob to attract females. Unreceptive females hop away sideways.

Distribution: South-eastern United States, restricted to Florida.
Habitat: Sandy areas, including pine, oak and rosemary scrub.
Food: Insects, spiders and other small arthropods.
Size: 9–14cm (3.5–5.5in).
Maturity: 1 year.
Breeding: 2–8 eggs laid in clutches of 4, with about 3 clutches per season in early summer.
Life span: Unknown.
Status: Common.

Eastern fence lizard

Sceloporus undulatus

The eastern fence lizard is so-named because it prefers to bask in a raised, sunny location, such as on top of a fence. It may also be spotted sunbathing on fallen logs, grassy dunes and open prairies, and in sunny woodland clearings. This lizard is perhaps most often seen on tree trunks, with its head pointing upwards so that it can run up into the branches if threatened.

This species occurs from Delaware on the east coast of the United States to northern Mexico. The range covers most of the southern states (except southern Florida) and extends to Utah and Arizona in the west. Eastern fence lizards are also found in Kansas and Missouri.

Fence lizards are diurnal. However, unlike many lizards that become most active at the hottest times of the day, this species heads for the shade. At night the lizards retreat to burrows and other hidden shelters. Eastern fence lizards hibernate through the winter and breed soon after emerging in spring.

This species is seen with various colourings, ranging from brown to grey. Often individuals have spots or streaks, and a dark band along the back of the thighs. Males have blue patches on the throat and belly. The scales are strongly keeled, each scale having a prominent spine.

Distribution: From Delaware west to Utah and south into north-central Mexico, including most of the south-eastern United States.
Habitat: Woodland and prairie.
Food: Insects, snails and other invertebrates.
Size: 9–19cm (3.5–7.5in).
Maturity: 1 year.
Breeding: Several clutches of up to 12 eggs each laid in summer.
Life span: Unknown.
Status: Common.

Leopard lizard

Gambelia wislizenii

Like the coat of a leopard, the skin of this long, slender lizard is covered in dark patches. Most leopard lizards are grey-brown, but they become darker in cold conditions. Females carrying eggs have orange spots and stripes. This species often takes up residence in rodent burrows, but it is perfectly capable of digging its own burrows when necessary. It occasionally climbs into bushes.

The leopard lizard lives in the region between the Rocky Mountains and the smaller coastal ranges closer to the west coast of North America. Many parts of its range are at high altitude and can be very cold, especially in the north around Idaho and Wyoming. Conditions are also very dry, because few of the rain clouds that come in from the ocean make it over the coastal mountains. Consequently, much of the leopard lizard's range is desert – especially in the south around the US–Mexico border. There are few plants in this habitat, and the soil is loose and sandy.

Leopard lizards are active during the day. Once warmed up, they are very agile hunters, and are often seen dashing from bush to bush as they actively search for insects and spiders. They also hunt by ambushing their prey, lying hidden beneath a shady bush and leaping out when prey approaches. They will eat small lizards too, and even members of their own species on rare occasions. When threatened, the leopard lizard hisses and may bite.

Distribution: North America, including California, Nevada and Utah to extreme western Texas and south to northern Mexico.
Habitat: Sandy and gravely areas.
Food: Mostly insects and spiders, but also other lizards and occasionally small rodents and plant matter.
Size: 22–39cm (8.5–15.5in).
Maturity: Unknown.
Breeding: Female lays 5–6 eggs in early summer, and sometimes again in late summer; hatching takes about 5–6 weeks.
Life span: Unknown.
Status: Common.

Diving lizard

Uranoscodon superciliosus

Distribution: Northern South
America, in the eastern and
northern Amazon region.
Habitat: Swampy forest.
Food: Invertebrates.
Size: 45cm (18in).
Maturity: Unknown.
Breeding: Up to 10 eggs laid.
Life span: Unknown.
Status: Common.

Despite being the sole member of its genus, this species is far
from rare. It is found across the northern and eastern Amazon
Basin, where it is often seen diving from branches into streams
and rivers. This behaviour is largely an escape tactic but,
being good swimmers, diving lizards do habitually enter the
water to move through the forest. Unusually for lizards,
they can also swim well underwater. Furthermore, like
basilisks they are able to run on water for short distances.

Diving lizards hunt in trees overhanging water, feeding on
arboreal insects and similar
invertebrates. Their dark
colouring helps to camouflage
them as they bask on tree
trunks and branches. When
danger threatens, they will remain
motionless, but if the threat
comes comes too close, they
plunge into the water and seek
refuge beneath submerged debris.

*The diving lizard has a slender
body and a long tail. The long legs
and toes enable it to move swiftly
on land and with great agility
through shrubs and trees. The
skin is brownish-grey, and there is
a crest that runs along the back.
In some individuals the back also
has golden flecks.*

Fringe-toed lizard (*Uma notata*): 12.7–23cm
(5–9in)
The comb-like fringes on this lizard's toes help it
to walk over fine sand in the deserts of southern
California, Arizona and northern Mexico. The
fringes act like snowshoes and spread the
lizard's weight, preventing its feet from sinking in
the shifting sand. When alarmed, the fringe-toad
lizard uses a swimming motion to bury itself in
the sand. It also heads underground to avoid the
worst of the sun's heat and, on rarer occasions,
any cold snaps. The lizard's upper jaw overhangs
the lower jaw to keep sand out of the mouth. It
also has valves to close the nostrils, flaps over
the ears and overlapping eyelids.

Mediterranean gecko (*Hemidactyus turcicus*):
10–12.5cm (4–5in)
Native to North Africa, southern Europe, the
Middle East and India, this lizard was introduced
to Texas and southern Florida, and it is now the
most conspicuous gecko in North America. This
nocturnal species has pads on its toes that help
it to grip on to very flat surfaces, such as leaves,
smooth tree trunks, walls and ceilings. The male
geckos produce tiny squeaks during fights.

Reef gecko (*Sphaerodactylus notatus*):
4.5–6.3cm (1.75–2.5in)
Reef geckos live in the Florida Keys, an archipelago
of islands at the state's southern tip. They also
live along the southern coast of the mainland.
Reef geckos prefer thick mangrove forest, and
they are also common in gardens. This species
is the smallest North American lizard. It is diurnal
and hunts for insects in leaf litter.

Bridled forest gecko

Gonatodes humeralis

This small lizard inhabits tropical forest across
northern South America, from Bolivia and
Brazil in the south to Colombia and the island
of Trinidad in the north. Although most
geckos are nocturnal hunters, this species is
diurnal. By night, the bridled forest gecko
sleeps on a large leaf or clinging to a stem.

The bridled forest gecko is most often
seen on the edges of forests and in clearings.
It has also been known to stray into human
houses. Unlike many geckos, especially those
in Europe, Africa and Asia, the bridled forest
gecko does not have toe pads. (These are used
to cling to smooth surfaces, even windows.)
As a result, this species is not so well adapted
to life among humans as many of its relatives.

Female bridled forest geckos lay single
eggs at irregular intervals
throughout the year. The
eggs have a hard shell,
and the young
hatch looking
like adults in
miniature.

Distribution: Northern South
America.
Habitat: Rainforest.
Food: Insects.
Size: 6–8cm (2.5–3.25in).
Maturity: Unknown.
Breeding: Several eggs laid
singly throughout the year.
Life span: Unknown.
Status: Common.

*Female bridled forest geckos are grey with dark
spots, while the males occur in a range of colours,
including olive bodies with red and blue spots. The
"bridle" is a pale band that runs from each eye
around the back of the head.*

Western banded gecko

Coleonyx variegatus

The western banded gecko is found in southern California, Arizona and northern Mexico, including half of the Baja peninsula. This slender-limbed, flexible-bodied lizard occupies rocky and sandy habitats such as the walls and beds of canyons. Agile and quick-footed, the Western banded gecko is active at night, when it forages for insects and spiders. Its days are spent sheltering in rocky crevices or rodent burrows.

The western banded gecko holds its tail in the air, rather like a cat, as it stalks insects and spiders. When trapped, this lizard makes high-pitched squeaks and, like many other geckos, it may shed its tail when attacked. There is a constriction at the base of the tail where the break occurs. The tail keeps moving for a short while after separation from the body. This behaviour is meant to confuse the predator, which may focus on the tail while the gecko makes its escape. The tail quickly regrows.

As well as the dark brown or black bands across the tan back, Western banded geckos can be identified by their moveable, protruding eyelids. The bands are most prominent in juveniles, and fade as the lizards get older.

Distribution: South-western United States to northern Mexico, including California, Arizona, and Baja California.
Habitat: Rocky deserts, also arid grassland and chaparral.
Food: Insects and spiders.
Size: 12–15cm (4.75–6in).
Maturity: Unknown.
Breeding: 3 clutches of 2 eggs laid in summer.
Life span: Unknown.
Status: Common.

Texas banded gecko

Coleonyx brevis

Texas banded geckos live in Texas, northern Mexico and parts of New Mexico. They are mainly found west of the Pecos River, in the so-called Trans-Pecos region. These geckos live in dry, rocky areas. They dig burrows in the sandy soil underneath flat rocks.

Texas banded geckos are nocturnal hunters. They feed on insects and spiders, which they stalk on the ground. Being cold-blooded, they have only a short time when their body is sufficiently warm enough to enable them to forage. They begin hunting at dusk, and generally finish about four hours later, by which time it is too cold for them to continue. The geckos find prey by tasting the air and ground to detect chemicals produced by nearby insects. They also locate prey by sight.

If the gecko is threatened by a predator, it turns around and waggles its tail at its attacker. When the predator strikes at the tail, the tail breaks away from the body, enabling the lizard to flee. The tail regrows, as it does in other tail-shedding species.

Distribution: Texas, New Mexico and Mexico.
Habitat: Rocky areas.
Food: Insects.
Size: 10–12cm (4–4.75in).
Maturity: Unknown.
Breeding: 2 clutches of eggs laid in late spring and early summer.
Life span: Unknown.
Status: Common.

Female Texas banded geckos are larger than males. As the lizards get older, the solid bands across the back break up into spots and blotches. In banded gecko species, the males have a pair of thorn-like spurs at the base of the tail.

Tropical house gecko

Hemidactylus mabouia

The tropical house gecko is one of many found in Africa, Asia and Europe. The wide pads on its toes help it to cling to tree trunks and other vertical surfaces.

Distribution: Amazon and southern Florida (introduced from Africa).
Habitat: Tree trunks and houses.
Food: Insects.
Size: 10cm (4in).
Maturity: 1 year.
Breeding: Several clutches of 2 eggs laid throughout year.
Life span: Unknown.
Status: Common.

The tropical house gecko has been introduced to the Amazon from Africa by human migrations. In the wild, these geckos flourish in the forests of Brazil and other Amazonian countries. However, as their name suggests, they have also become common in many settlements, including the largest South American cities.

House geckos are nocturnal hunters. They have very wide toe pads, which have scales arranged in tiny folds across the bottom. These folds give the toes a firm grip, even on extremely flat surfaces. House geckos often rest on tree trunks and walls in a head-down position, so that they are ready to escape to the safety of the forest floor (or another hiding place) should danger approach.

By day, tropical house geckos sleep on a leaf or in a sheltered nook. Their skin is darker at these times, but grows lighter when they forage for food. It has been observed that geckos hunting on white-washed walls become very pale in response to the white background.

Turnip-tailed gecko (*Thecadactylus rapicaudus*): 15–20cm (6–8in)
This gecko, the sole member of its genus, is the largest in South and Central America. It ranges from southern Mexico to southern Brazil and Bolivia. This gecko's name refers to the fact that when its tail is lost during an attack by a predator, it regrows in a rounded, turnip-like shape. Turnip-tailed geckos are largely forest-dwellers, but they often appear around rural settlements. Like many other geckos, they climb using retractable claws.

Amazon pygmy gecko (*Pseudogonatodes guianensis*): 5cm (2in)
This pygmy gecko is found across the Amazon Basin, being especially common in the Peruvian section. Its tail is about the same length as the body. If the tail is shed during an attack, the new tail does not reach the full length of the original. The Amazon pygmy gecko's small size makes it hard to spot, so it is likely that its numbers have been underestimated. Most geckos are nocturnal, but pygmy geckos are active by day, foraging on the forest floor for insects and other invertebrates. They lack the large toe pads of many larger species.

Coal skink (*Eumeces anthracinus*): 13–17.8cm (5–7in)
There are several disjointed populations of these diurnal lizards in central and eastern North America, the largest being in Oklahoma and Kansas. Other populations are found in the Mississippi Delta region, the Appalachians, Florida and Georgia. Coal skinks prefer damp areas with loose stones and leaf litter among which they can forage. They dive into water to avoid predators.

Mexican beaded lizard

Heloderma horridum

Mexican beaded lizards are the only close relatives of the gila monster. They are able to survive in deserts, just like the gila monster, but they also thrive in a number of other habitats. Their range extends from central Mexico to Guatemala and most of northern Central America. In the north of this range, beaded lizards live in rock-strewn semi-deserts. However, further south, where there is enough rainfall for trees and shrubs to grow, the lizards inhabit forests. Despite their large size, Mexican beaded lizards are accomplished climbers and are often seen high on ledges on the sides of canyons.

Mexican beaded lizards are hunters, preying on small vertebrates such as bird chicks, mice and smaller lizards. They also raid bird and reptile nests to eat the eggs. Most prey is swallowed whole. These lizards are venomous, and their bites become infected with bacteria from the lizard's saliva.

Distribution: Mexico and Central America.
Habitat: Semi-desert and woodland.
Food: Small mammals, birds, lizards, insects and eggs.
Size: 75–90cm (29.5–35.5in).
Maturity: Unknown.
Breeding: Up to a dozen eggs laid in early summer.
Life span: Unknown.
Status: Vulnerable.

Male Mexican beaded lizards are slightly larger than females. The species is named for its rounded, bead-like scales. Adults are black or brown, with yellow spots on the back and tail. The plump tail is a store of fat, which is used to keep the lizard alive when food becomes scarce.

Five-lined skink

Eumeces fasciatus

The five-lined skink ranges across eastern North America, from southern Quebec and Ontario just north of the Great Lakes to southern New England. The range extends south, covering most the eastern United States and Midwest to eastern Texas, however this species is not found in Florida. Five-lined skinks occupy a range of habitats within their extensive range. They prefer damp areas such as woodlands and meadows, but avoid areas that are prone to flooding or becoming too water-logged.

These lizards also require prominent basking sites, preferably rocky outcrops or tree stumps. They forage on the ground for insects and other invertebrates. They also eat small frogs, snails, baby mice and smaller lizards.

Male five-lined skinks are territorial and will not allow another adult male to come near. They advertise their ownership of an area using chemical markers, and also by displaying their brightly coloured bodies and tails.

Distribution: Eastern North America.
Habitat: Woodland.
Food: Insects, spiders and other invertebrates.
Size: 12.5–21.5cm (4.75–8.5in).
Maturity: 3 years.
Breeding: About 15 eggs laid in summer.
Life span: 6 years.
Status: Common.

This skink is named after the yellow stripes that run along its back. The stripes become lighter as the lizard ages.

Mole skink (*Eumeces egregius*): 8.9–16.5cm (3.5–6.5in)
The mole skink is found in southern Georgia, south-eastern Alabama and most of Florida (including the Keys but not the Everglades). This lizard is a good tunneller. It digs to find soil-dwelling prey such as insect larvae and spiders. The mole skink prefers areas with sandy soil in which it can dig with ease. Most of this soil is found on the coastal plain. Inland, the lizard is more restricted to lowland areas where sand gathers.

Broad-headed skink (*Eumeces laticeps*): 16.5–32.4cm (6.5–12.75in)
This skink has a very wide head. It occurs across the central and eastern United States, from Texas in the south to eastern Nebraska and southern Pennsylvania in the north. Broad-headed skinks live mainly in woodland, but also occur in open areas where there is plenty of plant debris or rocks to provide shelter. The young have wide white stripes across their back, which fade with age. Broad-headed skinks are active by day. They are known to hunt for insects high up in the trees, sometimes shaking the nests of paper wasps to dislodge the pupae inside. The wasps' stings cannot penetrate the lizard's thick scales.

Western skink (*Eumeces skiltonianus*): 16.5–23.7cm (6.5–9.25in)
The Western skink lives under rocks and in leaf litter in the Great Basin plateau of the western United States, which includes Nevada, Idaho and Oregon. The lizard's range also extends along the west coast to Baja California. The Western skink hunts by day for insects, spiders and earthworms.

Black-spotted skink

Mabuya nigropunctata

The black-spotted skink has pale and dark stripes along its sides, with dark spots underneath and brown scales above. The scales are smooth and shiny. There is a bluish tinge to the juveniles' scales.

The black-spotted skink is the only member of the skink family to be found in the Iquitos region of the Amazon Basin, which lies on either side of the Peru–Ecuador border and contains many of the Amazon River's major sources. From here, the skink's range extends throughout most of the Amazon watershed.

This species is a good climber, and it is sometimes found clambering through forest trees, especially when searching for a sunlit spot on which to bask. The black markings on its skin help it to absorb the sun's warmth more quickly.

Despite their tree-climbing abilities, black-spotted skinks are mainly terrestrial in habit. They hunt small invertebrates among the leaf litter of the forest floor, and may sometimes be seen foraging on village garbage tips. This species is viviparous, meaning that it gives birth to live young rather than laying eggs.

Distribution: Amazon Basin, including parts of Brazil, French Guiana, Venezuela, Peru, Ecuador and Bolivia.
Habitat: Forest.
Food: Insects, arachnids and other invertebrates.
Size: 17–23cm (6.75–9in).
Maturity: Unknown.
Breeding: Up to 8 young born in each litter, with 1 litter born per year.
Life span: Unknown.
Status: Common.

Six-lined racerunner

Cnemidophorus sexlineatus

This species is often just called the racerunner. The name is derived from this wary lizard's habit of running for cover whenever a person approaches. The racerunner lives across the lowland areas of south-eastern and central United States, from the east coast to the eastern foothills of the Rocky Mountains. It prefers to live in dry areas where sandy soil prevents thick vegetation from covering the ground. The lizard scurries around hunting for insects, snails and other soft-bodied invertebrates. It is almost never seen climbing trees.

Racerunners shelter under flat rocks and in other nooks and crannies. To avoid low temperatures at night and on cold days, they retreat into burrows. They sometimes dig burrows themselves, but they more often occupy burrows abandoned by other animals, especially those of moles. A racerunner's burrow has two entrances, one of which is always blocked up by the lizard when it is inside. In the north of this species' range, the lizards hibernate from autumn until late spring.

Distribution: Eastern and central United States.
Habitat: Sandy grasslands and woodlands.
Food: Insects.
Size: 30cm (12in).
Maturity: Unknown.
Breeding: 4–6 eggs laid in summer.
Life span: Unknown.
Status: Common.

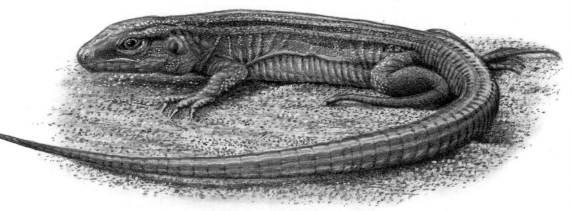

Despite their name, six-lined racerunners sometimes have seven pale stripes along the back. The males have green or blue throats, while the females have white throat patches.

Sonoran spotted whiptail

Cnemidophorus sonorae

The Sonoran spotted whiptail lives in the Sonoran Desert, which extends from north-western Mexico into southern Arizona. The lizard occupies the less arid upland areas in the eastern portion of the desert, where grasslands and woodland can grow.

The whiptail is a close relative of the racerunner, which is also a whiptail. However, there is one crucial difference that sets this lizard apart from other whiptails: there are no males of the species. Female Sonoran spotted whiptails reproduce by parthenogenesis. This is a form of asexual reproduction in which the lizards can produce eggs without mating. The young have exactly the same genes as their mothers. Egg production is stimulated by a ritual between two females that is similar to the courtship seen in sexual species. Asexual reproduction is a very efficient way of reproducing quickly and with the minimum of effort, but without a variety of genes in the population the species is less able to withstand changes in the environment.

Distribution: Sonoran desert, from southern Arizona to north-western Mexico.
Habitat: Dry grassland, desert scrub and mountain oak woodlands.
Food: Insects and other invertebrates, and smaller lizards.
Size: 20–28cm (8–11in).
Maturity: Unknown.
Breeding: 2–3 clutches of 3–4 eggs produced between mid-May and late July by parthenogenesis.
Life span: Unknown.
Status: Common.

All Sonoran spotted whiptails are female. They have six pale stripes on their dark, spotted back. The tail is paler than the back, and the belly is cream coloured. These lizards eat mainly insects and other invertebrates, but also prey on smaller lizards. They are most active in the first part of the morning. They rest during the intense midday heat, and resume activity in the afternoon.

Golden tegu

Tupinambis teguixin

The tail makes up two-thirds of a golden tegu's total length. The body has a dark background marked with yellow or golden rings. Juveniles are greener than adults, and adult males turn slightly blue.

The golden tegu is the largest lizard in the Amazon. These heavily built, ground-living hunters prey on all sorts of small animals, including mammals, other reptiles and amphibians, as well as large arthropods. They also supplement their diet with plant food. Golden tegus are diurnal hunters. They generally walk on four legs but can run at high speeds on their hind legs to escape from danger. Golden tegus retreat into burrows at night and when conditions are too cold for hunting. They occupy a range of habitats across the north of South America, from forest edges and river banks to thick jungle and cultivated fields.

Female golden tegus lay up to a dozen eggs, which apparently lie dormant for a few months before beginning to develop. As a result, the eggs take up to seven months to hatch.

Distribution: Amazon and Orinoco Basins in northern South America.
Habitat: Forests and cultivated areas.
Food: Small mammals, reptiles, amphibians, large arthropods, plants, some bird and caiman eggs and carrion.
Size: 95cm (37.5in).
Maturity: Unknown.
Breeding: Up to 12 eggs laid each year.
Life span: Unknown.
Status: Common.

Northern caiman lizard

Dracaena guianensis

This lizard leads a similar aquatic life to the crocodile tegu. The two species are not very closely related, but both resemble crocodilians. The caiman lizard is the larger and more robustly built species. It has three rows of spines on its tail and powerful jaws, which it uses to crush the shells of water snails and crustaceans. The northern caiman lizard is an Amazonian species. It is found in areas of flooded forest and in the many rivers and creeks that criss-cross the Amazon Basin. This northern species has a southern relative that lives south of the Amazon in the wetlands of Paraguay.

The northern caiman lizard often basks on the banks of rivers or on a large piece of floating debris. This lizard is a diurnal hunter with a specialized diet of water snails. It has powerful jaws with enlarged sites for muscle attachment and flat, molar-like teeth for crushing snails. The snail flesh is swallowed and indigestible fragments of shell are pushed out of the mouth by the tongue. In the dry season, when snails are less abundant, this lizard may climb trees to feed on eggs and invertebrates.

Female northern caiman lizards lay about a dozen large eggs in nests on land. These are sometimes in termite nests, perhaps to protect them from predators.

Distribution: Peru and Brazil.
Habitat: Flooded forest.
Food: Water snails; plus some invertebrates and eggs.
Size: 90–120cm (35.5–48in)
Maturity: Unknown.
Breeding: Up to 12 eggs laid beside a river.
Life span: Unknown.
Status: Common.

This species has a large head, which ranges in colour from green to orange. The body varies from olive brown to dark green. The belly is grey. The lizard's common name derives from the knobbly scales on its back, which resemble those of caimans.

Southern alligator lizard

Elgaria multicarinata

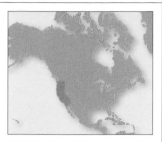

Distribution: West coast of North America.
Habitat: Grassland and woodland.
Food: Small mammals and insects.
Size: 25–43cm (9.75–17in).
Maturity: Unknown.
Breeding: Females lay 2–3 clutches of about 20 eggs during summer.
Life span: Unknown.
Status: Common.

The southern alligator lizard belongs to the anguid family. Most anguid lizards live outside of the Americas. They include monitor lizards and the fearsome Komodo dragon. American anguids, such as the alligator lizards, are much smaller than their foreign cousins.

The southern alligator lizard has a patchy range in the mountain woodlands along the west coast of North America. It is most common in California and Baja California, Mexico, but its range also extends north through the Cascade Mountains as far as southern Washington.

The southern alligator lizard is a diurnal hunter that often climbs in bushes, using its prehensile tail to grasp branches. The lizard eats anything it can catch, from small mammals and lizards to insects and other invertebrates.

Females lay more than one clutch of eggs per year during warmer periods. Each clutch contains about 20 eggs.

The southern alligator lizard has a distinct fold along its side, and dark crossbands on its brown back. The young have lighter bands.

Californian legless lizard (*Anniella pulchra*): 15.2–23.5cm (6–9.25in)
This is one of two lizards in North America. The other is found in the Baja peninsula. Legless lizards look like large worms or snakes. They are most closely related to the anguid lizard group, and should not be confused with amphisbaenians. The Californian species burrows in the soft soils of coastal California up to San Francisco Bay. It hunts for insects in the soil or the leaf litter that builds up in forest habitats. Its flexible legless form and blunt head make it a good tunneller. The California legless lizard is most active at night.

Granite night lizard (*Xantusia henshawi*): 10–14.5cm (4–5.5in)
This secretive, nocturnal lizard lives in the rocky deserts of southern California and Mexico's Baja peninsula. Its large, lidless eyes give it good night vision. Night lizards are viviparous, meaning that the young develop inside the females, nurtured by a placenta-like organ. They are born tail first. Most litters contain two young.

Crocodile tegu (*Crocodilurus lacertinus*): 60cm (23.5in)
The crocodile tegu has two rows of keel-like spines along its long tail, giving the animal a passing resemblance to a crocodile. The tail makes up about two-thirds of the lizard's overall length. Crocodile tegus frequently move in and out of water, although they also spend time in the trees. They occur right across the Amazon Basin, from the flooded forests of eastern Peru to the wetland region around the mouth of the Amazon River in eastern Brazil.

Large-scaled forest lizard

Alopoglossus angulata

This is one of several forest lizards that live in the Amazon. This particular species is found all over the region, and its range probably extends into surrounding areas as well. It seldom strays far from permanent bodies of water.

The forest lizards are characterized by having no ridges, or keels, on the scales of the head. This species is no exception, although its head scales are somewhat rough. The rest of the body, however, is covered in keeled scales.

Very little is known about the reproductive behaviour of this species, but it is thought that the females lay small clutches of eggs at varying times during the year.

Distribution: Amazon Basin.
Habitat: Moist forest.
Food: Insects.
Size: 10–13cm (4–5in).
Maturity: Unknown.
Breeding: Small clutches laid throughout the year.
Life span: Unknown.
Status: Common.

As its name suggests, the body of the large-scaled forest lizard is covered in large, rough scales. Even the lower eyelid has scales, although these are translucent to allow a little light to pass through even when the eyes are shut. (Most lizards, in contrast, have much more transparent scales on the lower eyelid.)

CROCODILIANS

Crocodilians are an ancient group of reptiles. They include crocodiles, alligators, caimans and gharials. They all live in or near water. Most crocodilians in North and South America belong to the alligator and caiman group. In fact only one type of alligator – the Chinese alligator – lives outside of the Americas. American crocodiles tend to be larger than their alligator and caiman cousins, and most are very rare.

American alligator

Alligator mississippiensis

Young American alligators feed on insects, small fish and frogs. As they get bigger, they begin to take larger prey, such as turtles and water birds. Adults feed on land as well as in water. They are opportunistic feeders, attacking anything that comes within reach. They even leap up to snatch birds perching on low branches.

During cold weather, American alligators become dormant in burrows dug into mud banks. In dry periods, they will travel long distances to find water, sometimes ending up in swimming pools.

After mating, the female makes a mound of vegetation and mud above the high waterline and lays her eggs in a hole in the top. When she hears the hatchlings calling, she breaks open the nest and carries her young to the water. They stay with their mother for about a year.

The American alligator has a broad snout. Unlike other crocodilians, the fourth teeth on either side of its lower jaw are not visible, since they fit into sockets in the upper jaw when the mouth closes.

Distribution: South-eastern United States.
Habitat: Swamps and rivers.
Food: Birds, fish and mammals.
Size: 2.8–5m (9.25–16.5ft).
Maturity: 5–10 years.
Breeding: Eggs laid in nest of mud and vegetation during spring.
Life span: 40 years.
Status: Common.

Black caiman

Melanosuchus niger

Black caimans are the largest alligators in the Americas. Young black caimans rely heavily on aquatic crustaceans for food, especially crabs and crayfish. Adults eat fish, such as catfish and piranhas, and often take large rodents called capybaras that live along the banks of rivers. At night, they may hunt on land, taking advantage of their excellent hearing and sense of sight to track large animals, which may include livestock and even humans.

Breeding takes place during the dry season, presumably to reduce the chance that the eggs become submerged while they incubate. The females build nest mounds that are about 1.5m (5ft) high. The nest mounds are built in a variety of places, some concealed, others in the open. Each female digs a conical hole in her nest and lays 30–65 eggs in the top. They hatch about three months later, at the beginning of the wet season.

As their name suggests, black caimans have dark bodies. They have grey-brown bands on their lower jaws. The young have yellow or white bands on their flanks, which fade as they age.

Distribution: Northern South America.
Habitat: Rivers and flooded forests.
Food: Fish, capybaras and other aquatic vertebrates.
Size: 4–6m (13–19.75ft).
Maturity: 5–10 years.
Breeding: Eggs laid in nest during dry season.
Life span: 40 years.
Status: Lower risk.

Spectacled caiman

Caiman crocodilus

Distribution: Central America and northern South America.
Habitat: Areas of still water.
Food: Fish, wild pigs and water birds.
Size: 1.5–2.5m (5–8.25ft).
Maturity: 4–7 years.
Breeding: Eggs laid in nests during wet season.
Life span: 40 years.
Status: Common.

Spectacled caimans live in a wide range of habitats from rivers to coastal wetlands. They prefer stiller waters than the black caimans that share parts of their range, and consequently they have taken up residence in many reservoirs.

Spectacled caimans rarely come out of the water, only attacking land animals when they come to the water's edge. They spend the day floating on the surface and hunt mainly at night. During periods of drought, they aestivate – enter a period of dormancy to avoid desiccation – in cool burrows dug deep into mud.

The breeding season coincides with the wet season in May and June. The dominant males get the best territories and attract most females. Females lay eggs in mounds of vegetation that they build on banks or rafts of plants. Several females may lay eggs in a single nest, which they guard together. The young live in large groups called crèches.

Spectacled caimans are smaller than most crocodilians. They get their name from ridges of bone located on their snouts between their eyes. The ridges appear to join the eyes together, looking similar to the frames of a large pair of spectacles.

Orinoco crocodile (*Crocodylus intermedius*): 4–7m (13.25–23ft)
These crocodiles live in the middle and lower reaches of the Orinoco River, Venezuela, where they prey on fish, birds and land animals. Females lay their eggs in holes dug into sandbars during low-water periods in January and February. The eggs hatch when the rains arrive about 70 days later. A mother will guard her young for up to three years.

Broad-snouted caiman (*Caiman latirostris*): 2–3m (6.5–11.5ft)
This medium-sized caiman has an even broader snout than the American alligator. It is found from Bolivia to southern Brazil and northern Argentina, in freshwater habitats and brackish coastal mangroves. Broad-snouted caimans eat aquatic snails, amphibians, small fish and even turtles. The female lays 20–60 eggs in a nest, sometimes on a river island. She guards them for 70 days, then breaks open the nest and carries the hatchlings to water.

Red caiman (*Caiman yacare*): 2.5–3m (8.25–9.75ft)
This species lives in the rivers, lakes and wetlands of northern Argentina, Paraguay, southern Brazil and Bolivia. Its alternative name, piranha caiman, refers the many teeth visible in its mouth. It feeds on water snails, fish and snakes. The female guards her 20–40 eggs, which she lays in an earthen nest.

American crocodile

Crocodylus acutus

American crocodiles live in fresh water, such as rivers and lakes, but will venture out into coastal waters, especially near estuaries and in lagoons, where the water is brackish. The crocodiles cope with the salty water by taking long drinks of fresh water when possible and removing salt from the body through glands on their faces – secreting "crocodile tears" in the process.

Feeding takes place at night, and the crocodiles occasionally come on to land to prey on livestock. They have also been known to attack humans. During periods of drought, the crocodiles burrow into mud and do not feed until the water returns.

Most females lay their eggs in holes dug in the ground, but they may build nest mounds in areas where the soil is likely to become waterlogged and thus chill the incubating eggs. Nesting takes place in the dry season. Between 30 and 60 eggs are laid, which hatch three months later as the rainy season begins. The mother guards her nest until the hatchlings have dispersed.

The American crocodile's diet consists mainly of fish and other small aquatic animals. Larger individuals may also eat small mammals, birds and turtles. American crocodiles often exceed the size of other crocodilians in North and South America.

Distribution: Southern Florida, Mexico, Central America and northern South America.
Habitat: Rivers and brackish water.
Food: Fish, turtles and birds.
Size: 4–5m (13–16.5ft).
Maturity: 5–10 years.
Breeding: Eggs laid in dry season.
Life span: 40 years.
Status: Vulnerable.

Dwarf caiman

Paleosuchus palpebrosus

The dwarf caiman, also known as Cuvier's dwarf caiman, is the smallest of all crocodile species. It lives throughout the Amazon Basin, from the foothills of the Andes in the east to the Atlantic in the west, and from Venezuela in the north to Paraguay in the south. Preferring fast-running, clear water, it is mainly found in rivers, but it also ventures into flooded forests, stagnant pools and swamps.

Dwarf caimans spend the day in burrows or basking in the open, becoming active at night, when they hunt for small animals such as frogs, snails, fish, aquatic mammals and crabs. Their short, curved teeth are particularly good at crushing shellfish. Younger individuals feed on smaller prey, including insects. Like all crocodiles, dwarf caimans have very strong stomach acid, which is capable of dissolving bone. They also swallow small stones (gastroliths) that help to grind the stomach contents into a more digestible paste.

Breeding takes place at the end of the dry season, when the males attract mates by roaring in shallow water with the head and tail raised above the surface. Females lay up to 25 eggs in mounds of rotting vegetation. (Well-fed females can lay eggs two or three times a year.) The young hatch after about 90 days, and the female opens the nest when she hears their cries.

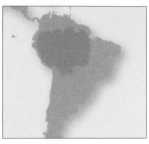

Distribution: Amazon Basin.
Habitat: Rivers and wetlands.
Food: Frogs, shellfish, snails and small fish.
Size: 1.2–1.6m (4–5.25ft).
Maturity: 10 years.
Breeding: Eggs laid in nests in dry season.
Life span: 30 years.
Status: Lower risk.

The dwarf caiman has more scutes, or osteoderms, than any other species. The scutes are bony plates that cover the skin and protect the body from damage by debris carried in fast-flowing water.

Schneider's dwarf caiman

Paleosuchus trigonatus

Schneider's dwarf caiman is the world's second smallest crocodile species. Males can reach more than twice the size of females, but are generally only slightly larger. This caiman prefers colder water than most crocodiles, which is why it is often found in the cooler, fast-flowing water under waterfalls and in rapids.

Schneider's dwarf caimans only gather together for breeding. Mating occurs at the end of the dry season. This ensures that the eggs – of which there are rarely more than 15 in a nest – hatch as the rains arrive, giving the young a better chance of survival. The nests are often built next to termite mounds, so that the heat from the mound helps to incubate the eggs. (This may be to compensate for the reduced incubating effect of the sun's rays in their shady rainforest habitat.) Female dwarf caimans become sexually mature when they reach 1.3 m (4.2ft), which may take between 10 and 20 years. They do not breed every year.

Schneider's dwarf caiman is also known as the smooth-fronted caiman, because it lacks the characteristic ridge between the eyes seen in other South American crocodiles. Hatchlings emerge from the eggs with a golden patch on their heads – hence the species' alternative name of crowned caiman.

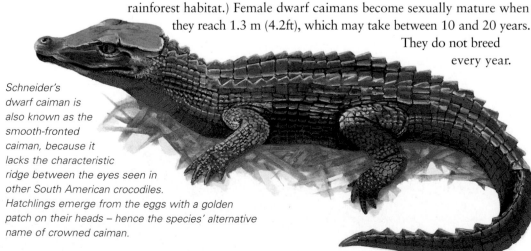

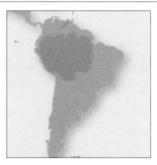

Distribution: Amazon and Orinoco Basins, from Peru in the west to French Guiana in the east, and from Venezuela south to Bahia state in Brazil.
Habitat: Fast-flowing water.
Food: Fish, birds, lizards and snakes, plus rodents and similar small mammals.
Size: 1.4–2m (4.5–7.5ft).
Maturity: 10–20 years.
Breeding: Eggs laid in nests before rainy season in early summer.
Life span: 25 years.
Status: Common.

Cuban crocodile

Crocodylus rhombifer

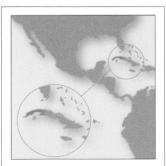

Distribution: Northwestern Cuba.
Habitat: Freshwater marshes.
Food: Fish, turtles and small mammals.
Size: Up to 3.5m (11.5ft).
Maturity: Not known.
Breeding: Eggs laid in holes or under mounds.
Life span: Not known.
Status: Endangered.

The rare Cuban crocodile is of medium size. It has unusually large legs, with keels of sturdy scutes that project from the back of the rear legs.

This crocodile has the smallest range of any species. It is only found in the Zapata swamp in northwestern Cuba and on Isla de Juventud. It was once found in other parts of the Greater Antilles, such as the Caymans and Bahamas, but is now extinct outside of Cuba. There are probably less than 6,000 Cuban crocodiles in the wild. After years of damage by humans, their swamp habitat has now been protected and hunting is banned. However, a large population is kept in zoos to ensure the species' survival.

Fossil records indicate that millions of years ago Cuban crocodiles preyed on the now-extinct giant ground sloths. Today, they mainly eat fish and turtles, whose shells they crush with their broad back teeth, and also small mammals. They are unusually agile on land, thanks to their strong legs and the reduced webbing on their feet. Using their powerful tails, they can propel themselves out of the water to snatch prey off waterside trees.

Little is known of the breeding behaviour of Cuban crocodiles, but they are reported to both dig nest holes and build mound nests, depending on the availability of suitable material. The normal clutch size is between 30 and 40 eggs. Many eggs and hatchlings are lost to predation by various mammals, reptiles and birds.

Morelet's crocodile

Crocodylus moreletii

Distribution: Mexico (Yucatan Peninsula), Belize and northern Guatemala.
Habitat: Freshwater swamps and rivers in forests.
Food: Lizards, turtles, fish and birds.
Size: 2–2.2m (7–7.25ft).
Maturity: 8 years.
Breeding: 20–45 eggs laid in nest at end of dry season.
Life span: 65 years.
Status: Endangered.

This rare North American crocodile has a blunt, alligator-like snout. Morelet's crocodile is similar to the American crocodile, but its skin is darker in colour.

Morelet's crocodile, also called the Mexican or soft-belly crocodile, lives on the eastern coastal plane of Mexico, ranging south along the Caribbean coast through Belize and also into Guatemala. It inhabits slow-flowing water in swamps and marshy areas, and sometimes in rivers that flow through forests. By day it basks in the sun, or lies submerged with just its eyes, ears and nostrils above the water. Hunting takes place mainly at night. As in all crocodile species, the diet changes with age. Young eat invertebrates, such as insect larvae and small fish, while juveniles feed on snails, small water birds and small mammals. Adults can tackle a range of prey, from turtles and lizards to small domestic animals, even dogs.

At the end of the dry season, the female Morelet's crocodile builds a nest of vegetation up to 3m (10ft) across and 1m (3.25ft) high close to water, occasionally on floating debris in the water itself. She remains nearby until the eggs hatch about 80 days later, and helps the youngsters out of the nest. Males sometimes assist with the early care of hatchlings. In hard times, hatchlings may be cannibalized.

NON-VENOMOUS SNAKES

Most snakes do not have a venomous bite and are completely harmless to humans. The largest American snakes – the boas – are non-venomous. They kill by coiling around prey and squeezing until their victims suffocate. Colubrids, typified by the garter snakes, are the largest group of snakes, with 1,700 species found worldwide. Most colubrids are non-venomous, although a few use their saliva to stun their prey.

Green anaconda

Eunectes murinus

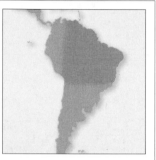

Distribution: Northern South America.
Habitat: Wetlands and flooded forests.
Food: Birds, caimans, deer and capybaras.
Size: 6–10m (20–33ft); 250kg (550lb).
Maturity: 6 years.
Breeding: 4–80 young born from mother.
Life span: 25 years.
Status: Common.

Green anacondas are the world's heaviest snakes, if not the longest. They are not venomous but kill by constriction, squeezing their prey in coils of their massive bodies.

Green anacondas spend most of their time in shallow water, being most common in open wetlands. Their eyes and nostrils are positioned on top of their heads, so that they can lie hidden underwater with only their heads breaking the surface. Anacondas are ambush predators: they wait for prey to come to the water's edge to drink, then they strike with lightning speed. Their bodies are powerful enough to squeeze the life out of a horse or a fully grown black caiman. Anacondas can kill humans, but only occasionally do so.

Male anacondas have claw-like spurs on their lower bodies, which they use to stimulate females. A single female may be tangled up with several males during mating. Like other boas, anacondas do not lay eggs but give birth to live young.

Compared to their huge bodies, green anacondas have small heads. Their bodies are covered in smooth olive scales, and they have black ovals on their backs. The males are smaller than the females. The young, born live from the mother, measure about 66cm (26in) at birth.

Emerald tree boa

Corallus caninus

Emerald tree boas spend their entire lives away from the ground, gripping tree branches with their coils. The snake's bright leaf-green body has flashes of white running across its back that help it to blend in with the forest foliage. This camouflage keeps the snake safe from predatory birds, such as owls and eagles.

Tree boas hang from sturdy branches and wait for small birds to fly by or small mammals to pass beneath them. The snake's eyes have vertical pupils. Just like small cats, this makes them better at sensing the movements of small prey in the gloom of the forest. Tree boas also have heat-sensitive pits on their snouts, which allow them to detect the body heat of prey moving near them. The snake waits, ready to pounce, with its upper body in an S-shape. When a prey animal comes close enough, the tree boa lunges forward and grabs it in its mouth. The snake's backward-curving teeth stop victims from struggling free.

During mating, the male entwines his tail with the female's. The female gives birth to between 3 and 15 young. The young snakes are red or orange for the first year of their lives.

Distribution: Northern South America.
Habitat: Rainforest.
Food: Birds and mammals.
Size: 1.5–2m (5–6.5ft).
Maturity: Not known.
Breeding: Young born live.
Life span: 40 years.
Status: Common.

The emerald tree boa has a long, slender body with a prehensile tail that is used for gripping branches. The snake's camouflaged body is reinforced down each side, like a girder, so it is powerful enough to reach across open spaces between branches.

Rosy boa (*Charina trivirgata*): 60–110cm (23.5–43in)
Rosy boas live in the deserts of the south-western United States and northern Mexico. The head is narrow for a boa species, and the body has smooth scales that form red and cream stripes. Rosy boas are nocturnal hunters that burrow under rocks and slither into crevices in search of prey. They mostly hunt on the ground, but occasionally climb into shrubs. They mainly eat small mammals and birds.

Amazon tree boa (*Corallus hortulanus*): 1.4–1.8m (4.5–6ft)
This boa occurs throughout the northern and eastern parts of the Amazon Basin. The Amazon tree boa hunts at night for tree frogs and lizards. Its long, slender body spreads its weight, so that the snake can move easily among all but the flimsiest of branches. When resting and digesting a meal, the snake wraps itself into a coil and hangs from a branch.

Western blind snake (*Leptotyphlops humilis*): 70–90cm (28–35in)
This small snake has a smooth, shiny, cylindrical body, and rudimentary eyes covered by large scales. It is found around the US–Mexico border, in dry habitats such as deserts, grasslands and canyons, where the soil is loose enough for burrowing. The snake spends the day underground and emerges on warm evenings to forage for ants and termites.

Kingsnake

Lampropeltis getulus

Kingsnakes are constrictors, killing their prey by squeezing them to death. They are very active hunters, slithering into rodent burrows and climbing through bushes to catch their diverse prey. They appear to be immune to the venom of other poisonous snakes, which they include on their menu. Kingsnakes are competent swimmers, and they often patrol riverbanks in search of frogs and small aquatic mammals.

As well as threatening many animals, these non-venomous snakes also have several enemies of their own, from large birds of prey to raccoons and other carnivores. If cornered, a kingsnake will try to bite its attacker. When captured, the snake's final defence is to smear its captor with foul-smelling faeces.

Kingsnakes live in a variety of climates and may be active during the day or night. They hibernate during cold periods, which may last for several months at the northern extent of their range.

The males bite their mates on the backs of their necks to restrain them during mating. About 12 eggs are laid under rotting vegetation.

Kingsnakes have different coloured bodies in different parts of their range. For example, Mexican kingsnakes are black, while those found in the deserts of Arizona have yellow bodies with black spots.

Distribution: Southern United States and northern Mexico.
Habitat: All land habitats.
Food: Birds, lizards, frogs and other snakes.
Size: 1–2m (3.25–6.5ft).
Maturity: Not known.
Breeding: Eggs laid in rotting vegetation.
Life span: 25 years.
Status: Common.

Texas thread snake

Leptotyphlops dulcis

The Texas thread snake, or Texas blind snake as it is also known, spends most of its life burrowing through the ground. Its body is well adapted for this lifestyle, being equipped with smooth scales and a blunt head for shoving earth out of the way.

The snakes feed on worms and other invertebrates that they come across, using their keen sense of smell to locate them. They also tunnel into the nests of ants and termites. When they enter a nest, the snakes begin to release the same chemical pheromones used by the insects themselves. This fools the normally aggressive insects into thinking the snakes belong there. The invading reptiles are free to slither about and feast on insect eggs and larvae. Texas thread snakes will come to the surface at night, especially after heavy rains, when the soil beneath is waterlogged.

After mating, the female lays only a handful of eggs and stays close to them while they incubate, often coiling around them. The thread snake family numbers 80 species in all.

The long, thin body of the Texas thread snake is covered in smooth, silvery scales. Even the snake's eyes are covered in thin scales.

Distribution: Southern United States and northern Mexico.
Habitat: Underground.
Food: Insects and spiders.
Size: 15–27cm (6–11in).
Maturity: Not known.
Breeding: Female incubates eggs in coils.
Life span: Not known.
Status: Common.

Boa constrictor

Boa constrictor

Boa constrictors are among the commonest large snakes in the Americas. They are found in a number of habitats, from northern Mexico all the way to Argentina. These snakes are equally at home in the branches of rainforest trees, in the grasses of open savannahs and among rocks in a desert. They are also frequently seen in many South American cities.

Boa constrictors hunt through the trees and on the ground for large lizards, small birds and medium-sized mammals. They kill by constriction, rather than with venom (although they will bite if handled). A boa wraps its body in coils around its prey and squeezes so hard that the animal eventually dies of suffocation. Each time the animal exhales, the snake tightens its grip. Boas find their prey using heat-sensitive pits on their face. Their preferred food is bats, which they catch by hanging from a branch or at the mouth of a roosting cave and knocking the bats to the ground as they fly past.

When they do not need to feed, these snake are fairly sedentary, and may remain in the same spot for several days. In colder parts of this species' range, the boas may have periods of inactivity that last for a number of weeks.

Boa constrictors occur in a range of patterns. Their coloration depends on where they live, but the background is often greyish or tan, with dark-red or brown blotches or saddle-shaped markings. The snake's muscular body is used for gripping branches when climbing and for constricting prey.

Distribution: From northern Mexico through Central and South America to Argentina; also found on the Lesser Antilles and other islands.
Habitat: Deserts, savannah and tropical forests.
Food: Lizards, small birds, bats, opossums, mongooses, rats and squirrels.
Size: 1–3m (3.25–10ft).
Maturity: Unknown.
Breeding: The female retains her eggs internally until they hatch, and gives birth to 20–50 live young, between 100 and 150 days after mating.
Life span: Unknown.
Status: Common.

Rubber boa

Charina bottae

This small snake is one of just two boas found in North America, where it lives in damp woodlands and mountain conifer forests in the west of the continent. Rubber boas are burrowers, as well as good swimmers, so they are especially common in sandy areas close to streams. Their small, blunt head and sturdy body help them to force their way through soft soil. Rubber boas are crepuscular, spending the day underground and coming to the surface around dusk or just before dawn.

The prey of rubber boas consists of small mammals, lizards, and birds, which the snakes kill by constriction. These snakes hunt on the ground, but they also use their slender, prehensile tail to climb into shrubs and the lower branches of trees. If danger threatens, a rubber boa will slither under a rock or burrow into sand or leaf litter.

This species does not lay eggs. Instead, the female retains the eggs inside her body until they hatch. When the young emerge, they are miniature versions of the adults. Young rubber boas prey on insects, salamanders, frogs and other small woodland animals.

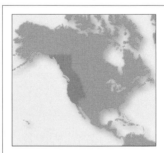

Distribution: British Columbia to Utah and southern California.
Habitat: Damp woodland and coniferous forest.
Food: Small mammals, birds and lizards.
Size: 35.5–84cm (14–33in).
Maturity: Unknown.
Breeding: 2–8 young born in late summer.
Life span: 10 years.
Status: Common.

With a short, rounded snout and an equally blunt tail, this snake looks as if it has two heads. The dark and matt scales on its body give the snake a rubbery appearance and texture.

Rainbow boa

Epicrates cenchria

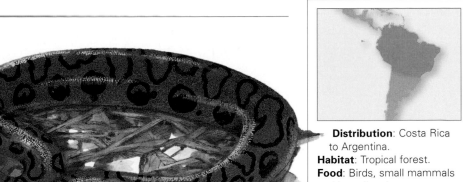

Rainbow boas live in tropical forests in parts of Central and South America. They also stray into agricultural areas. This species is closely related to the rare boas that live on the islands of the Caribbean. There are several subspecies of the rainbow boa, many of which have been bred in captivity. The two main wild forms are the Brazilian rainbow boa and the Peruvian rainbow boa, both of which are found in the Amazon Basin.

Rainbow boas hunt for small, warm-blooded animals such as mammals and birds. They hunt in the tree tops using their heat-sensitive pits to locate prey. Like other boas, they squeeze their victims to death. Younger rainbow boas tackle small rodents and nestlings, and they are also more likely to prey on tree frogs and lizards than their elders. At night, when they are most active, rainbow boas often become paler, especially around the flanks.

Distribution: Costa Rica to Argentina.
Habitat: Tropical forest.
Food: Birds, small mammals and large lizards.
Size: 1.5–2m (5–6.5ft).
Maturity: Unknown.
Breeding: 6–20 offspring produced.
Life span: Over 15 years.
Status: Common.

Rainbow boas exist in several subspecies. Most have an orange-brown body with dark rings that become paler in the middle. Some subspecies have solid rings.

Cuban wood snake (*Tropidophis melanurus*): 80–100cm (31.5–39.5in)
Also called the dusky dwarf boa, this is the only dwarf boa to be found on the Caribbean island of Cuba. It lives both in forests and alongside people. The Cuban wood snake is a welcome neighbour, since it is non-venomous and helps to keep down the numbers of rats and other pest rodents. However, when disturbed its defensive response is less appreciated: the snake rolls itself up into a ball and squirts a foul-smelling slime from its cloaca at the intruder. In the forest it preys on frogs and small snakes as well as rodents. Like other boas, this snake does not lay eggs, giving birth to about eight young at a time.

Mexican burrowing python (*Loxocemus bicolor*): 1–1.3m (3.25–4.25ft)
Despite its common name, this snake is no more closely related to the true pythons of Africa, Asia, and Australia than it is to the boas that inhabit North and South America. Like other burrowing snakes, this species has a narrow head and slender body to help it wriggle through loose soil and leaf litter. The Mexican burrowing snake lives in the forests of southern Mexico and much of Central America. It feeds on rodents, lizards and reptile eggs. Unlike boas, but like pythons, this species lays eggs in an underground chamber.

Red-tailed boa (*Boa constrictor constrictor*): 2.4m (8ft)
This boa is larger than other forms of the snake. It is named after the dark-red saddles on the rear of its body. The snake's coloration helps it to blend in with fallen leaves on the forest floor.

Brown snake

Storeria dekayi

The brown snake of eastern North and Central America occupies a range of habitats, from highland woods to salt-water marshes – in fact, anywhere with plenty of loose stones or other debris for it to hide beneath.

The brown snake spends most of its time underground. It hibernates through winter, often sharing its nest with other snakes, such as smooth green snakes and garter snakes. Mating takes place in spring, soon after the snakes emerge from their nests. The female produces a pheromone to attract males; a male will taste her with his tongue to check that she is the right species before mating.

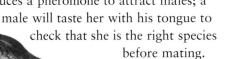

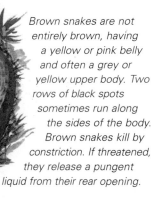

Distribution: Southern Canada to Honduras.
Habitat: Rocky areas, wetlands, woodland and cities.
Food: Earthworms and other soft-bodied invertebrates, including slugs and snails.
Size: 25–52cm (10–20.5in).
Maturity: 2 years.
Breeding: 10–20 young born in late summer.
Life span: 7 years.
Status: Common.

Brown snakes are not entirely brown, having a yellow or pink belly and often a grey or yellow upper body. Two rows of black spots sometimes run along the sides of the body. Brown snakes kill by constriction. If threatened, they release a pungent liquid from their rear opening.

Milksnake

Lampropeltis triangulum

Milksnakes range from Colombia and other northern parts of South America to southern Canada. They thrive in a wide range of habitats, including semi-desert and rainforest. They live high up in the Rockies and are also found in edge habitats, such as where farmland meets woodland. The longest milksnakes live in tropical regions. Those that are found in dry or cold areas to the north are barely half the size of their tropical cousins.

Milksnakes are nocturnal hunters, preying upon small rodents and amphibians. During the day, they hide out in leaf litter or under a rotting log, and sometimes in damp garbage. They live and hunt alone, but gather in large groups to hibernate together. Milksnakes mate while in their winter quarters and the females lay their eggs in early summer. They construct nests under rocks, in tree stumps and in other secluded spots.

Milksnakes are very colourful, with at least 25 different colour variants described so far. Many milksnakes mimic the bold, banded colours of venomous snakes, such as the coral snake, while others have mostly monochrome bodies, usually in tan, black or red. Hatchlings are particularly brightly coloured, but their markings become duller with age.

Distribution: Southern Canada and United States through Central America to Colombia, Ecuador and Venezuela.
Habitat: Desert, grassland and forests.
Food: Invertebrates, amphibians and small rodents.
Size: 0.6–0.9m (2–3ft).
Maturity: 3–4 years.
Breeding: 15 eggs laid in summer.
Life span: 21 years.
Status: Common.

Corn snake

Elaphe guttata

Corn snakes range from New Jersey to Florida and across to central Texas. They are most common in the south-eastern United States. These snakes live in woodland and meadows, and they are at also home around rural and suburban settlements.

Corn snakes hunt on the ground, up trees and among rocks. Like other members of the rat snake group, to which they belong, corn snakes have a wide underside that helps them grip onto near vertical surfaces such bark, rubble and even walls. They are not venomous, but when threatened these rattlesnake mimics will waggle their tail and rise up as if to strike. Corn snakes kill their prey – mainly small rodents – by constriction.

This species mates between March and May. Like other snakes, mating is more or less indiscriminate. The females lay eggs in rotting debris by midsummer. The heat produced by the rotting material incubates the eggs, helping them to hatch more quickly. The young corn snakes eat lizards and tree frogs; adults prey on rodents, bats, and birds.

Corn snakes belong to the rat snake group. Like their relatives, they occur in several colour forms. There are four subspecies, which tend to be more colourful in the south of their range.

Distribution: Eastern United States, from New Jersey to Florida and west into Louisiana and parts of Kentucky.
Habitat: Woodland, rocky areas and meadows.
Food: Mice, rats, birds and bats.
Size: 1–1.8m (3.25–6ft).
Maturity: 3 years.
Breeding: Between 10 and 30 eggs laid in summer; incubation takes around 60–65 days.
Life span: 20 years.
Status: Common.

Common rat snake

Elaphe obsoleta

Distribution: Eastern United States to Texas and Wisconsin.
Habitat: Grassland, forests and suburban areas.
Food: Small rodents and birds.
Size: 1.2–1.8m (4–6ft).
Maturity: Unknown.
Breeding: 20 eggs laid in summer.
Life span: 20 years.
Status: Common.

The common rat snake belongs to a group of three dozen rat snake species, which also includes corn snakes and fox snakes. This particular species is found across the eastern United States, from New England in the north to Texas, Nebraska and Wisconsin in the west. Common rats snakes are most abundant in the warmer parts of their range around the Gulf of Mexico and along the Atlantic coast.

The common rat snake occurs in three colour forms: almost completely black; yellow with black stripes; and orange with black stripes.

The common rat snake lives in a variety of habitats, with each of the many subspecies being adapted to a particular habitat type. For example, black rat snakes are found in highland regions, while yellow rat snakes inhabit oak woodlands and human habitations.

Rat snakes do not inject their prey with venom, but kill them by constriction. When threatened, these snakes coil themselves up and rustle dead leaves with their tail to imitate a rattlesnake. They also spread a foul musk with their tail to further discourage any attacker.

Kirtland's snake (*Clonophis kirtlandii*): 60cm (23.5in)
This rare snake lives in the Midwest of the United States, being most common in Ohio, Indiana and Illinois. Kirtland's snake is found in marshy areas and flooded fields. Although a water snake, it spends most of its time on dry land. Its diet consists of slugs and earthworms. To escape danger, this snake flattens its body and squeezes under rocks, where it shelters until the threat has passed.

Regal black-striped snake (*Coniophanes imperialis*): 30–51cm (12–20in)
This is one of several related species with two thin stripes running from the snout past the eyes and over the head. Black-striped snakes live in the extreme southern tip of Texas and along the Atlantic coast of Mexico and Central America. This species employs a mild venom to subdue prey such as frogs, toads, smaller snakes and mice.

Amazon egg-eating snake (*Drepanoides anomalus*): 60cm (24in)
This largely orange, Amazonian snake is most often seen on the edge of forests and in clearings. It mainly feeds on lizards' eggs, which are softer than birds' eggs. Snakes do not have chewing muscles in their jaws, so the eggs must be swallowed whole. Like most snakes, the Amazon egg-eating snake can separate its lower jaw, enabling it to stretch its mouth wide enough to accommodate large food items – sometimes even bigger than the snake's own head.

Common garter snake

Thamnophis sirtalis

This species has one of the widest ranges of any North American snake. At one extreme, the common garter snake lives on the southern shores of Hudson Bay in eastern Canada and survives the long and icy sub-Arctic winters. At the other end of its range, it lives in the humid, subtropical swamps of Florida.

Garter snakes are closely associated with water. They are able swimmers, but search for prey both in and out of water. Garter snakes are active hunters and generally have to pursue their victims. They seek out meals by poking their small heads into nooks and crannies and flushing out prey. The snakes' long bodies allow them to move with great speed, and their large eyes are well suited to tracking fleeing prey.

Garter snakes hibernate in burrows, and many snakes may crowd into a suitable hole. Mating takes place soon after hibernation. In northern regions with short summers, the pressure to mate quickly is very strong, while in the south of the range the snakes have a longer breeding season.

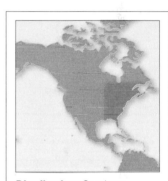

Distribution: Southern Canada to Florida.
Habitat: Close to water.
Food: Worms, fish and amphibians.
Size: 65–130cm (25–51in).
Maturity: Not known.
Breeding: Mate after hibernation.
Life span: Unknown.
Status: Common.

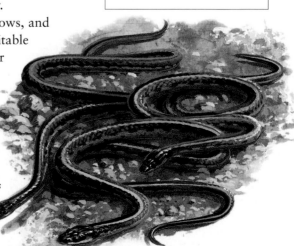

Common garter snakes have long bodies and small heads. They are found in a variety of colours, which provide camouflage in different habitats.

Rough green snake

Opheodrys aestivus

This slender species ranges along
the Atlantic coast of North
America, from
Connecticut to
Florida and inland to
Kansas and Ohio. Rough
green snakes prefer damp areas,
including flooded meadows and
around the edges of lakes, marshes and
streams, and they will occasionally enter
the water. They are good climbers and are
frequently found several metres above the
ground, often in trees and bushes that
overhang water, where they are well
hidden by their bright green coloration.

    Rough green snakes are non-venomous. They do not need to constrict their prey either,
since they eat only moths, grasshoppers, caterpillars and other soft-bodied invertebrates,
which they simply snatch and swallow. Mating occurs in spring, and in summer the females
produce about a dozen elongated, soft-shelled eggs, which are coated in an adhesive gel so
that they stick together. The eggs are laid under or in rotting logs and beneath moss or
rocks. Several females will often lay their eggs in the same place. The young, which are paler
than the adults, hatch from their eggs in August and September.

Distribution: Eastern and
southern United States.
Habitat: Wetlands.
Food: Insects and spiders.
Size: 71cm (28in).
Maturity: 2 years.
Breeding: Mates in spring.
Life span: Unknown.
Status: Common.

*This snake is a vibrant green,
with a paler, yellowish underside.
The scales are keeled (they have
a raised mid-line), a characteristic
that differentiates this species
from the smooth green snake,
its close relative, which is found
further north.*

Racer

Coluber constrictor

The racer occurs across southern North America, from the extreme south-west of Canada
to Florida. It is also found in parts of Mexico and all the way to Guatemala. This species
avoids the driest areas and is absent from large areas of the western United States. There
are at least 11 subspecies, all living in distinct ranges with subtle differences in colour.

    Racers are often seen basking in sunlit areas such as forest clearings and along
hedgerows. Their name suggests that these are fast-moving snakes, but they do not exceed
more than 6.5kmh (4mph), which is a fairly average speed for a snake. Because of this,
racers never stray far from dense undergrowth, into which they retreat to shelter from
danger. If a racer is caught by a predator, the snake will writhe to spread a vile-smelling
liquid over its body. Sometimes the writhing is so violent that the snake's tail breaks off,
startling or distracting the attacker long enough for the snake to escape.

Distribution: Southern
British Columbia to
Guatemala.
Habitat: Grasslands,
woodlands and rocky areas.
Food: Large insects, frogs,
lizards, small snakes, birds
and rodents.
Size: 86–195cm (34–77in).
Maturity: 2–3 years.
Breeding: Mating occurs
in spring.
Life span: 10 years.
Status: Common.

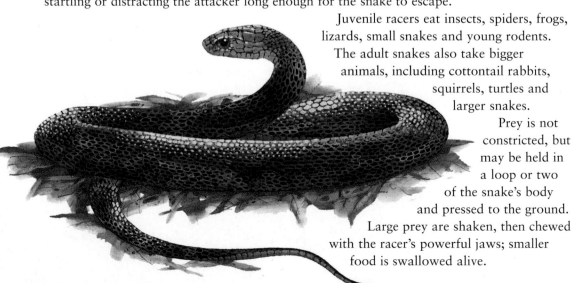

Juvenile racers eat insects, spiders, frogs,
lizards, small snakes and young rodents.
The adult snakes also take bigger
animals, including cottontail rabbits,
squirrels, turtles and
larger snakes.
Prey is not
constricted, but
may be held in
a loop or two
of the snake's body
and pressed to the ground.
Large prey are shaken, then chewed
with the racer's powerful jaws; smaller
food is swallowed alive.

*This species is often called the
blue racer, because its dark,
shiny scales often have a blue-
grey tinge. Jet black, greenish-
grey or light brown colorations
are also seen. Juvenile racers
have brown and red patterns on
their bodies, but these fade to
grey as the snake gets older.*

Sharp-tailed snake

Contia tenuis

The sharp-tailed snake is a secretive reptile that spends much of its time hidden in burrows or under rocks and logs. It is found mainly in the Sierra Nevada Mountains of western North America. The snake ranges from California (including the mountains of the Coastal Range) through Oregon and Washington state to southern British Columbia.

In the mountains, the sharp-tailed snake occupies a range of habitats. It prefers damp areas that have a large amount of leaf litter and other debris covering the ground. Unusually, it becomes more active in cooler and damper conditions. During the warmer parts of the year, the snake seeks refuge in mammal burrows and under logs. The sharp-tailed snake preys on slugs, and probably also eats snails and small lungless salamanders. Sharp-tailed snakes are most likely to be found after heavy rains, which bring their prey out into the open.

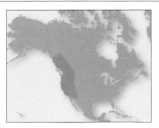

Distribution: Western North America.
Habitat: Mountains.
Food: Slugs.
Size: 25–48cm (10–19in).
Maturity: Unknown.
Breeding: Mating occurs in spring.
Life span: Unknown.
Status: Locally common.

The sharp spine on this snake's tail probably helps it to anchor its body when capturing its prey, while its needle-like teeth grip the slugs.

Mexican hook-nosed snake (*Ficimia streckeri*): 23–48cm (9–19in)
Identifiable from its a hook-shaped, upturned snout, this snake is found in the southern tip of Texas and in northern Mexico. It inhabits thorn forests in the north of its range and the cloud forests of the Sierra Madre Oriental mountains to the south. The Mexican hook-nosed snake spends most of the time underground, but regularly emerges after heavy rains to feed on spiders and centipedes. It probably lays its eggs in its burrow.

Night snake (*Hypsiglena torquata*): 30–66cm (12–26in)
This nocturnal species occurs across the deserts and dry prairies of the south-western United States and northern Mexico. Its range also stretches over the Rockies, into the Great Basin and up to the dry Scablands of the Columbia River Valley of Washington state. Despite its large range, it is rarely encountered. By day, it lies hidden under rocks or in leaf litter, while at night it hunts for frogs and lizards. When the night snake catches prey animals, it holds them using the large teeth at the back of its jaws. The snake's saliva stuns the victims slightly so that they struggle less and are easier to swallow.

Striped whipsnake (*Masticophis taeniatus*): 100–180cm (39.5–72in)
Striped whipsnakes live in the deserts and dry woodlands of northern Mexico, western Texas and up to Oregon and Washington, mainly on uplands in the south of their range. These slender, fast-moving snakes eat amphibians, lizards, smaller snakes, birds and eggs. They track down their prey by sight and smell.

Ring-necked snake

Diadophis punctatus

This small North American snake ranges from the maritime provinces of Canada to the Great Lakes, as well as along the coastal plain of the Atlantic seaboard and through the Appalachians to western Texas and northern Mexico. The ring-necked snake is found wherever there are plenty of hiding places.

This species preys on salamanders, frogs, worms and other small animals, plus young snakes of other species. Victims are partially constricted to stop them struggling free, and generally swallowed alive. Active at night, ring-necked snakes spend the day under logs and flat stones. In some places up to 100 snakes will share a refuge.

Mating takes place in spring. The females attract males by releasing pheromones. Eggs are laid in June or July, often in communal nests. The young emerge in August.

Distribution: Eastern North America.
Habitat: Moist areas.
Food: Worms, slugs, lizards, salamanders and newly hatched snakes.
Size: 25–76cm (10–30in).
Maturity: 2–3 years.
Breeding: Eggs laid in summer.
Life span: 20 years.
Status: Common.

This snake has a grey or light brown upper body and a yellow or red belly. The ring around the snake's neck may be yellow, cream or orange.

Rainbow snake

Farancia erytrogramma

The rainbow snake occurs in the south-eastern United States, south and east of the Appalachian Mountains. It is most common in South Carolina and Florida. This species lives near to water, especially on the sandy banks of rivers and streams. It is one of the most aquatic snakes in this part of the world, and is often found among floating plant debris.

Female rainbow snakes lay eggs in July. They make a small dip in the sand and deposit up to 50 eggs, each of which is about 4cm (1.5in) long. The snake stays with her eggs and incubates them for a while before they hatch.

Rainbow snakes are nocturnal hunters that lie in wait in water to ambush their prey. Adult rainbow snakes eat nothing but eels, but younger individuals eat salamanders, small fish, and tadpoles.

The spine at the end of the tail is used in self defence. The spine is pressed into an attacker's flesh, provoking a bite to the tail (the least important part of the reptile's anatomy) instead of a lethal strike at the snake's head.

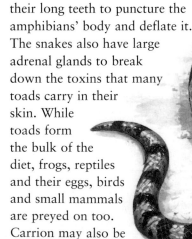

Distribution: Coastal plain of south-eastern United States.
Habitat: Sandy areas near water.
Food: Eels.
Size: 89–167cm (35–66in).
Maturity: Unknown.
Breeding: Eggs laid in July.
Life span: Unknown.
Status: Rare.

This burrowing snake has a cylindrical body with glossy dark scales. There are yellow or red strips along the edges of the belly. The underside is generally red. The spine at the tip of the tail is actually a pointed horny scale.

Western hog-nosed snake

Heterodon nasicus

The western hog-nosed snake is found across a swathe of North America, from northern Mexico to southern Canada. It inhabits the Great Plains region between the Mississippi River in the east and the Rocky Mountains in the west. This region is relatively dry, and the hog-nosed snake spends much of its time burrowing through loose, sandy soil, using its snout as a shovel to excavate soil.

Western hog-nosed snakes hibernate between September and March. Mating occurs soon after the snakes emerge in the spring. Females have multiple mates, and initiate the breeding season by moulting their skins and releasing an odour that attracts the males. About a dozen eggs are laid in soil in late summer, and these hatch just before the winter hibernation.

Hog-nosed snakes use their snout to dig up buried toads. Many toads puff themselves up when under attack, so the snakes use their long teeth to puncture the amphibians' body and deflate it. The snakes also have large adrenal glands to break down the toxins that many toads carry in their skin. While toads form the bulk of the diet, frogs, reptiles and their eggs, birds and small mammals are preyed on too. Carrion may also be consumed sometimes.

Distribution: Southern Canada to northern Mexico.
Habitat: Dry prairies and rocky areas.
Food: Mainly toads, plus other small vertebrate prey.
Size: 40–100cm (15.5–40in).
Maturity: 2 years.
Breeding: Eggs laid in summer.
Life span: 14 years.
Status: Common.

The snout of this snake is sharply upturned and pointed, so that it resembles a pig's nose. The western hog-nosed snake has three colour forms: brown, grey and tan. These forms closely resemble the eastern and southern hog-nosed species, which also have red forms.

Big-headed snail-eating snake (*Dipsas indica*): 100cm (40in)

As its common name suggests, this species eats snails. It extracts the snail's soft body from the hard shell by first biting the snail's fleshy foot and then hooking its lower jaw inside the shell to draw the snail out. The big-headed snail-eating snake lives in northern South America. It is most often seen in trees and will retreat to high branches when under threat. This species has a larger head than its relatives, and is thought to be able to eat larger snails that most.

Pine snake (*Pituophis melanoleucus*): 1.2–2.5m (4–8.25m)

The pine snake is found across western North America, from Mexico to southern Alberta and British Columbia. There is also a smaller population in the eastern United States, ranging from New Jersey to Kentucky and Florida. The pine snake hunts during the day. By night, it rests in the burrow of a tortoise or mammal. Its diet comprises rodents such as gophers – burrowing animals that are common in North America. Consequently, this species is often called the pine-gopher snake.

Queen snake (*Regina septemvittata*): 40–93cm (15.5–36.5in)

This brown-green snake lives in rivers and streams across the Midwest and southern US states. It is an excellent swimmer and drops or slips into water to escape from danger. Queen snakes eat mainly crayfish. They search rocky stream beds for crayfish that have recently shed an old shell and are still hardening their new one.

Northern water snake

Nerodia sipedon

This species occurs from New England and the Great Lakes through the central United States and south to the Mississippi Delta. Its range also extends down the Atlantic coast as far south as the Carolinas. The snake is found in all freshwater habitats, from swamps to rivers, as well as in the salt marshes of the Outer Banks in North Carolina.

Water snakes are a common sight, since they are active both day and night. They are often observed basking on sand banks and tree stumps, and in other open areas. By night, they may be seen feeding on minnows and other small fish in shallow pools.

Water snakes will bite if cornered, and their saliva contains an anticoagulant. When the saliva enters a bite wound, it prevents the blood from clotting properly, thus weakening the victim.

Distribution: New England to Colorado and Louisiana.
Habitat: Rivers and wetlands.
Food: Small fish, young turtles, salamanders and crustaceans.
Size: 56–134cm (22–53in).
Maturity: 2–3 years.
Breeding: Mating occurs in early summer.
Life span: 10 years.
Status: Common.

The body of the northern water snake is patterned in dark grey and reddish brown, with bands crossing behind the neck. When out of water, the pattern often fades as the snake's skin dries.

Coachwhip

Masticophis flagellum

One of the largest snakes in America, the coachwhip is found across the southern part of the United States and northern Mexico, where it mainly occupies arid habitats. The coachwhip is perhaps the fastest snake in North America, being able to race away over the ground at about 13kmh (8mph). It uses its speed to escape danger, but when foraging, the coachwhip moves slowly so as to not alert its prey, which includes grasshoppers, cicadas and other large insects, as well as lizards, small snakes and rodents. It keeps its head raised off the ground as it hunts, so that it can track prey by smell and sight.

When under threat itself, the coachwhip slithers up trees or into mammal burrows to escape. If cornered, it coils up and vibrates its tail to mimic a venomous rattler. It also bites its attacker repeatedly, often aiming for the face – behaviour that led early observers to believe that the snake killed its prey by whipping them to death.

Distribution: Southern United States and northern Mexico.
Habitat: Desert, scrubland and open woodland, and rocky areas.
Food: Birds, rodents, lizards, other snakes and insects.
Size: 90–260cm (35.5–102in).
Maturity: Unknown.
Breeding: Mating occurs in spring, egg-laying in summer.
Life span: 16 years.
Status: Lower risk.

This long, smooth, uniformly brown snake resembles a thick whip. Individuals in the eastern parts of the range, where the soil is less sandy, have darker bodies.

VENOMOUS SNAKES

About 10 per cent of snake species use modified fangs to inject prey with venom. One of the main groups of venomous snakes is the Viperidae *family – the vipers. There are about 230 viper species worldwide, including the American rattlesnakes and cottonmouths. The world's most venomous snakes, such as taipans, seasnakes and cobras, belong to the* Elapidae. *The most dangerous American elapids are the coral snakes.*

Sidewinder

Crotalus cerastes

Sidewinders are named for their unusual method of locomotion, in which they move sideways across loose ground, such as sand. Many snakes that live in similar habitats also "sidewind". This involves a wave-like undulation of the snake's body, so that only two points are in contact with the ground at any given moment. The snake progresses in a sideways direction across the ground (compared to the orientation of the body), leaving parallel S-shaped tracks in the sand.

Sidewinders are desert rattlesnakes that lie under shrubs and ambush small animal prey at night, using sensory pits below their eyes to detect their victims' body heat. They strike with lightning speed, injecting venom from glands in their upper jaws through their hollow fangs.

If the prey escapes a short distance before being overcome, the snake soon locates the corpse with its heat-sensitive pits.

Distribution: South-western United States and north-western Mexico.
Habitat: Desert.
Food: Lizards and rodents.
Size: 45–80cm (18–32in).
Maturity: Not known.
Breeding: Live young born in late summer.
Life span: Unknown.
Status: Common.

Sidewinders have wide bodies so that they do not sink into sand. Their tails are tipped with rattles that increase in length as the snakes age. Their heads are flattened and triangular.

Western diamondback rattlesnake

Crotalus atrox

Western diamondbacks are the largest and most venomous rattlesnakes in North America. The snake's rattle comprises dried segments, or buttons, of skin attached to the tail. The rattle is used to warn predators that the snake gives a poisonous bite. Although it will readily defend itself when cornered, the diamondback would prefer to conserve venom, and enemies, including humans, soon learn to associate the rattle with danger.

Like all rattlesnakes, diamondbacks are not born with a rattle. Instead they begin with just a single button, which soon dries into a tough husk. Each time the snake moults its skin, a new button is left behind by the old skin. The rattle grows in this way until it contains around ten buttons that give the characteristic noise when shaken.

Western diamondbacks have a very potent venom. They kill more people each year than any other North American snake, although this number rarely reaches double figures. The venom can kill even large prey, such as hares, in seconds. Like other rattlesnakes, diamondbacks can sense body heat using sensory pits on their faces.

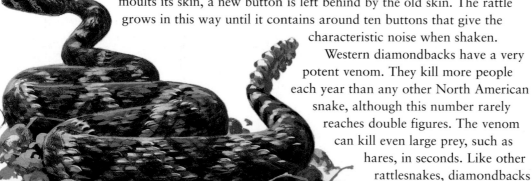

Distribution: Southern United States and northern Mexico.
Habitat: Grassland and rocky country.
Food: Vertebrate prey including small mammals, birds and lizards.
Size: 2m (6.5ft).
Maturity: 3–4 years.
Breeding: Young born live.
Life span: Unknown.
Status: Lower risk.

Diamondbacks are so named because of the brown diamonds, bordered with cream scales, seen along their backs.

Western coral snake

Micruroides euryxanthus

Distribution: South-western United States and northern Mexico.
Habitat: Desert.
Food: Snakes and lizards.
Size: 60–90cm (24–35in).
Maturity: 1–2 years.
Breeding: Eggs laid in summer.
Life span: Unknown.
Status: Common.

As they are relatives of cobras and mambas, western coral snakes have a similarly potent venom. Their bright bands warn potential predators that the snakes are very dangerous. The venom will kill most small animals. One in ten humans who leave a bite untreated are overcome by the toxins.

Coral snakes spend much of their time underground. Their thin, cylindrical bodies covered in smooth scales are ideal for this tunnelling lifestyle, and their rounded heads are used for burrowing through soft soil. However, the snakes also venture into the burrows of other animals to seek out resting snakes and lizards, their main source of food. They rarely come to the surface during the day, but may emerge to hunt in the cool of night. Western coral snakes mate in early summer; the females lay eggs about a month later. They are the only venomous snakes in the Americas to lay eggs rather than bear live young.

The western coral snake, with its brightly banded body, is typical among American coral snakes. Many non-venomous snakes mimic the colours of coral snakes to deter predators.

Green vine snake (*Oxybelis fulgidus*): 1.8m (6ft)
This is the largest vine snake in the tropical forests of the Amazon. It is also found throughout Central America and in Mexico. Like all vine snakes, this species is very long and slender, with a sharply pointed nose. The snake's thin green body allows it to move through even the flimsiest of branches unnoticed. The green vine snake sometimes hunts in the trees, but it is usually found in bushes close to the forest floor.

False coral snake (*Erythrolamprus aesculapii*): 65–78cm (25.5–31in)
This mildly venomous snake lives in Amazonian South America and Trinidad and Tobago. It mimics the brightly banded colours of highly venomous coral snakes. After one bad experience with a coral snake, a predator learns to avoid all snakes with a similar coloration – including false coral snakes. These snakes even behave like coral snakes when they are attacked, raising and coiling their tail as a warning. False coral snakes use their own mild venom to kill their lizard and snake prey.

Eyelash pit viper (*Bothriechis schlegelii*): 45–75cm (17.5–29.5cm)
This small, arboreal pit viper lives in the forests of Central America, as well as in parts of Colombia and Ecuador. It is most active at night, when it preys on tree frogs, lizards and small mammals, detecting prey in the dark using the heat-pits on its face. The snake sometimes hunts during the day, plucking hummingbirds from the air as they feed on flowers. It may also catch nectar-drinking bats at night in the same way. The "eyelashes" of this species are raised scales above the eyes.

Common mussurana

Clelia clelia

Common mussuranas are found across the Amazon Basin and also extend northward into Central America and south to the forests of northern Argentina. They are most commonly spotted in forest clearings and near to swamps. These snakes hunt on the ground but will also swim across rivers.

Mussaranas are mildly venomous. They inject venom into their prey with fangs located at the back of the mouth. These fangs also perform a holding function, keeping prey lodged firmly in the mouth until the venom subdues them. The snakes kill prey by constriction as well. Their diet includes lizards, small mammals and other snakes – many of them venomous. While mussuranas have only a weak venom, they seem to be largely resistant to the stronger venoms of their victims. Mussuranas lay up to 40 eggs in a single clutch, although the clutch size is usually smaller than this.

Distribution: Guatemala to Argentina.
Habitat: Forests near water.
Food: Lizards, snakes, ground birds and small mammals.
Size: 1.8–2m (6–6.5ft).
Maturity: Unknown.
Breeding: Up to 40 eggs laid.
Life span: Unknown.
Status: Common.

Mussaranas change colour as they get older. The young snakes are vivid red, while the adults are jet black. As the snake ages, the red changes to brown, then to green and finally to black.

Red pipesnake

Anilius scytale

This unusual snake is the only member of the *Aniliidae* family. It is included in this section on venomous snakes because its bright stripes convince predators that it is poisonous, however it is actually only mimicking venomous snake species such as the coral snake.

The red pipesnake is found only in the northern half of South America, ranging as far south as Amazonian Peru and southern Brazil. It prefers habitats with rich, moist soil, and uses its cylindrical body to tunnel underground or through deep leaf litter as it hunts subterranean animals, such as rodents and small snakes. Among its chief prey are caecilians and amphisbaenians, or worm lizards, which are common in the tropics of South America. It may also enter the water to find food, and in certain regions eels make up much of its diet.

Being burrowing animals, pipesnakes have small eyes and they are not able to rely on their sense of vision to locate prey. Furthermore, unlike their boa neighbours (and the pythons living elsewhere in the world), they do not have heat-sensitive pits to locate prey. Instead, they rely on their senses of touch and hearing, which are closely linked in snakes, to detect the movements of nearby animals.

Distribution: Northern South America.
Habitat: Tropical forests.
Food: Worm lizards, snakes, rodents and caecilians.
Size: 70–110cm (27.5–44in).
Maturity: Unknown.
Breeding: 3–13 live young.
Life span: Unknown.
Status: Lower risk.

Like many other tropical snakes, this species mimics the colours of the highly venomous coral snake. Its bright red and black stripes are rarely seen, however, because the species spends most of its time hidden underground. With dense, solid skull bones, the red pipesnake is well suited to a burrowing lifestyle.

Lancehead

Bothrops atrox

Lancehead snakes are pit vipers. Like rattlesnakes, they have heat-sensitive pits between the nostrils and eyes. Lanceheads are among the most dangerous snakes in the Americas. Others have more potent venom, but lanceheads are often found living alongside people, feeding on rats and other rodents, so they present more of a hazard. Although they prefer to avoid conflict, when disturbed they bite repeatedly in self defence. Lanceheads are especially common in plantations. In the wild they are found in forests, woodlands and grasslands. In some parts, such as the West Indies, these snakes are called fer-de-lance snakes.

Like many other vipers, male lanceheads tussle with each other over females. The females do not lay eggs but give birth to live young, producing up to 80 babies at a time, although less than half this figure is more usual. The young snakes, which are about 30cm (12in) long, are born with venom glands. Like their parents, they can give a dangerous bite.

Lanceheads ambush their prey. Their camouflaged scales keep them well hidden as they lie in wait. When prey comes near, they strike rapidly and aggressively with their long fangs. Lanceheads are good swimmers, and they may even climb trees to reach their prey.

Distribution: Central and northern South America.
Habitat: Tropical forests.
Food: Small mammals, birds, lizards and smaller snakes.
Size: 1–1.5m (3.25–5ft).
Maturity: Unknown.
Breeding: 10–25 babies born per clutch.
Life span: Unknown.
Status: Common.

Lanceheads are named after their arrow-shaped heads, which are typical among vipers. The snake's colouring varies between regions, ranging from grey to brown and green, with "geometric" markings that give effective camouflage. Lanceheads are mainly solitary. Breeding may occur all year round.

Copperhead

Agkistrodon contortrix

The copperhead is named after the solid copper of its triangular head. This colour continues along the rest of the body, where it is patterned with brown bands. Young copperheads have a bright yellow tip to the tail, which they use to lure frogs and lizards within striking range.

Copperheads are also called highland moccasins, being closely related to water moccasins (cottonmouths). Copperheads live across the United States, from Massachusetts to Nebraska in the northwest and Florida and the Big Bend region of the Rio Grande on the Texas–Mexico border.

Copperheads are less aquatic than their close relatives, although they do occasionally enter water. They are most often encountered in rocky areas, especially on hillsides – hence the species' alternative name – but also in lowland regions.

These snakes use heat-sensitive pits on their face to track prey at night. They inject prey animals with a venom that breaks down the victim's blood cells. Although the venom would eventually kill the prey, the snake does not wait for them to die but swallows them as soon as they are sufficiently subdued.

Distribution: Eastern United States to western Texas.
Habitat: Rocky outcrops in wooded areas.
Food: Small rodents, frogs and large insects.
Size: 56–135cm (22–53in).
Maturity: 2–3 years.
Breeding: Mating occurs in spring; about a dozen young are born in autumn.
Life span: About 18 years.
Status: Common.

Red-bellied snake (*Storeria occipitomaculata*): 20–40cm (8–15.5in)
This snake ranges across the whole of the eastern half of the United States, from North Dakota and eastern Texas to southern Florida and Nova Scotia in south-eastern Canada. It is a specialist slug- and snail-hunter. The red-bellied snake lives in damp habitats, such as woodlands and bogs, where its mollusc prey are common. Its westward range is limited by the dry prairies of the Great Plains. The snake hunts by day, locating prey by smell, and is most commonly seen after heavy rainfall. It can reach into a snail's shell with its small head to pull out the soft body, gripping the slimy, struggling prey with its long, backward-curving teeth. This species also has a mild venom that weakens the prey and also reduces the effect of their slimy secretions. Some red-bellied snakes eat only slugs, while others supplement their diet with worms and insect larvae.

Massasauga (*Sistrurus catenatus*): 45–100cm (17.5–39.5in)
This massasauga is an unusual rattlesnake that lives along the western side of the Appalachian Mountains, from the Great Lakes to southern Texas. It has nine large scales on its head, a stocky tail and only a small rattle. Massasaugas live in mossy bogs, swamps and woodlands in the north and east of their range. In other areas, they inhabit brushlands and dry grasslands. Massasauga means "great river mouth" in Chippewa, a Native American tongue, reflecting the fact that the snake is often seen in the swamps around river mouths and confluences.

Cottonmouth

Agkistrodon piscivorus

Cottonmouths, or water moccasins, are among the most venomous of all North American snakes. Although they rarely bite people, they are still persecuted and often killed on sight, along with many harmless water snakes, with which they are frequently confused.

These semi-aquatic snakes live in damp habitats near to swamps and streams in the lowland areas of south-eastern United States. The cottonmouth is a nocturnal hunter that catches a wide range of prey, from fish and frogs to baby alligators and small mammals. The snake holds cold-blooded victims in its jaws until the venom takes its effect, but it releases warm-blooded animals after it has delivered a bite. The victim runs away but dies nearby, and the snake locates the body using its sense of smell.

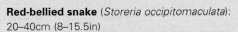

Distribution: South-eastern United States, including Florida, North Carolina and the Mississippi Valley and Delta.
Habitat: Swamps, streams and other wetlands.
Food: Amphibians, fish, birds, reptiles and small mammals.
Size: 51–190cm (20–75in).
Maturity: 3 years.
Breeding: Up to 12 young born in late summer.
Life span: Unknown.
Status: Common.

This snake has a striking cotton-white lining to the mouth, which it reveals when it gapes to warn off attackers. Adults are uniformly dark olive or black; juveniles are lighter with a banded patterning.

Timber rattlesnake

Crotalus horridus

The range of timber rattlesnakes extends north-east along the Appalachian Mountains to the Adirondacks of New York. Further south, they occur on either side of the mountains to the swampy Atlantic coastal plain between the Carolinas and northern Florida. They are also found across the Mississippi flood plain to eastern Texas and northern Mexico.

In the north and east, timber rattlesnakes live in forested rocky hills. They are often seen coiled on a tree stump waiting for passing prey such as tree squirrels, chipmunks and other rodents. In the south, the snakes are more common in damp meadowlands and swampy areas.

A timber rattlesnake on the lookout for food will remain motionless to avoid being detected by its prey, but it will also freeze when a threat approaches. The attack stance is only adopted at at the last minute, which itself is often enough to surprise the aggressor and deter it from attacking. If the danger persists, the snake raises its head and neck into an S-shape, before striking forward with exposed fangs. Timber rattlesnakes often gather in large groups to hibernate, sometimes with rat snakes and copperheads. Breeding occurs in spring, when the snakes emerge from their dens. At this time, rival males may tussle with each other, intertwining the rear part of their bodies while they raise the front half and try to push their opponent to the ground. The successful male then mates with the female.

Distribution: Eastern United States.
Habitat: Forests.
Food: Squirrels, mice, chipmunks and small birds.
Size: 89–190cm (35–75in).
Maturity: 9 years.
Breeding: Up to a dozen young born in late summer and autumn.
Life span: 30 years.
Status: Common.

In the northern part of their range, timber rattlesnakes are brown, grey and black, while those living further south are pink, tan and yellow. All timber rattlesnakes have black tails. Female timber rattlesnakes only breed every three to four years.

Pigmy rattlesnake

Sistrurus miliarius

Pigmy rattlesnakes are also called ground rattlers, because they are generally seen slithering along the ground in summer, or sunning themselves in quiet locations. They are rarely found far from a source of water, and they are good swimmers. Pigmy rattlesnakes range from southern Virginia to Oklahoma, and along the coast of the Gulf of Mexico to the Florida Keys.

Pigmy rattlesnakes spend a lot of time underground. However, these nocturnal snakes do not dig themselves but occupy burrows made by small mammals and tortoises. Although they are small, pigmy rattlesnakes often strike when disturbed. Unlike other types of rattler, this species does not rise up into a defensive posture. Instead, it sways its head from side to side before biting. The venom is rarely fatal to humans, but it is powerful enough to cause serious illness – and kill its prey.

Pigmy rattlesnakes hunt small animals such as mice, frogs and other snakes. They also eat insects, spiders, centipedes and newly hatched bird chicks.

Distribution: South-eastern United States.
Habitat: Woodlands near water.
Food: Lizards, snakes, mice and insects.
Size: 38–79cm (15–31in).
Maturity: Unknown.
Breeding: Mating occurs over winter; young born in August.
Life span: 15 years.
Status: Common.

This is one of the smallest of all rattlesnakes. Its tiny rattle is no louder than a buzzing insect, and cannot be heard from more than a couple of metres away.

Bushmaster

Lachesis muta

This species is the largest venomous snake in the Americas, and also the longest viper in the world. One in every five people bitten by a bushmaster dies, even if they get to hospital in time to be treated with antivenin drugs. This makes the bushmaster one of the deadliest snakes on the planet. Fortunately, it avoids contact with people whenever it can.

Like many other vipers, the bushmaster is an ambush hunter. It lies coiled up in the undergrowth along a trail or at the edge of a clearing, where it waits for small animal prey to wander by. The black-and-tan pattern along its back provides excellent camouflage, and this is another reason why bushmasters are rarely seen. Bushmasters rarely stray from the cover of pristine forests. They are most active at night, being more subdued during daylight. Unlike other vipers in South America, bushmasters lay eggs. Larger females lay more eggs than smaller ones. The female guards the eggs until they hatch.

Distribution: Northern South America and Central America.
Habitat: Tropical forest and scrubland.
Food: Small mammals.
Size: 3m (9.75ft).
Maturity: About 4 years.
Breeding: Up to 20 eggs laid in a burrow.
Life span: Up to 20 years.
Status: Common.

The bushmaster is the longest venomous snake in the Americas. The red-brown body is covered in crosses and diamonds, and there are spine-shaped scales on the tail.

Northern coral snake (*Micrurus fulvius*): 56–120cm (22–47in)
This is one of two North American species of coral snake. It ranges from North Carolina to Florida and around the Gulf of Mexico to central Mexico. This species is sometimes referred to as the eastern coral snake, to differentiate it from the western coral snake (or Arizona coral snake), which is also found as far north as the United States. Northern coral snakes are found mainly in forests, where they spend most of their time buried in damp soil or in leaf litter. These highly venomous snakes are often mistaken for harmless species that mimic their banded warning patterns.

Tropical rattlesnake (*Crotalus durissus*): 1.40m (4.5ft)
This snake, also known as the cascabel, has a greater range than any other rattlesnake. It is found in Mexico and much of Central America. In South America it lives on the edges of the Amazon Basin, from the coastal regions of Colombia and Venezuela to the monsoon forests of eastern Brazil and the scrublands of the Gran Chaco and Mato Grosso in Paraguay and northern Argentina. Tropical rattlesnakes are highly venomous: three-quarters of the people bitten by one of these snakes will die unless they get immediate medical attention. However, an effective antivenin has been developed so the chances of survival are high if treatment is given. Tropical rattlesnakes hunt in darkness, using the heat-sensitive pits on their face to track prey. The females give birth to live young, producing 6–12 offspring at a time.

Western Amazon coral snake

Micrurus spixii

One of the many elapid snakes that live in the Americas, the western Amazon coral snake is a relative of the cobras of Asia and Africa. It is just as deadly as its more famous cousins. In common with all coral snakes, this species advertises that it has dangerous venom by having bright rings round its body. However, as the snake gets older, the black base colour becomes stronger and the red and yellow rings begin to become less vivid.

Western Amazon coral snakes live across the Amazon Basin, from Venezuela to Peru and Bolivia. They inhabit rainforests and can be found resting under logs or other large debris. They are also able to swim.

Their diet consists of other smaller species of snakes and lizards. When threatened, western Amazon coral snakes coil up their body and bury their head under the coils for protection.

Distribution: Venezuela to Bolivia.
Habitat: Forests.
Food: Other snakes and lizards.
Size: 1.5m (5ft).
Maturity: 2 years.
Breeding: Eggs laid in summer.
Life span: Unknown.
Status: Common.

The red, black and yellow bands warn that this is a deadly snake. Many non-venomous snakes copy this coloration. In North America the rhyme "red to yellow, kill a fellow; red to black, venom lack" is used to tell true coral snakes apart from their mimics; it does not work in Central or South America, where there are many more coral snake species and mimics.

CATS

Cats belong to the Felidae *family of mammals. They fall into two main groups. The* Panthera *genus contains the big cats, such as lions and tigers, while* Felis *comprises the small cats, including the domestic cat. The majority of American cats belong to the second group, with the jaguar being the only big cat found on both continents. Most American cats are rarely seen, and some are threatened with extinction.*

Cougar

Felis concolor

Extremely strong and agile, cougar adults are able to leap more than 5m (16.5ft) into the air. Once they make a kill, their victims are dragged into secluded places and eaten over several days.

Cougars are also known as pumas, panthers or mountain lions, and have the most widespread distribution of any American species. They live in nearly all habitats, from the mountainsides of the Canadian Rockies to the jungles of the Amazon and the swamps of Florida.

The cougar is the largest of the small cats in America, with males up to 2m (6.5ft) long. They patrol large territories, moving both in the daytime and at night and taking shelter in caves and thickets. Their preferred food is large deer, such as mule deer or elk. They stalk their prey before bringing it down with a bite to the throat, or ambush it from a high vantage point. Cougars live alone, marking their territories with scent and by scraping visual signals in the soil and on trees.

Distribution: North, Central and South America from southern Canada to Cape Horn.
Habitat: Any terrain with enough cover.
Food: Deer, beavers, raccoons and hares.
Size: 1–2m (3.25–6.5ft); 60–100kg (132–220lb).
Maturity: 3 years.
Breeding: Every 2 years; litters of 3 or 4 cubs.
Life span: 20 years.
Status: Some subspecies endangered.

Margay

Felis wiedii

Distribution: Central America and Amazon Basin.
Habitat: Tropical forest.
Food: Birds, eggs, lizards, frogs, insects and fruit.
Size: 46–79cm (18–31in); 2.5–4kg (5.5–8.75lb).
Maturity: 1 year.
Breeding: Single cub or twins born once a year.
Life span: 10 years.
Status: Endangered.

Margays are small cats that live in the lush forests of Central and South America. These slender cats spend nearly all of their lives in the tree tops, rarely touching ground. They are active at night, searching through the branches for food, which ranges from small tree-dwelling mammals, such as marmosets, to insects and fruit.

Margays are very acrobatic climbers. They use their long tails to help them balance, and their broad, padded feet give them a good grip on flimsy branches. Margays are unique among cats because they can twist their hind feet right round so they face backwards.

Like most cats, margays live alone, defending large territories from intruders. They do, of course, pair up briefly with mates for breeding, but the males leave the females before litters are born. Breeding takes place throughout the year and most litters have one or perhaps two cubs.

Margays can climb down tree trunks head-first like squirrels, or hang upside down with the claws on their reversed hind feet embedded in tree bark.

Jaguar

Panthera onca

The jaguar is the only big cat in the Americas. It is smaller in length than the cougar, but much bulkier and heavier. Jaguars are usually a tawny yellow with dark rings, but they can also be black.

Jaguars prefer to live in areas with plenty of water for at least part of the year, although they will stray on to grasslands and into deserts in search of food. They live alone, taking refuge in secluded spots during the day and stalking prey at night. Despite being expert climbers, they hunt on the ground and drag their kills to hideaways before devouring them.

Female jaguars defend smaller territories than males, and a male's territory may overlap those of two or three females. The cats advertise their presence by scenting landmarks with urine or faeces and by scraping marks on tree trunks and rocks. When a female is ready to breed, she will leave her home range and be courted by outside males. Litters usually stay with their mother for about two years.

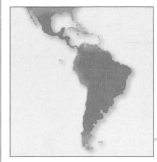

Distribution: South-western United States, Mexico, Central and South America to northern Argentina.
Habitat: Forests and swamps.
Food: Capybaras, peccaries, caimans and tapirs.
Size: 1.1–1.9m (3.5–6.25ft); 36–158kg (80–350lb).
Maturity: 3 years.
Breeding: Litters of 1–4 cubs born every 2 or 3 years.
Life span: 22 years.
Status: Lower risk.

Little spotted cat (*Felis tigrina*): 45–65cm (18–25.5in); 3.5kg (7.75lb)
Tawny coated, with rosette-shaped spots, these cats look similar to, but are smaller than, ocelots and margays. Little spotted cats are rare throughout their range, which extends from the north of Panama southward to northern Argentina. They are found in lowland rainforests and montane cloud forests up to 3,000m (10,000ft), but they may also be seen in drier regions, such as scrub and deciduous forests. Little spotted cats live alone and hunt at night, preying on small mammals, such as rodents, and small birds. In the Brazilian forests, they have also been known to catch small monkeys.

Northern lynx (*Felis lynx*): 80–100cm (31.5–39.5in); 5.1–30kg; (11.25–66.14lb)
Most of these cats live in Canada, although they spread south into Montana, Idaho and Washington, and there are small populations in New England and Utah. They prefer mature forests with thick undergrowth where they can lurk unseen, but they also venture into open habitats such as tundra. The fur is long, thick and yellow-brown, sometimes with dark spots. The tail is short, with dark rings and a black tip, and the ears are tufted. Lynx hunt at night, finding their food in a defended territory. They stalk prey such as snowshoe hares, rodents and birds, pouncing on their victims when they come within range. They also eat fish. A litter of two or three cubs is produced in early summer. The young are suckled for five months and stay with their mother for a year. The young lynx reach adulthood between the ages of two and three.

Ocelot

Felis pardalis

Ocelots are medium-sized small cats found across most of the American tropics. These agile hunters are most common in the dense jungles of the Amazon Basin, but are also found high on the slopes of the Andes and in the dry shrublands of northern Mexico.

An ocelot's typical day is spent sleeping in the cool of a shady thicket or on a leafy branch, but at night the cat comes out to hunt. Ocelots eat a wide range of animals, including rodents, snakes and even young deer and peccaries if the opportunity arises.

Ocelots are largely solitary animals, although males will maintain social links with a number of females in their local areas. They communicate with quiet mews, which become loud yowls during courtship. In the heart of the tropics, ocelots breed all year round, while at the northern and southern extremes of their range, they tend to mate during the late summer and fall.

Ocelots used to be hunted for their fur. They are now protected but are still threatened by deforestation.

Distribution: Mexico to northern Argentina.
Habitat: Tropical forest.
Food: Rodents, rabbits, birds, snakes and fish.
Size: 55–100cm (22–40in); 11.5–16kg (25.25–35.25lb).
Maturity: 18 months.
Breeding: Litters of 2–4 born once a year.
Life span: 15 years.
Status: Lower risk.

Bobcat

Felis rufus

Bobcats are found throughout North America, except its colder northern fringes. They are especially common in the south-eastern United States, where there is a population of more than one million. Bobcats survive in a range of habitats including forests, semi-deserts, mountains and brush – in fact, anywhere that has plenty of hidden spaces, such as hollow trees, thickets and crevices, in which the cats can make a den.

Bobcat fur varies from brown to tan, often marked with brown or black stripes and spots. In the past, bobcats were widely hunted for their pelts. Although it is still legal to hunt bobcats in some parts of their range, hunting is strictly controlled. Bobcats are solitary animals and most active at night, especially around dawn and dusk. They are good climbers but spend most of their time on the ground, using their exceptional vision, hearing and sense of smell to locate prey in the gloom. Rabbits and hares are favoured prey, but squirrels, chipmunks, rodents and birds are also eaten. In winter, when other prey is scarce, bobcats may hunt deer. Bobcats defend a territory, the size of which depends on the amount of food available in the area. Each cat marks the boundaries of its territory with urine, faeces and oils secreted from an anal gland. A male will control a large territory that overlaps the smaller territories of several females, but he will only interact with them during the mating season, when these normally quiet cats may vocalize with yowling and hissing.

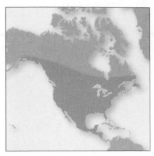

Distribution: From southern Canada to southern Mexico.
Habitat: Forest, semi-desert, mountains and brushland.
Food: Rodents, rabbits, small deer, large ground birds and reptiles.
Size: 65–105cm (25.5–41.5in); 4–15 kg (8.75–33lb).
Maturity: 8 months.
Breeding: Litter of 1–4 babies born once a year.
Life span: 12 years.
Status: Common.

Bobcats get their name from their short tails, which are generally only about one-fifth of the animal's overall body length. The tip of the tail and ears are black. Bobcats have hairy tufts on their ears, and sideburn-like tufts the side of the head, which extend from the base of the ears to the jowl.

Pampas cat

Felis colocolo

The pampas cat is the most widespread of all South American cats. The colour and patterns of the fur vary greatly across its range. The most conspicuous features are the ears, which are larger and more pointed than those of other American cats of a similar size.

Pampas cats are native to the pampas grasslands – the South American equivalent of the prairie or steppe – which are found mainly in Argentina, east of the Andes. These cats have also spread south into Argentina's cold and desolate Patagonia region. They are found in the forests of the Andes, too, and can even survive above the tree line. Pampas cats thrive in areas of swamp, but they are equally at home in drier regions, such as the Paraguayan Chaco – an arid shrubland that lies between the pampas and the fringes of the Amazon rainforest. Pampas cats are grey in the high Andes, with reddish stripes and spots. In Argentina, their coats are longer and yellow-brown. Brazilian pampas cats have long hair too, but their fur is also redder. These cats hunt at night for cavies and other small mammals, and also ground-nesting birds, such as tinamous. During the day, pampas cats rest in trees or in hidden dens.

Distribution: South America, from Ecuador, Peru and Brazil to southern Argentina.
Habitat: Mountains, cloud forest, brushland, woodland and pampas (grassland).
Food: Small mammals and ground birds.
Size: 57cm (22.5in); 5kg (11lb).
Maturity: 2 years.
Breeding: Single litter of 2–3 kittens born in summer.
Life span: 15 years.
Status: Common.

Jaguarundi

Felis yagouaroundi

Distribution: Texas to southern Argentina.
Habitat: Grassland, shrubland and tropical forest.
Food: Small mammals, reptiles, birds, frogs and fish.
Size: 77cm (30.5in); 9kg (19.75lbs).
Maturity: 2–3 years.
Breeding: Single litter of 1–4 cubs born in summer.
Life span: 15 years.
Status: Common, although rare in North America.

Jaguarundis live in a range of habitats, from arid shrublands and exposed grasslands to steamy jungles and mountain forests up to 3,200m (10,500ft). They are often found near waterways and swamps. With small heads, short legs and long bodies, jaguarundis most resemble the flat-headed cats of South-East Asia. Jaguarundis tend to have unspotted fur, either brownish-grey or reddish in colour. Cubs are sometimes spotted at birth but they lose these markings in their first two years.

In tropical regions, where food is available all year round, jaguarundis may produce two litters per annum. Elsewhere, breeding is confined to summer. When not breeding, they live a secretive and solitary existence. They hunt by day and return to dens at night.

With their long bodies, dark fur and rounded ears, jaguarundis have a passing resemblance to small mustelid carnivores, such as weasels and otters. This led early zoologists to name them "weasel cats".

Kodkod (*Felis guigna*): 40–50cm (16–20in); 2.2kg (4.75lb)
The kodkod (or guigna) – the smallest cat in the western hemisphere – lives in central and southern Chile and Argentina, in the temperate forests of the low Andes and coastal mountain ranges. Kodkods are arboreal, and typically occur in mature forests with many storeys of growth. Kodkods can survive in agricultural regions and areas of disturbed forest, but they are becoming less common as their primary-forest habitat is destroyed. Kodkods are grey-brown, with several black spots and some black streaks on their head and shoulders. The tail has black rings. Many kodkods are completely black, a condition called melanism. Kodkods hunt at night for tree-living mammals, birds and reptiles. It is possible that kodkods live in social groups, or packs, but very little is known about this. The cats become sexually mature at the age of two.

Mountain cat (*Felis jacobita*): 70–75cm (28–30in); 4kg (8.75lb)
Mountain cats, or Andean cats, range from northern Chile and north-western Argentina to southern Peru and Bolivia. They inhabit dry, sparsely vegetated rocky slopes at 3,000–5,000m (9,840–16,400ft). They feed mainly on chinchillas and viscachas, hunting them at night among the rocks and shrubs. Their fur is thick and silver or grey with rust-coloured spots. There are dark stripes on the back, and grey bars on the forelegs and chest. There are brown rings on the thick tail. Mountain cats are often mistaken for pampas cats, but they have a much longer tail, three times the length of the body. The long tail helps the cat to balance as it moves over rocky terrain.

Geoffroy's cat

Felis geoffroyi

Although Geoffroy's cat is sometimes seen in grasslands and savannahs, it prefers denser habitats. It occurs from lowland Amazon rainforests up to 3,500m (11,500ft) in the forests of the high Andes. Being primarily a forest dweller, Geoffroy's cat is an expert climber. It it also a good swimmer, and it often lives close to marshes and swamps.

The male cat controls a home range that encompasses the territories of several females, and he will breed with most of the females in that area. Smaller, weaker males cannot secure a territory, and usually do not reproduce.

This nocturnal cat hunts in the trees, on the ground and in water, taking frogs and fish as well as lizards, birds and small mammals. It will even hang upside down under branches to get at hard-to-reach prey.

Distribution: South America; southward from Bolivia and central Brazil to Patagonia.
Habitat: Scrubland, forests, open woodland and marshes.
Food: Birds, fish, amphibians, reptiles and small mammals.
Size: 54cm (21.5in); 4 kg (8.75lb).
Maturity: 18 months.
Breeding: Single litter of 1–4 cubs born in late summer.
Life span: 15 years.
Status: Common.

No larger than a domestic cat, Geoffroy's cat is small for a wild species. The tail is about half the length of the rest of the body. The coat is covered in black spots for camouflage.

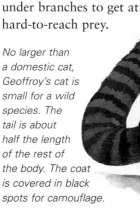

DOGS

Domestic dogs belong to the Canidae *family, which includes wolves (from which they are descended), foxes and jackals. Most types of wild canid live in large family groups called packs. Dog societies are very complex, because the animals must cooperate to survive, especially during winter. The dogs hunt together and take it in turns to care for the young.*

Maned wolf

Chrysocyon brachyurus

The maned wolf lives in areas of swamp and open grassland in central South America, east of the Andes. Its name comes from a dark swathe of hair on its nape and along its spine. The hairs in this mane stand erect when the animal is threatened.

Maned wolves form monogamous pairs throughout their lives. Males and females share territory and have dens hidden inside thick vegetation. Most of the time they stay out of each other's way, hunting alone at night. The pair only spend time together during the breeding season at the end of winter. Both parents help to raise the litter, regurgitating food at the den for the young to feed on.

Unlike other wolves, which run down their prey, maned wolves stalk their victims more like foxes. Despite having very long legs, maned wolves are not great runners. Instead, their height allows them to peer over tall grasses in search of prey.

Maned wolves have fox-like coloration, with a reddish-brown coat of longish fur. These canids are omnivorous, supplementing their diet with fruit.

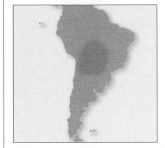

Distribution: Central and eastern Brazil, eastern Bolivia, Paraguay, northern Argentina and Uruguay.
Habitat: Grassland.
Food: Rodents, other small mammals, birds, reptiles, insects, fruit and other vegetable matter.
Size: 1.2–1.3m (4–4.25); 20–23kg (44–51lb).
Maturity: 1 year.
Breeding: Monogamous pairs produce litters of 2–4 cubs.
Life span: 10 years.
Status: Lower risk.

Grey wolf

Canis lupus

Grey wolves howl to communicate with pack members over long distances.

All domestic dogs are descended from grey wolves, which began living alongside humans many thousands of years ago. Grey wolves are the largest dogs in the wild, and they live in packs of about ten individuals. A pack has a strict hierarchy, with a male and female "alpha pair" in charge. The alpha dogs bond for life and are the only members of the pack to breed. The rest of the pack is made up of the alpha pair's offspring.

In summer, pack members often hunt alone for small animals such as beavers or hares, while in winter, the pack hunts together for much larger animals. Grey wolves are strong runners and can travel 200km (125 miles) in one night. They generally detect prey by smell and chase them down, taking turns to take a bite at the faces and flanks of their victims until they collapse from exhaustion.

Distribution: Canada and some locations in the United States and Europe, and across most of Asia.
Habitat: Tundra, pine forest, desert and grassland.
Food: Moose, elk, musk ox and reindeer.
Size: 1–1.6m (3.25–5.25ft); 30–80kg (66–175lb).
Maturity: 22 months.
Breeding: Once per year.
Life span: 16 years.
Status: Vulnerable.

Kit fox

Vulpes macrotis

Distribution: Western United States.
Habitat: Desert and scrub.
Food: Rodents, pikas, insects and fruit.
Size: 38–50cm (15–19.5in); 1.9–2.2kg (4.25–4.75lb).
Maturity: 1 year.
Breeding: Litters of 4–5 cubs.
Life span: 15 years.
Status: Vulnerable.

Kit foxes live in the dry desert and scrub areas of the high plateaux and valleys beside the Rocky Mountains in the United States. They generally live in breeding pairs, but social bonds are quite loose and pairs often split. The female does not leave her den – made in a disused burrow – while she is suckling her litter of four or five cubs. During this time she relies on the male for food, which is generally small rodents and rabbits, insects and fruit.

After three or four months, the young are strong enough to travel with their parents to other dens in their territory. A kit fox family's territory overlaps widely with those of other groups in the area. The size of the territory depends on the climate. Desert territories have to be large to supply enough food for the family. The kit fox is very similar in appearance and behaviour to the swift fox (*Vulpes velox*) which lives on the great plains farther east. It is possible that hybridization takes place where the ranges of these two dogs overlap.

The kit fox's large ears are lined with blood vessels that radiate heat to cool the animal down in hot desert climes.

Red wolf (*Canis rufus*): 100–130cm (39.5–51in); 20–40kg (44–88lb)
Red wolves once roamed over mountains, forests and wetlands across the whole of the south-eastern United States. Today they are critically endangered, and limited to the south-eastern tip of Texas and south-western Louisiana. The red wolf is smaller than its more common northern relative, the grey wolf, with longer legs and ears and shorter fur. It gets its name from the grizzled red hair on its underside; the rest of the fur is dark grey or black. Red wolves live in packs. Only the dominant male and female pair breed. Other pack members help to raise the young and find food. Red wolves hunt mainly at night, often alone. They prey on raccoons, rabbits, pigs, rice rats, nutria, and muskrats. When hunting together, they attack white-tailed deer.

Swift fox (*Vulpes velox*): 38–53cm (15–21in) 1.8–3kg (4–6.5lb)
This aptly named fox can run at 50kmh (30mph) when pursuing prey or fleeing predators. Once found from the Great Plains in western Canada to Texas, swift foxes became extinct in Canada in the 1930s. A tiny population has since been reintroduced. Today the largest populations live in Colorado, Kansas, New Mexico and Wyoming. The fox's decline was caused by the loss of its prairie habitat to farming. The swift fox is the smallest North American wild dog, about the size of a house cat. Its fur is light grey or tan, with white areas on the throat and chest; the bushy tail has a black tip. Between two and six pups are produced in a single litter. Adults begin to breed between the ages of one and two.

Bush dog

Speothos venaticus

Bush dogs live in wetlands and flooded forests in highly social packs of about ten dogs. Pack members hunt together, chasing ground birds and rodents. As with other pack-hunting dogs, the victims – which in this case include capybaras, agoutis and rheas – are often much bigger than the dogs themselves. These dogs are believed to be expert swimmers, sometimes diving into water in pursuit of their prey.

Bush dogs are diurnal (active during the day) and keep together by making high-pitched squeaks as they scamper through the dense forest. As night falls, the pack retires to a den in a hollow tree trunk or abandoned burrow. Little is known about the social system within the packs, but it is likely that there is a system of ranking.

Litters of two or three young are produced during the rainy season. The females only become ready to breed when they come into contact with male bush dogs.

Distribution: Northern South America, east of the Andes.
Habitat: Forests and swampy grasslands.
Food: Ground birds and rodents.
Size: 57–75cm (22.5–29.5in); 5–7kg (11–15lb).
Maturity: 1 year.
Breeding: Litter of 2–3 cubs born in rainy season.
Life span: 10 years.
Status: Vulnerable.

Bush dogs are unusual members of the dog family, looking more like weasels or mongooses than other dogs.

Coyote

Canis latrans

Coyotes live throughout North America and Central America, from the humid forests of Panama to the treeless tundra regions of Canada and Alaska. They are most common in the unpopulated desert areas of the south-western United States and northern Mexico.

These dogs look a little like small grey wolves. They are less likely to form packs than wolves, and are typically found alone, in pairs or in small family groups. Coyotes may dig their own den or enlarge the burrow of another animal. They are primarily nocturnal, being most active around dawn and dusk, but they do sometimes hunt during the day. They can reach speeds of up to 64kmh (40mph) when chasing swift jackrabbits and other prey.

These dogs are adaptable opportunistic feeders, and they are able to survive in farmland and suburban regions. They are increasingly coming into conflict with human communities expanding into the desert, which see them as pests.

Distribution: From Canada and the United States through Mexico to Panama.
Habitat: Desert, forest and tundra.
Food: Small mammals, such as rabbits, ground squirrels and mice, occasionally birds, reptiles and large invertebrates; carrion and some plant matter.
Size: 76–100cm (30–39.5in); 8–20kg (17.75–44lb).
Maturity: 1 year.
Breeding: Single litter of 6 pups born in early summer.
Life span: 10–14 years.
Status: Common.

Coyote fur varies from grey to yellow. The head and legs may have reddish hair on them. A black line runs along the back. The bushy tail is about half as long as the rest of the body. Coyotes are much smaller than wolves, but significantly larger than foxes.

Crab-eating fox

Dusicyon thous

The crab-eating fox inhabits woodland and grassland in the highlands around the Amazon Basin, although it is also found on the fringes of the region's lush lowland rainforests. It ranges from Columbia and Venezuela in the north to Paraguay, Uruguay and Argentina in the south.

Crab-eating foxes feed on both coastal and freshwater crabs, but the diet of this omnivorous animal also encompasses a wide range of other foods, including small mammals, insects, fruits and carrion. These nocturnal foxes locate crabs in the dark by listening for the rustling they make as they move through thick vegetation.

The foxes live in male-female pairs, and these pairings persist until one partner dies. Although they travel and den in pairs, they hunt alone. The pair will defend a territory, which grows during the dry season as food becomes more scarce. During this time of year, the territories of breeding pairs overlap considerably. Breeding may take place at any time of the year, although it is most common in late summer. The pups are weaned by about 90 days. Both parents share the task of finding food for the young and guarding them until they become independent, which occurs some five to six months after birth.

Distribution: South America; highlands around the Amazon Basin.
Habitat: Woodland and grassland.
Food: Land crabs, small mammals, birds, insects and other invertebrates, fruit and carrion.
Size: 60–70cm (23.5–27.5in); 6–7kg (13.25–15.5lb).
Maturity: 1 year.
Breeding: Single litter of 3–6 pups born in January or February.
Life span: 10 years.
Status: Common.

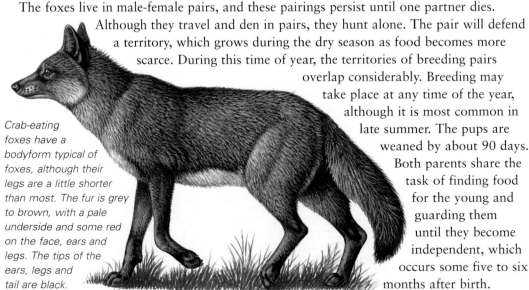

Crab-eating foxes have a bodyform typical of foxes, although their legs are a little shorter than most. The fur is grey to brown, with a pale underside and some red on the face, ears and legs. The tips of the ears, legs and tail are black.

Arctic fox (*Alopex lagopus*): 55cm (21.5in); 4kg (8.75lb)

The Arctic fox inhabits tundra, pine forests and mountain slopes in northern Canada and Alaska. It is also found in Greenland, Iceland, Siberia and Scandinavia. Arctic foxes are scavengers, taking whatever they can find. In summer they feed on small mammals, such as lemmings, but in winter they must diversify their diet to survive, eating invertebrates, berries, carrion, and even the faeces of other animals. While the land is iced over they rely on marine animals, such as sea birds and fish, for their meat. Arctic foxes have two colour forms: those in exposed tundra regions are more or less white all year around, becoming paler in winter; those in less-exposed areas have pale brown fur in summer, which becomes tinged with pale blue in winter.

Culpaeo (*Dusicyon culpaeus*): 90cm (35.5in); 10kg (22lbs)

Culpaeos, or coloured foxes, live from Ecuador to Chile, and even extend to Tierra del Fuego in Argentina. They are primarily found west of the Andes, where they live in pampas grasslands and high deciduous forests. The fur is a variety of colours, ranging from red to grey. Culpaeo females live in large sisterhoods that cooperate to raise the young of one dominant female. Males are solitary, but join the group to help care for the young in the breeding season. Pups are born in spring, in litters of about four. At a week old they start to establish a dominance hierarchy by fighting over milk and food. The ranking among the females established at this time lasts into adulthood.

Hoary zorro

Dusicyon vetulus

The hoary zorro lives in the tall-grass pampas and sparsely wooded savannahs of Brazil's Matto Grosso and Minas Gerais regions in the south of the country. It is referred to as the zorro – Spanish for fox – to avoid confusion with the royal, or hoary, fox (*Vulpes cana*) of South-east Asia.

Hoary zorros have short coats of grey and silver hairs. They shelter in burrows deserted by other animals, such as armadillos. These foxes hunt small mammals and birds, but much of their diet consists of insects such as grasshoppers and termites, especially in dry periods. Since the teeth are used for crunching small animals rather than ripping flesh, they are not as sharp as those of other foxes, and the grinding molar teeth are wider. Like many foxes, hoary zorros live in male-female pairs, with both parents raising the young.

The word "hoary" refers to the white hairs that are mixed in with the fox's grey coat, which produces a grizzled effect.

Distribution: Southern Brazil.
Habitat: Pampas and savannah grasslands.
Food: Small mammals, birds and insects.
Size: 59–64cm (23–25in); 4kg (8.75lb).
Maturity: 1 year.
Breeding: 2–4 pups produced in autumn.
Life span: Unknown
Status: Unknown.

Grey fox

Vulpes cinereoargenteus

Grey foxes are found in woodlands and forests, mostly in the southern half of North America. Their range continues down the western side of Central America to northern Colombia and Venezuela. They are not found in the Rockies and other mountain ranges of the western United States and Canada, nor in the highlands of Central America. They are also absent from the Great Plains region.

Male grey foxes are slightly larger than females. A mature fox has only one sexual partner during each breeding season, the timing of which depends on the location. For example, Canadian grey foxes breed in April, while those in the southern United States mate in February. The family group usually stays together until autumn, but the young will occasionally stay with their parents until the following breeding season to help raise the next litter. Grey foxes are unusual for dogs because they climb trees in search of prey such as insects and birds. They also eat fruits.

Distribution: Southern Canada to Venezuela.
Habitat: Woodland.
Food: Rabbits, other small mammals and birds.
Size: 80–112cm (31.5–44in); 3.6–6.8kg (8–15lb).
Maturity: 1–2 years.
Breeding: About 4 pups born in spring.
Life span: 8 years.
Status: Common.

Grey foxes have the bushy tail and large ears that typify foxes. The features that distinguish them from other foxes are the grizzled underparts and black tip to the tail.

BEARS

The world's largest land carnivore, the Kodiak bear – a subspecies of brown bear – lives in North America. It is a huge, hairy animal that can grow to 3m (10ft) tall. Despite their immense size and strength, bears are generally not the vicious predators many people think they are. Most eat more plant food than meat, and they are usually shy beasts, preferring to stay away from humans.

Polar bear

Ursus maritimus

Distribution: Arctic Ocean to southern limits of floating ice, and Hudson Bay.
Habitat: Ice fields.
Food: Seals, reindeer, fish, seabirds and berries.
Size: 2–2.5m (6.5–8.25ft); 150–500kg (330–1,100lb).
Maturity: 6 years.
Breeding: 1–4 cubs born every 2–4 years.
Life span: 30 years.
Status: Vulnerable.

Polar bears have proportionally longer necks than other types of bear so that they can lunge after seals and other aquatic prey.

Polar bears are semi-aquatic animals. They live on the fringes of the vast ice fields that surround the North Pole, where they feed on seals and other marine animals. The bears may cover large distances in search of food, sometimes coming far inland or swimming for several kilometres across open water. Their feet have hairy soles to keep them warm and give them a good grip on the ice. Their forefeet are also very broad, making them good paddles in water.

The bears' snow-white coats help them to blend in with their surroundings and stay hidden from their prey. The staple food of polar bears is the ringed seal. The bears either wait beside holes in the ice for seals to surface, or sneak up on them across the ice. They sometimes dig down into seal dens beneath the surface snow to get at new-born pups.

Polar bears put on a lot of weight in summer because they have less opportunity to feed in winter. They often take shelter from extreme weather in underground dens. Pregnant females sleep inside large dens for long periods during the winter months, before giving birth to their pups in spring. The young stay with their mothers for two years.

Brown bear

Ursus arctos

Brown bears live in many parts of the northern hemisphere, and although they belong to a single species, they look rather different from place to place. For example, the brown bears in Europe and Asia are smaller and darker than their American cousins. In North America, there are two subspecies of brown bear: Kodiaks and grizzlies.

Brown bears make their homes in cold places, such as northern forests, mountains and barren tundra. They feed on a range of fruits, plants and small animals. Only grizzlies regularly attack large animal prey, which may include deer and even smaller black bears.

Distribution: North America, Siberia, Europe and Caucasus Mountains.
Habitat: Tundra, alpine meadows and forests.
Food: Salmon, grasses, roots, mosses, bulbs, insects, fungi, rodents, deer, mountain sheep and black bears.
Size: 1.7–3m (5.5–10ft); 100–700kg (220–1,540lb).
Maturity: 6 years.
Breeding: 1–4 cubs born every 3–4 years.
Life span: 25–30 years.
Status: Endangered in some places.

Brown bears are generally solitary, although they may gather in groups around large food supplies, such as schools of salmon beneath waterfalls. As winter approaches, the bears dig themselves dens for semi-hibernation. Although they sleep during most of the winter, they often come out of the den for short periods between sleeps. Mating takes place in early summer. The female gives birth in spring, and her cubs stay with her for at least two years.

Brown bears have humps between their powerful shoulders, and longer claws than most other bears.

American black bear

Ursus americanus

Distribution: Alaska and Canada, and patchily throughout parts of the United States, from New England to Tennessee, Florida, Mississippi and western states. Also in northern Mexico.
Habitat: Forests.
Food: Fruits, nuts, grass, roots, insects, fish, rodents and carrion.
Size: 1.3–1.8m (4.25–6ft); 100–270kg (220–595lb).
Maturity: 6 years.
Breeding: 1–5 cubs born every 2 years.
Life span: 25 years.
Status: Lower risk.

American black bears are the smallest bears in North America. They live in the conifer forests of Canada and a few wilderness areas as far south as Mexico. They share these forests with grizzly bears and are sometimes eaten by them. Their main defence against this is to climb trees out of the reach of the less agile grizzly.

Black bears are most active at night. Three-quarters of what they eat is plant matter, with small animals, such as fish and rodents, making up the rest. Like other bears, black bears semi-hibernate through the winter in dens under fallen trees or in burrows. Although they sleep heavily, they often wake through the winter, going on excursions during breaks in the severe winter weather.

Although black bears generally forage for food alone, they will congregate around a large source of food. In general they stay away from each other, especially unknown bears. In the middle of summer, males and females come together for short periods. The male leaves soon after mating and cubs are born at the end of winter, while the mother is still in her winter den. The young stay with their mother until at least two years old, when they are usually driven away by the aggression of males courting their mother.

American black bears vary in coloration from black to dark or reddish-brown and pale tan. They differ from grizzlies in several respects, including their shorter fur and the lack of a shoulder hump. Black bears also have shorter legs and claws, which makes them far better tree climbers than grizzlies. The size of American black bears depends to some extent on the quality of food available in their locality.

Spectacled bear

Tremarctos ornatus

Distribution: Northern Andes Mountains, including Colombia, Ecuador, Peru, Bolivia and into Chile.
Habitat: Tropical mountain forest and alpine grassland.
Food: Fruits, epiphytes, bamboo hearts, corn, rodents and insects.
Size: 1.2–1.8m (4–6ft); 60–175kg (132–385lb).
Maturity: Unknown.
Breeding: 2 cubs born every 2–3 years.
Life span: 25 years.
Status: Vulnerable.

The spectacled bear is the only species of bear in South America. It lives mainly in the lush, high-altitude forests that clothe the slopes of the Andes Mountains from Colombia southward as far as northern Chile.

Spectacled bears are active at night, especially during the twilight hours. During the day they shelter in caves, under tree roots or on tree trunks. They are expert climbers and spend a great deal of time foraging in trees. Once up trees, the bears often build feeding platforms from broken branches. They use these platforms to reach more food.

The spectacled bear eats mainly fruit, and it will travel through the forest collecting ripe fruits. During periods when ripe fruit is unavailable, the bears eat epiphytes – plants that grow on other plants – called bromeliads, feasting on the soft edible hearts of the plants.

Being a tropical species, breeding occurs all year round. Pairs stay together for a few weeks after mating, and the cubs are born seven months later. The cubs stay with their mother for at least two years before being chased away by adult males seeking to mate with their mother.

Spectacled bears are so-named because of the large white circles or semi-circles of whitish fur around their eyes.

SMALL CARNIVORES

Most small carnivores belong to the Mustelidae *family. The mustelids are a diverse group, including otters, martens and badgers, which are adapted to aquatic, arboreal and subterranean lifestyles respectively. The world's largest and most successful mustelids live in the Americas, where they are found from the icy north to the humid tropics.*

Striped skunk

Mephitis mephitis

The striped skunk is well known for the foul-smelling spray it produces to ward off attackers. This spray comes out of two tiny apertures inside the anus. The discharge, known as musk, is squirted in spray form or as a directed arc of droplets.

The skunk will only spray when it has exhausted all other defensive tactics. These strategies include arching its back, holding its tail erect and stamping its feet. If these fail, the skunk will twist its body into a U-shape – so that its head and tail are facing the attacker – and release its musk. The musk, which can be smelled by humans over a mile away, causes discomfort to the eyes of an enemy.

Striped skunks are most active at night, foraging for food under the cover of thick vegetation. They spend the day in sheltered places, such as disused burrows. During the winter, skunks hibernate in their dens, staying underground for between two and three months. Mating takes place in springtime. Litters of up to ten young are born in summer.

The striped skunk is characterized by the broad white stripes that extend from the top of its head to the tip of its tail.

Distribution: North America.
Habitat: Woods, grasslands and deserts.
Food: Rodents, other small vertebrates, insects, fruits, grains and leaves.
Size: 28–30cm (11–12in); 0.7–2.5kg (1.5–5.5lb).
Maturity: 1 year.
Breeding: 1–10 young born every summer.
Life span: 6 years.
Status: Common.

American mink

Mustela vison

American mink are small carnivores that live close to water, where they feed on small aquatic animals. They originally came from North America, but were brought to Europe and Asia to be farmed for their fine fur. They have since escaped into the wild and are now a common pest. They are also competition for the similar, but very rare, European mink.

Mink prefer to live in areas with plenty of cover. Their river-bed dens are generally deserted burrows made by other river mammals, but mink will dig their own burrows if necessary. Mink are active at night and dive into water to snatch their prey. They live alone and will defend their own stretches of riverbank against intruders. Two months after mating a litter of up to five young is born in a dry underground nest lined with fur, feathers and leaves. The young begin to fend for themselves in autumn.

Mink are known for their luxurious fine fur, which is used for clothing. Several domestic varieties of mink have been bred, each with different-coloured fur.

Distribution: North America. Introduced to northern Europe.
Habitat: Swamps and near streams and lakes.
Food: Small mammals, fish, frogs and crayfish.
Size: 33–43cm (13–17in); 0.7–2.3kg (1.5–5lb).
Maturity: 1–1.5 years.
Breeding: 5 young born in late spring.
Life span: 10 years.
Status: Common.

Wolverine

Gulo gulo

Wolverines are giant relatives of weasels. As well as being found in the conifer forests of North America, these mustelids occur in northern Europe and Siberia, where they are known as gluttons due to their catholic feeding habits.

Wolverines are generally nocturnal, but will forage by day if they need to. Their diet varies throughout the year. In summer, they feed on small animals, such as rodents and ground-living birds, and readily feast on summer fruits. In winter, when most other carnivores are hibernating, wolverines may tackle bigger prey, such as deer. The wolverines' wide feet act as snowshoes and allow them to walk over deep snow; deer, by contrast, flounder in the snow and find it difficult to escape from the wolverines. Wolverines mate in early summer and the young are born in underground dens the following spring. They leave their mothers in the autumn.

Wolverines have large heads and heavily built bodies. Their dense coats have hairs of different lengths to prevent winter snow and ice from getting too close to the skin and causing heat loss.

Distribution: Canada, northern United States, Scandinavia and Siberia.
Habitat: Tundra and conifer forest.
Food: Carrion, eggs, rodents, berries, deer and sheep.
Size: 65–105cm (25–41in); 10–32kg (22–70lb).
Maturity: 2–3 years.
Breeding: Litter of 2–4 born in early spring every 2 years.
Life span: 10 years.
Status: Vulnerable.

Eastern spotted skunk (*Spilogale putorius*): 29cm (11.5in); 600g (21.25oz)
Eastern spotted skunks live throughout the eastern United States. They range as far west as Minnesota and south into Mexico, and are especially common in the mid-western states and the Appalachian Mountains. These skunks prefer woodland or other habitats with plenty of cover, such as areas of tall grass and even rocky regions. They dig burrows, possibly expanding a den abandoned by another animal. Several skunks will occupy each burrow. The eastern spotted skunk has short legs, so its body is held close to the ground. The head is small relative to the body size. This skunk is named after the spots on its head and rear.

Pygmy spotted skunk (*Spilogale pygmaea*): 22cm (8.5in); 500g (17.5oz)
The pygmy spotted skunk is restricted to a small area of woodland along Mexico's Pacific coast, where it lives in burrows or in trees. The black coat has white stripes over the back, which break into spots on the rump. Two large scent glands beside the anus spray a cloud of foul-smelling droplets to scare off predators. This is a tactic of last resort: the skunk's initial response to a threat is to lift its tail and make itself appear larger by raising its outer hairs. Then it stands on two legs and marches toward the attacker. Only if this is unsuccessful will it release the spray. Pygmy spotted skunks mate between February and March, and their young are born in May. They hunt at night, preying on smaller mammals, birds and reptiles. They also eat carrion, insects and fruits, and may climb trees to reach birds' eggs.

American badger

Taxidea taxus

American badgers are tough animals that live in the open country in the Great Plains region of North America. They are expert burrowers and use this skill to dig out their preferred foods – rodents, such as prairie dogs and ground squirrels. They rest in their own burrows during the day and emerge to feed at night. During the coldest weeks of the year, American badgers do not hibernate, but they sleep underground for several days at a time.

The badgers may bury some of their food so that they can eat it later, or even dig holes big enough for both themselves and their prey to fit into. American badgers and coyotes are known to hunt together in teams. The coyotes sniff out the buried prey and the badgers dig them out. Both parties then share the food.

Mating occurs in summer and early autumn, and births take place in the following spring. The young leave home after two months.

American badgers have a white stripe running from the nose along the back. In northern badgers the stripe runs to the shoulders, while on those in the south of the range it runs all the way along the back.

Distribution: Central and southern North America.
Habitat: Dry, open country.
Food: Rodents, birds, reptiles, scorpions and insects.
Size: 40–70cm (16–28in); 4–12kg (9–26.5lb).
Maturity: Females 4 months; males 1.3 years.
Breeding: 1–5 young born in spring.
Life span: 14 years.
Status: Lower risk.

Sea otter

Enhydra lutris

Sea otters live in the cold coastal waters around the northern Pacific Rim. They do not need to come on to land to survive, but often do. Unlike other marine mammals, sea otters do not have thick blubber under their skins for insulation. Instead, they rely on a layer of air trapped by their soft fur to insulate them against the cold. Pollution, such as oil in the water, can reduce the fur's ability to trap air, and otters may die of hypothermia as a result.

The otters spend a minute or two at a time underwater, collecting food such as shellfish and urchins. They then float on their backs to feed. They smash the hard shells against stones to get at the soft meat inside, using their chests as tables.

Sea otters are active during the day. At night they wrap themselves in kelp before going to sleep to prevent themselves from floating away. They sometimes put their forepaws over their eyes while sleeping.

Sea otters live alone and only tolerate each other when mating. A male will defend his territory, but fights are unusual, since most disputes are settled by splashing and vocal contests.

Breeding occurs all year round. Pups are carried on the female's chest for about two months, when they begin to feed themselves. They are independent by the time they are six months old.

Sea otter fur comprises 100,000 hairs per 1sq cm (0.15sq in), making it the densest fur of any mammal. This keeps the animal warm in the cold ocean. The hind feet are webbed and flipper-shaped.

Distribution: Northern Pacific coasts from California and Baja, Mexico, to Japan. Sea ice limits their northern range.
Habitat: Temperate coastal waters up to 20m (60ft) deep and less than 1.6km (1 mile) from shore.
Food: Fish and shellfish, such as sea urchins, abalones, crabs and molluscs.
Size: 1–1.2m (3.25–4ft); 15–45kg (33–99lb).
Maturity: Females 4 years; males 6 years.
Breeding: Single pup every 1–3 years.
Life span: 20 years.
Status: Threatened.

Giant otter

Pteronura brasiliensis

The giant otter is the largest mustelid in the world, although it is not as heavy as the sea otter. This semi-aquatic mammal inhabits the tropical river basins of South America. It lives in groups of about six, each communicating with chirping sounds. Generally, the group comprises an adult pair and their offspring of various litters. Each group controls its own stretch of stream, preferring those areas with plenty of cover.

The giant otter swims at high speed by waving its tail and body up and down, using its webbed feet to steer. On land it is far less agile, and is often seen sitting grooming itself. Giant otters are diurnal – only active during the day. They catch prey in their mouths and hold it in their

forepaws to eat it on the shore. During the dry season, the otter groups are restricted to small areas of water, but when the rains come to flood the forest, the otters can roam over larger areas. Little is known about the mating habits of giant otters, other than that the young stay with their parents for a few years before reaching adulthood.

The giant otter's fur has a velvety appearance, more like the pelt of a seal than an otter. Its feet are large and have thick webbing, and the tail is flattened into a flipper-like shape.

Distribution: Central America and South America from Venezuela to Argentina.
Habitat: Slow-moving rivers and creeks in forests and swamps.
Food: Fish, fish eggs, crabs, birds and small mammals.
Size: 0.8–1.4m (2.5–4.5ft); 22–34kg (48.5–75lb).
Maturity: Unknown.
Breeding: 1–3 young produced every year.
Life span: 15 years.
Status: Vulnerable.

North American river otter

Lutra canadensis

Distribution: Widespread across most of North America.
Habitat: Rivers and lakes.
Food: Amphibians, fish, crayfish and aquatic insects.
Size: 60–110cm (23.5–43in); 3–14kg (6.5–30lb).
Maturity: 2–3 years.
Breeding: 1–5 young born every year.
Life span: 20 years.
Status: Lower risk.

North American river otters rarely stray far from the banks of shallow rivers. They live alone or in pairs, but often play with other individuals in the area. This play strengthens social ties. Each of the otters has an individual scent which it uses to mark its territory. River otters communicate with each other through sounds such as whistles, growls, chuckles and screams.

North American river otters are known for their boundless energy, and they must eat frequently. They catch fish in their mouths and detect other prey by feeling with their whiskers along the bottoms of streams. Unlike many other otters which chew their food, the river otter's prey is gulped down immediately.

Mating takes place in March and April. The young are born almost a year later. The females give birth in dens close to the water's edge. They drive the males away soon after the birth of their young, but the dog otters return later to help raise the offspring. The young depart at the age of one year.

River otters have streamlined bodies with dark fur, thick tails and short legs with webbed feet.

Marine otter (*Lontra felina*): 90cm (35.5in); 4.5kg (10lb)
The marine otter, or sea cat, lives on South America's Pacific coast, from its southern tip to northern Peru. Small populations also exist on the South Atlantic coast of Argentina. This is the smallest of the American river otters, which form a separate genus to the Old World otters and the sea otter. It is the only river otter that lives exclusively in the sea. It occupies exposed rocky coasts, sheltering from rough seas and strong winds in caves and crevices. Marine otters eat fish and shellfish such as crabs and mussels. They sometimes catch birds and small mammals.

Neotropical river otter (*Lontra longicaudis*): 36–66cm (14–26in); 5–15kg (11–33lb)
This river otter lives in tropical regions from north-western Mexico to Argentina. It is the most common otter in Mexico. Further south other, larger otters predominate, but this species is more widespread than any of its relatives. It spends the night in a burrow. By day it forages for fish, crustaceans and molluscs. It will also eat insects, reptiles, birds and small mammals.

Southern river otter (*Lontra provocax*): 66–110cm (26–43in); 6–9kg (13.25–19.75lb)
Southern river otters live in southern Chile and parts of Argentina, in both marine and fresh water habitats with plenty of vegetation cover. Chilean otters eat mainly fish and crustaceans; those in Argentina eat less fish, but supplement their diets with molluscs and birds. These otters live in family groups, consisting of an adult female and her young. Males are solitary.

Fisher

Martes pennanti

The fisher, or pekan, lives in the thick forests of North America. Despite its name, it feeds on small land animals, such as mice and porcupines. Fishers have no permanent dens, but take shelter in hollow trees, holes in the ground and even abandoned beaver lodges.

They are active during the day and night, and despite being expert climbers, spend most of their foraging time on the ground. When they come across suitable prey animals, they rush forward and kill them with bites to the back of the neck. Larger animals are killed with repeated bites to the face.

Males seek out mates during the spring breeding season and litters are born about ten months later. As with many mustelids, the fertilized eggs do not begin to grow immediately inside the females. Their development is delayed for several months so that they are born at the right time of year. Unusually, births always take place in trees.

Distribution: Canada and northern United States.
Habitat: Conifer forest.
Food: Birds, rodents, carrion.
Size: 49–63cm (19–25in); 1.3–3.2kg (2.75–7lb).
Maturity: 1–2 years.
Breeding: 3 young born every spring.
Life span: 10 years.
Status: Lower risk.

Fishers have dark fur that is coarser than that of most mustelids. Nevertheless, they are still hunted by humans for their fur.

Black-footed ferret

Mustela nigripes

Before the prairies of the North American West were cultivated for farmland and turned into cattle pasture, black-footed ferrets would have been a common sight. The burrows that they and their prey made in the ground formed dangerous obstacles to grazing cattle and farm machinery, so the animals were methodically exterminated by pioneer farmers. Today the ferrets – the only species of ferret native to North America – occur wild in just three places in Montana, South Dakota and Wyoming (all reintroduced populations).

Black-footed ferrets live on and under prairies that have short or medium-length grasses. Each ferret occupies about 40ha (100 acres) of prairie, in which it finds all its food, but a nursing mother needs two or three times this space. Black-footed ferrets take up residence in burrow systems abandoned by prairie dogs, their main food. In places where prairie dogs form large communal "towns", the ferrets may actually live among their prey.

The breeding season is in late spring. The young remain underground for a month after they are born. Mother and young forage together in late summer, generally at night, and by autumn the young begin to drift away. Males take no part in raising the young.

Distribution: Historically southern Canada to northern Mexico; today reintroduced populations exist in Montana, South Dakota and Wyoming.
Habitat: Prairie.
Food: Mainly prairie dogs, along with some mice, ground squirrels and other small animals.
Size: 38–60cm (15–23.5in) 645–1,125g (22.75–39.75oz).
Maturity: 1 year.
Breeding: Single litter of 1–6 young produced in early summer, after a gestation of 35–45 days.
Life span: 5 years.
Status: Endangered.

As well as having black feet, these ferrets have a black "mask" over their eyes. The underside of the body is covered in yellowish fur. Male black-footed ferrets are slightly larger than females.

Greater grisón

Galictis vittata

Distribution: From Mexico through Central and South America to Brazil and Bolivia.
Habitat: Grasslands and rainforest, often near water.
Food: Small mammals including chinchillas, viscachas, agoutis and mice; occasionally reptiles, birds and some fruits.
Size: 51cm (20in); 2kg (4.5lb).
Maturity: 1 year.
Breeding: 2–4 young born between March and October
Life span: 5 years.
Status: Rare.

The greater grisón's range stretches from southern Mexico to Brazil and Bolivia. These animals are found mainly in lowland areas, rarely ascending to more than 1,500m (5,000ft) above sea level. Within its large range, the greater grisón lives in a variety of habitats, from dry savannahs and grasslands to more verdant areas, including rainforests. The grisón makes its home in secluded spots, such as under tree roots or in rock crevices, and it sometimes takes over the abandoned burrows of armadillos.

Like other small carnivores, the grisón has a long, powerful body, with short legs and a short tail. While the bodyform limits the animal to slow running speeds, it does enable it to wriggle into tight spaces, such as the burrows of its prey. The ears are small, so they do not get snagged in tight spots, and the claws are wide and very long for digging and extracting food.

Grisóns have more robust bodies than weasels. The greater grisón's most obvious feature is the white stripe across its face and around its ears. This stripe divides the black face from the grey forehead, giving the animal's face a banded appearance. The rest of the body is grizzled grey and black. Greater grisóns may live alone, in pairs or in small groups. These agile predators despatch their prey with a bite to the neck.

Stoat

Mustela erminea

Although rarely seen, stoats are common in the countryside, where they mainly feed on rodents. The large males will often prey on rabbits, even though rabbits are considerably larger. Stoats are said to mesmerize their prey by dancing around them, before nipping in for the kill. This is not just a rural myth. Stoats have been observed leaping around near rabbits in a seemingly deranged fashion. This curious "dance" seems to have the effect of confusing the rabbits, which just watch the stoat draw slowly closer and closer, until it is too late to escape. The stoats then grasp the prey with their sharp teeth.

In mild climates, stoats have chestnut fur all year round. In colder areas, their coats change to pure white by the time the first snows have fallen. White stoats are known as ermines, and their fur was once prized for its pure colour and soft feel.

Stoats are distinguished from their smaller cousins, weasels, by having black tips to their tails.

Distribution: Widespread in northern and central Europe, extending into Asia and across northern North America. Introduced to New Zealand.
Habitat: Anywhere with enough cover.
Food: Mammals up to the size of rabbits.
Size: 16–31cm (6.25–12.25in); 140–445g (5–15.75oz).
Maturity: 1 year.
Breeding: Single litter of 5–12 young.
Life span: 10 years.
Status: Common.

Colombian weasel (*Mustela felipei*): 22cm (8.5in); 140g (5oz)
Living in the highlands of Colombia, this is one of only three weasels native to South America. Little is known about the Colombian weasel because only a few specimens have ever been handled, and even fewer observed in the wild. The coat is dark brown or black on top, with a reddish-tan underside. The webbed feet have naked soles, suggesting that the weasel spends a lot of time foraging in mountain waterways.

Tropical weasel (*Mustela africana*): 32cm (12.5in); weight unknown
This is another poorly understood species. It has been found in Peru, east of the Andes, and in Brazil it probably ranges across most of the Amazon lowlands. With continued destruction of Amazon rainforests, the tropical weasel is now classed as endangered. The coat is red-brown, becoming lighter on the underside. Like the Colombian weasel, this species has naked feet. Zoologists initially classified the tropical and Colombian weasels in their own genus. Now, however, all weasels are grouped together.

Lesser grisón (*Galictis cuja*): 45cm (18in); 1kg (2.2lb)
Lesser grisóns occur across central and southern South America, from southern Peru, Paraguay and central Chile to northern Patagonia in Argentina. They are at home in a range of habitats, including the arid scrubland of Paraguay's Chaco region, as well as moister grasslands and forests. This species closely resembles the greater grisón, having the same banded face. The lesser grisón is found at altitudes up to 4,000m (13,120ft).

Least weasel

Mustela nivalis

Least weasels are common throughout Canada and Alaska. Their North American range extends to the forests of the Carolinas and the prairies of Wyoming. They are also found throughout much of the northern hemisphere, with the exception of most islands and Arabia. Least weasels survive in a wide variety of habitats, but they avoid thick forests, sandy deserts and any exposed spaces.

Least weasels have a very long body, with a long neck and flat head. This allows them to move with ease over broken ground and inside burrows. The size of this weasel varies with its distribution across the globe. The largest least weasels are found in North Africa, while those in North America have the smallest bodies.

Least weasels live alone outside of the breeding season. Males occupy territories that are home to two or more females. They forage for food at all times of the day or night. They watch carefully for movements caused by prey, before launching an attack and dispatching their victims with a bite to the neck.

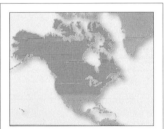

Distribution: Arctic to North Carolina; also found in Northern Asia, Africa and Europe.
Habitat: Forest, prairie, farmland and semi-desert.
Food: Rodents, eggs, nestlings and lizards.
Size: 16–20cm (6.25–8in); 30–55g (1–2oz).
Maturity: 8 months
Breeding: Two litters of up to 7 young, born in spring and late summer.
Life span: 7 years.
Status: Common.

In summer, the least weasel's brown fur is about 1cm (0.4in) long, but the winter coat is more than double this length. In the far north, the coat also turns white in winter.

American marten

Martes americana

The American marten lives in the cold northern pine forests of Canada, ranging from Newfoundland in the east to the US state of Alaska in the west. Martens also live in the high-altitude mountain areas of the continental United States, where conditions are similar to the cold north. The fur of the American marten is highly valued, and although the species is not endangered, hunting and the destruction of its conifer-forest habitat have caused a severe decline in numbers in many parts of its range.

American martens spend the day in nooks and crannies in the forest, and move through the trees and along the ground in search of food at night. To compensate for the low light levels, martens have large eyes, and large ears (for a mustelid) that resemble those of a cat. They kill their prey with their long, curved claws and sharp teeth. Their diet includes small mammals, carrion, fruits and insects.

Young martens are born in spring. Animals of breeding age locate each other by scent, releasing a strong odour from their anal glands. They live alone for the rest of the year.

Distribution: Canada to northern California and Colorado.
Habitat: Pine forests.
Food: Small mammals, carrion, fruits and insects.
Size: 32–45cm (12.5–18in); 0.3–1.3kg (0.75–2.75lb).
Maturity: 2 years.
Breeding: Up to 5 kits produced in March or April.
Life span: 10 years.
Status: Lower risk.

The American marten has a long, slender body, and large eyes and ears. The fur on the head is light brown or grey, while the legs, tail and upper surface of the body are dark brown or black. The underside is pale yellow or cream.

Tayra

Eira barbara

This unusual species is found from central Mexico to northern Argentina, and also on the island of Trinidad. It lives in thick forests, from lowland regions to about 2,400m (7,900ft) above sea level. A few tayras are known to live in areas of tall grass.

Tayras forage for food on the ground and also in the trees, where their long tail helps them to balance as they move through the branches. As well as being nimble climbers and agile on the ground, these weasels can also swim well. Tayras are mainly active during the day. They make their nests in hollow trees or logs, grassy thickets, or in the burrows of other animals. Most tayras live alone or in pairs. Sometimes they form small groups of up to four individuals. Members of the group may work together to prey on animals such as large rodents and small deer. When they are being chased by predators, tayras will evade capture by running up trees and leaping from branch to branch.

Tayras can be tamed, and they are sometimes kept as pets. Indigenous people once used them to control rodents pests in homes.

Distribution: From Central Mexico to Bolivia and Argentina; also found on the island of Trinidad.
Habitat: Tropical deciduous and evergreen forests,
Food: Mainly rodents, but also rabbits, small deer, birds, reptiles, invertebrates, honey and fruits.
Size: 100cm (40in); 4–5kg (8.75–11lb).
Maturity: 2 years.
Breeding: 3 kits born between March and July; however, some authorities claim that breeding is non-seasonal.
Life span: Unknown.
Status: Lower risk.

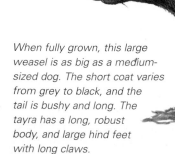

When fully grown, this large weasel is as big as a medium-sized dog. The short coat varies from grey to black, and the tail is bushy and long. The tayra has a long, robust body, and large hind feet with long claws.

Long-tailed weasel

Mustela frenata

This species has the largest range of any American weasel, from southern Canada through the United States and Central America to the lower slopes of the Bolivian Andes.

Long-tailed weasels occupy a range of habitats, from farmland and gardens to woodland. However, they avoid dense forests and desert areas. The weasels are most easily spotted emerging from their burrows, which tend to be inside tree hollows, under rocks and in other secluded spots. They often take over the burrow of one of their prey, enlarging the accommodation if necessary. Long-tailed weasels are good climbers and swimmers. They hunt at night, tracking prey by scent.

The fur is red-brown, with a yellowish underside. In colder regions, where snowfall is common, the weasel develops a white winter coat.

This weasel's tail is particularly bushy compared with those of other weasels. Apart from this, the form is fairly typical, with short legs, small ears and a long, flexible body.

Distribution: From southern Canada to Bolivia.
Habitat: Grassland, shrubland and open woodland.
Food: Small rodents, rabbits, birds and reptiles.
Size: 20–26cm (8–10in); 80–350g (3–12oz). Males are larger than females.
Maturity: 6 months.
Breeding: 6 young born in spring.
Life span: 5 years.
Status: Common.

Western hog-nosed skunk (*Conepatus mesoleucus*): 55cm (21.5in); 1.9kg (4.25lb)
Western hog-nosed skunks live in the south-western United States and Mexico, from Colorado to the highlands of northern Mexico. This species is most often found on low hills with brush or open woodland, but rarely ventures into exposed territory, such as desert, or more dense habitats, such as forest. The fur is dark brown with a stripe running from the head to the base of the bushy tail. The long snout has a naked patch that gives the species its common name.

Eastern hog-nosed skunk (*Conepatus leuconotus*): 75cm (29.5in); 3.25kg (7.25lb)
Less common than its western relative, the eastern hog-nosed skunk is limited to southern Texas and eastern Mexico. It lives in a wide range of habitats, including woodlands, grasslands, cactus forests and thorny brush areas, where it dens in fallen trunks or among rocks. This species is the largest of the North American skunks. It resembles the western hog-nosed skunk, but is about 25 per cent larger. The back stripe is slightly thinner and often does not reach the tail.

Striped hog-nosed skunk (*Conepatus semistriatus*): 57cm (22.5in); 1.6kg (3.5lb)
The striped hog-nosed skunk, or Amazonian skunk, ranges from southern Mexico to northern Peru and eastern Brazil. It occupies a variety of habitats duirng the dry season, but in the wet season it spends most of its time in deciduous mountain forests. Like other hog-nosed skunks, it has a bald patch on its snout. Two white stripes run from the nape of the neck along the black back.

Patagonian weasel

Lyncodon patagonicus

The Patagonian weasel ranges from the southern and western parts of Argentina into Chile. It is most commonly found in the pampas – areas of tall grass and few trees in the colder, dryer regions. This weasel has a short, bushy tail and legs that are short even for a mustelid. This accentuates the appearance of the long, slender body.

Most of the animals of the pampas live in burrows or at least depressions in the ground. Patagonian weasels are known to enter burrows to get at their prey, which comprise insects and small burrowing mammals such as rodents and insectivores. The weasel's small ears and short legs are designed to help it move easily through narrow burrows.

Patagonian weasels defend territories. A male weasel will occupy an area that covers the territories of several females. When a female is ready to mate with the male in the area, she produces a signalling odour to attract him.

The Patagonian weasel's coat comes in a range of colours, from white to brown and black. A white or yellow band runs along the back.

Distribution: Argentina and Chile.
Habitat: Pampas and desert.
Food: Small burrowing animals.
Size: 30–35cm (12–14in); 225g (8oz).
Maturity: 1 year.
Breeding: Unknown.
Life span: Unknown.
Status: Common.

RACCOONS AND RELATIVES

Raccoons and their relatives belong to a family of mammals called the Procyonidae. *Procyonids are small opportunistic feeders and scavenging animals. Many live in trees, but the most successful – the raccoons – live mainly on the ground. Most procyonids live in the Americas, where they range from the cold northern forests of Canada to the humid, tropical swamps of the Amazon.*

Common raccoon

Procyon lotor

Raccoons live in woodland areas and rarely stray far from water. They are more active at night than during the day. Periods of rest are spent in dens in tree hollows or other sheltered places. When on the move, raccoons will readily swim across streams and rivers and climb into trees in search of food. They use their touch-sensitive hands to grab prey and then break it into mouth-sized pieces.

Raccoons do not hibernate in warmer parts of their range, although in cooler northern parts they may do so. In fact, they only semi-hibernate, popping out every now and then to feed during breaks in the severest weather.

Males are largely solitary but will tolerate the presence of females living in or near their territories. Mating takes place in spring, and young are born a couple of months later. The young stay with their mothers until the following spring.

The common raccoon is well known for its black "bandit" mask across the eyes and its tail ringed with black hoops. The animal's footprints look similar to those of a human infant.

Distribution: Southern Canada throughout the United States to Central America.
Habitat: Forests and brushland.
Food: Crayfish, frogs, fish, nuts, seeds, acorns and berries.
Size: 41–60cm (16–23.5in); 2–12kg (4.5–26.5lb).
Maturity: 1 year.
Breeding: 3 or 4 young born in summer.
Life span: 5 years.
Status: Common.

Olingo

Bassaricyon gabbii

Distribution: Central America to northern South America as far as Brazil.
Habitat: Tropical forest.
Food: Fruits, insects and small mammals.
Size: 35–48cm (14–19in); 0.9–1.5kg (2–3.25lb).
Maturity: 21 months.
Breeding: Single offspring.
Life span: 5 years.
Status: Lower risk.

Olingos live in the trees of tropical forests. They are active at night and spend the day in nests of leaves high up inside hollow trees. Equipped with long claws, olingos are expert climbers, and they rarely descend to the ground. They can also jump long distances through the tree tops, using their long tail to keep them balanced.

An olingo's diet comprises mainly fruit, although the animal will seek out insects and small vertebrates, such as lizards, on occasion. Olingos live alone, although they are often found living alongside kinkajous – procyonids that are close relatives – as well as opossums and night monkeys.

Olingos mark objects in their territories with urine, although it is not known whether this is to ward off intruders or to help them navigate in the darkness. Mating takes place all year round. Gestation lasts about ten weeks and generally results in a single offspring.

Olingos have thick, pinkish fur. These procyonids have long bodies with short limbs and flattened tails.

Ring-tailed coati

Nasua nasua

Distribution: Northern South America as far as Argentina.
Habitat: Woodland.
Food: Fruits, insects, rodents.
Size: 41–67cm (16–26.5in); 3–6kg (6.5–13.25lb).
Maturity: 2 years.
Breeding: 2–7 young born in rainy season.
Life span: 10 years.
Status: Common.

Coatis have long muzzles compared to raccoons and other procyonids. They use these to root out food from rocky crevices and from knots in trees. Coatis forage both on the ground and in trees. On the ground they hold their long tails erect, with the tips curled. In trees, coatis' tails are prehensile enough to function as a fifth limb. The tips curl around branches to provide support in more precarious locations.

Ring-tailed coatis are most active during the day. When there is plenty of fruit on the trees, they will eat little else. However, during seasons when fruit is less abundant, they come down to the forest floor to forage for insects and rodents.

Ring-tailed coatis tend to congregate in bands of up to 20 females and young. Adult males live alone and are only allowed into bands during the breeding season, which is the time when there is plenty of fruit available. When fruit is not as easy to find, male coatis may try to eat smaller members of their band, and consequently are expelled by the adult females.

Like all coatis, this species has a long and pointed muzzle with an articulated tip. Ring-tailed coatis have long, coarse fur, and tails banded with white stripes.

Cozumel Island raccoon (*Procyon pygmaeus*): Length unknown; 3–4kg (6.5–8.75lb)
The world's smallest raccoon, this species is also known as the pygmy raccoon. It lives solely on Cozumel Island off Mexico's Yucatan Peninsula, inhabiting the mangrove swamps that fringe the island's coast. The Cozumel Island raccoon is about one-third of the size of the common raccoon of the American mainland. This raccoon is considered endangered because of its small range and the continued coastal development on Cozumel to cater for tourism. Some zoologists think that the Cozumel Island raccoon is not a distinct species, merely an unusual population of common raccoons introduced to the island by humans in prehistoric times.

Guadeloupe raccoon (*Procyon minor*):
Size unknown
Another endangered animal, this raccoon lives on the island of Guadeloupe in the French West Indies. Thought to be of a similar size to the common raccoon, the Guadeloupe raccoon has paler fur than its mainland relative. Like other island raccoons, including *Procyon maynardi* of Nassau in the Bahamas, some zoologists argue that this "species" is merely the remains of an introduced population of common raccoons.

Tres Marias raccoon (*Procyon insularis*):
Size unknown
The Tres Marias raccoon is found on Maria Madre Island and Maria Magdalene Island off the western coast of Mexico. Until recently, these raccoons were thought to be a variety of the common raccoon, rather than a separate species.

Kinkajou

Potos flavus

Kinkajous are almost entirely arboreal (tree-living). Thanks to their long claws and prehensile tails, they are very agile climbers. Kinkajous are nocturnal and spend the day in dens inside hollow trees. On the hottest days they emerge from their stifling dens to cool off in the open on branches.

At night, kinkajous race around the trees in search of fruit. After searching through one tree, they will cautiously move to the next before beginning to forage again. They use their long tongue to reach the soft flesh and juices inside the fruit.

Kinkajous tend to return to the same roosting trees each dawn. They travel alone or in breeding pairs. However, groups of kinkajous may form in trees that are heavy with fruit. Kinkajous leave their scent on branches, probably as a signal to potential mates. They also give shrill calls to communicate with partners. Mating takes place all year round, and single offspring are born after four months.

Distribution: Mexico to central Brazil.
Habitat: Forests.
Food: Fruits, insects and small vertebrates.
Size: 40–76cm (15.5–30in); 1.4–4.6kg (3–10.25lb).
Maturity: 1.5–2.5 years.
Breeding: Single offspring.
Life span: 15 years.
Status: Endangered.

Kinkajous have soft and woolly fur, with rounded heads and stockier bodies than most of their relatives. They are sometimes mistaken for the African primates known as pottos.

Mountain coati (*Nasuella olivacea*): Head and body 35–45cm (14–18in); 2kg (4.5lb)
Mountain coatis closely resemble other coatis, but they tend to be smaller and have shorter tails. They are very rare and live in tropical forests on the slopes of the Andes Mountains in northern South America. They feed on insects, fruits and small vertebrates, which they find in the trees and on the ground.

Allen's olingo (*Bassaricyon alleni*): 42–47cm (16.5–18.5in); 1.6kg (3.5lb)
Allens's olingo is very similar to the common olingo (*Bassaricyon gabbii*). It lives in a similar range and is about the same size, if not slightly larger. The most distinguishing feature of Allen's olingo is that its tail is bushier than that of the common olingo. This species is a nocturnal forager, moving through the treetops in search of food. Allen's olingo mainly feeds on fruits and insects, but it occasionally eats small arboreal mammals and lizards.

Other olingos
While Allen's olingo and the common olingo are not currently considered to be in danger of extinction, the three other olingo species are much more threatened. These three species also live in Central and South America: *Bassaricyon lasius* is found in Costa Rica, *Bassaricyon pauli* lives in the forests of Panama, while *Bassaricyon beddardi* is native to Guyana. This last species is sometimes considered to be a subspecies of Allen's olingo. All are on the endangered list.

Cacomistle

Bassariscus sumichrasti

Sometimes called ringtails (but not to be confused with *Bassariscus astutus*, their close relative) cacomistles have a small, cat-like body and a bushy, black-and-white-striped tail. They range from southern Mexico to Panama. They prefer to live in forested areas, especially in mountainous regions where the ground is broken by rocky outcrops.

Cacomistles seldom stray far from water and are most active at night, foraging mainly for insects, rodents and fruit. Being agile climbers, they move up and down cliffs with ease. As with many other climbing animals, a cacomistle's hind feet can twist around 180 degrees. This allows the animal to climb down trees and rocks headfirst, with the claws on the hind feet clinging to the surface behind them. Breeding can occur all year around, but most young are born in summer.

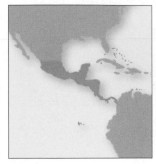

Distribution: From southern Mexico to Panama.
Habitat: Rocky areas.
Food: Insects, rodents and fruits.
Size: 30–42cm (12–16.25in); 0.8–1.3kg (1.75–2.75lb).
Maturity: 10 months.
Breeding: 1 offspring born in early summer.
Life span: 10 years.
Status: Vulnerable.

The feet of cacomistles have naked soles. This helps them to grip on to rocky surfaces and tree branches as they move around their varied habitat.

Crab-eating raccoon

Procyon cancrivorus

The crab-eating raccoon, or mapache, lives in swamps or by streams across much of South America east of the Andes and north of Patagonia. Southern Costa Rica is the most northerly extent of the raccoon's range. This species has much shorter hair and a more slender body than most of its raccoon cousins.

Although they prefer being close to water, crab-eating raccoons also survive in a range of other habitats, including scrubland and even Amazonian rainforest. They search the water for food at night, detecting prey – crabs, crayfish, fish and worms – with their touch-sensitive paws. Raccoons also have excellent night vision, which not only helps them to locate prey but also makes it easier to spot ripe fruits in the dark.

A male crab-eating raccoon will occupy a territory that encompasses the home ranges of several females. He will control mating access to all these females until a younger, stronger male arrives to take control of the territory.

Crab-eating raccoons are smaller and slimmer than common raccoons, because they lack thick, insulating underfur.

Distribution: Costa Rica to northern Argentina; only found east of the Andes.
Habitat: Forests.
Food: Crustaceans, worms, fish, frogs, fruits and seeds.
Size: 45–90cm (18–35.5in); 2–12kg (4.5–26.5lb).
Maturity: 1 year.
Breeding: Single litter of 3–4 young born between July and September.
Life span: 5 years.
Status: Common.

Ringtail

Bassariscus astutus

This species is named after its bushy tail, which is ringed with black and white stripes, much like the tails of raccoons. However, ringtails have more agile, cat-like bodies than raccoons. Both the ringtail and the cacomistle, its relative, are largely solitary, and become aggressive towards intruders into their territory. A ringtail scent-marks its territory by regularly urinating at specific sites.

Ringtails are found from the western United States to southern Mexico. They are most commonly found in highland forests. They prefer rocky areas, such as canyons, but also occupy a range of lowland habitats, including deserts, woodland and shrubland. Although they prefer dry environments, they are also common near rivers, where food is easier to find. When ready to give birth, females make a den under a boulder or in a hollow tree. The young are suckled for ten weeks, after which the mother has to find food for the young. The father may stay nearby – and be tolerated by the female – and play with his offspring as they grow. The young disperse after about ten months.

Ringtails are most active at night, spending most of their time foraging. They are excellent climbers, and literally search high and low for rodents, squirrels, insects and other small animals. When they finish eating, they groom themselves by licking their fur, wiping their head clean with damp paws. If threatened, their tail bristles and arches over their head, making them look larger.

Distribution: From southern Oregon and eastern Kansas in the western United States to southern Mexico, including Baja California.
Habitat: Rocky areas, woodland and shrubland, and montane conifer forest.
Food: Small mammals, insects, birds, lizards, frogs, nuts and fruits.
Size: 30–42cm (12–16.5in); 0.8–1.4kg (1.75–3lb).
Maturity: 10 months.
Breeding: Single litter of 1–4 young born between April and July
Life span: 7 years.
Status: Common.

White-nosed coati

Nasua narica

The white-nosed coati is found in a variety of forest types, from rainforest to drier, high-altitude woodland. The silver hairs mixed into the grey-brown fur produce a grizzled look. The snout, which is long and flexible, has a white band near its tip. There are also white spots above and below each eye, and one on each cheek. The long tail, which has black rings, is raised above the body when the animal walks.

White-nosed coatis are most active during the day. They forage for insects on the ground and then retreat to the trees to spend the night. Males live alone, while females form bands of up to 20 individuals. Males under the age of about two are tolerated by the females, but once they approach sexual maturity the males are chased away.

In early spring, the most dominant male in the area is accepted into the female band. He mates with each of the females in a tree, after which they chase him off. Before giving birth, a female will leave the band and build a secluded nest in a tree. After about five weeks, the mother and her young rejoin the band. New bands form when existing ones become too large and split.

Distribution: From Arizona to Columbia and Ecuador.
Habitat: Forests.
Food: Insects.
Size: 40–70cm (15.75–27.5in); 3–5kg (6.5–11lb)
Maturity: 3 years.
Breeding: Up to 7 young born in summer.
Life span: 10 years.
Status: Common.

This species has plantigrade feet, meaning that its bodyweight is spread over the whole foot. This provides stability as the coati moves through the trees. (Only a few species are plantigrades, including bears and humans.) The long, semi-prehensile tail aids balancing and climbing.

RODENTS

The Rodentia *order is the largest, most widespread and most diverse mammal group. There are more than 2,000 species of rodent, making up almost half of all mammal species. The secret of the rodents' success is their teeth. Their long, chisel-shaped incisors keep growing throughout their lives. These teeth are self-sharpening, enabling rodents to eat almost any food, from wood to meat and even household rubbish.*

Grey squirrel

Sciurus carolinensis

Distribution: Eastern North America. Introduced to parts of Europe.
Habitat: Woodlands.
Food: Nuts, flowers and buds.
Size: 38–52cm (15–20.5in); 0.3–0.7kg (0.75–1.5lb).
Maturity: 10 months.
Breeding: 2 litters born each year with 2–4 young per litter.
Life span: 12 years.
Status: Common.

Grey squirrels are native to the open woodlands of eastern North America. They have also been introduced into parts of Europe, where they have out-competed the smaller red squirrels for food and breeding sites.

Grey squirrels feed primarily on the nuts and buds of many woodland trees. In summer, when they are most active just after dawn and before dusk, grey squirrels also eat insects. In winter, when most animals of their size are hibernating, grey squirrels spend their days eating stores of food which they buried throughout the previous summer. Grey squirrels may make dens in hollow trees, but are more likely to make nests, or dreys, from twigs and leaves in the boughs of trees.

There are two breeding seasons each year: one beginning in midwinter, the other in midsummer. Males begin to chase females through the trees a few days before they are receptive to mating. When females are ready, their vulvas become pink and engorged. Litters of three are born six weeks later.

Grey squirrels have, as their name suggests, greyish fur, although many individuals have reddish patches. Their tails, which have many white hairs, are bushier than those of most other squirrels.

Woodchuck

Marmota monax

Woodchucks are the largest squirrels in North America. These stocky-bodied rodents are well adapted to burrowing, with short, legs and curved claws.

Woodchucks are also called groundhogs or whistlepigs – the latter because of the shrill alarm call they make when threatened. Unlike most other squirrels, they eat the green parts of plants rather than the seeds and buds. They also eat bark and small twigs. Their natural habitat is the edge of forests or other open areas where there is plenty of cover. With the growth of agriculture, woodchucks have increased in number, making use of hedges beside open fields. They live alone, unlike most other ground squirrels.

Woodchucks hibernate in winter, living off the fat reserves that they build up over summer. Their winter sleep is much deeper than that of most squirrels. Mating takes place soon after hibernation ends. Female woodchucks have a single litter every year and males mate with more than one female. Young woodchucks are thrown out of their mother's burrow after a few months.

Distribution: Southern Canada southward through eastern North America.
Habitat: Woodland or open areas that have plenty of ground cover.
Food: Plant leaves and stems.
Size: 45–65cm (17.5–25.5in); 2–5kg (4.5–11lb).
Maturity: 2 years.
Breeding: 3–5 young born in May.
Life span: 6 years.
Status: Common.

Northern pocket gopher

Thomomys talpoides

Northern pocket gophers have robust, tubular bodies with short legs. Their forefeet have long claws and their tails are naked at the tip. Male gophers are much larger than females.

Pocket gophers spend a great deal of their time burrowing. They feed on the underground parts of plants, such as roots, tubers and bulbs. The gophers access their food by digging temporary feeding tunnels out and up from deeper and more permanent galleries, located 1–3m (3.25–10ft) underground. Gophers keep their burrow entrances blocked with earth most of the time, and rarely appear above ground during the day. At night they may move around on the surface.

Gophers carry food in pouches inside their cheeks to storage or feeding sites in their burrow systems. They do not drink water, and so get all of their liquid from plant juices.

Only during the mating season will a male be allowed into a female's burrow. Litters are born just 18 days after mating, which generally takes place in summer.

Distribution: Western North America from Canada to Mexico.
Habitat: Burrows under desert, prairie and forest.
Food: Roots, bulbs and leaves.
Size: 11–30cm (4.5–12in); 50–500g (1.75–17.75oz).
Maturity: 1 year.
Breeding: 1–10 young born in summer.
Life span: 2 years.
Status: Common.

Hoary marmot (*Marmota caligata*): 45–57cm (18–22.5in); 3.6–9.1kg (8–20lb)
This species occurs in the northern Pacific region of North America, from Idaho and Washington to Alaska. It inhabits the pine forests typical of cold climates and high mountains, and also the alpine meadows that bloom above the tree line in summer. It is called hoary because of the white hairs that grizzle its black fur, giving it a silver-grey appearance. Like other ground squirrels, the hoary marmot is an expert digger, using the long, robust claws on its forefeet for excavation. It hibernates through winter in large burrows.

Yellow-bellied marmot (*Marmota flaviventris*): 34.5–48cm (13.5–19in); 1.5–5kg (3.3–11lb)
These marmots occur in western North America, from south-western Canada to the US–Mexico border, typically in meadows, prairies and around forest edges. Their underside is lined with yellow fur, and there are yellow speckles on the neck. Yellow-bellied marmots live in extensive burrows, in groups comprising an adult male and two or three females. Hibernation burrows are dug several metres down to avoid ground frost. The diet consists of fruits, seeds and some insects.

Plains pocket gopher (*Geomys bursarius*): 19–36cm (7.5–14in); 300–450g (10.5–16oz)
This brown, burrowing animal lives on the plains between the Mississippi River and the Rocky Mountains, from Texas and north-eastern Mexico to the Canadian border. Common in open habitats, it also occurs in sparsely wooded areas where tree roots do not dominate the soil. It prefers deep sandy soils supporting plants that produce storage tubers and roots – the gopher's main food.

American beaver

Castor canadensis

Beavers are among the largest of all rodents. Family groups of beavers live in large nests, called lodges, in or near forest streams or small lakes. Beavers eat wood and other tough plant foods, which have to be soaked in water before being eaten.

They use their large front teeth to gnaw through the base of small trees. Sections of these logs are transported back to the lodge via a system of canals dug into the forest. If necessary, beavers will also dam a stream with debris to make a pool deep enough to store their food. A beaver colony may maintain a dam for several generations. The lodge has underwater entrances so beavers can swim out to their food supply even when the pool is frozen.

A beaver has webbed hind feet, a flattened tail for swimming and large front teeth for gnawing through wood. Its fur is coated with oil to keep it waterproof.

Distribution: North America.
Habitat: Streams and small lakes.
Food: Wood, leaves, roots and bark.
Size: 60–80cm (23.5–31.5in); 12–25kg (26.5–55lb).
Maturity: 1.5–2 years.
Breeding: 2–4 young born each spring.
Life span: 24 years.
Status: Locally common.

Alaska marmot

Marmota broweri

Alaska marmots are found only in small areas of the Brooks Mountains in northern Alaska, where they live amid rock slides and on boulder-strewn slopes. The marmots occupy the spaces formed under the rocks, burrowing into the permafrost with their strong foreclaws to make a living area. The plants that grow on the broken, rocky ground resemble those of tundra and alpine areas, and they provide the marmots with most of their food.

Alaska marmots are social animals living in colonies of up to 50 individuals. The colony shares and maintains a tunnel system, although each marmot has its own den. Within a few metres of each den is an observation post, where a marmot can keep a lookout for predators such as wolverines and bears. Members of the colony take turns to keep watch. The larger the colony, the less time each animal has to spend on sentry duty, and the more time it can devote to sunbathing, feeding and grooming. When danger is spotted, sentries let out a warning call and the colony disappears below ground.

The Alaska marmot has thick, coarse hair, which makes its heavyset body appear even more rounded. It is adapted to a burrowing lifestyle, with powerful legs and strong, sharp claws for digging. Its body weight varies during the year, since it has to build up substantial fat reserves in summer to see it through hibernation, when it loses one-fifth of its bodyweight.

Distribution: Brooks Mountains of northern Alaska.
Habitat: Scree, rocky outcrops and boulder fields.
Food: Grasses, forbs, fruits, seeds, legumes and occasionally insects.
Size: 54–65cm (21.5–25.5in); 2.5–4kg (5.5–8.75lb).
Maturity: 2 years.
Breeding: Single litter of 3–8 young born in spring, after a gestation period of about 5 weeks.
Life span: 14 years.
Status: Common.

Southern flying squirrel

Glaucomys volans

Southern flying squirrels inhabit woodlands, and their range extends from Quebec in eastern North America to Honduras in Central America. Their bodies resemble those of other squirrels, except that they have loose folds of skin that run along their sides and attach to their elongated arms and legs. When the limbs are outstretched, these skin folds are pulled tight to form wing-like membranes.

The flying squirrel cannot actually fly, since the lift force created by the flaps of skin is not enough to keep the animal aloft. It can, however, glide down from tall tree tops to lower branches or to the ground. The squirrel uses its flattened tail as a rudder during glides. For example, when it is time to land, the tail is lifted, altering the animal's centre of gravity and tilting the body upward. This causes the skin membrane to act as a brake, slowing the squirrel for a safe landing. Once on the ground, the squirrel scurries around to the other side of the tree to avoid predators that may have spotted the glide. To get back up the tree, it climbs in conventional squirrel fashion. Flying squirrels are nocturnal. As a result, they have large eyes that enable them to see well enough in the dark to perform complex and risky gliding manoeuvres.

Distribution: South-eastern Canada to Central America.
Habitat: Woodland.
Food: Nuts, seeds, fruit, insects, leaf buds, bark, young birds, young mice and fungi.
Size: 21–26cm (8.25–10.25in); 50–180g (1.75–6.5oz).
Maturity: 1 year.
Breeding: 2–3 young born twice a year, in spring and autumn.
Life span: Up to 10 years.
Status: Common.

The fur-covered flap of skin between a flying squirrel's fore and hind legs is called the gliding membrane. It extends along the side of the body from the ankle to the wrist, and tightens when the animal spreads its limbs during a "flight".

Black-tailed prairie dog

Cynomys ludovicianus

Distribution: From south-western Canada to north-eastern Mexico.
Habitat: Grassland.
Food: Grasses and forbs.
Size: 28–33cm (11–13in); 0.7–1.4kg (1.5–3lb).
Maturity: 2 years.
Breeding: 3–6 young born in early spring.
Life span: 5 years.
Status: Low risk.

This species of prairie dog inhabits the great prairies that roll south from south-western Canada to north-eastern Mexico. Black-tailed prairie dogs live in large colonies that excavate extensive communal burrows called towns. In frontier times, one huge town in west Texas was estimated to contain 400 million prairie dogs. Today, these rodents are much rarer. They have been exterminated in many places, partly because they devour cereal crops, and partly because grazing livestock injure themselves in the prairie dogs' burrow holes.

Prairie dogs are the most social of all ground squirrels. Each town is divided into smaller neighbourhoods, or coteries. Females stay in the coterie they were born in, forming a band of sisters and female cousins. However, young males set up home in the surrounding coteries. Generally there is one adult male per coterie, although brothers sometimes occupy a particularly large coterie.

This rodent is actually a type of ground squirrel, but it is referred to as a prairie "dog" because of its barking call. Black-tailed prairie dogs moult twice a year. After each moult, their hairs are a slightly different mixture of colours, ranging from red and yellow to silver and black. The tail has a black tip.

Olympic marmot (*Marmota olympus*): 46–53 cm (18–21in); 3–9kg (6.5–19.75lb)
Olympic marmots live on the rock-strewn alpine meadows of the Olympic Peninsula, Washington State, in the north-west of the United States. They live in groups of a about a dozen, made up of an adult male plus two or three females and their offspring. Females produce litters every two years. The marmots forage throughout their territory by day for seeds, fruits and insects. At dusk they follow scent trails back to their burrows.

Northern flying squirrel (*Glaucomys sabrinus*): 27–34cm (10.5–13.5in); 75–180g (2.5–5oz)
The northern flying squirrel is smaller than its southern relative, but it has the same gliding membrane for swooping between trees. It occurs from Alaska down North America's Pacific coast to California. Inland it is found in the Rockies, the Appalachians, across the Great Lakes and New England, and as far south as the Sierra Nevada of Mexico. This species inhabits a variety of woodland, from the pine-clad peaks of the sub-Arctic to the lowland deciduous forests of the Midwest. It eats nuts, fungi, fruits and lichens.

White-tailed prairie dog (*Cynomys leucurus*): 34–37cm (13.5–14.5in); weight unknown
Slightly larger than the black-tailed prairie dog, this rodent lives in the grasslands of the western United States. It does not live in such large social groups as its black-tailed cousin. White-tailed prairie dogs hibernate from late summer to spring, and breed as soon as they emerge from their winter burrows.

Mountain beaver

Aplodontia rufa

The main populations of mountain beavers are found in two mountain ranges, one extending from southern British Columbia to northern California, and the other from California to western Nevada. Although these forest-dwelling rodents can be found right up to the tree line at 2,200m (7,200ft), they are more common at lower levels. They prefer to be near a source of water, and they also need areas of deep soil in which they can dig their burrows. The burrows are often located under fallen logs.

Mountain beavers live solitary lives and rarely stray more than a few metres from their burrows. They rely on their senses of smell and touch to orientate themselves. Their diet consists of very tough plant food, and they have to digest it twice in order to get all the nutrients out of it. This involves eating pellets of faeces.

Despite their name, these animals are not true beavers, and they do not dig canals, fell trees or build dams.

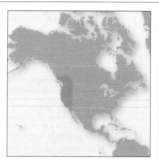

Distribution: British Columbia to California and Nevada.
Habitat: Forest and alpine meadows.
Food: Forbs, grasses and ferns.
Size: 30–46cm (12–18in); 0.8–1.5kg (1.75–3.25lb).
Maturity: 1 year.
Breeding: 2–3 young born in spring.
Life span: 5–10 years.
Status: Lower risk.

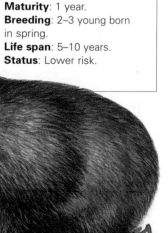

American red squirrel

Tamiasciurus hudsonicus

American red squirrels live in a range of forest habitats, from the pine forests of Canada's cold northern regions to the deciduous woodlands that grow further south as far as Arizona. Although the squirrel's name suggests that it has red hairs, in reality the fur changes colour throughout the year, ranging from a dark brown to ginger. The belly is covered in much paler fur. Each eye has a white ring around it.

Red squirrels live alone. They forage for food during the day and do not hibernate, although they become less active in the coldest regions during winter, when they survive on caches of food. They make their homes in tree hollows and similar small hideaways, including the abandoned holes of woodpeckers. In areas prone to severe frosts, red squirrels den in underground burrows to escape from the freezing temperatures.

During the breeding season, females are receptive to males for just one day. After mating, the male and female separate, and the female cares for the young on her own. Red squirrels eat a wide range of foods. Their diet largely consists of vegetable matter, but they will also feed on eggs, young birds and small mammals when the opportunity arises.

The tail of the American red squirrel is less bushy than those of related species, and it is more than half the length of the body. The squirrel's coat varies in colour, depending on the time of year.

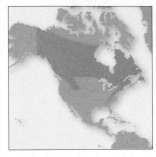

Distribution: North America, including Canada, New England, the Appalachian Mountains and northern Rockies.
Habitat: Forest.
Food: Seeds, fruits, nuts, bark, buds, shed antlers, small animals.
Size: 16–23cm (6.25–9); 140–250g (5–8.25oz).
Maturity: 1 year.
Breeding: Up to 8 young born in late winter. In warmer climates there are two breeding seasons, in the late winter and mid-summer.
Life span: 7 years.
Status: Common

White-tailed antelope squirrel

Ammospermophilus leucurus

Distribution: South-western North America, from Oregon to New Mexico and Baja California, Mexico.
Habitat: Deserts and scrublands.
Food: Leaves, seeds, plant stems, roots and fruits, as well as some insects and carrion.
Size: 18–24cm (7.4–9.4in); 96–117g (3.4–4oz).
Maturity: 1 year.
Breeding: Up to 10 young born in spring.
Life span: Unknown.
Status: Common.

White-tailed antelope squirrels inhabit the deserts of the south-western United States and Mexico's Baja California peninsula, and the arid scrub and grasslands of the Great Basin of the north-western United States. They prefer areas with sandy or gravel soils that can be dug into easily. The squirrels burrow into the loose soil to avoid the most intense heat of the day. They also enlarge the abandoned dens of other burrowing desert rodents, such as those of kangaroo rats.

White-tailed antelope squirrels are solitary for most of the year. They forage at dawn and in the late afternoon to avoid the worst of the heat. They retreat to shaded areas to eat, carrying food in their cheek pouches. At the height of summer, when it is especially hot, the squirrels lie underground, pressing their underside to the cool floor of the burrow. In the northern part of their range, winter temperatures often plummet to below freezing. In these situations, the squirrels huddle together in small groups to conserve their body heat.

The body of the white-tailed antelope squirrel is typical of ground squirrels, although the legs are slightly longer than in most species. The underside of the tail is white. This surface may reflect sunlight when the tail is held over the body.

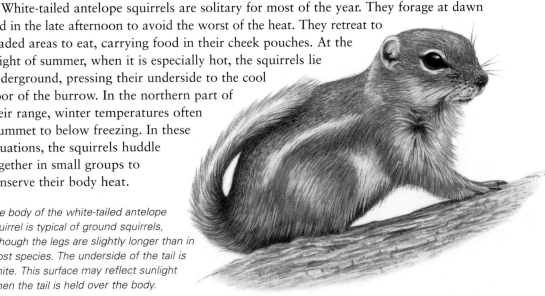

Cliff chipmunk (*Tamias dorsalis*): 21–25cm (8.5–10in); 61–74 g (2.15–2.6oz)
The cliff chipmunk is found in south-western United States and northern Mexico. It lives near cliffs in high desert hills covered by scrub, and makes dens under rocks. This solitary species is grey with dark stripes on the back. By day, the cliff chipmunk forages over a wide area, defending a relatively large territory for such a small animal. It searches for seeds, acorns and juniper berries. Up to six young are produced in spring.

Eastern fox squirrel (*Sciurus niger*): 45–70cm (18–27.5in); 0.7–1.2kg (1.5–2.5lb)
The eastern fox squirrel is an average-sized, tree-dwelling squirrel. Its back is usually covered in yellow-orange fur, but many individuals are completely black. In winter, the squirrel's ears grow tufts. This squirrel ranges from eastern Canada through the eastern and central United States and into northern Mexico. It is found in all forest types, but does best in those with a variety of tree species. This diurnal, largely solitary species eats a range of foods, from nuts, fruits and buds to insects, young birds and even dead fish.

Variegated squirrel (*Sciurus variegatoides*): 22–34cm (8.5–13.5in); 430–900g (15.25–32.75oz)
Variegated squirrels range from Chiapas in southern Mexico to Panama. They live in all types of tropical forest, from moist evergreen forests to drier deciduous or monsoon forests. The coats of variegated squirrels display a variety of bands and other patterns. These solitary animals spend most of their time up in the branches. They eat mainly plant matter such as nuts, fruits and flowers.

Grey-collared chipmunk

Tamias cinereicollis

Grey-collared chipmunks are not a widespread species, although they are common within their range in the south-western United States. Their preferred habitat is relatively dry mountain conifer forest, where they are rarely found below 1,950m (6,400 ft). However, grey-coloured chipmunks have also adapted to living in suburban areas at lower altitudes, following the recent rapid expansion of human settlements in the region. Here, the chipmunks are often found living under patios and in the foundations of buildings.

Grey-collared chipmunks are diurnal, being most active in the cool of the morning and evening. They live alone in burrows. In winter, they spend long periods underground to avoid the worst of the weather. They mate soon after emerging from their burrows in spring, and breed again in autumn before preparing for hibernation.

Grey-collared chipmunks, so called because of the distinctive colour bands on their body, have dextrous hands and unusually protruding incisors. They hold food in their hands and remove any unwanted material with their teeth, before pushing the food into a cheek pouch.

Distribution: Arizona and New Mexico.
Habitat: Mountain conifer forests.
Food: Nuts, berries, seeds and insects.
Size: 8–16cm (3.1–6.3in); 55–70g (2–2.5oz).
Maturity: 1 year.
Breeding: Litters of 2–5 born in spring and autumn.
Life span: 3 years.
Status: Common.

Eastern chipmunk

Tamias striatus

These rodents are found in eastern North America. They live in woodland and bushy habitats, feeding on nuts, seeds, mushrooms and fruits during the daytime. These solitary animals retire to burrows at night. The burrows are only just below the surface, but their tunnels may extend for several metres. The burrow entrances are hidden (the excavated earth is scattered), and they are often located in secluded areas to avoid discovery by predators such as foxes, snakes and birds of prey.

Eastern chipmunks forage for food in a small territory around the burrow. They chase away any intruders looking for food in that area. These chipmunks sleep through the winter in their burrows, waking regularly to feed on caches of food made during the autumn.

Chipmunks are named after the "chip chip" noises they frequently make, and often gather in groups to "sing" to each other. These noises and other vocalizations are used by chipmunks in communication.

Eastern chipmunks are larger than most chipmunks. Their most obvious feature is the pouched cheeks located inside their mouths. These pouches are used to store food.

Distribution: Eastern North America, from Quebec and Ontario to Iowa and Illinois
Habitat: Woodland.
Food: Nuts, seeds, mushrooms and fruits.
Size: 13–19cm (5.25–7.5in); 70–140g (2.5–5oz).
Maturity: 1 year.
Breeding: About 4 young are produced in early spring, and again in summer.
Life span: 1 year.
Status: Common.

North American porcupine

Erethizon dorsatum

North American porcupines are nocturnal animals that spend most of the night looking for food on the ground. However, they occasionally climb slowly into trees to find food. They cannot see very well, but have sensitive noses for detecting danger.

During the daytime, porcupines rest in hollow trees, caves or disused burrows. They regularly move from den to den throughout the year. They do not hibernate and keep feeding throughout the winter, but they will stay in their den during periods of harsh weather.

Porcupines live solitary lives, but do not defend territories, although they may attempt to drive away other porcupines from trees laden with food. When cornered by predators, porcupines turn their backs on their attackers and thrash around with their spiky tails. If the barbed quills penetrate the attacker's skin, they detach from the porcupine and work their way into the assailant's body.

In early winter, males seek out females and shower them with urine before mating. The males are chased away by the females after mating. They give birth to their litters in summer.

Porcupines have sharp, barbed quills (thickened hairs) on their rumps and short tails. In New World porcupines the quills are set individually in the skin; in Old World species they are grouped into clusters.

Distribution: North America, including Alaska and Canada, south to northern Mexico.
Habitat: Forest and brush.
Food: Wood, bark and needles in winter; buds, roots, seeds and leaves in summer.
Size: 64–80cm (25–31.5in); 3.5–7kg (7.75–15.5lb).
Maturity: 2.5 years.
Breeding: Single young born in summer.
Life span: 18 years.
Status: Common.

Capybara

Hydrochaerus hydrochaeris

Capybaras are the largest rodents in the world. They live in herds of about 20 individuals, feeding by day on the banks of rivers and in swampy areas. These grazing herbivores use their incisors to clip the grasses off at ground level. Although they are well suited to being in water, with eyes and nostrils high on the head and webbed hind feet, capybaras do not feed for long periods in water. They tend to use water as a refuge from predators and as a means of keeping cool on hot days. If startled, capybaras gallop into water and may swim to the safety of floating plants. When they surface, only their eyes and nostrils are visible.

Capybaras do not make permanent dens, but sleep in waterside thickets. Each herd contains several adults of both sexes plus their offspring, all conforming to a hierarchy. A single male leads the herd. Only he can mate with the females in the herd. Fights often break out between the other males as they attempt to improve their rank.

Capybaras can breed all year round, but mating is most common at the start of the rainy season. Usually females give birth to one litter, but two may be produced if conditions are favourable. The young are well developed at birth, and soon able to follow their mother and eat grass. They are weaned after about four months.

Distribution: Central America to Uruguay.
Habitat: Thickly vegetated areas around fresh water.
Food: Grass, grains, melons and squashes.
Size: 1–1.3m (3.25–4.25ft); 27–79kg (59–174lb).
Maturity: 15 months.
Breeding: Single litter of 5 young born at any time of year.
Life span: 10 years.
Status: Common.

Capybaras have bodies similar to guinea pigs, except that they are much bigger and more heavyset. The males possess large sebaceous (oil) glands on their short rounded snouts.

Pygmy mouse

Baiomys taylori

Pygmy mice are the smallest rodents in the Americas, little more than the size of a person's thumb. They live in areas where plants, logs and rocks provide them with plenty of cover. The mice create networks of runs through undergrowth and under rocks, leaving piles of droppings at junctions. These may act as signposts or be signals to other mice in their network. Pygmy mice are most active at dawn and dusk, but will also feed throughout the day.

At night they sleep in nests made from plants and twigs. They do not live in groups as such, but will tolerate the presence of other mice close by. Pygmy mice can breed at a young age. Females can become pregnant after just a month of life. They breed throughout the year, often producing several litters per year. Both parents care for the young, which are born in nests inside shallow dips dug into the ground or in secluded cavities under logs or rocks.

The pygmy mouse's ears are smaller and rounder than those of most mice. It has black and brown hairs on its back with lighter red and brown fur underneath.

Distribution: South-western United States to central Mexico.
Habitat: Dry scrub.
Food: Stems, leaves, insects and seeds.
Size: 5–8cm (2–3.25in); 7–8g (0.2–0.3oz).
Maturity: Females 28 days; males 80 days.
Breeding: Several litters of 1–5 young each year.
Life span: 2 years.
Status: Common.

Prehensile-tailed porcupine (*Coendou prehensilis*): 30–60cm (12–23.5in); 0.9–5kg (2–11lb)
Primarily a forest dweller, this porcupine is found from Venezuela to southern Brazil and the foothills of the Bolivian Andes, and also on the Caribbean island of Trinidad. It occurs in lowland and coastal areas, and up to 2,500m (8,200ft). Prehensile-tailed porcupines eat plants, especially tender leaves, stems and flowers. They gnaw at the young wood under bark, and sometimes raid commercial fruit crops. After spending the day resting in trees they forage in darkness, winding their tail around branches for extra support when moving through the trees. The porcupines rely on their sharp quills to ward off predators, but they may try to frighten aggressors away by stamping their feet. If all else fails, they curl up into a ball to protect themselves from attack.

Bahamian hutia (*Geocapromys ingrahami*): 20–60cm (8–23.5in); 5kg (11lb)
This unusual rodent lives in the Bahamas; subspecies are found on other Caribbean islands and on the Venezuelan mainland. Bahamian hutias live in forested habitats, spending time both on the ground and in trees. They are mainly vegetarian, eating eat bark, nuts, leaves and fruits. The body is rat-like in form, although the species is more closely related to cavies and coypus.

Southern mountain cavy (*Microcavia australis*): 22cm (8.5in); 275g (9.75oz)
This species, a relative of domestic guinea pigs, is found in Argentina, southern Chile and southern Bolivia, where it lives in dry brush habitats. It is rarely seen, since it moves through runs hidden among the thick vegetation. Where the cover is less thick, southern mountain cavies dig burrows. They feed during the day, climbing in shrubs to get at the most tender leaves.

Guinea pig

Cavia aperea

Guinea pigs, or cavies as they are also known, are most active in the twilight hours – around dawn and dusk. At these times, most predators are less active because their eyes cannot cope with the rapidly changing light levels. Guinea pigs are found in a wide range of habitats and altitudes, even living high up in the Andes Mountains.

Guinea pigs generally rest underground or in thickets. They may dig their own burrows, but are more likely to take over holes made by other animals. When on the move, these rodents follow well-trodden paths to areas where food is available.

Guinea pigs live in small groups of fewer than ten individuals. Many groups may crowd around a large supply of food, forming a temporary mass of rodents. The groups have hierarchies, with single males and females ruling over the others. Contenders for the top positions in the group may fight each other to the death. Breeding takes place throughout the year.

Distribution: Colombia to Argentina, excluding the Amazon Basin.
Habitat: Grassland, swamp and rocky areas.
Food: Plants.
Size: 20–40cm (8–15.5in); 0.5–1.5kg (1–3.25lb).
Maturity: 3 months.
Breeding: Up to 5 litters per year.
Life span: 8 years.
Status: Common.

Although domestic guinea pigs often have long, soft coats of many colours and patterns, wild specimens have shorter and coarser fur, generally made up of grey, brown and black hairs.

Mara

Dolichotis patagonum

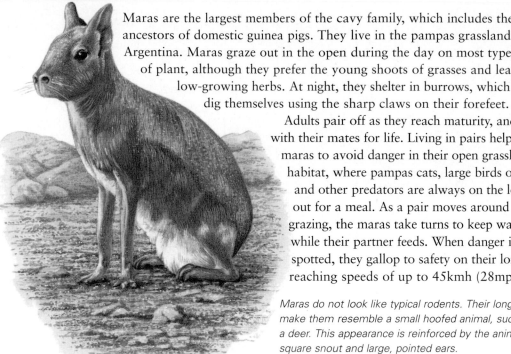

Maras are the largest members of the cavy family, which includes the wild ancestors of domestic guinea pigs. They live in the pampas grasslands of Argentina. Maras graze out in the open during the day on most types of plant, although they prefer the young shoots of grasses and leafy, low-growing herbs. At night, they shelter in burrows, which they dig themselves using the sharp claws on their forefeet.

Adults pair off as they reach maturity, and stay with their mates for life. Living in pairs helps the maras to avoid danger in their open grassland habitat, where pampas cats, large birds of prey and other predators are always on the look out for a meal. As a pair moves around grazing, the maras take turns to keep watch while their partner feeds. When danger is spotted, they gallop to safety on their long legs, reaching speeds of up to 45kmh (28mph).

Maras do not look like typical rodents. Their long legs make them resemble a small hoofed animal, such as a deer. This appearance is reinforced by the animal's square snout and large, pointed ears.

Distribution: Central and southern Argentina.
Habitat: Open pampas grassland and dry scrub.
Food: Grass and herbs.
Size: 73–80cm (29–32in); 8–16kg (18–36lb).
Maturity: 6 months.
Breeding: Litters of up to 3 young born two or three times a year.
Life span: 15 years.
Status: Lower risk.

Northern viscacha (*Lagidium peruanum*): 30–45cm (12–18in); 0.9–1.6kg (2–3.5lb)
While these animals resemble rabbits, with long pointed ears and large hind feet, they are actually relatives of chinchillas. Living high up the Peruvian Andes, they occupy dry rocky areas that exist between the tree line and the snow line. Viscachas live in large colonies of up to 80 individuals. They survive by eating the grasses, lichens and mosses that grow in the harsh alpine conditions.

Green acouchi (*Myoprocta acouchy*): 32cm (12.5in); weight unknown
These relatively large, long-legged rodents are related to agoutis. The fur is often greenish, but it can also be red or grey. Green acouchis live in the forests of the Amazon Basin and the surrounding highlands. They are most active by day, and bury food to be used in times of drought. They eat fruits, nuts, succulents and roots, and may be pests in cassava and peanut plantations.

Social tuco-tuco (*Ctenomys sociabilis*): 18–24cm (7–9.5in); 180g (6.5oz)
This grassland species of southern Argentina occurs between the Andes Mountains and the Patagonian Desert. Social tuco-tucos feed on the grasses and sedges that grow around their burrow entrances. These rodents live in colonies containing many small family groups. Each group comprises several closely related females. During the breeding season, a male is accepted into the group's den and allowed to breed with the females. He is then chased away, and moves to another group elsewhere in the colony.

Chinchilla

Chinchilla lanigera

The chinchilla's dense coat helps it to survive on the bleak, windswept Andean mountain slopes. In the past, chinchillas were hunted for their striking blue-grey fur in an unsustainable fashion. As a result, wild chinchillas, which once ranged across the High Andes from Peru and Bolivia to Chile, are now only found in the mountains of northern Chile. Today, chinchillas are a protected species. They are bred in captivity for their fur (and make good pets), although wild animals are still occasionally hunted illegally.

Chinchillas shelter in rock crevices by day. They eat alpine plants, and do most of their feeding in the gloom of dawn and dusk. They may form colonies of up to 100 individuals. On sunny days, colony members can be seen sunbathing at the entrances to their dens.

Chinchilla fur is thick and soft, with about 60 hairs growing out of each follicle. Coats made from chinchilla fur were once highly valued. Hunting wild chinchillas for their fur is now illegal.

Distribution: Northern Chile.
Habitat: Arid mountain slopes.
Food: Grass, seeds, insects and birds' eggs.
Size: 22–38cm (8.5–15in); 500–800g (17.75–28.25oz).
Maturity: 8 months.
Breeding: Litters of 2–3 young born in spring and summer.
Life span: 10 years.
Status: Vulnerable.

Brazilian agouti

Dasyprocta leporina

Brazilian agoutis are found throughout Brazil and the surrounding South American countries, from dense rainforests to suburban back gardens. They prefer areas with plenty of cover, and are most common close to bodies of water.

Brazilian agoutis are cautious creatures. They are rarely seen out in the open, preferring to move slowly but surely through undergrowth. They are primarily diurnal, although they do feed on bright moonlit nights. Their diet consists mainly of seeds and fruit. When they sense danger, the agoutis dash away on their long, powerful legs. These animals pair up for life. They travel in small groups made up of the breeding pair and their offspring. The young, which can run within an hour of birth, remain with their parents until they are five or six months old. Males are more likely to leave the family group than females. These lone males are often forced to set up home in unsuitable open territory, where they are more likely to be picked off by ocelots and other predators.

Distribution: Northern South America, east of the Andes.
Habitat: Areas with plenty of cover, mainly forests.
Food: Seeds, fruits, leaves and insects.
Size: 41–62cm (16–24.5in); 3–6kg (6.5–13.25lb).
Maturity: 1 year.
Breeding: Litters of up to 3 pups born twice a year.
Life span: 15 years.
Status: Common

Brazilian agoutis are also known as red-rumped agoutis because of the red patch on their hind quarters. Their relatively long legs make them look different from most other rodents. They often squat on their back legs, like squirrels, when feeding.

Coypu

Myocastor coypus

Coypus, or nutrias, live in wetland habitats from southern Brazil and Bolivia to Tierra del Fuego at the southern tip of South America. They have very large, orange-tinged incisors. These are always visible, since the mouth closes behind them in order to keep out water when the animal is swimming.

Coypus are nocturnal feeders, foraging for food both in and out of the water. These small, largely herbivorous rodents eat aquatic plants, but they will occasionally take freshwater molluscs such as mussels and water snails. They are able to remain submerged for up to 10 minutes. When not feeding, the coypus sunbathe and groom each other on platforms of floating vegetation. They may shelter in the burrow of another animal or dig their own burrow, which can be a simple tunnel or a complex system of chambers and passages.

Coypus live in groups of a single adult male, several females (often related to each other) and up to a dozen of their young. Females may produce their single litter at any time of year, and the males play no part in raising the young. Females tend to stay with their family group, while young males disperse.

Distribution: Southern South America, east of the Andes; introduced to the Mississippi Delta.
Habitat: Marshes; river and lake banks.
Food: Water plants and freshwater molluscs.
Size: 47–58cm (18.5–23in); 5–10kg (11–22lb).
Maturity: 6 months.
Breeding: Single litter of about 6 young born at any time of year.
Life span: 6 years.
Status: Lower risk.

Coypus look like large water rats, with soft, thick underfur covered by longer, well-oiled hairs. The hind feet are webbed to help with swimming and moving through boggy ground. The unwebbed forefeet are used for holding food.

Brown lemming

Lemmus sibiricus

Contrary to popular belief, lemmings do not commit suicide. During favourable years, the lemmings' ability to reproduce very quickly leads to population explosions of amazing proportions. As the population size goes up, space becomes more and more difficult to find, and young are pushed away from the best habitat, down the mountains and into the valleys. Lemmings are good swimmers when they have to be, but they have their limits. During dispersal, young lemmings often try to cross large bodies of water that are beyond their swimming capabilities, drowning in the process. It is this behaviour that gave rise to the misconception that they kill themselves.

In summer, lemmings spend much of their time underground in burrows, but when the ground starts to freeze in autumn, they cannot dig through the ground and are forced to forage on the surface. They do not hibernate in the harsh winter, but tunnel under the snow in search of food. The tunnels keep them out of sight from predators such as snowy owls, which are heavily reliant on lemmings as a source of food.

Unlike other lemming species, the brown lemming does not change the colour of its winter coat.

Distribution: Arctic mainland and islands of northern Canada, Alaska and Siberia.
Habitat: Arctic tundra grassland and sub-Arctic tundra above the treeline.
Food: Mosses, grasses and sedges.
Size: 13–18cm (5–7in); 50–140g (2–4.75oz).
Maturity: 5–6 weeks.
Breeding: These prolific breeders may produce as many as 8 litters per year, each of up to 12 young; gestation is about 3 weeks.
Life span: Less than 2 years.
Status: Common.

Southern bog lemming

Synaptomys cooperi

With their dark, thick hair, bog lemmings look almost round. However, their bodies are small and they are no more robust than other lemmings or voles. They have powerful jaws and the long, orange-coloured incisors typical of rodents, which are kept sharp by frequent gnawing. The fur is grey-grizzled by silver hairs mixed in with the darker ones. Female southern bog lemmings have six nipples, while in northern bog lemmings, their closest relatives, the females have eight.

Southern bog lemmings live in the eastern region of North America, from Labrador to Ontario and Kansas to North Carolina. They are most often found in bogs, generally sphagnum bogs, so-called because of the large amounts of thick sphagnum moss that dominate the habitat. However, these lemmings are also found in less water-logged areas, such as pine forests and cultivated fields.

Southern bog lemmings may be active by day or night, but they are largely nocturnal. They eat a wide range of plant foods. By gnawing through the base of the stems, they fell tall plants so that they can eat the tender leaves, shoots and fruits growing higher up. Bog lemmings construct tunnels and subsurface runways, or utilize those made by other small mammals. They use dried grass and sedge to build concealed nests in clumps of grass, or under tree stumps and sphagnum mounds.

Bog lemmings breed up to three times a year, although in northern areas more than once is probably unlikely.

Distribution: Eastern North America.
Habitat: Bogs and wet grasslands.
Food: Grasses, moss, sedges, fruits, mushrooms and roots.
Size: 11–14cm (4.25–5.5 inches); 20–50g (0.75–1.75oz).
Maturity: 5 weeks.
Breeding: Litters of 1–8 young (average 3) are produced 2–3 times a year; most young are born between April and September.
Life span: 2 years.
Status: Common.

Muskrat

Ondatra zibethicus

Distribution: Northern Canada and Alaska to Gulf of Mexico.
Habitat: Swamps and other wetlands.
Food: Water plants.
Size: 22–33cm (8.5–13in); 0.7–1.8kg (1.5–4lb).
Maturity: 7 months.
Breeding: 6 young born in summer.
Life span: 3 years.
Status: Common.

Muskrats live in most of Canada and the United States, excluding the high Arctic region. At the beginning of the last century, muskrats were introduced to Eurasia, and they have thrived in parts of Scandinavia and northern Russia, as well as in warmer parts of Siberia.

Muskrats live in large family groups along riverbanks and in marshes, particularly where there is plenty of bankside vegetation to provide shelter. They dig burrows into the banks, which they access through underwater entrances. When living in more open wetlands, they make domed nests from grass. Muskrats are largely nocturnal, but crepuscular (active at dawn and dusk) as well.

In the south of their range, muskrats breed at all times of the year. In the northern areas, the long winters limit the breeding season to the summer.

Muskrats are semi-aquatic animals, spending time both in and out of water. Their fur is oily to make it waterproof, and the hind feet are webbed. These rodents use their scaly tails for steering while swimming. Muskrats eat water plants and small aquatic animals, including mussels and crayfish.

Round-tailed muskrat (*Neofiber alleni*): 38–54cm (15–21.5in); weight unknown
The round-tailed muskrat, or Florida water rat, occurs from southern Georgia and across Florida, including the islands off the Florida coast. It is smaller than other muskrats, which also have more flattened tails. Round-tailed muskrats live in swamps, lakes and other wetland areas. They build a dome-shaped lodge from felled vegetation, with a grass-lined chamber inside. Round-tailed muskrats are declining as their habitat is lost to development along Florida's coast.

Black rat (*Rattus rattus*): 16–22cm (6.25–8.5in); 70–300g (2.5–10.5oz)
Originally from India, this rat is found wherever humans have settled, including throughout the Americas. It even survives in Arctic settlements, but no sustainable population exists in Antarctica. Adaptability is the secret of the black rat's success. Its medium-sized body makes it a good climber, jumper, swimmer and runner. Its long teeth allow it to tackle almost any food, and its intelligence means that it can investigate new areas quickly and remember the location of food sources.

Brown rat (*Rattus norvegicus*): 20–30cm (8–12in); 275–575g (9.75–20.25oz)
The brown rat, or Norway rat, has spread from its native forest habitat in China and is now common on all continents except Antarctica. Brown rats share the characteristics that make its relative the black rat a success. A female brown rat can produce 60 offspring in one year if conditions are right, illustrating just how quickly these rodents can take over a new habitat.

Hairy-tailed bolo mouse

Bolomys lasiurus

Hairy-tailed bolo mice occur throughout central South America, from Bolivia and Brazil to northern Argentina. They live in dry grasslands and savannahs, and sometimes around the edges of forests. More than four-fifths of their diet is made up of grass seeds. The rest consists of leaves and insects. The mice become especially dependent on insects after the savannahs have been swept by fires at the end of the dry season.

Hairy-tailed bolo mice are most active during the daytime. They produce extensive burrow systems with several entrances, giving easy access to the safety of the burrow when predators approach. Male mice occupy a large territory that includes the home ranges of several females. They prevent rival males from entering the territory. Most mating occurs in the rainy season.

Distribution: Central South America.
Habitat: Savannah.
Food: Seeds, leaves and insects.
Size: 18cm (7in); 35g (1.25oz).
Maturity: Unknown.
Breeding: 3–6 young per litter; most litters produced in wet season (January–March), although breeding occurs all year round.
Life span: Unknown.
Status: Common.

These mice are named for their hair-covered tail. Unusually for mice, the tail is shorter than the body length. The male hairy-tailed bolo mice are slightly larger than the females.

Meadow jumping mouse

Zapus hudsonius

Meadow jumping mice have enormously long tails – up to 16.5cm (6.5in) or more – that are much longer than their body length. They also have large hind feet, up to 3.5cm (1.4in) long, with which they propel themselves forward in great bounds. The fur on the back is greyish-brown, the flanks are yellowish-brown, and the underside is whitish. The tail lacks the white tip seen on woodland jumping mice. The meadow jumping mouse is the only mammal species with 18 teeth. Females are sometimes larger than males.

Meadow jumping mice live across the northern part of North America, from the Atlantic coast of the United States to the Great Plains east of the Rocky Mountains. These mice are also found as far south as New Mexico. Meadow jumping mice live in any area with a layer of undergrowth in which they can move around unnoticed. Despite their name, they do live in woodlands, but prefer the more open habitat of grasslands.

Meadow jumping mice live solitary lives. They are most active during the night, and make their way through the dense undergrowth by following the runways made in the grass by voles. They can hop a considerable distance, up to 15cm (6in) in one bound. These mice can also climb trees, swim across streams and dig into the ground.

They forage for food over a wide area, resting in nests made of grass during the day. Their diet consists mainly of seeds, but insects are important in spring. In winter, they hibernate in deep underground burrows. They begin breeding soon after emerging in spring.

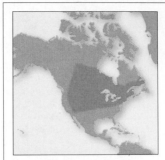

Distribution: Northern North America, from southern Alaska to Labrador and northern Georgia; isolated populations occur in the mountains of Arizona and New Mexico.
Habitat: Moist grasslands.
Food: Seeds, berries, fruits and insects.
Size: 7.5–11cm (3–4.3in); 12–30g (0.5–1oz).
Maturity: 2 months.
Breeding: 2–3 litters of 5 or 6 young born in spring and summer; gestation is about 18 days.
Life span: 1 year.
Status: Common.

Woodland jumping mouse

Napaeozapus insignis

Woodland jumping mice live in the north-eastern region of North America, from central Canada to Labrador, and to the Appalachian Mountains of the United States. They live in forests, being most common in the pine forests that grow at higher latitudes and on high mountains. In the southern part of their range, many of the forests have been reduced in size by agriculture, so these mice are only found in the small patches that remain.

Woodland jumping mice are nocturnal, but often come out to feed on cloudy days. They dig their own burrows and build grass-lined nests inside. When out foraging, the mice cover the entrances to their burrows with vegetation.

This species hibernates underground for at least six months of the year, during which time it may lose more than one-third of its bodyweight.

When the mice awake, they breed immediately. In warmer parts of their range, the mice may produce two litters if warm weather persists for long enough. The young are weaned when they are about five weeks old.

Like the meadow jumping mouse, the woodland jumping mouse has a long tail, which can measure up to 16cm (6.3in) long. The fur is arranged in three coloured bands. The underside is pale, almost white. The sides of the body are pale brown, with long, black guard hairs. The upper surface has a wide, dark brown stripe from the head to the base of the tail. Females are slightly larger than males, and mice in the northern parts of the range tend to be about 12 per cent larger than individuals from southern parts.

Distribution: North-eastern North America, from south-eastern Manitoba to Labrador and Pennsylvania and south along the Appalachians to northern Georgia.
Habitat: Pine and mixed forests.
Food: Fruits, seeds, fungi and insects.
Size: 8–10cm (3–4in); 17–35g (0.5–1.25oz).
Maturity: 8 months
Breeding: 1–2 litters of 2–7 young produced in summer; gestation is 23–29 days.
Life span: 3 years.
Status: Common.

Giant pocket gopher

Orthogeomys grandis

Distribution: Central America and Mexico
Habitat: Burrows under forests.
Food: Roots, turnips, tubers, nuts and seeds.
Size: 22–28cm (8.5–11in); 830g (29.25oz).
Maturity: 3 months.
Breeding: Up to 10 young born in a single litter at any time of year.
Life span: 2 years.
Status: Common.

Giant pocket gophers are found in Mexico and Central America. They spend most of their time in tunnels that they excavate under forests and farmland. Their body is adapted for moving through burrows in soft ground. Flaps close their ears to keep out dirt, while the eyelids seal the eyes and thick tears wash away any soil from the eye's surface. As the gophers use their teeth to cut through soil, the mouth closes behind the teeth, so they do not swallow earth.

Giant pocket gophers dig two kinds of tunnel. Long, winding tunnels just below the surface are used to find food. Deeper tunnel networks are used to make dens, where young are born and food is stored. Large mounds of earth mark the entrances to these tunnels. The entrances are generally sealed so that flood water and predators, such as snakes, cannot get in. Pocket gophers are named after the fur-lined pockets on the outside of their cheeks, which these rodents use for transporting food. The pockets can be turned inside-out for cleaning.

The gopher's body is covered in sensitive whiskers that can detect vibrations made by other gophers moving through tunnels. The naked tail is also highly sensitive to touch, and is used to feel objects in the dark. When the tunnels get too hot, excess body heat is released through the tail.

Pale kangaroo mouse (*Microdipodops pallidus*): 6.5–7.5cm (2.5–3in); 10–17g (0.25–0.5oz)
Pale kangaroo mice are found in western Nevada and the dry regions of eastern California. They prefer dry shrublands and semi-deserts with sandy or gravel soils, often digging their burrows at the base of shrubs. The kangaroo mouse moves by hopping on its long hind feet, using its tail for balance. The soles of the hind feet are covered in hairs that make them much wider, preventing the mouse from sinking in soft sand. This species has long, silky, tan-coloured fur. Pale kangaroo mice eat mainly seeds, nibbling off the hard husks with their front teeth and carrying the food back to their burrows inside cheek pouches. They feed at night and live alone.

Bristle-spined rat (*Chaetomys subspinosus*): 42cm (16.5in); 1.3kg (2.75lb)
These rodents are sometimes called three-spined porcupines. They live in northern and central Brazil, where they occupy both bushlands and forest habitats. Unlike true porcupines, the hairs of bristle-spined rats are more like stiff bristles than sharp quills. These bristles cover the head, neck and forelimbs of the rodent. The tail is long and scaly. Bristle-spined rats are slow-moving animals that jump and climb through trees looking for food, which is mostly made up of fruits and nuts. The rats are nocturnal, sleeping in tree hollows or rock crevices. Bristle-spined rats are found only in small areas of Brazil. Their habitats are gradually being destroyed by logging, agriculture and industry, and this species is now classified as vulnerable.

Desert kangaroo rat

Dipodomys deserti

Desert kangaroo rats live in arid regions of the south-western United States and Mexico, where there is very little vegetation. They inhabit some of the hottest and driest places on Earth, including Death Valley in California. They are also found on desert peaks up to about 1,700m (5,600ft). Desert kangaroo rats only survive where there are wind-blown sand-dunes. These sand-dunes contain enough food for the rats, including old plants covered by sand and seeds blown into the dune by the wind. The rats do not need to drink water, because they get all the water they need from the plants they eat.

Desert kangaroo rats dig complex burrows inside the sand-dunes. The burrows have a central nest chamber and several side spaces for storing food. These solitary rodents only emerge at night, and so avoid the heat of the day. With reduced front limbs, they leap around on their long back legs like kangaroos. The tail may be up to 21cm (8.5in) long.

Distribution: South-western North America.
Habitat: Sand-dunes.
Food: Seeds and dried leaves.
Size: 12–16cm (5–6.5in); 95–135g (3.3–4.7oz).
Maturity: 2 months.
Breeding: 2–3 litters of up to 6 young born January–July.
Life span: 5 years.
Status: Common.

This species stores seeds and other foods inside its fur-lined cheek pockets. Male desert kangaroo rats are slightly larger than females. Curiously, desert kangaroo rats have thicker hair than species of kangaroo rat that live in cooler regions.

Red tree vole

Arborimus longicaudus

Red tree voles live in well-established forests. Most of the forests in their range, which stretches from northern California to southern Washington, are populated with fir and spruce trees. They also prefer areas that get a lot of rain. The voles spend almost their entire lives up trees. Only the males regularly come to the ground, where they den in burrows at the foot of trees. The females build their nests among the branches at all heights, from the lowest branches to the very tops of trees.

Apart from mothers raising young, red tree voles are solitary animals. However, they sometimes live in loose clusters or colonies, in which individuals avoid interaction with each other but gather together in one tree or stand of trees. These voles are nocturnal. They collect needles (predominantly those of the Douglas fir) and bring them back to their nests, then feed on their store of needles during the day. They obtain the water they need from the needles and the dew that forms on them. At night they are cautious creatures. If they are disturbed, the voles will leap to lower branches and head down to the ground, where they hide in the undergrowth.

These small rodents have fur that ranges from ginger to cinnamon. The females tend to be larger than the males. Red tree voles only have claws on four of their five digits. The first digit has a nail instead. They nest high up in fir trees.

Distribution: Pacific North-west region of United States; west of the Cascade Mountains, from southern Washington to northern Carolina.
Habitat: Conifer forests.
Food: Conifer needles.
Size: 9.5–11cm (3.75–4.3in); 25–50g (1–1.75oz).
Maturity: 2 months.
Breeding: 3 litters of up to 3 young born mainly in spring and summer.
Life span: 2 years.
Status: Common.

Western heather vole

Phenacomys intermedius

The colour of this heather vole's long, soft fur varies across its range, but it is largely greyish brown, with a slightly lighter underside. There are sometimes orange hairs growing on the ears. At 2.5–4cm (1–1.6in), the short tail is only about as long as the hind feet. The heather vole so closely resembles another species, the meadow vole, that the two can sometimes only be identified by examining their skull characteristics and teeth.

The western heather vole occurs across the western United States as far south as New Mexico. In Canada, the range extends to the Yukon and eastward to the Atlantic coast of Labrador. As its name suggests, this vole lives in highland meadows and more exposed alpine tundras, where heather is common. However, this species is also found in alpine and northern lowland forests, where conifers such as aspen and spruce predominate.

Unusually for a small species living in such a northerly range, heather voles do not hibernate and are active all year round. During the summer, they construct an underground burrow with an entrance hidden by fallen leaves. In winter, the voles cannot dig into the frozen ground. Instead they make nests in the snow, generally underneath a shrub or log for added protection from the elements. The voles keep warm by lining their snow holes with moss, lichens and twigs.

These voles are solitary except during the breeding season, when males fight with each other and females with young become aggressive toward intruders.

Distribution: Western United States, as far south as New Mexico, and across Canada, from the Yukon to Labrador.
Habitat: Highland meadows, spruce, pine and aspen forests.
Food: Bark, buds, heathers, twigs, seeds, berries, lichens and fungi.
Size: 9–12cm (3.5–4.8in); 30–50g (1–1.75oz).
Maturity: 6 weeks.
Breeding: Up to 3 litters of about 4 young each are produced in summer; gestation is 19–24 days.
Life span: 1 year.
Status: Common.

Azara's grass mouse

Akodon azarae

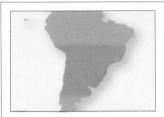

Distribution: Central and southern South America.
Habitat: Undergrowth.
Food: Leaves, fruits, insects and seeds.
Size: 7.5–15cm (3–6in); 10–45g (0.25–1.5oz).
Maturity: 2 months.
Breeding: 2 litters of 3–4 young produced in summer.
Life span: 1 year.
Status: Lower risk.

Azara's grass mouse lives in the tall-grass pampas of central Argentina and southern Brazil. It is also found in Bolivia, Paraguay and Uruguay. These mice dig their burrows in the undergrowth close to habitat boundaries, where thick vegetation gives way to more open terrain. Here, they can return to the safety of the plant cover after foraging in the open. This sort of habitat is common in artificial landscapes such as gardens and along roadsides. In winter, this species is also often found in flooded lowland areas. However, at warmer times of year the mice head for high ground.

Azara's grass mice live in groups made up of both males and females. Mice born in autumn will survive for about a year, but those born in spring are unlikely to last more than eight months, because many adult mice struggle to find shelter during winter.

The tail of Azara's grass mouse can be up to 10cm (4in) long. Being a small mammal, it can fluctuate in weight easily. It is heaviest in spring, but may be half this weight by the autumn.

House mouse (*Mus musculus*): 6.5–9.5cm (2.5–3.75in); 12–25g (0.5–1oz)
From its original range, which stretched from the Mediterranean Sea to China, the house mouse has now spread around the world, making its home wherever humans live. The key to its success is its ability to make use of whatever food sources people provide. Today, house mice are considered to be a major pest, causing billions of dollars' worth of damage to food stores worldwide every year. They also damage buildings, woodwork, furniture and clothing, and are known to carry various diseases, including typhus and salmonella. However, house mice are virtually unrivalled in their capacity to adapt to new surroundings. Their generalist habits, rapid breeding rate and talent for slipping into places unnoticed has enabled them to become possibly the most numerous mammal species in the world today.

Mexican volcano mouse (*Neotomodon alstoni*): 10–13cm (4–5in); 40–60g (1.5–2oz)
The Mexican volcano mouse inhabits the volcanic mountains of central Mexico, where it is found in pine forests between 2,600m and 4,600m (8,500–15,000ft). These forests differ from conifer habitats found further north because they have a layer of grass beneath the trees. Mexican volcano mice live in burrows under the rocks that stud the grass. These opportunistic feeders eat seeds, insects, leaves and many other foods. Young are produced between June and September, with about three mice in each litter. The young mice are ready to breed themselves after about five months, which is a slow maturation for a mouse species. Observations also suggest that these mice live for a long time, perhaps up to five years.

Bushy-tailed woodrat

Neotoma cinerea

Distribution: Western North America, from Arctic Canada to Arizona.
Habitat: From woodland to desert.
Food: Insects, bark, fruits and succulent plants.
Size: 13–29cm (5–11.5in); 170–580g (6–20.5oz).
Maturity: Not known.
Breeding: 3 litters of up to 6 young born in spring and summer.
Life span: 1 year.
Status: Common.

Bushy-tailed woodrats have a huge range. They can be found from the dry scrub of northern Arizona and New Mexico to the icy forests at the edge of the Arctic in Canada. No other woodrat lives in such cold environments as this species. Within this range, bushy-tailed woodrats occupy a number of habitats, including near-desert and dense pine forest. As odd as this may sound, the woodrat has similar problems to overcome in both environments, since both deserts and frozen forests have little running water. Woodrats are most common in mountainous regions.

Like all woodrats, this species builds middens, where the rodent deposits its waste nest material and faeces, which are solidified with calcium carbonate and calcium oxalate crystals from the woodrat's urine. Many generations of woodrat will use the same midden, and nests may even be made within it.

Male bushy-tailed woodrats are nearly twice as heavy as females. Woodrats that live in cooler, more northerly parts of the range tend to be larger than those that live in warmer areas to the south. The tail of this species can reach about 25cm (10in) in length.

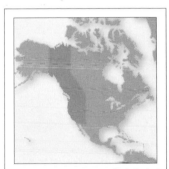

RABBITS

Rabbits, hares and pikas belong to the mammal order Lagomorpha. *Most of the lagomorphs that live in the Americas are found north of Mexico. Unlike their cousins in Europe, most American rabbits do not dig burrows. Like hares, they generally shelter above ground. The only rabbit to dig its own burrow is the pygmy rabbit, which is also the smallest rabbit in the world.*

Pika

Ochotona princeps

The pikas of North America live in areas of scree – fragments of eroded rock found beneath cliffs or mountain slopes. They shelter under the rocks and feed on patches of vegetation that grow amongst the scree. Pikas may forage at all times of the day or night, but most activity takes place in the early mornings or evenings.

During the winter, pikas survive by eating "ladders" of grass and leaves that they have collected during the late summer. These ladders are piles made in sunny places, so that the plants desiccate into alpine hay. Like most of their rabbit relatives, pikas eat their primary droppings so that their tough food is digested twice, in order to extract all of the nutrients.

Adult pikas live alone and defend territories during the winter. In spring, males expand their territories to include those of neighbouring females. Most females produce two litters during each summer. When preparing for winter, the females chase their mates back to their own territories and expel their mature offspring.

Pikas are small relatives of rabbits. They do not have tails, and their rounded bodies are covered in soft red and grey fur. Unlike those of a rabbit, a pika's hind legs are about the same length as its forelegs.

Distribution: South-western Canada and western United States.
Habitat: Broken, rocky country and scree.
Food: Grass, sedge, weeds and leaves.
Size: 12–30cm (4.75–12in); 110–180g (4–6.25oz).
Maturity: 3 months.
Breeding: 2 litters of 2–4 young born during summer.
Life span: 7 years.
Status: Common.

Snowshoe hare

Lepus americanus

Like most hares, snowshoe hares do not dig burrows. Instead they shelter in shallow depressions called forms, which they scrape in soil or snow. Snowshoe hares are generally nocturnal, and rest in secluded forms or under logs during the day. When dusk arrives, the hares follow systems of runways through the dense forest undergrowth to feeding sites. They maintain these runways by biting away branches that block the way and compacting the winter snow.

In summer, the hares nibble on grasses and other green plant material. They survive the long winter by supplementing their diet with buds, twigs and bark. Over several years, the overall population of snowshoe hares can rise and fall dramatically. At the low points there may be only two animals per square kilometre. At the peak there may be as many as 1,300 in the same area.

Snowshoe hares are more social than other hares. During the spring breeding season, the male hares compete with each other to establish hierarchies and gain access to mates. Conflicts often result in boxing fights – hence "mad March hares".

Distribution: Alaska, Canada and northern United States.
Habitat: Conifer forest.
Food: Grass, leaves, buds and bark.
Size: 40–70cm (15.5–27.5in); 1.35–7kg (2.75–15.5lb).
Maturity: 1 year.
Breeding: 4 litters of 2–4 young produced per year.
Life span: 5 years.
Status: Common.

In summer, the snowshoe hare's fur is a rusty or greyish-brown, but in areas with heavy winter snow the fur is white as a camouflage against predators.

Eastern cottontail

Sylvilagus floridanus

Eastern cottontail rabbits do not dig burrows, although they may shelter in disused ones dug by other animals. Generally they shelter in thickets or forms – shallow depressions made in tall grass or scraped in the ground. Cottontails forage at night, grazing mainly on grasses, but also nibbling small shrubs. Unlike hares, which rely on their speed to outrun predators, cottontails freeze when under threat, blending into their surroundings. If they have to run, they follow zigzag paths, attempting to shake off their pursuers.

In warmer parts of their range cottontails breed all year round, but farther north breeding is restricted to summer. Males fight to establish hierarchies, with top males getting their choice of mates. A pregnant female digs a shallow hole, which is deeper at one end than the other. She lines the nest with grass and fur from her belly. Once she has given birth, she crouches over the shallow end and her young crawl up from the warm deep end to suckle.

Female cottontails are larger than the males. The name "cottontail" is derived from their short, rounded tails, which have white fur on their underside. Their upper bodies are covered in grey, brown and reddish hairs.

Distribution: Eastern Canada and United States to Venezuela.
Habitat: Farmland, forest, desert, swamp and prairie.
Food: Grass, leaves, twigs and bark.
Size: 21–47cm (8.5–18.5in); 0.8–1.5kg (1.75–3.25lb).
Maturity: 80 days.
Breeding: 3–7 litters per year, each of up to 12 young.
Life span: 5 years.
Status: Common.

Pygmy rabbit (*Brachylagus idahoensis*): 21–27cm (8.5–10.5in); 200–450g (7–16oz)
These rabbits live on an arid plateau in the north-west of the United States. Pygmy rabbits are related to cottontails, but they are about half the size. They dig burrows under thickets of sagebrush – the only North American rabbit to do so – and move through a network of runways above ground. They eat the sagebrush, and are most active at dawn and dusk.

Swamp rabbit (*Sylvilagus aquaticus*): 45–55cm (18–21.5in); 1.5–2.5kg (3.25–5.5lb)
Swamp rabbits live in the wetlands around the Mississippi Delta and other rivers in the southern United States. Unlike most rabbits, the males and females of this species are about the same size. Swamp rabbits build nests of dead plants and fur at ground level. They maintain territories by calling to intruders and marking their areas with scent. They breed all year round. Female swamp rabbits may produce up to 40 young per year.

Collared pika (*Ochotona collaris*): 18–20cm (7–8in); 130g (4.5oz)
Collared pikas inhabit the cold mountains of central and southern Alaska and also north-western Canada, where they are found in scree and other rocky areas above the tree line. There is a greyish "collar" around the neck and shoulders. These diurnal animals feed on herbs and grasses, and make hay piles to eat during winter. Collared pikas produce about three young in each litter.

Jackrabbit

Lepus californicus

Jackrabbits are actually a type of hare and so share many of the hare's characteristics, from long ears to large, hairy hind feet. Jackrabbits live in dry areas with only sparse plant cover. This has benefited the species in the past. Overgrazing of the land by cattle in the arid south-west of the United States and Mexico has created an ideal habitat for jackrabbits.

Unlike other hares, jackrabbits make use of burrows. They do not dig their own, but they modify underground shelters made by tortoises. Jackrabbits feed on grasses and herbaceous plants, which also supply them with nearly all the water they need.

Distribution: South-western United States to northern Mexico.
Habitat: Dry grasslands.
Food: Grass.
Size: 40–70cm (15.5–27.5in); 1.3–7kg (2.75–15.5lb).
Maturity: 1 year.
Breeding: 3–4 litters of 1–6 young each year.
Life span: 5 years.
Status: Common.

Female jackrabbits are larger than males. They have grey fur with reddish and brown flecks. Their undersides are paler, and their tails and the tips of their huge ears are black. Like other hares, male jackrabbits indulge in frenzied fights during the breeding season.

Arctic hare

Lepus arcticus

The winter coat of the Arctic hare is white, with black tips to the ears. In summer, the fur is a variety of colours, depending on where the hare lives. In the tundra, for example, the hares are blue-grey. The long claws are used for digging in ice and snow.

Arctic hares live in northern North America, from Labrador and Newfoundland in the south to the Mackenzie River Delta in northern Canada. They also live on the many islands of the Canadian Arctic province of Nunavut. The hares occupy both lowland an upland regions. In the far north, both these landscapes are covered by tundra, where the vegetation is mostly small, ice-resistant plants such as mosses and hardy grasses. The hares make their homes in areas of broken ground, where rocks provide some shelter. In summer, larger plants grow in these sheltered spots, and in winter they do not freeze as deeply as exposed areas.

Arctic hares are most active at dawn and dusk. They forage on their own, but sometimes form loose colonies of up to 300 animals, probably to give some protection against Arctic foxes, polar bears and other predators.

Distribution: Northern Canada and Greenland.
Habitat: Tundra.
Food: Mosses, lichens, leaves, berries, roots and carrion.
Size: 40–76cm (15.5–30); 1.2–5kg (2.5–11lb).
Maturity: 1 year.
Breeding: Mating occurs in April and May; single litter of up to 5 young born in summer.
Life span: 5 years.
Status: Common.

Alaskan hare (*Lepus othus*): 50–70cm (19.5–27.5in); 2–5kg (4.5–11lb)
Alaskan hares live in northern and western Alaska. Some reports also place them across the Bering Straits in eastern Siberia. This species is most often found on tundra and barren mountain slopes, and rarely in lowland areas. Alaskan hares produce just one litter each year. Although this is less than other hares, it is no mean feat in the harsh conditions of their sub-Arctic home. They mate in spring and up to eight young are born two months later. These hares are active at dawn and dusk. Their main foods are leaves, shoots, bark and roots, plus grasses in summer.

Antelope jackrabbit (*Lepus alleni*): 48–63cm (19–25in); 2–5kg (4.5–11lb)
This jackrabbit lives in southern Arizona and along the Pacific coast of northern Mexico. It occupies highland areas in the Sonoran Desert, and is especially common on mesas – the steep-sided tables of rock that project from the ground in this region. There is no breeding season, and female antelope rabbits produce several litters per year, each of about three young. Antelope jackrabbits are nocturnal. They do not hide in burrows during the day, but rely on their high-speed running to escape from predators.

Tehuantepec jackrabbit (*Lepus flavigularis*): Size unknown
These nocturnal jackrabbits are found only on the northern coast of the Gulf of Tehuantepec in southern Mexico. Tehuantepec jackrabbits live in the forests that grow on sand dunes surrounding salt-water lagoons.

White-sided jackrabbit

Lepus callotis

White-sided jackrabbits occur from southern New Mexico into central Mexico. They live in the high plateaus that are common in this region. These uplands are covered by dry grasslands, with a few shrubs also growing.

White-sided jackrabbits are crepuscular, (active at dawn and dusk), but they are also at large on cloudy days and bright, moonlit nights. They tend to occur in male-female pairs, and this pair bonding is most evident during the breeding season.

When threatened by a coyote or another predator, this hare initially leaps straight up in the air and extends its hind legs to flash its white sides. This behaviour is meant to startle the attacker and give the jackrabbit a chance to flee. If successful, the hare makes its escape with high bounds, propelled by its long hind feet.

Female white-sided jackrabbits are slightly larger than males. In winter, the white areas of fur darken into a dull grey. The black line down the lower part of the back also fades at this time of year.

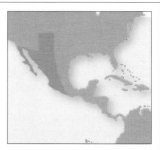

Distribution: New Mexico and north-western Mexico.
Habitat: Grassy plateaux.
Food: Grasses and sedge.
Size: 43–60cm (17–23.5) 2–3kg (4.5–6.5lb).
Maturity: 2 years.
Breeding: 2–3 young born in spring or summer.
Life span: 5 years.
Status: Lower risk.

Black jackrabbit

Lepus insularis

Black jackrabbits occur only on the volcanic island of Espiritu Santo in the Gulf of California, off western Mexico. The island has rocky hills and steep-sided valleys, but little running water; consequently, only desert shrubs and cacti survive there, along with some grasses.

Black jackrabbits are solitary animals. They do not dig burrows into the rocky volcanic soil, but take shelter in shallow hollows, often scraped out under the shade of a bush.

By day, the jackrabbits are very easy to spot moving around against the pale background of the islands' vegetation and rocky slopes, making them vulnerable to predatory birds such as American kestrels and caracaras. They are therefore most active during the night, when they can move more freely under the cover of darkness.

Black jackrabbits feed almost exclusively on grasses. However, at the driest time of year, when green vegetation is most scarce, these hares survive by gnawing bark. They obtain all the water they need from their plant food.

Black jackrabbits usually have a few white hairs on the tops of their otherwise black heads. The dark fur extends down the back and the rest of the body is covered with glossy brown fur, which is grizzled with long cinnamon guard hairs. The soles of the feet have heavy padding. As in other hare species, female black jackrabbits tend to be larger than the males.

Distribution: Restricted to Espiritu Santo Island in the Gulf of California off western Mexico.
Habitat: Steep valleys with shrubs and cacti.
Food: Mainly grasses, plus some bark.
Size: 57cm (22.5in); 1.5kg (3.25lb).
Maturity: 1 year.
Breeding: Up to 3 litters of 2–4 young from January to July; gestation is 41–43 days.
Life span: 5 years.
Status: Near threatened.

Mountain hare

Lepus timidus

Distribution: Northern hemisphere, from Alaska, northern Canada and Greenland to northern Europe and eastern Siberia.
Habitat: Tundra, forest and moorland.
Food: Leaves, twigs, lichen, grass and heather.
Size: 43–61cm (17–24); 2–6kg (4.5–13lb).
Maturity: 1 year.
Breeding: Breeding season is from end of January to September. Litters of 1–6 young produced twice a year (sometimes more) in spring and summer; gestation varies from 47 to 54 days.
Life span: 5 years.
Status: Common.

Mountain hares, often regarded as a subspecies of Arctic hare, are found at northern latitudes across the globe, from Alaska, northern Canada and Greenland to Scandinavia, northern Russia and Siberia. Small populations also live in Japan, Ireland, Scotland and even the European Alps. They inhabit tundra, conifer forest and moorland in highland regions. In winter, the hares usually move to the shelter of the forest.

These hares are nocturnal, resting by day in a form (a depression dug into the ground). They do not dig their own burrows, but often take over the burrows of other animals when they need to shelter their young. When not on the move, mountain hares "hook" before resting. This involves making a final jump to the side so that predators cannot follow the hare's tracks.

Mountain hares are mainly solitary, but in severe weather or at sites where food is plentiful they may congregate in large groups of up to 70. In the breeding season, several males will compete for access to a single female. If a male approaches an unreceptive female too closely, he may be aggressively rebuffed, with the female rising up on her hind legs and batting at him with her paws, claws extended. If the male persists, a longer fight may ensue, with both hares "boxing" and biting at each other.

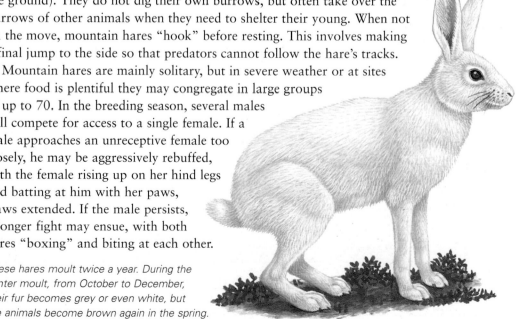

These hares moult twice a year. During the winter moult, from October to December, their fur becomes grey or even white, but the animals become brown again in the spring.

Desert cottontail

Sylvilagus audubonii

Despite their name, desert cottontails do not just live in desert habitats, but are also found in grasslands and woodlands. They range from Montana in the north to central Mexico in the south, and from altitudes of 1,800m (5,900ft) in the Rocky Mountains of the east to the Pacific coast in the west.

Desert cottontails tend to live alone and avoid interacting with one another. Males rarely tolerate another male near them, but females are sometimes seen gathering in an area with plenty of food without coming into conflict. In general, however, a single rabbit occupies a territory of about 3 hectares (8 acres). Most feeding takes place in early morning and at dusk. As the heat of the day increases, the cottontails spend as much time as possible under cover. When startled, this rabbit will either freeze or run. If it bolts, it follows a zig-zag path to evade pursuers.

Breeding occurs between December and late summer. The female digs a shallow nest hole in the ground and lines it with fur and grass. They young cottontails leave the nest when they are about two weeks old.

Distribution: Western North America.
Habitat: Deserts, prairie and woodland.
Food: Grass.
Size: 38cm (15in); 840–990g (29.5–35oz).
Maturity: 3 months.
Breeding: Litters of 3 young produced in spring and summer; gestation is 28 days.
Life span: 5 years.
Status: Common.

Female desert cottontails are slightly larger than their male counterparts. Both sexes have the characteristic short, white tail that earns this species and its relatives the name cottontail.

Brush rabbit

Sylvilagus bachmani

Brush rabbits are found along the Pacific coast of the United States, from the south side of the Columbia River Valley along the northern border of Oregon to the deserts of southern California. Their range does not penetrate far inland, only reaching the eastern side of the Cascade and Sierra Nevada ranges.

As their name implies, these rabbits are found living in brush habitats, which are particularly common in the deserts of California. The rabbits stay hidden among the low plants, and are rarely spotted in open country. They feed in large groups but do not have strong social interactions. Grasses comprise the bulk of the diet, but other plant foods may be eaten according to the season, including clover, leaves, forbs, berries and scrubs.

Like many rabbits and hares, brush rabbits are most active in the twilight of dawn and dusk. The rest of the time they lurk in the safety of the brush, digging simple burrows and tunnel networks, or forming runways through the thick vegetation. When a brush rabbit senses danger, it thumps the ground rapidly with its feet to warn other rabbits in the area. It is able to sit still for long periods of time to avoid detection by predators. If chased, it can reach speeds of 12–15 kmh (20–25mph) as it flees, constantly changing direction to wrong foot the pursuing animal. Brush rabbits may even climb trees and scrubs to put themselves out of an attacker's reach.

Distribution: Western United States, from Oregon to southern California.
Habitat: Brushy cover.
Food: Grass and berries.
Size: 28–37cm (11–14.5in); 0.7kg (1.5lb).
Maturity: 6 months.
Breeding: 3 litters of 2–4 young produced from late winter to late summer; gestation is about 27 days.
Life span: 5 years.
Status: Endangered.

This rabbit belongs to the same genus as cottontails. However, unlike many of its fluffy-tailed relatives, the brush rabbit's tail is small and dark on top. Compared to other cottontails, brush rabbits are also quite small. Females are usually slightly larger than males.

Volcano rabbit

Romerolagus diazi

This rabbit species is found only on the slopes of two volcanic mountain ranges in central Mexico. These mountains harbour an unusual habitat known as zacaton. This is a dry, high-altitude pine woodland where clumps of grass grow under the trees. Volcano rabbits live in small colonies in rocky areas of the zacaton, feeding on tender herbs and grasses. They shelter in burrows by day and follow networks of runways through tall grasses when feeding at night. Up to five rabbits share each burrow. The burrows are several metres long and about 40cm (15in) under the surface. The volcanic soil is dark and very rocky.

Volcano rabbits are most active at dawn and dusk. They forage in large groups, like pikas. They also communicate with a series of squeaks and other high-pitched calls. This species breeds mainly in summer. Young are born six weeks after mating.

The volcano rabbit is an unusual rabbit species, and resembles pikas in many ways. It is the only member of its genus, and is one of the smallest of all rabbits, with short ears, short legs and no visible tail. The dark fur on the back and flanks has yellowish hairs mixed in. The underside is a light grey.

Distribution: Mountains in central Mexico.
Habitat: Pine forest with grass undergrowth.
Food: Grass.
Size: 27–31cm (10.25–12.5in); 370–600g (13–21.25oz).
Maturity: 1 year.
Breeding: Litters of 1–3 young produced at any time, but mostly in summer; gestation is 38–40 days.
Life span: 5 years.
Status: Endangered.

Mountain cottontail (*Sylvilagus nuttallii*): 35–39cm (14–15.5in); 0.7–1.2kg (1.5–2.5lb)
This species lives in the woodland and brush that grows on hill and mountain slopes in the western United States, and also on exposed rocky mountainsides. Mountain cottontails forage at dawn and dusk, usually near running water. They eat grasses, sagebrush and juniper. These rabbits live alone, because otherwise the competition for food would be too great. They are active all year around, and breed in summer. If frightened, a mountain cottontail will run back on itself in a semicircle to confuse its attacker.

New England cottontail (*Sylvilagus transitionalis*): 38–42cm (15–16.5in) 1.4kg (3lb)
Also known as the wood rabbit, the New England cottontail lives along the eastern coast of the United States, from Maine to Alabama. Its main habitat is dense deciduous forest, where it often lives alongside eastern cottontails. This species eats plant stems and leaves, but individuals in colder areas are forced to rely on twigs and bark in winter. The coat is pinkish-buff, with a patch of black between the ears. These rabbits generally take over the burrows abandoned by other animals, since they are not able to dig their own.

Tapeti (*Sylvilagus brasiliensis*): 35cm (14in); 0.7–1kg (1.5–2.2lb)
The tapeti, or forest rabbit, ranges from southern Mexico to northern Argentina. It lives around the edges of the Amazon Basin. As well as tropical forest, this species also inhabits scrublands such as the Chaco of Paraguay. The tapeti is nocturnal and feeds on low-growing forest plants.

Marsh rabbit

Sylvilagus palustris

Marsh rabbits are cottontail rabbits that live throughout the south-eastern United States, from Virginia to the tip of Florida. This region is characterized by wetlands, especially around the Mississippi Delta. Marsh rabbits live in these swamps and bogs, and also near deeper and faster-running bodies of water.

These rabbits build platforms of rushes and other aquatic vegetation to hold their dens. Marsh rabbits swim regularly, and will also hide from danger in water. They never stray far from solid ground, since they are often forced to take cover in the thick undergrowth that grows along the banks.

Despite their semi-aquatic lifestyle, marsh rabbits forage on land at night for bark and leaves. They eat their hard pellets to extract as much goodness as possible from their tough food. Marsh rabbits are solitary, but when it is time to mate the males organize themselves into a hierarchy by fighting each other.

Compared to other cottontails and hares, marsh rabbits have short, rounded ears.

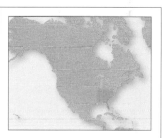

Distribution: South-eastern United States.
Habitat: Swamps and waterways.
Food: Bark and leaves.
Size: 35–45cm (14–18in); 1–2kg (2.2–4.75lb).
Maturity: 1 year.
Breeding: 6 litters of 2–8 young produced spring and summer; gestation is 30–37 days.
Life span: 5 years.
Status: Endangered.

BATS

Bats are grouped together in the Chiroptera *order of mammals. They are the only mammals that can truly fly. Their wings are made from thin membranes of skin stretched between elongated arms and legs. Most bats are active at night and "see" the world through sound. They emit high-pitched calls and interpret the echoes that bounce back to build up pictures of their surroundings.*

Common vampire bat

Desmodus rotundus

Within their range, vampire bats are found in most types of habitat where there are large animals to feed upon, and they have become common in areas where livestock is being raised. They feed on the blood of animals such as cattle and donkeys and sometimes domestic poultry.

They begin to feed soon after nightfall, flying silently from their roosts in caves and hollow trees. Vampire bats will travel several kilometres to find blood. Once they locate suitable host animals, they lick the target area – usually on the neck or leg – and bite off hairs or feathers to clear a patch of skin. Then the bat cuts away a circle of skin with its long teeth and laps up the blood flowing from the wound.

Vampire bats swallow about 20ml (7fl oz) of blood each day. They return to their roosts to digest their food during the day. Roosts may contain as many as 2,000 bats. Single males mate with small groups of females. They need to guard them, however, because they are often usurped by other males. Births of single young take place in spring or autumn.

Vampire bats have dark upper bodies with grey undersides. Their upper front teeth are very long and pointed, and their limbs are adapted for walking along the ground.

Distribution: Mexico to Uruguay.
Habitat: Caves, hollow trees and disused buildings.
Food: Blood.
Size: 7–9cm (2.75–3.5in); 15–50g (0.5–1.75oz).
Maturity: 10 months.
Breeding: Single birth in spring or autumn.
Life span: 10 years.
Status: Common.

Tent-building bat

Uroderma bilobatum

Tent-building bats have four white stripes on their faces, with pointed "nose leaves". Up to 20 females may share a tent.

Tent-building bats live in areas with enough palm or banana trees for them to roost in. They make tents from the broad fronds by nibbling through the central, supportive ribs so that the fronds flop down over them. The tents shelter the bats from the sun and wind while they sleep during the day. The fronds eventually die and fall off the trees because their vascular systems have been damaged by the bats. Consequently, the bats build themselves new shelters every two or three months.

Tent-building bats mainly eat fruit, which they chew up, drinking the juice. They also alight on flowers to grab insects, and will eat any nectar and pollen available. Males roost alone or in small groups, while females rest in groups of 20 or more. Breeding takes place at all times of the year. Nursing mothers leave their single young in their tents while they go on their nightly foraging trips.

Distribution: Southern Mexico and northern South America to Brazil.
Habitat: Palm or banana forests.
Food: Fruit, pollen, nectar and insects.
Size: 5.5–7.5cm (2.25–3in); 13–21g (0.5–0.7oz).
Maturity: Unknown.
Breeding: Single young born throughout the year.
Life span: Unknown.
Status: Common.

Velvety free-tailed bat

Molossus ater

Velvety free-tailed bats are nocturnal insect-eaters, tracking their prey by echolocation. Echolocation is a system in which the bats bounce chirps of ultrasound off objects and listen to the echoes to build an image of their surroundings.

Velvety free-tailed bats live in damp forests, but will venture out into more open country to find food. They roost by day in tree hollows, in rock overhangs or under palm fronds. At dusk, the bats set off in search of food, which they store in pouches inside their cheeks. When the pouches are full, the free-tailed bats return to their roosts to digest their food.

These bats sometimes use their mobile tails as feelers by crawling backwards along the ground, waggling their tails from side to side. With wings adapted for twisting and turning in pursuit of prey, free-tailed bats are not very good at taking off from the ground. Instead, they take to the wing by climbing up trees and dropping into the air.

Velvety free-tailed bats are so-named because of their soft fur and because, unlike most bats, they do not have membranes of skin joined to the sides of their tails.

Distribution: Northern Mexico to Argentina in South America.
Habitat: Forests and open woodland.
Food: Insects.
Size: 5–9.5cm (2–3.75in); 10–30g (0.3–1oz).
Maturity: 1 year.
Breeding: Single offspring produced once or twice per year.
Life span: Unknown.
Status: Common.

Ghost bat (*Diclidurus albus*): 5–8cm (2–3.25in); 20–35g (0.7–1.25oz)
This species of bat ranges from southern Mexico to Peru and northern Brazil. Ghost bats have white or grey fur and are found in tropical forests, seldom far from running water. They roost by day under large palm leaves, and pursue moths and other insects by night. Ghost bats live largely solitary lives, but do congregate at roosts, especially during the breeding season in late summer.

Fishing bulldog bat (*Noctilio leporinus*): 10–13cm (4–5in); 60–80g (2–2.75oz)
The males of this species of bat, which lives in Central America, have bright orange fur, while the females are dull grey or brown. They have pointed muzzles with heavily folded lips and long hind legs with well-developed claws. These claws are used for catching fish. Fishing bulldog bats hunt over ocean surf as well as lakes and rivers. They even follow flocks of pelicans and snatch small fish disturbed by the birds.

Peter's disc-winged bat (*Thyroptera discifera*): 3.5–5cm (1.5–2in); 40–60g (1.5–2oz)
Also known as the New World sucker-footed bat, this species ranges from Nicaragua to Peru and northern Brazil. Its name refers to the suction cups located on short stalks on the soles of its forefeet. The bats use these suckers to hang from smooth leaves in their rainforest habitat. Unusually for bats, which generally hang upside down, sucker-footed bats roost upright.

Pallid bat

Antrozous pallidus

Pallid bats prefer to live in areas with plenty of rocky outcrops, in dry scrubland or forest terrain in western North America. They roost in caves and hollow trees during the day and do not emerge until well after dark. They go on two foraging trips each night, returning to their roosts in between to digest their food. They hunt for food on the wing, frequently descending to about 2m (6.5ft) above the ground before taking a long glide over the terrain. This behaviour is suited to locating slow-moving and ground-based prey, such as beetles and crickets.

Some pallid bats may migrate from cooler parts of their range to warmer areas in winter. Others hibernate during the coldest months. Pallid bats live in large social groups. They call to one another as they return to the roosts after feeding, and communicate as they jostle for position inside their roosting sites. During the summer, males live in male-only roosts. Mating takes place in autumn, soon after that year's young have dispersed from their mothers' roosts. Births, usually of twins, take place in summer.

Pallid bats have cream to yellow fur, with whitish patches on their underside. Their ears are very large in proportion to their head.

Distribution: Western North America from British Colombia to Mexico.
Habitat: Forests and arid scrubland.
Food: Insects, spiders and lizards.
Size: 6–8.5cm (2.5–3.25in); 17–28g (0.6–1oz).
Maturity: 1 year.
Breeding: Twins born in summer.
Life span: 9 years.
Status: Vulnerable.

Mexican free-tailed bat (*Tadarida brasiliensis*):
Length 6–7cm (3.5–4in); 12.3g (0.4oz)
This species ranges from southern Texas and
Mexico through Central America to Brazil. The
largest colony is found in Braken Cave near San
Antonio, Texas, with an estimated 20 million bats
occupying this single roost during summer. This is
the largest known gathering of mammals. Several
other caves in the region host more than 1 million
bats. The fact that so many bats can fly through
narrow caves in such huge numbers is testament
to the accuracy of their echolocation sonar.
Mexican free-tailed bats eat small flying insects
such as mosquitoes and other flies.

Broad-eared bat (*Nyctinomops laticaudatus*):
5–9cm (3.5–5.5in); weight unknown
A relative of the free-tailed bats, this species has
long jaws and nostrils that end in small tubes.
Broad-eared bats live in the tropical parts of
Central and South America, mainly in lowland
forests. They roost in human dwellings and
caves, as well as on cliffs, and they feed on
flying beetles. Unusually for bats of this size,
some of the calls they make are so low pitched
that they are audible to humans. The species is
threatened, but not high risk.

Big free-tailed bat (*Nyctinomops macrotis*):
12–16cm (4.75–6.25in); 22–30g (0.8–1oz)
The big free-tailed bat has a huge range,
stretching from northern British Columbia and
South Carolina to the whole of South America.
Big free-tailed bats live in rugged habitats where
there are plenty of rocky crevices for roosting in.
They mainly feed on large moths.

Thumbless bat

Furipterus horrens

Thumbless bats range from Costa Rica to
Peru and Brazil, including the island of
Trinidad. These bats generally roost in caves
or hollow trees. They hunt at night near
rivers and streams, where they fly 1–5m
(3.25–16.5ft) above the ground, plucking
moths and other insects from the air. Like
nearly all small bats, thumbless bats use
echolocation to find their prey. This involves
making short, high-pitched chirrup calls
(too high for the human ear to detect) and
moving the ears from side to side to scan
the night sky for echoes bouncing
back off large flying
insects. The ears can
be moved independently
if necessary.

Thumbless bats live in
colonies numbering up to
300 individuals. While
roosting, the bats in a colony
will sometimes form smaller
subgroups, each made up of
about 20 individuals.

*The thumbless bat is so called
because it lacks a thumb claw (most
bats have claws sticking out of the
leading edge of the wing). The long
fur on the head covers the mouth.*

Distribution: Central America
and northern South America,
plus Trinidad.
Habitat: Caves in forests.
Food: Insects.
Size: 4cm (1.5in); 3g (0.1oz).
Maturity: 1 year.
Breeding: Unknown.
Life span: Unknown.
Status: Lower risk.

Dwarf bonneted bat

Eumops bonariensis

Dwarf bonneted bats live in the Veracruz region of Mexico
and spread south through Central America and northern
South America to Paraguay and Uruguay. A few can be
found further south in eastern Argentina. They inhabit
deciduous tropical forests and thorn scrub in lowland areas.

These bats roost in hollow trees and under the roofs
of forest dwellings. They are a common house bat in the
southern portion of their range. They hunt at night using
echolocation to sense their surroundings and
catch insects such as beetles and moths on
the wing. Many of the prey insects are fast
flyers, so the bats need to be quick in the
chase. Their long wings and ability to
shorten their tail membrane allow them to
achieve higher flight speeds than many species.
Dwarf bonneted bats can fly at 65kmh (40mph)
when flying alone; when flying in groups,
they can reach speeds of around 95kmh
(60mph), because there is less drag.

*This is the smallest of the eight
bonneted bat species. The hair
is pale at the base and white
at the tip. The hair is long for a
bat, reaching up to 5mm (0.2in).
Bonneted bats have smaller eyes
than most other types of bat.*

Distribution: From Mexico
through Central America to
Uruguay and Paraguay in
South America.
Habitat: Dry forest.
Food: Beetles, moths
and other insects.
Size: 5–7cm
(2–2.75in); 7–13g
(0.2–0.5oz).
Maturity: 1 year.
Breeding: 1 young born
in summer.
Life span: Unknown.
Status: Common.

Western bonneted bat

Eumops perotis

The western bonneted bat, also known as the mastiff bat, occurs in small patches across its range, which stretches from Nevada in the western United Sates and south through Texas and Arizona into central Mexico. The bat is also found on the Caribbean islands of Cuba.

The broken pattern of distribution reflects the bat's need for habitats with steep cliffs, on the side of which the bat roosts. The cliffs must be sheer or overhanging so that, when it is time to hunt, the bat can simply let go of its foothold and drop into the air. It freefalls to gain sufficient airspeed before using its wings. This species is unable to get airborne from the ground.

Beneath the cliffs, western bonneted bats hunt in a variety of open habitats, including desert, scrub and even dry woodlands. They spend several hours each night foraging for flying insects. Unusually for bats, this species hunts in cold weather, only becoming inactive when temperatures reach 5°C (41°F).

The western bonneted bat has large, linked ears that stand high above the head and project forward beyond the end of the snout. If this species finds itself on the ground, it must climb a tree or other object to gain the 5m (16.5ft) or so in height that it needs to launch itself into the air again.

Distribution: Southern California, Nevada, New Mexico and Texas; also Mexico and Cuba.
Habitat: Cliffs.
Food: Insects.
Size: 8cm (3.25in); 57g (2oz).
Maturity: 1 year.
Breeding: 1 young born in summer.
Life span: Unknown.
Status: Common.

Pocketed free-tailed bat

Nyctinomops femorosaccus

The pocketed free-tailed bat lives in the region either side of the US–Mexico border. It is most commonly found in desert habitats, where it feeds on flying insects. It eats a range of prey, including moths, crickets, flying ants and lacewings. Many of its prey are pests that feed on crops, and the bat's presence is encouraged by local farmers.

The pocketed free-tailed bat is a swift, high-flying species that is most active in the hours just after dusk and just before dawn. It uses echolocation to find its way around and locate insect prey. It prefers small moths, but will also take crickets, beetles, flying ants, stinkbugs, froghoppers, and lacewings. The bat's ears are joined together, so they move as a single unit when detecting echoes. Prey is usually caught on the wing.

Small colonies of pocketed free-tailed bats, usually fewer than 100 bats, roost in caves and on rugged cliffs, tall rocky outcrops and buildings. Like western bonneted bats, they must drop for a few metres before they achieve the airspeed necessary to stay aloft in powered flight. As well as emitting echolocation calls, this species often makes high-pitched chattering social calls, especially in the first few minutes of flight and while roosting. Pocketed free-tailed bats can frequently be observed flying swiftly over ponds and other watercourses, making audible whistling and fluttering sounds with their wings. To drink, these bats will impact with the water's surface while in flight and scoop up a mouthful of water.

Distribution: Southern California, south-eastern New Mexico, western Texas and Michoacán state, Mexico.
Habitat: Deserts.
Food: Insects.
Size: 11cm (4.25in); 12g (0.4oz).
Maturity: 1 year.
Breeding: 1 young born in June or July.
Life span: Unknown.
Status: Common.

Being a free-tailed bat, this species has a tail that extends beyond the skin membrane which forms the wing and other flight surfaces. The "pockets" referred to in the bat's common name are produced by folds in the skin that joins the legs to the arms.

Ghost-faced bat

Mormoops megalophylla

This species lives in Arizona and Texas in the north and south, through Mexico and Central America to Peru in the west and Venezuela in the east. It typically roosts in caves and smaller nooks and crannies, and often makes its home in artificial structures, such as tunnels and mines. It does not roost in buildings very often because they tend to be too dry. The bats prefer places with a high humidity to stop their wings from drying out too much.

Ghost-faced bats eat large insects such as moths. Little is known about how they catch their prey. It is likely that they take them on the wing, but they may also swoop down and snatch them off the ground.

During the day, ghost-faced bats roost in vast colonies numbering up to half a million individuals. A colony of this size needs an enormous roosting space, since each bat prefers to have about 15cm (6in) between itself and its neighbours. In winter, it is likely that bats in cooler areas migrate toward the warmer regions near the tropics.

The ears of this medium-sized, reddish-brown or dark brown bat are joined along their inner edges. Together they can be twisted to point in a variety of directions when scanning for sonar echoes from small prey. The ghost-faced bat has relatively small eyes, and its lips are wrinkled into a funnel-like shape. Conspicuous leaf-like flaps of skin protrude from the bat's chin, giving rise this species' other common names: leaf-chinned bat and old man bat.

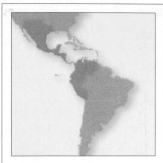

Distribution: From Arizona and Texas in the United States through Central America to Peru and Venezuela in South America.
Habitat: Desert.
Food: Large-bodied moths and other large insects.
Size: 6.5cm (2.5in); 13–19g (0.5–0.7oz).
Maturity: 1 year.
Breeding: 1 offspring produced in May or June.
Life span: Unknown.
Status: Common.

Mexican funnel-eared bat

Natalus stramineus

Mexican funnel-eared bats are found in the tropical region of the Americas on either side of the equator. The northern limit of their range is the Sonoran desert in north-western Mexico, while the southern extent is eastern Brazil. These bats also live on several Caribbean islands, including the Lesser Antilles, Hispaniola (Haiti and the Dominican Republic) and Jamaica.

Mexican funnel-eared bats prefer a deciduous forest habitat, and tend to be absent from the lush tropical forests that grow in equatorial lowlands and on the sides of mountains. The bats roost in colonies of up to 300 individuals, which is relatively small by bat standards.

Mexican funnel-eared bats are most active in the first few hours after sunset. They hunt small flying insects at night, typically in the understorey – the layer of shrubs and small trees that grows near to the ground in forests. These swift, agile flyers twist and turn in flight to avoid the foliage as they pursue their prey. Between hunts, the bats rest in trees for a short while. They return to the roost before dawn.

The sexes appear to separate when the young are born, forming maternity colonies in which the females care for their offspring. The baby bats are comparatively large, often weighing more than 50 per cent of the adult mass.

This small bat is so called because of its large, funnel-shaped ears. Both sexes have a moustache, and the adult males have a gland on the forehead. Biologists are uncertain what this gland is for. This species is slim bodied with long, slender wings, legs and tail.

Distribution: From north-eastern Mexico patchily through Central America to eastern Brazil; also found on Caribbean islands, including Hispaniola, Jamaica and the Lesser Antilles.
Habitat: Dry deciduous and semi-deciduous forest; occasionally evergreen forest.
Food: Small flying insects.
Size: 3.8–4.6cm (1.5–1.75in); 3–6g (0.1–0.2oz).
Maturity: 1 year.
Breeding: 1 young, usually born at the end of the dry season; gestation probably lasts 8–10 months.
Life span: 20 years.
Status: Common.

Lesser bulldog bat

Noctilio albiventris

Like most American bats, the lesser bulldog bat is limited to the tropics. It ranges from southern Mexico to eastern Brazil and the northern tip of Argentina. While this species has been spotted in a range of habitats, it is most common in forests, and never strays far from running water. Lesser bulldog bats roost in tree hollows, thick bushes and in the roofs of houses. They often share roosts with mastiff bats.

Lesser bulldog bats often hunt in small groups of 8–15 bats. Each bat has a personalized echolocation call, which helps it to identify the echoes produced by its own high-frequency clicks. It is uncertain whether the bats make use of the echoes of other bats to help them orientate themselves. A more likely scenario is that hunting in groups increases the chance of finding food. The bats eat insects that fly over water, plucking them out of the air. If the insects drop to the water's surface, the bats scoop them up in their mouths or grab them by trailing their hind claws through the water.

Male bulldog bats are bright red, while the females are dull brown. These bats have very pointed snouts, but no nose leaf. The tail protrudes beyond the tail membrane. Roosting groups of lesser bulldog bats consist of a single male with multiple females. These social groups of bats remain intact throughout the whole year.

Distribution: Southern Mexico through Central America to northern Argentina and Peru.
Habitat: Forests, near running water.
Food: Insects.
Size: 5.7–8.5cm (2.25–3.25in); 18–44g (0.6–1.5oz).
Maturity: 1 year.
Breeding: 1 young born in April or May.
Life span: 10–12 years.
Status: Common.

Big bonneted bat (*Eumops dabbenei*): 16.5cm (6.5in); 76g (2.75oz)
This insect-eating South American species occurs east of the Andes, from Colombia to northern Argentina, but is absent from Amazonia. Big bonneted bats roost in tree holes and buildings near forests. It is likely that these rare bats are becoming endangered by habitat degradation. The males have a large throat sac, which swells up in the mating season and fills with a pheromone that attracts females. Most females produce a single pup each year, although twins occasionally occur. A few females produce two litters annually.

Parnell's moustached bat (*Pteronotus parnellii*): 7.3–10cm (2.75–4in); 10–20g (0.3–0.7oz)
Parnell's moustached bat occurs from southern Mexico to northern Brazil. It lives on the edge of forests and is found in both lowland and mountain habitats. The bat's name derives from the hairs sticking out from its muzzle. At night it hunts moths and flying beetles, flying low and hugging the terrain. By day it roosts in caves.

Gervais's funnel-eared bat (*Natalus lepidus*): 35–55cm (13–21.5in); 5–10g (0.2–0.3oz)
Native to lowland forests in the Bahamas and Cuba, Gervais's funnel-eared bats roost in large caves and mines, forming colonies of several hundred bats. The inner surface of the large, funnel-shaped ears is greatly curved and almost covers the eyes. The males have a gland on their forehead, the function of which is unclear. In the mating season, the bats roost in single-sex colonies. These insect eaters take insects on the wing over shrubs and low-growing vegetation.

Greater bulldog bat

Noctilio leporinus

The greater bulldog bat shares its range with its smaller relative, the lesser bulldog bat. Also like its relative, this species hunts over water, such as rivers, lakes and even among the waves breaking along the coast. However, it is not primarily an insect eater, preferring fish, crustaceans and other water animals. The bat hunts by making low, zig-zagging flights over the water, using its sonar system to detect disturbances on the surface. It drags its hind feet, which are equipped with long claws, through the water in an attempt to hook fish. Such behaviour can net fish up to 10cm (4in) long. This hunting technique probably evolved from a method of catching insects on the water's surface, similar that used by the lesser bulldog bat. A successful bat eats its meal on the wing. This species stores any uneaten fish in pouches inside its elastic cheeks.

Distribution: Southern Mexico to northern Argentina and south-eastern Brazil; also found on the Greater and Lesser Antilles, as well as the Bahamas.
Habitat: Near water and coasts.
Food: Fish.
Size: 10–13cm (4–5.25in); 60–78g (2–2.75oz).
Maturity: 1 year.
Breeding: 1 young born in January.
Life span: Unknown.
Status: Common.

Male greater bulldog bats are slightly larger than females. They have red or orange fur, while females are grey or brown. These bats get their name from the fold of skin between the lips and nostrils, which gives them a bulldog-like appearance.

Antillean fruit-eating bat

Brachyphylla cavernarum

The upper body has yellow or ivory hairs with golden brown tips, while the underside is brown. The small nose leaf has a V-shaped groove. The tail is completely surrounded by the wing membrane.

This species is found on the Caribbean island chain known as the Lesser Antilles. Its range extends south along the chain to Barbados and St Vincent. It is also found further west, on the larger island of Puerto Rico. Antillean fruit-eating bats roost in caves and, increasingly, in artificial structures. They hunt and forage at night in the dense forests that grow on parts of these islands.

As well as insects, these bats will also feed on fruit, pollen, nectar and flowers. Their main source of energy is nectar, a sugary liquid produced by flowers. In return for the nectar, the flowers use the bats to transfer pollen grains from flower to flower as they feed. This form of pollination is more commonly performed by insects. Flowers that are pollinated by bats open at night, not by day. Since bats cannot see very well, the flowers do not need to be brightly coloured. Adult Antillean fruit-eating bats are often aggressive while feeding, hitting, biting and scratching one other.

Colonies of Antillean fruit-eating bats contain 2,000–3,000 individuals. Maternity colonies form during the mating season, and mainly comprise females and their young, with few males and non-breeding females.

Distribution: Puerto Rico and the Lesser Antilles south to St Vincent and Barbados.
Habitat: Forests.
Food: Fruits, pollen, nectar, flowers and insects.
Size: 6.5–12cm (2.5–4.75); 45g (1.5oz).
Maturity: 1 year.
Breeding: 1 young, usually born May–June; gestation is about 4 months. In good years, a second young may be produced later in the year.
Life span: Unknown.
Status: Lower risk.

Hairy-legged vampire bat

Diphylla ecaudata

Hairy-legged vampire bats live in tropical America, from southern Texas to Peru and Brazil south of the equator. They live in a range of habitats, including deserts and grasslands, but are most commonly seen in forests.

By day, hairy-legged vampire bats roost out of sight in caves, mines and hollow trees. However, the roosts are very small, containing only about 12 individuals. The bats tend to spread out when roosting, rather than huddling together as other species do.

At night, these blood-sucking bats seek out warm-blooded animals using heat sensors on their noses. Their favoured hosts are birds, but the bats will also suck the blood of large mammals. First they select an area of the skin that has plenty of blood vessels near the surface. Then they lick the skin and bite, making a small wound. The bat's saliva contains an anti-clotting substance, and the bat laps up the blood that flows from the wound. Most of the bats' victims are unaware that they have been bitten.

These vampires have smaller bodies and ears than other species of vampire bat. The incisors are longer than the canine teeth, a highly unusual arrangement. The incisors are used to draw blood from prey. These social bats regularly groom each other, and a bat may even regurgitate blood to feed a fellow bat with which it has a strong bond.

Distribution: Tropical regions, from southern Texas in the United States through Central America to eastern Peru and southern Brazil in South America.
Habitat: Typically forests, but also grassland and deserts
Food: Blood of birds, including domestic chickens, and occasionally livestock.
Size: 8.5cm (3.5in); 30–40g (1–1.5oz).
Maturity: 9 months.
Breeding: 1–2 young born at any time of the year; gestation is 6–8 months.
Life span: Unknown.
Status: Common.

Geoffroy's tailless bat

Anoura geoffroyi

Distribution: Central Mexico to central South America.
Habitat: Rainforests and savannah.
Food: Insects, fruit, nectar, and pollen.
Size: Length unknown; 15g (0.5oz).
Maturity: 1 year.
Breeding: 1 young born in November or December.
Life span: 10 years.
Status: Common.

Geoffroy's tailless bats are found across Central America and northern South America, and on the islands of Trinidad and Grenada. They roost in caves or similar humid spaces, and are equally at home in tropical rainforest and savannah, where they fly between the distantly spaced trees.

This species is an agile flyer, and can even hover for short periods. Without a tail, the bat does not suffer from high drag forces. Colonies usually consist of small, same-sex groups that tend to occupy the same roosting site throughout their lives.

Geoffroy's tailless bat eats nectar and pollen. It also snaps up any insects that happen to be feeding on the flowers or the surrounding leaves. As well as using echolocation like other small bats, this species uses its sense of smell to locate suitable flowers. Smell is also important for communicating with other bats in the roost, such as mates and young.

This species lacks a tail completely. Females appear to have longer wings than males. This makes the females very powerful flyers, and allows them to carry their young on flights until the pup is able to fly on its own.

Cuban fruit-eating bat (*Brachyphylla nana*):
Length unknown; 45g (1.5oz)
A close relative of the Antillean fruit-eating bat, this species is found on different Caribbean islands, including Cuba, Grand Cayman and Hispaniola. Cuban fruit-eating bats roost in deep, humid caves in colonies containing several thousand individuals. Some of the islands in their range possess no suitable caves, so the bats roost wherever they can, generally in smaller groups. These bats sniff out ripe fruits and blooming flowers to feed on nectar and pollen.

Seba's short-tailed bat (*Carollia perspicillata*):
Length unknown; 25g (0.9oz)
Seba's short-tailed bats are found from southern Mexico to Bolivia and south-east Brazil. They are commonly found in evergreen and dry forests, generally in lowland areas. These fruit-eaters roost in groups of up to 100 in tree hollows or small caves. In dry periods, when food is scarce, the bats enter a state of torpor – an inactive state similar to hibernation – during which their energy consumption falls by about 99 per cent.

White-winged vampire bat (*Diaemus youngi*):
8.5cm (3.25in); 35–45g (1.25–1.5oz)
This blood-drinking bat occurs throughout tropical South America in forests, plantations and farmland. It is the only bat species to have 22 teeth. (Other vampires have fewer teeth, but most bats have more.) The white-winged vampire lives for up to nine years in the wild – several years longer than most species. Like other vampires, it probably crawls along the ground to creep up on its victims, such as domestic chickens and turkeys.

Mexican long-tongued bat

Choeronycteris mexicana

The Mexican long-tongued bat has a large range, which extends from the southern United States through to Colombia and other northern areas of South America. It is most common in Mexico, where it occupies dry habitats such as deserts and alpine scrublands. They roost most often in caves and rocky crevices, but can also be found hanging from the cliffs of desert canyons. In Mexico, this bat has adapted to built-up environments, where it occupies abandoned buildings.

Mexican long-tongued bats eat fruits and pollen, and probably some insects. However, their main source of food is nectar, especially from the flowers of cactus and agave plants, which open their large blooms at night. The bats are important pollinators of these plants, since they transfer pollen from plant to plant while feeding. The bats migrate south in the winter to follow the flowering pattern of the plants.

Distribution: Mexico to northern South America.
Habitat: Deserts, mountains, rivers and scrublands.
Food: Fruits, pollen, and nectar.
Size: 8.5cm (3.25in); 25g (0.9oz).
Maturity: 1 year.
Breeding: 1 young born in later spring and summer.
Life span: Unknown.
Status: Lower risk.

This bat's large eyes help it to seek out nectar-producing flowers. It uses its long tongue, which can extend to one-third of the body length, to lick the sweet liquid from the heart of the flower.

Southern long-nosed bat

Leptonycteris curasoae

The southern long-nosed bat lives in the Sonoran desert, which stretches from the south-western region of the United States to central Mexico. It can also be found in arid areas further south in Mexico. In some parts of its range, the bats inhabit mountain woodlands. By day, the southern long-nosed bat roosts in caves in large numbers, and it occasionally takes up residence in abandoned mines. Roosts may contain tens of thousands of individuals, but despite such vast gatherings, the members of this species do not cooperate with each other.

After dark, the bats can often be seen around flowering cacti, from which they obtain pollen and nectar. They also eat the pulp of cactus fruits. A single bat may visit up to 100 cacti per night, and make a round trip of 30km (18 miles). The cacti tend to flower earlier in the south, so the bats migrate slowly from south to north through their range following blooming patterns. Although cacti are the main food source, the bats will also feed on other plants, including agave and bindweed. Some plants are only pollinated by this species of bat.

This southern long-nosed bat uses its long tongue, which is the same length as its body, to lick nectar and pollen out of large flowers. Unlike most blooms, the flowers on which bats feed open at night.

Distribution: South-western United States and Mexico.
Habitat: Desert, arid grassland, scrubland, tropical dry forest and mountain woodland.
Food: Nectar and pollen.
Size: 8cm (3.25in); 23g (0.8oz).
Maturity: 1 year.
Breeding: 1 pup born in December and January; gestation is probably about 5 months.
Life span: Unknown.
Status: Vulnerable.

Banana bat

Musonycteris harrisoni

These bats are found in banana groves along the Pacific coast of Mexico, west of the Isthmus of Tehuantepec in the south of country. They are found from sea level to 1,700m (5,600ft). Within this small range, banana bats are restricted to dry deciduous forests and thorny shrubland. The species was first described feeding in a banana grove, hence its common name.

Banana bats feed on nectar and pollen, often from banana plants, but not exclusively. Like many flower-feeding bats, they migrate over small distances to find freshly flowering plants. While feeding on nectar at a flower, they may also suck up any insects that they find there. Pollen from the flower clings to the bats' fur, and they swallow this as they lick their fur during grooming.

Young banana bats are cared for by their mothers only. They develop rapidly and are weaned and able to fly within a few weeks. Raccoons, snakes, ringtails, and small cats prey on roosting banana bats, while hawks and owls may catch them when they emerge to feed at dusk.

The banana bat has the longest rostrum of any bat. The rostrum is the bone that extends from the skull and forms the bridge of the nose. The banana bat also has a long tongue covered in a ridge of bumps, which helps it to collect pollen from its fur.

Distribution: Pacific coast of Mexico, in the states of Jalisco, Colima, Guerrero, Mexico, Michoacán and Morelos.
Habitat: Thorn scrub and dry forest.
Food: Nectar, pollen and insects.
Size: 7–8cm (2.75–3.25); weight unknown.
Maturity: 1 year.
Breeding: 1 pup born in late summer.
Life span: Unknown.
Status: The bat's restricted range and the loss of its habitat due to human activity have led to this species' classification as vulnerable.

Big-eared woolly bat

Chrotopterus auritus

Distribution: Southern Mexico to Paraguay and northern Argentina.
Habitat: Lowland forests near streams.
Food: Small mammals, reptiles and amphibians; insects and fruit.
Size: 13.5cm (5.25in); 200g (7oz).
Maturity: 1 year.
Breeding: 1 young born in July.
Life span: Unknown.
Status: Lower risk.

Big-eared woolly bats range from southern Mexico to Paraguay and northern Argentina. They populate lowland forests and cloud forests that grow on the sides of tropical mountains. The bats roost in small groups of only about five individuals. Each bat will regularly move to a new roost.

This large species is unusual in that it preys on vertebrates as well as insects. It also eats a small amount of fruit. Although the big-eared woolly bat uses echolocation to sense its surroundings, it does not rely on this system to locate prey. Instead, it uses its sensitive ears to listen for noises made by prey animals such as mice, birds, lizards, and even smaller bat species. The bat kills its prey by biting it around the head and neck. It then eats the dead animal head first. Some small animals are carried back to the roost to be eaten during the day.

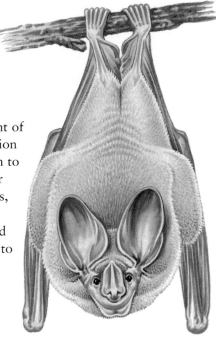

This is one of the largest of the insect-eating bats – only the fruit bats, or flying foxes, are larger. The big-eared woolly bat can be identified by its large nose leaf, tiny tail and white wingtips.

Mexican long-nosed bat (*Leptonycteris nivalis*): 7–9cm (2.75–3.5in); 18–30g (0.6–1oz)
This bat ranges from the southern United States to Guatemala and Honduras. It is most often found on mountain slopes where alpine scrub and pine woodlands grow. The bat's diet consists mainly of pollen and nectar from agave flowers, and the occasional insect, although it also feeds on cacti, berries and fruits. Agave flowers open just once, on a single night, and then perish. Consequently, the Mexican long-nosed bat must migrate to follow the blooming of its prime food source. The species is classed as endangered, because its habitat is diminishing and the agave plants it feeds on are becoming harder to find.

Thomas's nectar bat (*Lonchophylla thomasi*): 4.5–6cm (1.75–2.5); 6–14g (0.2–0.5oz)
Thomas's nectar bat is found in Panama and from Peru in western South America to the Brazilian Amazon in the east. It lives in lowland forests, especially near streams and larger watercourses. This bat roosts in caves and hollow trees, usually in small groups. Being a nectar and pollen feeder, it is equipped with a long snout to probe into flowers, and a bumpy tongue for licking up pollen.

Tomes's sword-nosed bat (*Lonchorhina aurita*): 5.3–6.7cm (2–2.5); 10–16g (0.3–0.6oz)
Named after the shape of its nose leaf, this forest bat lives in southern Mexico and Central America, and ranges south to Peru and Brazil. It feeds on insects, using its prominent nose leaf to direct echolocation calls and its large ears to detect the echoes returning from its prey.

Long-legged bat

Macrophyllum macrophyllum

The long-legged bat is found throughout northern and central South America. Its range also stretches north through the eastern part of Central America to southern Mexico. The southern limit is the north-eastern tip of Argentina. The long-legged bat occupies a variety of habitats. It is generally found close to ponds and lakes in all types of forest. It roosts alone or in small groups in hollow trees and, increasingly, in artificial structures, including in drainage tunnels and under bridges.

These bats feed on small insects that live on the surface of water or flutter close to it. The bats have a large nose leaf (a fleshy flap on the face), which is used to direct their echolocation calls to locate prey more precisely. A large tail membrane spans the long legs and toes. The bats use this membrane to skim insects off the water's surface and scoop them into their jaws.

Distribution: Eastern Central America and South America.
Habitat: Forests near water.
Food: Aquatic insects.
Size: 8–10cm (3.25–4in); 7–11g (0.2–0.4oz).
Maturity: 1 year.
Breeding: 1 pup born at all times of year.
Life span: 500 days.
Status: Common.

As well as long legs and large hind feet, this species has a long tail surrounded by a membrane of skin joining the two back legs. This membrane is covered with dotted lines that each end in a bump on the trailing edge. The fur is sooty-brown above and paler below. On the wing, long-legged bats have a fluttering flight, rather like a butterfly.

Striped hairy-nosed bat

Mimon crenulatum

This bat has a patchy range that includes southern Mexico, the island of Trinidad and most of tropical South America east of the Andes. It is found in lowland forests, where it is most often seen flying near streams. It also frequents the pools that form in bromeliad plants, which grow on the sides of trees. These pools are used for reproduction by the bat's insect prey. As well as insects, the striped hairy-nosed bat also feeds on spiders and small lizards. Prey is often snatched from the surface of leaves.

Striped hairy-nosed bats roost in hollow trees and logs. The roosts contain small family groups of about four bats. Like many other bat species, the striped hairy-nosed bat uses scent to communicate in roosts, and most roosting sites are obvious by the strong smell coming from them. Comparatively little is known about this species' breeding habits. It is thought that the bats form monogamous pairs that reproduce and forage together. The single offspring, which is born at the beginning of the wet season, is nursed by its mother for approximately nine months.

The young of this species are dark brown-red. As they get older, their fur becomes yellow, orange and red, and a pale line develops along the spine.

Distribution: Southern Mexico, Panama, Trinidad and northern South America.
Habitat: Near streams in rainforests.
Food: Insects, spiders and other arthropods, plus small reptiles.
Size: 5–7.5cm (2–3in); 12–13g (0.4–0.5oz).
Maturity: 1 year.
Breeding: 1 pup born between December and July.
Life span: 20 years.
Status: Common.

Spectral bat

Vampyrum spectrum

As the bat's scientific name suggests, this species was once thought to feed on the blood of other animals. The spectral bat is now known to be one of the many "false vampires", being a meat-eater rather than a blood-drinker. It is a powerful hunter that preys on other bats, small rodents, including mice and rats, and also birds, such as parakeets, orioles and wrens. The bat locates prey more by smell than by sight or echolocation. It stealthily creeps up on its victim – it is surprisingly agile on all fours – before pouncing or dropping down a short distance on to the animal and killing it with a bite from its sharp teeth. Fruits and insects may also form part of the spectral bat's diet.

The spectral bat lives in forests in the northern parts of South America and Central America, as far north as southern Mexico. It seldom strays far from water. The bat roosts in hollow trees in small family groups. Each group consists of a breeding pair, their latest offspring and two or three of the offspring from the year before.

Spectral bats form monogamous breeding pairs, possibly for life. Both parents take part in the rearing of the single young, licking their offspring incessantly and foraging for food to bring back to the roost. The adults feed morsels of chewed animal flesh to the young bat when it is being weaned. While roosting, the male spectral bat may wrap his huge wings around both the mother and their offspring.

This is the largest species of bat in the Americas. It has an average wingspan of about 90cm (35.5in), but in larger individuals this can be as much as 1m (3.3ft). The bat has large ears and a large nose leaf, but no tail. The short, fine fur is reddish-brown above and slightly paler below.

Distribution: From southern Mexico through Central America to Peru, Bolivia and central Brazil; also found on Trinidad.
Habitat: Near rivers and swampy areas.
Food: Birds and bats, as well as rodents such as mice and rats; possibly some fruit and insects.
Size: 12.5–13.5cm (5–5.25in); 170–180g (6–6.5oz).
Maturity: 1–2 years.
Breeding: 1 pup probably born at the beginning of the wet season, mainly between May and July.
Life span: 5 years.
Status: Lower risk.

Wrinkle-faced bat

Centurio senex

Distribution: From Mexico through Central America to northern South America; also found on Trinidad.
Habitat: Dense forest.
Food: Fruits.
Size: 5.3–7cm (2–2.75in); 13–28g (0.5–1oz).
Maturity: 1 year.
Breeding: 1 pup born between February and August.
Life span: Unknown.
Status: Common.

Even for a bat, this species has a very wrinkled and ugly face. It has a very small nose but large eyes compared to other bats. Its favoured food is overripe fruits that are beginning to liquefy, especially mangoes and bananas. The bat sucks the sweet juices directly from the fruit. This may explain the strange facial features, which help the bat to make a strong seal around the fruit as it sucks. The fruit juice is filtered through extensions on the lips and gums, which remove unwanted mush. The bat's wrinkled face enables the cheeks to be greatly distended, and the bats use this extra cheek space to store fruit pulp so that they can eat it when they return to the roost.

The wrinkle-faced bat lives in dense forested areas of Central and South America, where fruits are most abundant. It roosts during the day in pairs or trios under the leaves of large trees.

The folds of naked skin around the bat's face are the source of its common name. There is also a "beard" of white fur surrounding the lower face.

California leaf-nosed bat (*Macrotus californicus*): 8–9cm (3.5–3.75in); 8–17g (0.3–0.6oz)
This species has short wings, large ears and eyes, and a large nose leaf. The nose leaf is a fleshy projection on the snout that acts like a megaphone, amplifying and directing the bat's echolocation calls. Leaf-nosed bats often hunt fast-moving insects – the hardest prey to track accurately. The California leaf-nosed bat is no exception, feeding on ground-dwelling insects, such as grasshoppers and cicadas. It often hovers in the air before striking. These bats live in northern Mexico, southern California, Nevada and Arizona.

Greater spear-nosed bat (*Phyllostomus hastatus*): 10–13cm (4–5in); weight unknown
Ranging from Honduras to Peru and Paraguay, the greater spear-nosed bat occurs near streams in both forests and more open habitats. This species has a long, spear-shaped nose leaf, and a V-shaped groove in its lower lip. Males have a large throat sac, which is probably a gland that produces pheromones in the summer mating season. Spear-nosed bats sleep in hollow trees, termite nests and caves, roosting in groups of up to 100. They mainly eat mice, lizards and other small vertebrates, plus pollen and fruits.

Fringe-lipped bat (*Trachops cirrhosus*): 7–10cm (3–4in); 32g (1oz)
Named after the bumps on its lips and muzzle, this omnivorous species lives in tropical Central and South America. Its habitat is lowland rainforest, and it roosts in hollow trees, caves and artificial structures such as culverts.

Ipanema bat

Pygoderma bilabiatum

This species is found in the tropical region of South America, from northern Argentina in the south to Bolivia in the west and Surinam in the north. Ipanema bats are found mainly in tropical forests, where they roost in trees. They have increasingly begun to colonize human dwellings as people encroach into the forest. Their range includes the Ipanema neighbourhood of Rio de Janeiro, where they are commonly found feeding on garden fruit trees.

Analysis of the stomach contents of these bats has revealed that they eat almost no fibrous plant material, such as leaves, seeds or stalks, but only energy-packed fruits. The fruits are probably only eaten once they are very ripe, by which time the fruit tissues are beginning to break down, so the bat can absorb their nutrients more quickly. Ipanema bats may also eat pollen and nectar.

Distribution: Tropical regions of South America.
Habitat: Tropical forest.
Food: Fruits, probably also pollen and nectar.
Size: 6–8.5cm (2.5–3.25in); 27.5g (1oz).
Maturity: 1–2 years.
Breeding: 1 offspring born in the wet season.
Life span: Unknown.
Status: Common.

The Ipanema bat has dark brown fur on its back and grey hairs on its chest. There are also white patches on each shoulder. This bat has no tail, merely a membrane of skin that connects the legs.

Spix's disc-winged bat

Thyroptera tricolor

Spix's disc-winged bat lives in tropical parts of the Americas, wherever dense rainforests and other jungles grow. The bat's range extends from southern Mexico through Central America to the lower fringes of the Amazon Basin in southern Brazil. This is one of just two species of disc-winged bats. The other – Peter's disc-winged bat – lives in the same area. Disc-winged bats have suction cups on their thumbs and ankles, enabling them to cling to the surfaces of smooth leaves. The cups are controlled by tiny muscles, which can expand the cups to reduce the pressure of the air trapped inside. The difference between the air pressure outside and inside the cup is what holds the bat in place. A single cup can carry the bat's entire weight. Spix's disc-winged bats roost inside the leaves of *Heliconia* trees. When young, these leaves are curled up, providing a sheltered hideaway where the bats roost head-up during the daytime, with usually one or two bats per leaf, but sometimes as many as eight. Unlike most bats, this species roosts in a head-up position.

Spix's disc-winged bat has red fur on its back and pale cream hairs underneath. Instead of a nose leaf, the bat has wart-like bumps on its snout.

Distribution: From southern Mexico through Central America to south-eastern Brazil.
Habitat: Tropical forests.
Food: Mainly insects, especially beetles and flies, plus jumping spiders and other invertebrates.
Size: 2.7–3.8cm (1–1.5in); 4–5g (0.1–0.2oz).
Maturity: 1 year.
Breeding: 1 pup born twice a year.
Life span: Unknown.
Status: Common.

Big brown bat

Eptesicus fuscus

Female big brown bats are slightly larger than males. These bats have 32 sharp teeth inside their large, powerful jaws, which can deliver a painful bite when the bats are handled. The teeth are used to crush the tough outer skeletons of the bats' insect prey. Big brown bats can only feed during the warmer months when their insect prey are active. They eat as much as they can to lay down enough fat reserves to see them through the winter, when their body weight can fall by as much as one-third.

The big brown bat, which hibernates in winter, is one of the largest bats of North America. It is a common resident of artificial structures, and can even be found in the heart of cities. Its natural habitat, however, is heavy forest. The nature of these forests changes considerably across this species' range. In the southern limit, at the northern tip of South America, the forests are dense jungles. Moving north, deciduous forests take over from jungles, especially in the eastern United States. At the northern limit, along the southern fringe of Canada, deciduous trees give way to conifers.

During summer, when the female bats rear their young, the sexes roost separately. This is a common feature of hibernating bat species. The sexes come together to mate at the end of summer, before forming large, mixed-sex winter roosts. The development of the young is delayed over the winter. The embryos begin to grow in spring, and pups are born in summer. The young bats are able to fly within three to four weeks.

Distribution: Southern Canada to Panama and the northern tip of South America; also found in the West Indies.
Habitat: Heavy forest; often found in urban areas.
Food: Insects, especially beetles, plus moths, flies, wasps, flying ants, lacewing flies, and dragonflies.
Size: 11–13cm (4.25–5in); 50g (1.75oz).
Maturity: 1 year.
Breeding: 1–2 offspring born in June and July.
Life span: 19 years.
Status: Common.

Jamaican fruit-eating bat (*Artibeus jamaicensis*): c.10cm (4in); 30–50g (1–2oz)
This species ranges from Mexico to Bolivia and Brazil. It is also found on the Lesser and Greater Antilles island chains. The bat is not restricted to one habitat. It is often seen hunting in open areas. Roosting sites include houses, hollow trees and caves. In forested parts of its range, the bat roosts under "leaf tents", which it creates by nibbling through the central vein of a large leaf so that the leaf bends in the middle. This species roosts in harems of as many as 14 females with just one male. Its diet consists mainly of fruit, including bananas, avocados and figs, but it will also eat nectar, pollen and petals, as well as any insects that it finds on flowers.

Little white-shouldered bat (*Ametrida centurio*): 3.5–4.7cm (1.5–1.75in); 7.8–12.6g (0.3–0.4oz)
The little white-shouldered bat is found in Central America and northern South America. It lives in rainforests, and is most often seen flying near running water. The female is 50 per cent heavier than the male. This size difference resulted in the bat's initial classification as two species. Both sexes have pale shoulder patches, and males have fleshy pads under their eyes. The diet probably consists of fruit and some insects.

Visored bat (*Sphaeronycteris toxophyllum*): 5.7cm (2.25in); 17g (0.6oz)
These tailless, fruit-eating Amazonian bats live in forest clearings. They get their name from a roll of loose skin under the chin, which can be rolled over the face. The also have fleshy, horn-shaped nose leafs, which are longer on the males.

Spotted bat

Euderma maculatum

Spotted bats occur in small areas of a large range that extends from northern Mexico to British Columbia in south-western Canada. They live in many habitats, including the marshes of the southern United States and the dry hill forests in the south-west.

These bats use low-frequency echolocation calls, some of which are audible to humans as clicks. The low frequency means that the calls only form clear echoes on bigger objects, and consequently they give a relatively basic representation of the bats' surroundings. Because of this, spotted bats only catch large insects such as moths, and they prefer to occupy open habitats where there is plenty of space between obstacles. In densely forested areas, the bats would have difficulty avoiding branches in their flight path. Spotted bats are still expert hunters in the right environment. They have been recorded catching prey every 45 seconds, and are known to hunt for at least four hours each night.

This species gets its name from the three white spots on its shoulders and rump. The rest of the back is covered by black fur.

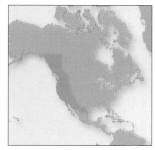

Distribution: British Columbia to northern Mexico.
Habitat: Dry, open forests and marshlands.
Food: Flying insects, especially large moths.
Size: 12.6cm (5in); 16–20g (0.6–0.7oz).
Maturity: 1 year.
Breeding: 1 young born in June.
Life span: Unknown.
Status: Unknown.

Allen's big-eared bat

Idionycteris phyllotis

Distribution: South-western United States and central Mexico.
Habitat: Mountain pine forests.
Food: Insects, especially moths.
Size: 10–12cm (4–4.75oz); 8–16g (0.3–0.6oz).
Maturity: 1 year.
Breeding: Single pup born in summer.
Life span: Unknown.
Status: Vulnerable.

These rare bats occupy the pine and oak forests that grow on the dry mountainsides of the south-western United States and central Mexico. The bats need to roost near springs or water holes, so that they can easily replace the moisture they lose through the surface of their wings while roosting. This is important, since most of the roosting sites in their habitat are dry places, compared to the humid surroundings adopted by the majority of bats. Big-eared bats roost in small colonies under overhanging cliffs or in crevices between boulders. The sexes separate during the summer, with the females forming maternity groups, and the males possibly remaining solitary.

Allen's big-eared bats are agile flyers and flit through the tight spaces of their rocky habitats. They often hover before swooping down on moths and other insect prey as they rest on the ground. These bats are useful predators of insect pests that threaten crops. Some people also use the bats' droppings as fertilizer.

Allen's big-eared bat is most notable for its large ears, which are up to 4.5cm (1.75in) long. Lappets – hanging fringes of skin – extend from the base of the ears and over the forehead.

Red bat

Lasiurus borealis

The hairs of this bat's red coat are white at the tips, giving the bat a frosted, grizzled appearance. The coloration of the coat helps to camouflage the bat in sycamore, oaks, elm, and box elder trees, which prove popular roosting sites. The rear part of the skin membrane is covered in fur to help keep the bat warm.

Red bats range across the Americas, from southern Canada to Chile and Argentina. They are commonly found living alongside humans in rural and suburban areas. Red bats hang in trees during the daytime, often by one foot, and are easily mistaken for dead leaves. In colder parts of their range, they may hibernate in hollow trees or migrate south for the winter.

Red bats are fast flyers, with a medium-sized body and long wings. The head is small, and the jaws are equipped with 32 small, sharp teeth. These insect-hunting bats catch their prey on the wing, and they are often seen feeding in brightly lit areas that attract a wide range of insects. The bats fly through the swarming insects, selecting a target 5m (16.5ft) away. They strike every 30 seconds, and catch about half of their intended victims.

The red bat is one of the few bat species that is regularly preyed on in flight. Since red bats often fly around lights, they make easy targets for owls. Opossums, snakes and racoons also prey on them as they roost in buildings and other structures.

Distribution: From southern Canada through Central America to Chile and Argentina.
Habitat: Suburban and rural areas.
Food: Insects.
Size: 9.3–11.7cm (3.7–4.5in); 7–13g (0.2–0.5oz).
Maturity: 1 year.
Breeding: Mating is in August and September; litter of 2–3 (maximum 4) pups born in summer.
Life span: Unknown.
Status: Common.

South-western myotis

Myotis auriculus

These bats have distinctive long, brown ears. Their brown fur lacks the glossiness seen on many other species. The south-western myotis lives in the same area as many of its close relatives. It is easy to identify, because the trailing edge of its tail membrane has no hairs. South-western myotis are able to hover and pluck insect prey from surfaces. They are believed to make seasonal migrations and hibernate in parts of their range.

Several species of small brown bat share the common name myotis. The group is also known as the mouse-eared bats. South-western myotis occur throughout Mexico and north to New Mexico and Arizona. They live in dry woodlands and desert scrublands. In high-altitude areas, they inhabit chaparral – forests of small trees. These bats are most common in rocky areas where there is a supply of water. They roost on cliffs, in sheltered rock crevices or in rotting trees.

South-western myotis, particularly females, concentrate their hunting along watercourses. They specialize in catching moths and other flying insects that are 3–4cm (1.25–1.5in) long. Moths are taken in flight or snatched up while resting. Foraging trips are alternated with rest periods, when the bats can digest their food. The bats need to drink large amounts of water to wash away the toxic nitrogen waste produced by digesting their high-protein diet, and also to replace water lost from their bodies by evaporation in their arid habitats.

Distribution: South-western United States to southern Mexico.
Habitat: Dry woodlands and desert.
Food: Insects, particularly moths.
Size: 27cm (10.5in); 5–8g (0.2–0.3oz).
Maturity: 1 year.
Breeding: Mating probably occurs in autumn; 1 pup, usually born in June or July, but later in southern parts of range (timing of births shows considerable geographic variation).
Life span: 3 years.
Status: Common.

Evening bat

Nycticeius humeralis

Distribution: North America, from the Great Lakes Basin south to Texas and Florida.
Habitat: Forest and near rivers.
Food: Insects.
Size: 8.6–10.5cm (3.5–4.25in); 6–14g (0.2–0.5oz).
Maturity: 1 year.
Breeding: 2 pups born in summer.
Life span: 2 years.
Status: Common

The name evening bat is given to a great many bats belonging to the *Vespertilionidae* family. Their alternative name of vesper bats was acquired because many species would roost in dark church belfries and be seen flying off to hunt while vespers, the evening service, was being conducted. This particular evening bat is found across eastern North America, from the Great Lakes to Texas and Florida. It may live in churches and other buildings, but its natural roosting site is in the hollow of a rotting tree. It forms harems comprising one male roosting with up to 20 females.

This species is medium-sized and dark brown. Like all vesper bats, it lacks a nose leaf. Evening bats catch flying insects, such as beetles, flies and moths. They appear to hunt high up during twilight hours, gradually descending as it gets darker. This may be a defence against owls. In the north of their range, the bats migrate southward in autumn.

These dark brown bats never live in caves, even in winter. Instead, they are found in hollow trees, under loose bark and in buildings.

California myotis (*Myotis californicus*): 7–9.4cm (2.75–3.75in); 3.3–5.4g (0.1–0.2oz)
This species has one of the most northerly ranges of all the North American bats. The California myotis is found in south-eastern Alaska and stretches south along the Pacific region of Canada and the United States to southern Mexico. It lives in a range of habitats, from the semi-deserts of the southern parts of its range to the damp coastal forests further north. In open lowland areas, this little bat has pale fur. Higher up, where it lives in forests, the coat is darker. In summer, California myotis roost in small groups, but during winter they form larger colonies in deep caves and other places to avoid the worst of the cold weather. Amazingly, these bats can still fly at temperatures below freezing. They are insect eaters, catching prey on the wing as they make swooping flights.

Little brown bat (*Myotis lucifugus*): 8.5cm (3.5in); 7–13g (0.2–0.5oz)
This Myotis species lives all over North America, from Alaska to northern Mexico. Little brown bats often inhabit houses, spending the summer roosting in lofts. They feed in open areas and woodlands, and also over water, catching gnats, beetles, wasps and other small insects. These nocturnal bats are most active a few hours after dusk and just before dawn. In winter they head for humid caves or mines. One pup is born between May and July, which the mother keeps beneath a wing while she is roosting. The pup starts to fly and is weaned at about four weeks old. The mother distinguishes her own offspring from the other pups by its scent and call.

Western pipistrelle

Pipistrellus hesperus

Pipistrelles form another large group of vesper bats. This species lives in the western United States and most of Mexico, where it is most commonly found in dry, rocky habitats. In summer, these bats roost by day in crevices and buildings, but during winter they seek out more secluded, damp hideaways, often ending up in caves and mines.

Western pipistrelles eat a range of insect prey. They search for an insect swarm and then spend the night feeding, consuming up to one-fifth of their body weight in insects. Being small, this bat must eat large quantities of food to survive. (In general, large animals need to eat a smaller proportion of their body weight to stay alive. This is because they lose heat more slowly, and so expend less energy keeping their bodies warm.) Consequently, the western pipistrelle must hibernate, including in the warmer parts of its range, because it cannot tolerate any period when food is even slightly scarce.

Distribution: From southern Mexico, including Baja peninsula, to Texas and California in the United States.
Habitat: Canyons, cliffs and rocky areas.
Food: Insects.
Size: 6.6–7.3cm (2.5–2.75in); 3–6g (0.1–0.2oz).
Maturity: 1 year.
Breeding: 1 pup born in June or July.
Life span: Unknown.
Status: Common.

These bats are small compared to other species found in the region. They have distinctive black and leathery skin on their face, ears and wing membranes. Females are slightly larger than males.

ARMADILLOS AND RELATIVES

Armadillos, anteaters and sloths belong to a group of mammals called the Xenarthra *(formerly named* Edentata, *meaning toothless). Most xenarths live in South and Central America. Only one, the long-nosed armadillo, lives as far north as Texas. These animals are taxonomically related to one another but do not share evident common physical characteristics, except for unique bones that strengthen their spines.*

Giant armadillo

Priodontes maximus

Like all armadillos, the giant armadillo has bands of bony plates running from side to side across its body to serve as armour. These plates are covered in leathery skin, and a few thick hairs stick out from between them.

The giant armadillo is the largest of all armadillos. It is nocturnal and shelters by day in burrows dug with the mighty claws on its forefeet. Most of the burrows are dug into the side of termite mounds. Giant armadillos also dig to get at their prey. They typically excavate termite mounds and ant nests, but they also dig out worms, subterranean spiders and occasionally snakes.

Unlike many other armadillos, giant armadillos cannot curl up completely to protect their soft undersides with their armoured upper bodies. Instead, these giants rely on their considerable size to deter predators. If they are attacked, giant armadillos try to dig themselves out of trouble. Armadillos live alone. They breed all year round, and mate when they chance upon the opposite sex during their travels. One or two young are born in a large burrow after a four-month gestation.

Distribution: Venezuela to northern Argentina.
Habitat: Dense forest and grassland near water.
Food: Termites, ants, spiders and other insects, worms, snakes and carrion.
Size: 0.7–1m (2.25–3.25ft); 60kg (132lb).
Maturity: 1 year.
Breeding: 1–2 young born throughout the year.
Life span: 15 years.
Status: Vulnerable.

Long-nosed armadillo

Dasypus novemcinctus

Distribution: Southern United States to northern Argentina.
Habitat: Shaded areas.
Food: Arthropods, reptiles, amphibians, fruit and roots.
Size: 24–57cm (9.5–22.5in); 1–10kg (2.2–22lb).
Maturity: 1 year.
Breeding: 4 young born in spring.
Life span: 15 years.
Status: Common.

Long-nosed armadillos are found in a wide range of habitats, but always require plenty of cover. In the warmer parts of their range they feed at night. In colder areas they may be active during the day, especially in winter. These armadillos build large nests at the ends of their long burrows. The nests are filled with dried grasses. In areas with plenty of plant cover, long-nosed armadillos may also build their nests above ground.

Long-nosed armadillos search for their animal prey by poking their long noses into crevices and under logs. They also eat fallen fruit and roots. When threatened, the animals waddle to their burrows as fast as possible. If cornered, they will curl up.

Long-nosed armadillos forage alone, but they may share their burrows with several other individuals, all of the same sex. The breeding season is in late summer. Litters of identical, same-sex quadruplets are born in the spring.

The long-nosed armadillo is also called the nine-banded armadillo because it typically has that number of plate bands along its back, although specimens can possess either eight or ten bands.

Three-toed sloth

Bradypus tridactylus

Distribution: Eastern Brazil.
Habitat: Coastal forest.
Food: Young leaves, twigs and buds.
Size: 41–70cm (16–27.5in); 2.25–5.5kg (5–12lb).
Maturity: 3.5 years.
Breeding: Single young born throughout the year.
Life span: 20 years.
Status: Endangered.

Three-toed sloths spend most of their lives hanging upside down from trees. They are very inactive creatures, but they do climb down to the ground once or twice a week to excrete or move to other trees.

Three-toed sloths feed by pulling on flimsy branches with their forelegs, to bring them close to their mouths. They spend long periods waiting for their tough food to digest. Because they are so inactive, sloths have a lower body temperature than other mammals – sometimes as low as 24°C (75°F). Their fur is sometimes tinged with green because algae are growing in it. The sloths may absorb some of the algal nutrients through their skin, and the green colour helps to camouflage them among branches and leaves.

Sloths have very simple societies. They live alone and females only produce offspring every two years. Mating can occur throughout the year though, with both partners still hanging upside down. Mothers give birth in this position too, and the young cling to the hair on their mothers' breasts.

Unlike other mammals, three-toed sloths have long, grey hairs that point downwards when the animals are hanging upside down from tree branches. This ensures that rainwater runs off the fur easily. The sloths climb using their strong, hook-like claws.

Pichi (*Zaedyus pichiy*): 26–34cm (10–13.5in); 1–2kg (2.2–4.5lb)
The pichi is a small armadillo that lives on the grasslands of southern Argentina and in the alpine meadows of the Chilean Andes. Its armoured head, body and tail have long hairs growing out from behind each plate. When threatened, a pichi withdraws its legs under its body so that the serrated edges of its armour dig into the ground. It uses this technique to anchor itself in its burrow. Pichis probably hibernate in colder parts of their range. Between one and three young may be born at any time of the year. This species eats carrion, small insects and worms.

Silky anteater (*Cyclopes didactylus*): 18–20cm (7–8in); 375–410g (13.25–14.5oz)
The silky anteater is found in forests from southern Mexico to Bolivia and Brazil. It lives in ceiba trees, which have large seed pods filled with silky fibres. The seed pods provide the perfect camouflage for the anteater, since the animal's silky fur blends in with the tree's shiny pods, making it almost invisible – even to sharp-eyed predators such as harpy eagles and owls. The anteater rarely leaves the safety of its tree. It rests during the day in a tree-hollow nest; by night, the silky anteater moves slowly through the branches eating ants, termites, beetles and other tree-dwelling insects. In one day, a silky anteater can consume as many as 8,000 ants, which it licks up with its long, sticky tongue. When threatened, this species stands on its back legs and steadies itself by grasping a branch with its prehensile tail. This posture frees up the clawed forelimbs for fighting off predators.

Giant anteater

Myrmecophaga tridactyla

Giant anteaters live wherever there are large ant nests or termite mounds in abundance. They use their powerful claws to rip the colonies apart, then they use their sticky tongues to lick up the insects and their eggs and larvae. A single giant anteater can eat over 30,000 ants or termites in one day.

Despite being powerful diggers, giant anteaters shelter in thickets, not burrows, because of their awkward shape. They spend most of their time alone searching for food, with their long noses close to the ground. While on the move, they curl their forelimbs under their bodies so that they are actually walking on the backs of their forefeet and their claws do not hinder them.

Females often come into contact with one another, but males keep their distance. Breeding can take place all year.

Distribution: Belize to northern Argentina.
Habitat: Grasslands, forests and swamps.
Food: Ants, termites and beetle larvae.
Size: 1–1.2m (3.25–4ft); 18–39kg (39.75–86lb).
Maturity: 2.5–4 years.
Breeding: Single young born throughout the year.
Life span: 25 years.
Status: Vulnerable.

Giant anteaters have powerful digging claws on their forelimbs and incredibly long tongues – often over 60cm (24in) – inside their snouts. They have white stripes along their flanks and a long, bushy tail.

Six-banded armadillo

Euphractus sexcinctus

Six-banded armadillos live in the savannahs of South America. They are active by day, unlike most other armadillos. They prefer arid areas, where it is easier to dig burrows in the dry soil, although some are found in wetter, often muddy areas. These armadillos are omnivores, meaning they eat all types of food. They dig for tubers and roots, and forage for the fruits of succulent plants and palm nuts. Although plant foods make up the majority of their diet, the armadillos will also eat ants and termites, along with other insects and carrion. They even kill small vertebrates, including mice or lizards. Without any proper biting or chewing teeth, eating flesh is difficult for the armadillos. They solve this problem by standing on the dead body and ripping off the meat with their jaws. Six-banded armadillos mark their burrow and other key features in their territory with a smelly liquid produced by a scent gland under the base of the tail.

Distribution: South America east of the Andes, Brazil to northern Argentina.
Habitat: Dry savannahs.
Food: Fruits, tubers, palm nuts and insects.
Size: 40cm (15.5in); 5kg (11lb).
Maturity: 1 year.
Breeding: 1–3 young born throughout the year.
Life span: 8–12 years.
Status: Common.

This species is also called the yellow armadillo because of the pale tone of its armour. It has between six and eight moveable bands on its back.

Pink fairy armadillo (*Chlamyphorus truncatus*): 8–10cm (3–4in); 80–100g (2.75–3.5oz)
The smallest of all the armadillo species, this animal lives on sandy plains in Argentina, where it is known as the pichiciego. Burrows are usually dug close to ant nests and termite mounds, which are the pink fairy armadillo's main sources of food. It also eats snails, worms and roots. This solitary, nocturnal species remains underground during the daytime. If it rains, the armadillo evacuates its burrow to avoid drowning.

Chacoan fairy armadillo (*Chlamyphorus retusus*): 14–17.5cm (5.5–7in); 1kg (2.2lb)
Slightly larger than the pink fairy armadillo, this species shares many of the same characteristics. It lives in the Gran Chaco scrub region of central South America. Chacoan fairy armadillos are expert burrowers and are seldom spotted above ground, because they quickly bury themselves when alarmed. Once underground, the animal's rear is protected by a circular plate of armour, which presents an effective shield to any predator that tries to dig out the armadillo. Like other armadillos, this species is omnivorous.

Andean hairy armadillo (*Chaetophractus nationi*): 22–40cm (8.5–15.5in); 0.75–1kg (1–2.25lb)
This armadillo is found in Bolivia and Chile, on the grasslands of Andean slopes up to 3,500m (11,500ft). Thick hairs stick out between its scales, and the legs and underside are also hairy. In summer, the Andean hairy armadillo is nocturnal in habit, sheltering from the daytime heat in the cool of its burrow. However, during winter it reverses its behaviour, foraging by day and keeping warm in its burrow at night.

Southern three-banded armadillo

Tolypeutes matacus

An inhabitant of South American grasslands, this species ranges from central Argentina northward into Paraguay and southern Brazil, and to Bolivia in the west. Southern three-banded armadillos are sometimes found in marshes or other boggy areas. As a general rule, these habitats are seldom far from drier habitats such as savannahs or forests. The armadillos make dens inside old ant nests.

When threatened, the armadillo can roll itself into a ball. The only unprotected area is between the head and tail section. If a curious predator tries to poke its paw into this space, the armadillo clamps the intruder between its armour plates.

This species eats mainly ants and termites. It uses its powerful forelegs and strong claws to excavate ant nests and termite mounds or lever off tree bark. Then it licks up insects with its long, sticky tongue.

Distribution: South America.
Habitat: Grasslands and marshes.
Food: Ants and termites.
Size: 30cm (12in); 1.4–1.6kg (3–3.5lb).
Maturity: 9–12 months.
Breeding: Single young born between November and January.
Life span: 8–12 years.
Status: Common.

This species and the Brazilian three-banded armadillo can roll up into an armoured ball for protection against attack. Contrary to popular belief, this is an unusual behaviour – no other armadillos can roll themselves up so completely.

Large hairy armadillo

Chaetophractus villosus

Armadillo means "little armoured one" in Spanish. The armour is made of plates of bone covered in a layer of horny skin. The plates are joined together by flexible skin, so they form a tough but supple covering. Unlike most other armadillos, this species has long, thick hairs.

Distribution: Central South America, from northern Paraguay and southern Bolivia to central Argentina.
Habitat: Semi-desert.
Food: Insects, invertebrates, small vertebrates, plants and carrion. Plant matter makes up about half of its diet during winter, much less at other times of year.
Size: 22–40cm (8.5–15.5in); 2kg (4.5lb).
Maturity: 9 months.
Breeding: Litter of 2 young born once or twice per year.
Life span: 30 years.
Status: Common.

This species is found in northern Paraguay and southern Bolivia. It also ranges south into central Argentina. This part of South America is called the Gran Chaco – a dry, sandy region of unique but inhospitable scrubland. Although the area gets enough rain for grasslands and savannahs to grow, much of the soil's water is lost by evaporation due to the high winds and baking sun. Large hairy armadillos escape from the heat by burrowing into the ground, since it is considerably cooler just below the surface. The loose sand makes it easy for armadillos to dig deep holes in a short time, so this is also the main method of avoiding attack by predators. Once in the hole, an armadillo relies on its armoured back to protect it from further danger.

Large hairy armadillos are omnivores. They forage at night for insects, other invertebrates and the occasional small mammal or lizard. They also eat plant food and carrion. They have been known to dig underneath large carcasses to feast on the maggots and grubs growing inside the rotting flesh.

Northern naked-tailed armadillo

Cabassous centralis

Distribution: South America, from northern Argentina to Colombia and Venezuela; Central America, from Panama to southern Mexico.
Habitat: Grasslands and woodlands.
Food: Insects, mainly ants and termites; rarely bird eggs, earthworms, and small reptiles and amphibians.
Size: 30–50cm (12–20in); 2–3kg (4.5–6.5lb).
Maturity: Unknown, probably about 1 year.
Breeding: Single babies.
Life span: 8–12 years.
Status: Common.

This species has a large range that extends from northern Argentina through Central America, reaching as far north as southern Mexico. It is most commonly found in grasslands and woodlands, wherever there is enough thick undergrowth to hide from predators. The armadillo digs its own burrow, often in the side of an embankment.

Northern naked-tailed armadillos are solitary creatures, like most armadillos. They do sometimes gather in small groups in areas with a good supply of food. However, in these situations they are tolerating the presence of others rather than grouping together for a reason. They are active at night, and never leave their burrows before sunset.

This species has a diet made up almost exclusively of insects, which it apparently locates by scent. The armadillos dig up beetle grubs and excavate termite and ant nests, and then use their long tongue to extract the small insects from their tunnels. The sickle-like claw on each front foot is used to cut through roots to reach the insect prey. Sometimes the armadillos completely bury themselves with soil while digging for food.

The protective armour so characteristic of these animals is not found on the tail of this armadillo – a feature it shares with three other species. It is also known as the eleven-banded armadillo.

Southern tamandua (*Tamandua tetradactyla*): 53–88cm (21–34.5in); 2–7kg (4.5–15.5lb)
Superficially very similar to its northern relative, the southern tamandua lives in South America, from Trinidad and Venezuela to northern Argentina. In the south of its range, it has a "vest" pattern to its black and blonde coat, which resembles that of the northern tamandua. In the northern part of the range, the fur is of a single colour, ranging from black to blonde and brown. These animals are mainly arboreal, using their long claws to grip tree bark as they climb. On the ground, they walk on the sides of their feet, because the claws would stick into the soles if they walked flat-footed. When cornered, a tamandua uses its claws as weapons. It stands on its hind legs with its back against a tree trunk and stretches out its powerful forelegs. In this position it can deliver slashing blows to any predator that approaches.

Brown-throated three-toed sloth (*Bradypus variegatus*): 55–60cm (21.5–24in); 3.5–4.5kg (7.5–10lb)
This species lives in the tropical forests of Central and South America, mainly east of the Andes. It feeds on the foliage of cecropia trees. The sloth's legs are designed to allow the animal to hang from trees; as a result, it is severely disadvantaged on the ground, since its legs are too weak to carry its body weight. In common with other three-toed sloths, this species has three more neck vertebrae than other mammals. These extra bones enable sloths to turn their heads through 270 degrees. Male brown-throated sloths have yellow or orange patches on their backs.

Northern tamandua

Tamandua mexicana

Sometimes called lesser anteaters, tamanduas have a long snout with a tiny mouth, and long, curved claws. They use their claws and prehensile tails to climb through the branches of trees in search of food. They do forage and rest on the ground, but out of the trees they are more clumsy and vulnerable to attack.

Like other anteaters, tamanduas lack teeth, so they grind up their insect food using a muscular stomach sac called a gizzard. The gizzard also contains little pebbles and pieces of grit that are swallowed along with the ants. These hard objects help to break down the food into a digestible paste.

Tamanduas are traditionally known as stinkers of the forest, thanks to the foul-smelling secretions from their anal gland, which they use to mark territories. They also communicate with hisses.

Distribution: Central and South America.
Habitat: Rainforest, drier forests and grasslands.
Food: Termites and ants.
Size: 47–77cm (18.5–30.5in); 2–7kg (4.5–15.5lb).
Maturity: 1 year.
Breeding: Single young born in spring.
Life span: 9 years.
Status: Common.

A V-shaped marking down the back of the neck makes this species look as though it is wearing a vest – hence its alternative name of vested anteater.

Maned three-toed sloth

Bradypus torquatus

This rare species is found only in what remains of the coastal forests of eastern Brazil. Like so many species from this mixed habitat of deciduous and evergreen trees, it is being endangered by deforestation. Although renowned for being slow moving, these sloths occupy a surprisingly large territory, moving through the rainforest along lianas that grow between the crowns of the trees.

The long, thick fur makes it hard for these sloths to regulate their temperature internally. When they are cold, the animals climb up to the highest branches to sunbathe. To cool off, they move down inside the crown of the tree to find a shady spot.

The maned sloth is a leaf eater. Leaves are not very nutritious, so sloths must spend long periods eating and digesting their food. Consequently, they move very slowly to conserve energy. Their metabolic rate is about half that of other similar-sized mammals.

The long, grey mane of fur on the neck often has traces of green in it. This colour is produced by blue-green algae, a plant-like form of bacteria. The maned sloth has three claws on each foot.

Distribution: Eastern coast of Brazil, South America
Habitat: Coastal forest.
Food: Leaves, twigs and buds.
Size: 55–60cm (21.5–24in); 3.5–4.5kg (7.5–10lb).
Maturity: 3 years.
Breeding: Single young born once a year.
Life span: 12 years.
Status: Endangered.

Southern two-toed sloth

Choloepus didactylus

While three-toed sloths have very short tails, two toed sloths have no tail at all. Their front feet have two toes while their hind feet have three. All the toes have long, curved claws, which the animal hooks over branches. The sloths move with a hand-over-hand action.

Southern two-toed sloths live in the rainforests of northern South America as far south as Peru and Amazonian Brazil. They spend almost their entire lives hanging in the crowns of tall trees. They occasionally climb down to the ground, either to empty their bowels or to move to a tree that contains more food.

On the ground they are very awkward, and have to drag themselves along. Their body is adapted to life hanging upside down in trees. Everything takes place upside down, including feeding, mating and giving birth.

When resting, the sloths hang in a ball that looks like a wasp nest, termite nest or branch stump. Southern two-toed sloths live alone, only ever interacting during mating or with young. However, several two-toed sloths may feed in a large tree. These animals eat leaves, twigs and fruits. Because they lack sharp biting teeth, the sloths have hard lips that cut through leaves and twigs. The back teeth grind the hard food. These teeth are continually worn down and grow throughout the animal's life.

Distribution: South America east of the Andes, from eastern Venezuela and the Guianas south into northern Brazil and the upper Amazon Basin of Ecuador and Peru.
Habitat: Rainforests.
Food: Leaves, berries, twigs and fruits.
Size: 54–74cm (21.5–29in); 4–8.5kg (8.75–18.75lb).
Maturity: 4–5 years.
Breeding: Single offspring born every year.
Life span: 12 years.
Status: Vulnerable.

Hoffmann's two-toed sloth

Choloepus hoffmanni

Distribution: Central America and northern South America. There are two distinct populations: the first extends from Nicaragua to Venezuela, the second ranges from Peru to southwestern Brazil and central Bolivia.
Habitat: Tropical forests.
Food: Leaves, twigs and fruit.
Size: 54–90cm (21.5–36in); 4–8.5kg (8.75–18.75lb).
Maturity: 4 years.
Breeding: Single young born approximately every 18 months.
Life span: 12 years.
Status: Status unknown.

Hoffmann's two-toed sloths live in the rainforests of northern South America as far south as Brazil and Bolivia, and into Central America as far north as Nicaragua. Unlike their three-toed cousins, they have only two digits on each forefoot, but their hind feet have three. Like other sloths, this species lives a slow, nocturnal life, hanging from high branches.

When feeding, Hoffmann's two-toed sloth uses its long arms to pull branches within reach of the mouth. Its diet consists of leaves, fruit and twigs, which do not provide the sloth with large amounts of nutrients or energy. Consequently, it cannot rely on summoning the energy to run from danger. Instead, it hides by staying perfectly still during the day. As in all the sloths, the hair shafts of this species have a long groove that collects blue-green algae, which makes the hairs appear green. The green hair adds to a motionless sloth's camouflage, helping it to blend in with the foliage. If the camouflage fails to prevent attack from harpy eagles, jaguars, or other predators, the sloth may fight back with its claws.

It has been suggested that the sloth may also gain nutrients from the algae, obtained either by absorption through the skin or by licking the hair.

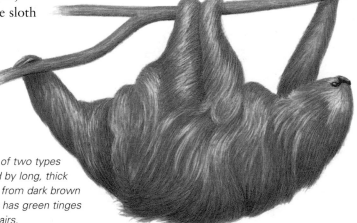

The sloth's shaggy coat is made up of two types of fur. The short underfur is covered by long, thick guard hairs. The hairs vary in colour from dark brown to pale yellow, although the fur also has green tinges produced by bacteria living on the hairs.

MARSUPIALS

Marsupials are a group of mammals that brood their young in pouches on their bellies, rather than in wombs like placental mammals. The overwhelming majority of marsupials are found in Australia and New Guinea, but several species live in the Americas. However, fossil evidence has led zoologists to conclude that marsupials first evolved in South America, and subsequently spread to Australasia.

Water opossum

Chironectes minimus

Water opossums have short waterproof coats with a grey and black pattern. Their hind feet are webbed, and both sexes have pouches opening to the rear.

Water opossums, or yapoks, live beside bodies of fresh water in tropical forests. They make dens in burrows in the banks of streams or lakes, with entrances just above water level. Unusually, both sexes have pouches. A female can close her pouch using a ring of muscles to keep her developing young dry while she is underwater. A male's pouch is always open and he uses it to protect his scrotum while in water or when moving quickly through forest.

Water opossums are superb swimmers, using their hind feet to propel themselves through the water. However, they also forage on land or in trees. They spend the night in their dens, but may rest in bundles of leaves in secluded places on the forest floor between daytime feeding forays. Most births take place between December and January. After their birth, the young opossums spend a few more weeks in the pouch until they are fully developed.

Distribution: Central and South America from southern Mexico to Belize and Argentina.
Habitat: Fresh-water streams and lakes.
Food: Crayfish, shrimp, fish, fruit and water plants.
Size: 27–40cm (10.5–15.5in); 600–800g (21.25–28.25oz).
Maturity: Unknown.
Breeding: 2–5 young born in summer.
Life span: 3 years.
Status: Lower risk.

Virginia opossum

Didelphis virginiana

Distribution: United States, Central America and northern South America.
Habitat: Moist woodlands or thick brush in swamps.
Food: Plants, carrion, small vertebrates and invertebrates.
Size: 33–50cm (13–19.5in); 2–5.5kg (4.5–12.25lb).
Maturity: 6–8 months.
Breeding: 2 litters per year.
Life span: 3 years.
Status: Lower risk.

Virginia opossums generally live in forested areas that receive plenty of rain. However, the species is very adaptable and is making its home in new places across North America. Many survive in more open country beside streams or in swamps, while others make their homes in people's sheds and barns.

Virginia opossums are most active at night. By day they rest in nests of leaves and grass, hidden away in crevices, hollow trees and sometimes in burrows. By night, the marsupials hunt for food. They are good climbers, using their prehensile tails to cling to branches.

Virginia opossums do not hibernate, but they do put on fat as the days shorten with the approach of autumn. They rely on this fat to keep them going during the periods of harshest winter weather, when they cannot get out to feed. In the very coldest parts of their range, these marsupials sometimes suffer frostbite on their naked tails and thin ears.

Mating takes place in both late winter and spring. The young are only 1cm (0.4in) long and underdeveloped at birth. Over 20 are born, but the mother can only suckle 13 at once, so the weaker offspring die.

Virginia opossums have white faces, often with darker streaks. Their bodies are covered in shaggy coats of long grey and white hairs, but their tails are almost naked.

White-eared opossum

Didelphis albiventris

Distribution: South America.
Habitat: Most habitats.
Food: Invertebrates, fruits
and seeds.
Size: 30–50cm (12–20in);
0.4–1.3kg (1–2.75lb).
Maturity: 9 months.
Breeding: Up to 6 young
born in litters produced twice
each year.
Life span: 3 years.
Status: Common.

These highly adaptable marsupials live throughout South America east of the Andes, occupying all habitats that contain enough food. Although they avoid deserts and drier areas, they can survive in a range of temperatures and humidity, including in the mountains of Patagonia and on open areas such as pampas. However, white-eared opossums are most common in deciduous forest. They can survive such diverse habitats because they are generalist feeders. Their diet includes invertebrates, fruits, seeds and small mammals and reptiles. In some parts of their range, the opossums even eat highly venomous pit vipers.

White-eared opossums are nocturnal creatures, sleeping in tree hollows and other hidden spots by day, and foraging at night. They live alone and will not tolerate the presence of another opossum. Males are particularly aggressive, except towards females that are ready to mate. It is possible that individuals form alliances with each other and organize themselves into a loose hierarchy.

Male white-eared opossums are larger than females. Their bodies are rat-like, although they are not related to these rodents. The females have a pouch on their underside, in which the young are carried.

Central American woolly opossum (*Caluromys derbianus*): Length unknown; 200–400g (7–14oz)
With a range extending from central Mexico to western Colombia and northern Ecuador, this species occupies lowland rainforests and similar tropical forests that grow in upland areas. This is the largest of the woolly opossums, which are named after their long, dense fur. It has a black stripe from the top of the head to the tip of the snout. The long, prehensile tail has a naked tip to help grip branches. The opposable thumb, or hallux, on the paws is clawless to avoid damaging the foot pad. This species eats a range of foods, including seeds, fruits and insects.

Southern opossum (*Didelphis marsupialis*): 26–45cm (10–17.5in); 0.6–2.4kg (1.25–5.25lb)
The southern opossum is a close relative of the Virginia opossum of North America, but it is found further south, ranging from eastern Mexico to north-eastern Argentina. Like other opossums, it is a generalist feeder that occupies a variety of habitats. Southern opossums are typically forest-dwellers, but they also venture into cultivated areas such as coffee plantations. Southern opossums are often seen in urban and suburban areas, where they eat garbage.

Agile gracile mouse opossum (*Gracilinanus agilis*): 11–14cm (4.25–5.5in); weight unknown
This tiny marsupial lives in Peru, Brazil and northern Argentina. It lives in forests, where it forages and nests alone. It does not dig its own burrow, but occupies a nest abandoned by another animal. Its prehensile tail and opposable big toe help to make it an excellent climber.

Big-eared opossum

Didelphis aurita

This opossum lives along the Atlantic coast of Brazil and extends inland to Paraguay and northern Argentina. It is found in the unique Atlantic rainforests that grow in this region, as well as in other types of forest that clothe the highlands further inland. Many of these habitats, especially the Atlantic rainforest, are under grave threat. However, this adaptable opossum seems to be largely unaffected by deforestation and human settlement. Being a generalist feeder, it can survive just as well by rooting through rubbish tips as it can by eating fruits and insects deep in the forest. The big-eared opossum also eats other mammals, small birds and fish.

This opossum is nocturnal and lives alone. It looks for food on the ground or by climbing through undergrowth and the lower branches of forest trees. In flooded parts of its range, it spends long periods living in trees.

This species has a distinctive black line that runs down the middle of the forehead. The large ears are hairless. The long, prehensile tail has long black and white fur at the base.

Distribution: Eastern South America.
Habitat: Coastal forest.
Food: Insects and fruit.
Size: 31–39cm (12–15.5in);
0.7–1.9kg (1.5–4.25lb).
Maturity: 6 months.
Breeding: 2–3 litters of up to 7 offspring each, born at all times of the year.
Life span: 2 years.
Status: Lower risk.

Black-shouldered opossum

Caluromysiops irrupta

Distribution: Andes Mountains.
Habitat: Humid forest.
Food: Fruit and nectar.
Size: 25–30cm (10–12); 2–5kg (4.4–11lb).
Maturity: Unknown.
Breeding: Several young in each litter.
Life span: Unknown.
Status: Common.

This opossum lives in the misty forests that grow along the Andes Mountains of South America. It is more arboreal than many of its relatives and rarely comes to the ground, since it mates, feeds and gives birth in the trees. Its eats mainly fruits, but relies on nectar in the dry season, when fruits are less common.

Black-shouldered opossums are solitary, only coming into contact with other members of the species to breed. Mating takes place at all times of the year. As in other marsupial species, the mother lacks a uterus and cannot carry her young for long, so they are born in an underdeveloped state. The mother guides her young to the pouch by licking a path through the fur from the birth canal. Once in the pouch, the young remain attached to a teat for three or four months.

The black-shouldered opossum's tail is a little longer than the rest of its body. The two black lines on the upper body run from the forefeet and join together at the shoulders, then they divide again and run along either side of the back all the way to the hind feet.

Mexican mouse opossum (*Marmosa mexicana*): 24–43cm (9.5–17in); 20–140g (0.7–5oz)
Mexican mouse opossums are found in Central America, from Panama to southern Mexico. They live in dry monsoon forests, which receive most of their rain during a specific wet season. The opossums live in the lower branches of the trees and rarely venture down to the ground. This species is one of the few marsupials that does not have a pouch. Female marsupials lack a uterus where the embryos can develop. As a result, newborn marsupials are often very undeveloped, so they seek refuge in their mother's external pouch until they are more fully grown. However, mouse opossums are small enough to reach a relatively advanced stage of development before being born, after which they travel on their mother's back. As many as 13 young are born in each litter, although many of them die before reaching maturity.

Red-legged short-tailed opossum
(*Monodelphis brevicaudata*): 16cm (6.25in); 67–95g (2.25–3.25oz)
This species ranges from northern South America to Bolivia and southern Brazil, occupying forests and dense shrublands. Unusually for an American marsupial, its tail is non-prehensile and shorter than rest of its body. The red-legged short-tailed opossum is a solitary forager, being most active by day. It spends most of its time on the ground, although it will also hunt in trees. Cockroaches and grasshoppers are the opossum's favourite foods, supplemented by fruits and seeds.

Lutrine opossum

Lutreolina crassicaudata

The word lutrine in this species' common name means "like an otter", referring to the fact that this opossum is a regular swimmer and is often found near water. It is even at home in flooded forests. Not only is its behaviour lutrine, but it also has a body shape resembling that of a small carnivore, such as an otter or weasel.

Lutrine opossums are also known as thick-tailed opossums. They live in two populations. The larger group occurs in Bolivia, east of the Andes, and in Brazil. The smaller population is found in forests north of the Amazon Basin, from the Guianas to northern Colombia. Lutrine opossums also occur on the pampas of northern Argentina.

These animals are more social than other opossum species, although most live alone. They are active at night, when they climb or swim in search of food. Their varied diet is made up largely of small mammals, birds, fish and insects, but they also eat crabs and other aquatic invertebrates, as well as fruits.

Distribution: Eastern Bolivia, southern Brazil and northern Argentina; also in Guyana, Venezuela and Colombia.
Habitat: Grassland and flooded woodland.
Food: Small mammals, birds, reptiles, fish, insects and aquatic invertebrates.
Size: 20–40cm (8–15.5in); 500g–1kg (1.25–2.25lb).
Maturity: Unknown.
Breeding: 2 litters of about 10 offspring produced in spring and summer.
Life span: 3 years.
Status: Common.

These hunting marsupials have small ears, a long, slender body, short, stout legs and a long, thick tail. The tail, which can measure about 30cm (12in) long, is not as prehensile as that of other opossums.

Grey slender mouse opossum

Marmosops incanus

Distribution: Eastern Brazil.
Habitat: Humid forest.
Food: Insect.
Size: 24–43cm (9.5–17in);
20–140g (0.75–5oz).
Maturity: 6 months.
Breeding: Litters born from
September to December.
Life span: 1–1.5 years.
Status: Not known.

*These small opossums have a
mouse-like body. In the more
southerly parts of its range, the
fur is considerably longer in winter
than in summer. Males may be
much larger than females.*

This is another marsupial species that lives in the forests that grow along Brazil's Atlantic coast. It is also found on a few of the islands that exist along this stretch of coastline. The grey slender mouse opossum is most common in the damp forests of lowland areas, although it also occurs in the drier monsoon and gallery forests that grow further inland.

Grey slender mouse opossums feed almost exclusively on insects, especially beetles and grasshoppers. They are scansorial animals, which means that they are highly curious and will climb over all parts of their environment, exploring every nook and cranny for feeding opportunities. They are just as at home in the trees as they are on the ground, and they frequently move between the two.

The grey slender mouse opossum has a short life cycle. Breeding takes place between September and December, after which all the males die, so that none are left alive by February. The females give birth and then die themselves in May. The young are helpless at birth but develop rapidly. By August the young born that year have reached maturity, and are ready to mate in the forthcoming breeding season.

Brown four-eyed opossum

Metachirus nudicaudatus

Distribution: Nicaragua to
eastern South America.
Habitat: Forest and brush.
Food: Primarily fruits, but
also insects, amphibians,
reptiles, molluscs, birds,
eggs, and small mammals.
Size: 19–31cm (7.5–12.25in);
0.8kg (1.75lb).
Maturity: Unknown.
Breeding: Litters of up to 9
young; young are born at all
times of year, and each
female may produce several
litters annually.
Life span: 3 years.
Status: Common.

This species ranges from Nicaragua in Central America to Paraguay and northern Argentina in South America. Brown four-eyed opossums are found in dense lowland forests, where they move between the branches and the forest floor. They also live in more open brushlands, including the Gran Chaco of Paraguay and Argentina. In this habitat they remain hidden in thick undergrowth.

Brown four-eyed opossums are nocturnal. They always remain in their nests until after dark. The nests are round formations of leaves and twigs that are generally built among tree branches or under rocks and logs. These opossums appear to be very curious foragers. They do not occupy a distinct territory, but travel far and wide in search of food. Brown four-eyed opossums regularly move to new areas in search of better food supplies. Their diet is made up mainly of fruits, but they are also known to eat a range of other foods, from insects to eggs and lizards. They are sometimes said to damage fruit crops.

*The white spots over this
opossum's eyes are the source
of its unusual common name.
The short, dense, silky fur is
brown on the back and sides,
with traces of black on the rump.
The tail measures 19–39cm
(7.5–15.3in). Females weigh about
one-third less
than males.*

INSECTIVORES

Insectivores, or insect-eaters, belong to the Insectivora *order of mammals. The first mammals to develop their young in uteruses belonged to this group, and most insectivores still resemble these small, primitive animals. However, insectivores have evolved to live in a wide range of niches, including subterranean, terrestrial, aquatic and arboreal habitats.*

Giant mole shrew

Blarina brevicauda

Giant mole shrews live in most land habitats within their range, but they are hard to spot. They use their strong forepaws and flexible snouts to dig deep burrows in soft earth and, when on the surface, they scurry out of sight beneath mats of leaves or snow. However, they do climb into trees in search of food on occasion.

These small mammals feed at all times of the day and night. They rest in nests of grass and leaves made inside their tunnels or in nooks and crannies on the surface. Giant mole shrews will eat plant food, but they also hunt for small prey, such as snails, mice and insects. Their saliva contains a venom that paralyzes prey animals. In the mating season, which takes place between spring and autumn, they expand their territories so that they overlap with those of the opposite sex.

Giant mole shrews have stout bodies with long, pointed snouts covered in sensitive whiskers. Their eyes are very small because they spend most of the time underground, and their ears are hidden under thick coats of grey hairs.

Distribution: Central Canada to south-eastern United States.
Habitat: All land habitats.
Food: Insects, small vertebrates, seeds and shoots.
Size: 12–14cm (5–5.5in); 15–30g (0.5–1oz).
Maturity: 6 weeks.
Breeding: Litters of 5–7 young born throughout the summer.
Life span: 2 years.
Status: Common.

Star-nosed mole

Condylura cristata

Distribution: Eastern Canada to south-eastern United States.
Habitat: Muddy soil near water.
Food: Aquatic insects, fish, worms and crustaceans.
Size: 10–12cm (4–5in); 40–85g (1.5–3oz).
Maturity: 10 months.
Breeding: 2–7 young born in summer.
Life span: Unknown.
Status: Endangered.

Star-nosed moles live in waterlogged soil. They dig networks of tunnels in the soil, which generally reach down as far as the water table. They push the mud and soil out of the entrances of the tunnels, making molehills in the process. The moles construct nests at the ends of tunnels, which are lined with dry grass.

Star-nosed moles are expert swimmers. They search for food at the bottom of streams and pools, using their sensitive snouts to feel their way and detect prey. In winter, star-nosed moles use tunnels with underwater entrances to get into ponds that are iced over. They feed in water both in the daytime and at night, but they are only really active above ground during the hours of darkness.

Most births take place in early summer. The young already have the star of rays on their snouts. Breeding pairs of males and females may stay together throughout the winter and breed again the following year.

Star-nosed moles have unusual fleshy rays that radiate from each nostril. These are sensitive feelers that the moles use in the darkness below ground. The moles' dark, dense fur is coated with water-repelling oils.

Hispaniolan solenodon

Solenodon paradoxus

Distribution: Hispaniola.
Habitat: Woodland and bushy areas.
Food: Insects.
Size: 28–33cm (11–13cm); 0.6–1kg (1.25–2.2lb).
Maturity: Unknown.
Breeding: 2 litters of up to 3 offspring born at all times of year.
Life span: 11 years.
Status: Endangered.

This highly unusual species of mammal lives on Hispaniola, a large Caribbean island in the Greater Antilles. The island is divided into Haiti and the Dominican Republic. Most solenodons are found in the north of the island, in wooded and brush areas. By day the solenodons shelter in extensive tunnel systems that they excavate themselves. They will also rest in tree hollows and caves. As night falls, the solenodons leave their dens to look for insects, other invertebrates and fruits. Their main foods are millipedes, beetles, grasshoppers, snails and worms.

Solenodons forage by sniffing out prey with their long snout. The Hispaniolan solenodon's snout is unique among mammals, because it is connected to the skull by a ball-and-socket joint, which makes it extremely flexible. As it forages, the animal uses its clawed feet to overturn stones and rip off bark to expose insects.

Looking like a huge shrew, this rare species uses its large forelegs for digging tunnel networks. All the feet have long claws. The Hispaniolan solenodon has 40 teeth for cutting up insect prey. Some of these teeth can inject venomous saliva when the animal bites its victims.

Cuban solenodon (*Solenodon cubanus*): 28–39cm (11–15.5in); 1kg (2.2lb)
The lesser known of the two solenodon species, the Cuban solenodon is found in eastern Cuba, where it occupies caves and hollows in wet mountain forests. Cuban solenodons live in small family groups, probably made up of a mother and her assorted offspring. Although these solenodons do not have a joint inside their snout like their Hispaniolan relatives, the snout is still extremely flexible. They are believed to have toxic saliva, which is delivered into wounds when the animal bites an attacker. There is no evidence that this venom is used in hunting. The females carry their young while they are still attached to their teats (most insectivores and other mammals carry young in their mouth or on their back). This species has more catholic tastes than the Hispaniolan solenodon: as well as insects, it eats small reptiles, roots and leaves.

Elliot's short-tailed shrew (*Blarina hylophaga*): 9.2–12cm (3.6–4.75in); 15g (0.5oz)
Elliot's short-tailed shrew lives in the Midwest region of the United States. It inhabits forests and grasslands, and has adapted to life in the huge wheat and corn fields that cover its range. It requires soft soil for burrowing through and is common close to the banks of rivers, where the damp earth is looser than in drier areas. However, the shrew never takes to the water. It is a skilled climber and forages for insects and plant food all year round. It does not hibernate and generally survives for no more than a year. It relies on stores of food laid down in autumn to get it through the winter.

Southern short-tailed shrew

Blarina carolinensis

This species ranges from southern Illinois to Florida. It prefers to live in damp habitats with well-drained soil for burrowing. It is especially common in woodlands, where the roots of trees create good conditions for digging tunnels.

The southern short-tailed shrew is the smallest in its genus, with members of the species having as few as 36 chromosomes, while their larger relatives, the giant mole shrews, have between 48 and 50.

Southern short-tailed shrews are nocturnal. Even when active, they are often hidden away in tunnels and runways among leaf litter and grass. They are most likely to be seen just after rainfall. The rain water trickles though the soil, flooding lower levels, and this forces insects and worms that are living underground up to the surface, where the shrews are ready and waiting. The shrews also supplement their diet with berries.

Young shrews are born blind and helpless, and are cared for in a nest of grass and other dry vegetation under a log, stump or underground.

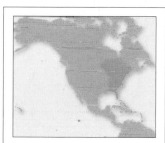

Distribution: South-eastern North America.
Habitat: Moist woodlands.
Food: Insects and worms.
Size: 7.5–10.5cm (2.9–4.1in); 15–30g (0.5–1oz).
Maturity: 12 weeks.
Breeding: Several litters produced in summer.
Life span: 1 year.
Status: Common.

This is the smallest of the short-tailed shrews. Its fur is almost a completely uniform grey, which becomes slightly paler in summer. As with most shrews, this species has a long flexible nose for probing through loose soil.

Least shrew

Cryptotis parva

Least shrews live south of the Great Lakes across the eastern United States. They also occur through eastern Mexico to northern Nicaragua in Central America. Within this vast area the shrews occupy a variety of habitats. In northern parts of the range, least shrews are found in grasslands, meadows or areas covered in a thick layer of brush. Further south, where it is generally drier, these shrews are more common in the vegetation that grows along the banks of streams and lakes.

Least shrews move through the plant cover in tunnels called runways, which connect their nests together. The nests are constructed underground in burrows dug by the shrews, and then lined with leaves. Least shrews will also take over and extend burrows made by other animals. Rather unusually for shrews, this species is relatively social. The nests are shared, and more than 30 shrews have been found living together in a single nest.

Least shrews are almost exclusively flesh eaters. They have been seen to open up the abdomens of insects such as grasshoppers to eat only the most nutritious internal organs.

Distribution: From eastern United States south to northern Nicaragua in Central America.
Habitat: Grass and brush.
Food: Insects, worms, slugs and snails, plus some plant matter.
Size: 5–8cm (2–3in); 4–6.5g (0.1–0.2oz).
Maturity: 5 weeks.
Breeding: Several litters of about 5 young produced in summer.
Life span: 1.5 years.
Status: Common.

This mammal has black fur on its back and white fur on its underside. In summer, the upper fur often pales slightly to brown. The milk teeth of young shrews fall out while the animals are still in the womb.

Desert shrew

Notiosorex crawfordi

The desert shrew ranges across the arid south-west of the United States. It is also found in the drier areas parts of Mexico. Although it can survive in desert conditions, this shrew can also be found in a range of other habitats, including marshland.

The desert shrew preys mainly on invertebrates such as worms, spiders and insects, but it also eats lizards, birds and small mammals such as mice. The shrew must consume three-quarters of its own body weight in food each day to survive. (This is actually a relatively small amount for a shrew.) In the driest parts of its range, the desert shrew can survive on the water it gets from its food. However, it is most often found close to a supply of drinking water.

Desert shrews hunt at night, restricting themselves to areas with thick brush to avoid owls and other predators. They rest in the burrow of another animal during daylight hours. In the hottest part of the day, the shrews enter a torpor – an inactive state similar to hibernation.

In this state, they use only a fraction of the energy that they would do when normally active. The female makes a crude nest from hair, grass and other vegetation. The blind, hairless young develop rapidly and may accompany their mother for a short period before they disperse.

Distribution: South-western United States, from California to Texas and Colorado; also Baja California and northern and central Mexico.
Habitat: Deserts, semi-arid grasslands, chaparral, woodland and marshland.
Food: Invetebrates such as insects, spiders and worms; also lizards, small mammals and young birds.
Size: 5–6cm (2–2.5in); 4.5–8g (0.2–0.3oz).
Maturity: 2 months.
Breeding: 1–2 litters of 3–5 young born each year.
Life span: Unknown.
Status: Common.

The desert shrew's tail is at least half as long as its small body. Desert shrews are often found living in garbage dumps around human settlements.

Arctic shrew

Sorex arcticus

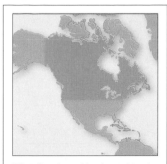

Distribution: Northern North America.
Habitat: In forests near fresh water.
Food: Invertebrates.
Size: 6–7cm (2.5–2.75in); 5–13g (0.2–0.5oz).
Maturity: 2 years.
Breeding: Up to 9 young born in one litter in April or May.
Life span: Unknown.
Status: Common.

This species ranges south from Canada's North-west and Yukon Territories to Minnesota in the US Midwest and east to Nova Scotia on the Atlantic coast of Canada. It is most often spotted near to supplies of fresh water. Its preferred habitats are forests growing on boggy ground, which are populated with trees such as wet spruce and tamarack. Such marshy woodland is alive with invertebrates, providing the shrew with an excellent supply of food throughout the year.

Like most shrews and other small, warm-blooded animals, the Arctic shrew must eat huge quantities of food to supply its body with the energy it needs to survive. This is especially true in the colder northern parts of this species' range, where it will die if it goes without food for more than two hours. Consequently, Arctic shrews will eat virtually anything. Most of their diet is made up of invertebrates, mainly insects such as beetles and their larvae, but they also eat earthworms, spiders, snails, seeds and leaves.

The distinctive three-coloured fur makes the Arctic shrew easy to identify. There is a black band running along the back from nose to tail. The sides are brown, and the underside is grey.

Giant Mexican shrew (*Megasorex gigas*): 8–9cm (3.25–3.5in); 10–12g (0.3–0.4oz)
Although members of this species are consistently large, they are not by any means the largest of the shrews. They get their "giant" moniker from the fact that they are the last surviving member of the *Megasorex* genus, which once contained truly giant shrews. Giant Mexican shrews live in tropical forests and grasslands in western Mexico. They find worms, grubs and other invertebrate prey by rooting through loose soil and leaf litter with their pointed snout.

Gaspé shrew (*Sorex gaspensis*): 9.5–12.5cm (3.75–5in); 2.2–4.3g (0.1oz)
This shrew is found on the Gaspé Peninsula of eastern Quebec, and in two small ranges in New Brunswick and on Cape Breton Island in Nova Scotia. Gaspé shrews live in mountain conifer forests, where they forage among the leaf litter or mosses that grow on the forest floor. They are grey all over, with a very narrow snout. Their diet comprises mainly grubs, maggots and spiders, but they also eat worms, snails, slugs and plant matter.

Masked shrew (*Sorex cinereus*): 7cm (2.75in); 2.5–4g (0.1oz)
This is North America's most widespread shrew, ranging across Canada and Alaska and much of the northern United States. Masked shrews occupy a range of habitats, wherever there is adequate ground cover. They are most commonly found in wet areas, such as near to streams or in marshes. Among American mammals, only the pygmy shrew is smaller than this species.

Long-tailed shrew

Sorex dispar

The long-tailed shrew is found as far north as Nova Scotia in eastern Canada. From there it ranges south to Tennessee and North Carolina in the southern United States. This shrew can survive in a range of forest types, although most of the forests within its range are cool and damp. The long-tailed shrew is especially abundant in mountain forests, on ranges such as the Appalachians and Adirondacks. It makes its dens in cool rock crevices and under boulders and scree.

Long-tailed shrews forage for food both day and night. They do not hibernate. Like most shrews, they lead a solitary life and chase away any shrew that comes near. A long-tailed shrew must eat twice its body weight in food every day to stay alive. The diet consists of insects, spiders, centipedes and other invertebrates, as well as plant foods such as seeds.

Distribution: Eastern North America.
Habitat: Damp forest.
Food: Invertebrates and plants.
Size: 4.6–10cm (1.75–4in); 4–6g (0.1–0.2oz).
Maturity: 4 months.
Breeding: Several litters of about 5 young produced between April and August.
Life span: 2 years.
Status: Common.

Long-tailed shrews are often mistaken for smoky shrews, but long-tailed shrews tend to be more slender and have a longer tail.

Pygmy shrew

Sorex hoyi

Because of its small size, the pygmy shrew is able to occupy a range of microhabitats, such as moss, leaf litter, root systems, rotting stumps and the burrows of larger animals. It can even travel in the tunnels of large beetles. The coat of the pygmy shrew varies from grey-brown in winter to grey in summer; the underparts are light grey.

Although this is the smallest American mammal, it is by no means the smallest mammal in the world. The white-toothed shrews living in the so-called Old World – Europe, Africa and Asia – are almost half the weight of this species, and the hog-nosed bat of Thailand is equally small, at about half the weight of a penny coin or a dime.

Pygmy shrews occupy a wide range of habitats, but they are sparsely distributed and often hard to locate. They feed on small invertebrates such as ants and spiders, and will also eat carrion if the opportunity arises. These tiny creatures live life at a feverish pace. They forage in short bursts of just a few minutes and then rest for a similar amount of time. They nose through soil and leaf litter in search of prey, and often venture into the tunnels of larger animals to look for food. When threatened, pygmy shrews release a musky odour from glands on their sides. This smell not only deters the attacker, but also alerts any shrews nearby to the potential danger.

Distribution: From Alaska and eastern Canada to the Rockies and Appalachian Mountains in the United States.
Habitat: Forest, swamp and grassland.
Food: Insects.
Size: 5–6cm (2–2.5in); 2–4g (0.1oz).
Maturity: 1.5 years.
Breeding: One litter of about 5 young born in summer, about 18 days after mating.
Life span: Unknown.
Status: Common.

Water shrew

Sorex palustris

Distribution: Northern North America.
Habitat: Near streams and other fresh-water habitats.
Food: Insects.
Size: 8cm (3in); 8–18g (0.3–0.6oz).
Maturity: 1 year.
Breeding: 2–3 litters of 3–10 young produced in spring and summer.
Life span: 18 months.
Status: Common.

One of the most aquatic of all shrews, this species occurs throughout Alaska and Canada. It extends south into high, mountainous regions of the United States, most notably along the Rockies, where climatic conditions are similar to those found further north. This shrew is often found in or close to water. It also lives in damp conifer forests.

Water shrews live alone and are known to hunt for insects. Most of their prey are the aquatic youngsters of insects such as crane flies and caddis flies. While under water, the shrews detect the movements of prey using whiskers on their snouts. They grab the food with their forefeet or mouth. In captivity, water shrews have been seen feeding once every ten minutes. In the wild, they will die if they go without food for about three hours.

Males of this large shrew species tend to be longer than females. The thick fur traps a layer of air around the body to keep the animal warm while diving in cold water.

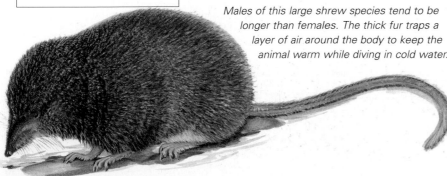

Montane shrew (*Sorex monticolus*): 6–8cm (2.5–3in); 5.9–7.2g (0.2–0.25oz)
This solitary species, also called the dusky shrew, occurs from northern Alaska southward to New Mexico, and from the west coast to Manitoba in the east. It occurs in a variety of habitats, including tundra in the far north, prairies in drier parts of the range and also mountain forests. All these habitats have some ground vegetation in which the shrews can hide from predators. Montane shrews feed on insect larvae, spiders, earthworms and occasionally small salamanders. They also eat non-animal foods such as seeds and mushrooms.

American shrew mole (*Neurotrichus gibbsii*): 7–9cm (2.75–3.5in); 8–14.5g (0.3–0.5oz)
The smallest American mole, this species is the size of a large shrew. Shrew moles range from northern California to southern British Colombia. They tunnel in soft, deep peaty soils, especially those formed by the highly fertile rainforests of North America's northern Pacific coast. They must eat about one-and-a-half times their body weight in insects and worms each day to survive.

Townsend's mole (*Scapanus townsendii*): 18–24cm (7–9.5in); 100–170g (3.5–6oz)
Confined to a small range between the Cascade Mountains and the Pacific coast of California, Oregon and Washington, Townsend's mole is the largest mole in North America. This species lives in lowland areas with deep, loamy soil. The mole preys on earthworms and insect larvae by patrolling their territories through a permanent network of tunnels.

Eastern mole

Scalopus aquaticus

Distribution: Eastern and central United States and southern Canada.
Habitat: Fields, meadows and open woodland.
Food: Earthworms, insects and roots.
Size: 11–17cm (4.25–6.75in); 32–140g (1.25–5oz).
Maturity: 1 year.
Breeding: One litter of 2–5 young produced per year; the breeding season is from March to April in most of the range, but begins in January in the south.
Life span: 3 years.
Status: Common.

The eastern mole ranges from Wyoming and South Dakota in the north and west to Texas and Florida in the south and New England in the east. There is also a smaller, isolated population in Mexico. This mole needs to dig its burrows in soil that is relatively free of large roots and rocks, so it avoids thick forest and stony ground, preferring areas of moist sandy or loamy soils. When it burrows, the mole thrusts its front limbs forward, then pulls them outward and back to force the loose dirt out of the way.

Most of the eastern mole's diet consists of earthworms, although it will eat adult and larval insects as well as roots. Being a large insectivore, the mole needs to consume just a quarter of its bodyweight in food each day – far less than smaller insectivore species. Eastern moles find their food using their sense of smell and by detecting vibrations in the floor and walls of their tunnels made by the movements of prey. Although the ears are covered by a layer of skin to keep earth out, the moles are still able to hear. The eyes are light-sensitive, even though they cannot form images, so the moles can at least tell when they break the surface.

The size of this species varies according to geographical location. The largest moles live in the north-east, in areas such as New England, while the smallest individuals are generally found in the south-west, notably Texas.

Hairy-tailed mole

Parascalops breweri

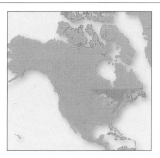

Distribution: Eastern Canada to the Appalachians.
Habitat: Forests and meadows.
Food: Insects and worms.
Size: 11.5–14cm (4.5–5.5in); 40–85g (1.5–3oz).
Maturity: 10 months.
Breeding: One litter of 4–5 young produced in summer.
Life span: 3 years.
Status: Unknown.

This mole differs from other mole species by having a much shorter snout and a hairy tail. It also lacks the protuberances on the snout used by many species to detect the movements of prey.

The hairy-tailed mole ranges from southern Quebec and Ontario to central Ohio and western North Carolina. It lives in open woodland and meadows. In the south of its range, it occurs at high altitudes in the Appalachian Mountains, which have a colder and wetter climate than lowland areas.

Hairy-tailed moles are most active during the day, when they tunnel under the ground in search of food. They may also move around at night, sometimes emerging from their tunnels to forage on the surface. In winter, each mole occupies its own network of tunnels and will close up any links with the tunnels of other moles. However, during summer the males, females and young all share a network of tunnels.

Having mated in the spring breeding season, the female builds an underground nest out of a ball of dry vegetation approximately 25cm (10in) below the surface. Gestation is about four to six weeks. The newborn young remain in the nest for up to a month, by which time they have been weaned on to solid food.

NEW WORLD MONKEYS

Most New World monkeys are found in South America, but some species live as far north as southern Mexico. There are 30 species of New World monkey, including howler monkeys and capuchins. The features that differentiate New World Monkeys from species living in Africa and Asia are their flattened noses, which have broadly spaced nostrils, and their prehensile tails, which they use like a fifth limb.

Brown capuchin

Cebus apella

Like some other capuchin species, brown capuchins have a cap of dark hair on the top of their heads, with thick tufts or "horns" above the ears.

Capuchins are sometimes called ring-tails. This is because they often curl the tip of their semi-prehensile tail into a ring. Capuchins are among the most intelligent and adaptable of all monkeys. They are found in a wide range of habitats, from dense jungles to towns and cities. Some even live on the seashore, where they collect crabs. Capuchins sometimes break open hard nuts by pounding them with stones – an example of animals using tools. This species lives in troops of about 12 monkeys. Most troops have a single adult male, who fathers all the children. The monkeys chatter and squeak a great deal, telling each other of their location and warning of danger. Since they lack a set breeding season, capuchin mothers may give birth to their single babies at any time of the year. Each young capuchin initially clings to its mother's chest, then rides on her back until it becomes more independent.

Distribution: From Colombia to Paraguay.
Habitat: Rainforest.
Food: Fruit, nuts, flowers, bark, gums, insects and eggs.
Size: 30–56cm (12–22in); 1.1–3.3kg (2.5–7.25lb).
Maturity: Females 4 years; males 8 years.
Breeding: Single young born throughout the year.
Life span: 30 years.
Status: Lower risk.

Squirrel monkey

Saimiri boliviensis

Squirrel monkeys live in many types of forest. They spend most of their time in trees, rarely coming down to the ground. However, some populations of squirrel monkeys have made their homes in areas cleared of trees for agriculture. These monkeys tend to live close to streams for reasons of safety. Squirrel monkeys form complex social groups, or troops, which are larger than those of any other monkey species in the Americas. In pristine rainforests, the troops can number up to 300 individuals.

Males do not help in raising the young and during the mating season (the dry part of the year) they establish hierarchies by fighting each other. Only dominant males get to mate with the females. Soon after giving birth to their single offspring, the new mothers chase away the breeding males, which reform their bachelor subgroups. Adolescent males, too old to stay with their mothers, eventually join these subgroups, having fought their way in.

Squirrel monkeys have black, hairless snouts and helmets of dark fur around their pale faces. Their ears are covered in pale fur. The rest of the body is more brightly coloured, in hues of pale yellow and red, and the mobile tail has a black tip. The body is slender in shape. Squirrel monkeys travel through the forest on all four legs.

Distribution: Central America to Upper Amazon Basin.
Habitat: Tropical forest, close to streams.
Food: Fruit, nuts, flowers, leaves, gums, insects and small vertebrates.
Size: 26–36cm (10–14in); 0.75–1.1kg (1.65–2.4lb).
Maturity: Females 3 years; males 5 years.
Breeding: Single young born from June–August.
Life span: 20 years.
Status: Lower risk.

Black-handed spider monkey

Ateles geoffroyi

Spider monkeys are the most agile of the American primates, not least because their long prehensile tails function as a fifth limb. The animals can pick up food or hold on to branches with their tails. It is not unusual to see one of these monkeys hanging from its tail alone.

Spider monkey troops live high up in forest canopies, and almost never visit the ground. They are most active early in the morning, spending the rest of the day relaxing and digesting tough plant food.

Troops usually contain about 30 individuals, with equal numbers of males and females. However, larger groups of more than 100 have been reported. The males in the troops defend large territories by regularly patrolling the perimeters, while females and young tend to stay close to the centre.

Males tend to stay in the troops they were born into, while females move to other troops in the area. Breeding occurs all year round. Spider monkeys reportedly have a unique defensive strategy: when potential predators approach – including humans – the monkeys drop heavy branches on top of them.

Spider monkeys have very long, prehensile tails and similarly long legs, hence their name. This allows them to be extremely agile in the treetops.

Distribution: Mexico to Colombia.
Habitat: Tropical forest.
Food: Fruit, seeds, buds, leaves, insects and eggs.
Size: 38–63cm (15–25in); 6–8kg (13.25–17.5lb).
Maturity: 4–5 years.
Breeding: Single young born throughout the year.
Life span: 30 years.
Status: Vulnerable.

Black-bearded saki (*Chiropotes satanas*): 40–51cm (16–20in); 2–4kg (4.5–8.75lb)
The black-bearded saki has a long, thick beard on its elongated chin. Its head, beard and tail are black, while its shoulders, back, hands and feet are reddish-brown to black. This species lives in Guyana, Venezuela and Brazil north of the Amazon. The black-bearded saki eats fruit, the seeds of unripe fruit, leaves, flowers and a few insects. It lives in troops of up to 30 individuals. The monkey's tail is non-prehensile, but the animal is capable of a very strong grip with its hands and feet. It often hangs by a single limb while foraging high in the trees.

White-nosed bearded saki (*Chiropotes albinasus*): 38–42cm (15–16.5in); 2–3kg (4.5–6.5lb)
This species lives south of the Amazon River in central Brazil. The white-nosed bearded saki inhabits a range of forests, and is mainly found in the emergent layer, where tall trees poke out above the upper forest canopy. This bearded saki is diurnal and rests in the boughs of trees at night. To avoid being attacked by predators, it never sleeps in the same place for two consecutive nights. The body is covered by black hair, except for the nose and upper lip, which have white fur. When a mature female is ready to mate, her vulva becomes bright red as a signal to males. Matings usually take place in December and June, with the female producing a single young each year. White-nosed bearded sakis live in large troops of up to 30 monkeys. They communicate with whistles and chirps.

Common woolly monkey

Lagothrix lagotricha

Common, or Humboldt's, woolly monkeys are among the largest of all New World monkeys. (Only the muriqui, or woolly spider monkey, is appreciably bigger.) These monkeys live in high forests on the slopes of the Andes Mountains and Mato Grosso in Brazil. They spend much of their time at the top of the tallest trees, which protrude from the forest canopy. On the ground, they may walk on their hind legs, using their heavy tails to keep them upright. They are diurnal animals and eat mainly fruit and insects, but they can survive on leaves and seeds if necessary.

Common woolly monkeys live in groups of about eight individuals. They communicate using a range of facial expressions and calls. Males, which are heavier than females, often display their long canine teeth with wide yawns to warn off rivals.

The fur is thick and black, and the body is very heavyset compared to other tree-dwelling monkeys. Older monkeys grow a fringe of long hair on the backs of their arms and legs.

Distribution: Northern South America.
Habitat: Tropical forest.
Food: Fruits, leaves, seeds and insects.
Size: 40–70cm (16–28in); 5–10kg (11–22lb).
Maturity: 5–8 years.
Breeding: 1 young produced every 2 years.
Life span: Unknown.
Status: Vulnerable.

Red howler monkey

Alouatta seniculus

Howlers are large monkeys that live in the trees of tropical forests. They are known for the roaring howls that fill South American forests. The monkeys have very wide jaws, which allow them to open their mouths wide and make such loud calls.

Howler monkeys roar first thing in the morning before setting off to look for food. Although they eat fruits, such as figs, when they are available, howler monkeys rely for long periods on just leaves. Few other monkeys have such an unvaried, indigestible diet. After a rest in the middle of the day, the monkeys feed some more before travelling back to their sleeping trees while howling to each other again.

Howler monkey troops contain about eight or nine individuals. Larger troops form when there are more fruits available. Males compete with each other to join troops, and the victors may kill the young of the males they depose. The howling call is thought to be a mechanism for locating nearby troops. These monkeys breed all year round. The young ride on their mothers' backs for up to a year. Both males and females leave their mothers' troops when they are sexually mature and join others.

Distribution: Northern South America.
Habitat: Rainforest and mangroves.
Food: Leaves and figs.
Size: 55–92cm (21.5–36in); 4–10kg (8.75–22lb).
Maturity: 4–5 years.
Breeding: Single young born throughout the year.
Life span: 20 years.
Status: Endangered.

Howler monkeys typically have reddish-brown hair, although some have a more yellowish or dusky coloration. Their strong prehensile tails have naked patches on their undersides to help them grip branches. The males are larger than the females and generally have darker hair. The loud calls of these monkeys, especially by the males, are made possible by a specialized larynx in the throat, which amplifies the sound.

White-faced saki

Pithecia pithecia

Distribution: Northern South America from Venezuela to north-eastern Brazil.
Habitat: Tropical forest.
Food: Fruit, honey, leaves, mice, bats and birds.
Size: 30–70cm (12–27.5in); 0.7–1.7kg (1.5–3.75lb).
Maturity: 2–3 years.
Breeding: Single young born in the dry season, which remains with its parents until it is mature.
Life span: 14 years.
Status: Common.

White-faced sakis live high up in trees. They feed during the daytime and almost never come down to the ground. Although they do occasionally leap from tree to tree, sakis are not the most agile of monkeys. They climb down trunks backwards and generally run along thick branches on all fours. Sometimes, however, sakis have been seen walking on their hind legs with their arms held above their heads.

A lot of the saki's diet consists of vegetable matter and fruit. However, these monkeys do also catch small vertebrate animals, such as birds and bats. The sakis rip their victims apart with their hands before skinning and eating the pieces of flesh. The monkeys have sharp teeth that are useful for biting into forest fruits and slicing up meat.

A saki group is based around a pair of breeding adults. The rest of the group, which may contain up to five individuals, will generally be the chief pair's offspring of different ages. The breeding pair produces a single baby once a year. Most births occur in the dry season at the end of the year.

Only male white-faced sakis have the white faces after which they are named. The females have black or dark brown faces. Most saki monkeys have broad, round faces with hooded eyebrows.

Southern night monkey

Aotus nigriceps

Night monkeys, which are also known as douroucoulis, are the only nocturnal monkeys in the world. These rare monkeys live in most types of forest, except those close to water. Biologists used to think there was a single species, but it is now known that there are several living across South America.

The large eyes of these monkeys collect enough light for them to see in the gloom. Night monkeys can only see in monochrome (black and white), but this still allows them to run and jump through the trees even on the darkest nights. By day, they rest in nests made from dry leaves and twigs.

Night monkeys live in family groups, with one adult pair and two or three of their young. Family members warn each other of approaching danger, such as tree snakes or birds of prey, with long "wook" alarm calls. The monkeys have loose sacs of skin under their chins, which they inflate to amplify these calls. At night the monkeys rely on scent as well as calls to communicate with other monkeys and with nearby groups. The scent comes from their urine, and also from glands on their chests, which the monkeys rub against branches.

Night monkeys have large eyes which give them good night vision. Their thick, woolly fur gives them a rounded appearance, and their tails, which are not prehensile, are thickened and furry at their tips.

Distribution: Central and South America from Panama southward to Brazil, but patchily distributed.
Habitat: Forests.
Food: Fruit, nuts, leaves, bark, flowers, gums, insects and small vertebrates.
Size: 24–37cm (9.5–14.5in); 0.6–1kg (1.25–2.2lb).
Maturity: 2 years.
Breeding: Single young born throughout the year.
Life span: 18 years.
Status: Vulnerable.

Northern night monkey (*Aotus trivirgatus*): 24–47cm (9.5–18.5in); 0.8–1.3kg (1.75–2.75lb)
Northern night monkeys have a brown or grey back and a pale red underside. Like their close relatives, the southern night monkeys, they are nocturnal. (The niche of feeding at night is taken by lemurs, bushbabies and other non-monkey primates in Africa and Asia.) Northern night monkeys range from southern Panama to northern Argentina, and from the Andes to the Atlantic coast. They live in lowland rainforests and mountain cloud forests, moving slowly from tree to tree as they feed on fruit and insects. They have the best-developed sense of smell of all the New World monkeys. Individuals hoot into the darkness to attract mates. Night monkeys form monogamous pairs. A single young or twins are born in January. The males do more than the females to raise the young. The young stay with their parents for several months after weaning, forming a small family group.

Black uakari (*Cacajao melanocephalus*): 30–50cm (12–19.5in); 2.4–4kg (5.25–8.75lb)
This more common relative of the bald uakari lives east of the Japura River up to the Negro and Branco Rivers (all tributaries of the Amazon). It lives in flooded forests as well as highland forests. There is black fur on its head and back, but the tail is paler, even yellow in some individuals. Black uakaris eat mainly seeds, which they collect when the fruits are still on the trees. They climb down to the ground to feed on fallen nuts if other food is scarce.

Bald uakari

Cacajao calvus

Uakaris only live in tropical rainforests that are flooded or filled with many slow-flowing streams, and consequently they are very rare. They are active during the day, running on all fours through the tops of large trees. They mainly feed on fruit, but will also eat leaves, insects and small vertebrates. Although they are quite agile, uakaris rarely jump from branch to branch. They almost never come down to the ground.

Uakaris live in large troops of 10–30 individuals. In areas where forests have not been damaged by human activity, groups of over 100 have been reported. Uakari troops often get mixed in with those of other monkeys, such as squirrel monkeys, during daytime feeding forays.

Each troop has a hierarchical structure, which is maintained by fighting among both sexes. The dominant males control access to females in a troop during the breeding season. Females give birth to a single young every two years.

Distribution: Upper Amazon from Peru to Colombia.
Habitat: Beside rivers in flooded forests.
Food: Fruit, leaves and insects.
Size: 51–70cm (20–27.75in); 3.5–4kg (7.75–8.75lb).
Maturity: Females 3 years, males 6 years.
Breeding: Single young born in summer every 2 years.
Life span: 20 years.
Status: Endangered.

Bald uakaris have hairless, red faces fringed with shaggy fur, hence their name. The long fur on the body is pale but looks reddish-brown, and a few have white fur. Their clubbed tails are proportionally shorter than those of other New World monkeys.

Muriqui

Brachyteles arachnoides

The muriqui, or woolly spider monkey, is the largest New World monkey. This extremely rare monkey lives in the coastal forests of south-eastern Brazil. These forests contain a mixture of deciduous and evergreen trees. They have been heavily deforested as land is cleared for agriculture and settlement, and now few areas of forest are large enough to support populations of the muriqui. Despite the decline of their natural habitat, muriquis are adaptable enough to survive in all but the most damaged forests. For example, although they prefer to live almost exclusively in the canopy layer, they will readily troop across open ground to reach isolated pockets of forest.

Little is known about muriqui society. The animals are thought to live in promiscuous groups, where all adults mate freely with each other. Females seem to have more control over mating times than males. With females holding dominant positions, it is they who leave the groups of their birth to join neighbouring ones. The males stay in the same group for their whole lives.

Muriquis eat leaves, flowers and seeds, but fruit is their preferred food. In fact, if a group of muriquis find a rich source of unripe fruit, they may wait for days, feeding on leaves, until the fruit becomes edible. Muriquis are occasionally preyed on by jaguars, ocelots and harpy eagles, and they are hunted by humans for their meat.

Distribution: South-east Brazil.
Habitat: Coastal forest.
Food: Fruit, leaves, flowers and seeds.
Size: 45–65cm (18–26in); 12–15kg (26.5–33lb).
Maturity: 6–11 years.
Breeding: Single young born every 2–3 years.
Life span: 12–25 years.
Status: Critically endangered.

Like most New World monkeys, this species has a long prehensile tail, which can grip branches. As it swings through the trees, the muriqui hangs from its fingers. Its thumbs are very small and almost useless. The coat is a greyish-gold, and the face a sooty-black. Both males and females have a pot-bellied appearance.

White-bellied spider monkey

Ateles belzebuth

The white-bellied spider monkey lives in Colombia, Venezuela, Peru, and Ecuador, and ranges into Brazil along the northern fringes of the Amazon Basin. It lives in the rainforests that grow in the region's lowlands. It is rarely found in forest more than a few hundred metres above sea level.

The white-bellied spider monkey lives in groups of between 20 and 40 individuals. There are generally three adult females for every male group member. (The other males live in small male-only groups and wait for an opportunity to join a mixed troop.) Each female will mate with one or all of the males in the group in quick succession, generally on the same day.

The monkeys forage during the day. They are able to hang from branches by their highly prehensile tails and pick fruits and other foods with their free hands. These little monkeys move around the forest by using their forelimbs to swing from branch to branch.

This species has very long arms and legs, which are longer than its body. The prehensile tail is used for picking up food and holding branches.

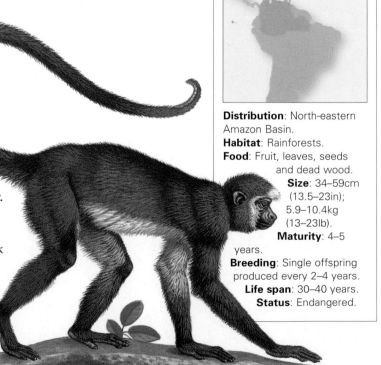

Distribution: North-eastern Amazon Basin.
Habitat: Rainforests.
Food: Fruit, leaves, seeds and dead wood.
Size: 34–59cm (13.5–23in); 5.9–10.4kg (13–23lb).
Maturity: 4–5 years.
Breeding: Single offspring produced every 2–4 years.
Life span: 30–40 years.
Status: Endangered.

Dusky titi monkey

Callicebus moloch

Dusky titi monkeys exhibit a variety of fur colours, ranging from grey to red to gold. Their tails are long and bushy, but not prehensile. When resting, a pair of monkeys will entwine their tails together.

Dusky titi monkeys occur in most forested parts of Brazil around the Amazon Basin, reaching into Colombia and Venezuela, around the headwaters of the Orinoco River. They tend to live in the lower trees near riverbanks, often climbing down to the shrub plants near the ground to feed on fruit, leaves, birds' eggs, and invertebrates. In periods of drought, these monkeys survive by eating figs, which are among the few forest fruits that are abundant in the dry season. As night falls, dusky titis climb higher into the trees to escape predators. This species lives in family groups, each of which is dominated by a single adult pair. A baby titi monkey is quite large, so the male carries it for most of the time, only giving it to the female for suckling. This ensures that a higher percentage of the young survive than if the females were to raise them alone.

Distribution: Central Brazil to Colombia and Venezuela.
Habitat: Rainforest.
Food: Fruits, insects, leaves, eggs and rodents.
Size: 24–61cm (9.5–24in); 0.5–0.75kg (1–1.75lb).
Maturity: 3 years.
Breeding: 1 young born between December and April.
Life span: 12–25 years.
Status: Common.

Brown-headed spider monkey (*Ateles fusciceps*):
40–60cm (15.5–24in); 9kg (19.75lb)
These spider monkeys live in the rainforests of Central America and the northern tip of South America. They occupy the upper branches of trees, often hanging by their prehensile tail as they forage. Their favoured foods are fruits and leaves, but they will also eat nuts, insects and even birds' eggs. The fur is shaggy, and different subspecies display a variety of colour forms. Brown-headed spider monkeys lack thumbs, enabling them to grip surfaces more firmly while climbing. They move by swinging from branch to branch or by walking along thicker branches on all fours. These monkeys are expert jumpers, being able to leap across gaps of about 9m (30ft). They live in groups of about 20 individuals. Group members rarely all gather in one place, but move around a home range in smaller subgroups.

Black spider monkey (*Ateles paniscus*):
49–58cm (19–23in); 7–9kg (15.5–19.75lb)
Black spider monkeys inhabit lowland rainforest in Central and South America, and extend farther south than brown-headed spider monkeys. The males are among the largest American primates. Black spider monkeys have long black hair, and their faces vary from pink to black. Like other spider monkeys, they lack thumbs and have long arms and flexible shoulder joints – all adaptations for an arboreal existence. Black spider monkeys live in groups of about 20 adults, with three females for every male. The males, which mate with several females, co-operate to prevent males from other groups from having access to the females.

Masked titi

Callicebus personatus

Masked titis inhabit the mixed forests that grow along the Atlantic coast of Brazil south of the mouth of the Amazon. They prefer forests with a broken canopy, where enough light reaches the ground for a thick understorey (undergrowth layer) to grow. Masked titis live in widely distributed groups, with only a few monkeys occupying large areas of forest. The destruction of coastal forests has meant that the populations of this species are now small, isolated and increasingly vulnerable.

Like other titi species, masked titis form monogamous pairs that mate for life. The male does the bulk of the carrying once the single young is produced, and he is responsible for nearly all of the parental care after weaning. Young masked titis stay with their parents for at least a couple of years, helping to raise their younger siblings.

Distribution: Atlantic coast of Brazil.
Habitat: Coastal forests.
Food: Fruit, insects, birds' eggs and mice.
Size: 31–42cm (12–16.5in); 0.97–1.65kg (2.2–3.75lb).
Maturity: Unknown.
Breeding: Single young born between August and October.
Life span: 20 years.
Status: Vulnerable.

There are five subspecies of masked titi, each with a differently coloured coat. Most have black foreheads and sideburn-like tufts around their dark faces. Their bodies have a range of grey or yellow-orange fur. The tail is not prehensile.

Central American squirrel monkey (*Saimiri oerstedii*): 22–30cm (8.5–12in); 0.5–1.1kg (1–2.5lb) Found along the Pacific coast of Panama and Costa Rica, this species occurs in a variety of habitats, from rainforest to mangrove swamps and thickets. Like other squirrel monkeys, it has a slender body and a long, prehensile tail. The predominantly yellow fur is slightly paler on the underside, and there is a black crown on the head. Central American squirrel monkeys travel in small troops. They occasionally gather in larger groups, when monkeys may move between troops.

White-fronted capuchin (*Cebus albifrons*): 33–44cm (13–17.5in); 1.1–3.3kg (2.5–7.25lb) Superficially similar to the white-faced capuchin, this monkey is found to the south of its relative. The ranges of the two species may overlap in northern Colombia and Ecuador, but the white-fronted capuchin is more likely to be found at lower altitudes in well-developed rainforest. This capuchin eats mainly fruit, along with insects and other arthropods. Troops contain 15–35 members, and are dominated by a single breeding pair.

Black howler monkey (*Alouatta caraya*): 51–67cm (20–26.5in); 4–10kg (8.75–22lb) This monkey lives in the forests of central South America, from northern Argentina to southern Brazil and eastern Bolivia. It inhabits either flooded gallery forests beside rivers or dry deciduous forests that grow in patches close to savannahs. Like other howlers, this species is a folivore – a leaf eater. Black howler monkeys live in family groups with a few more females than males. Male offspring are chased away as they mature.

Monk saki

Pithecia monachus

These monkeys are found in north-western Brazil, Colombia, Ecuador and Peru. Because they live at the very tops of rainforest trees, they are very difficult to study. Like the majority of New World monkeys, monk sakis are most active during the day. They leap from tree to tree in search of fruits, which they cut up with their long canine teeth before eating them.

Monk sakis live in small family groups of about four or five. Each group contains an adult breeding pair and their offspring of varying ages. A newborn saki clings to its mother's belly. As it grows larger, it rides on her back, until it is able to move around independently. Members of the family communicate using calls, mainly to let each other know where they are. At night, several families will sleep together in the same tree.

Saki monkeys have very thick tails for their relatively small bodies. The tail is not prehensile and is used for balance. There is a gap between the second and third digit on both the front and rear feet.

Distribution: Northern South America.
Habitat: Forest.
Food: Fruit, seeds, nuts and insects.
Size: 30–50cm (12–19.5in); 1–2kg (2.2–4.5lb).
Maturity: Unknown.
Breeding: 1 young born every year.
Life span: 12–25 years.
Status: Lower risk.

White-faced capuchin

Cebus capucinus

These monkeys are characterized by white fur around the face, as well as on the chest and upper arms. Unlike most New World monkeys, the thumb is opposable and is used to hold a range of foods.

The white-faced, or white-throated, capuchin ranges from Honduras in Central America and south to the Pacific coast of Colombia. It occupies well-developed rainforests with dense canopies and little undergrowth. This intelligent and adaptable species also lives in mangroves and drier, more open forests.

Capuchins have a cap of dark hair on the head that resembles the hood, or capuche, worn by friars. The tail is slightly prehensile, but it is not the "fifth limb" of certain New World monkeys. The tail is carried coiled up – hence the nickname ringtail.

White-faced capuchins live in troops of about 12 individuals. The females in a group are all related, but the males are drawn from different troops. Upon maturity, males are driven away by older males and presumably join other troops.

A troop splits if it grows too large for its territory. The two new, smaller groups are able to locate food more easily.

Distribution: Northern Colombia and Central America.
Habitat: Montane forest.
Food: Fruits, nuts, insects, rodents, lizards, frogs, birds and shellfish.
Size: 33–51cm (13–20in); 1.1–3.3kg (2.5–7.25lb).
Maturity: 4–8 years.
Breeding: 1 offspring born every 2 years at any time of year.
Life span: 12–25 years.
Status: Common.

Weeping capuchin

Cebus olivaceus

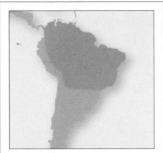

Distribution: South America.
Habitat: Forests.
Food: Fruits, palm, nuts, insects, spiders and small vertebrates.
Size: 35–50cm (14–20in); 2.5–2.8kg (5.5–6.25lb).
Maturity: 4–7 years.
Breeding: 1 young born every 2 years.
Life span: 35 years.
Status: Common.

The tail of the weeping capuchin is only semi-prehensile, unlike many other capuchin species, which have more dextrous tails. The tail is often carried with the section near the tip coiled up.

Weeping capuchins live across the whole of tropical South America east of the Andes Mountains. They are most commonly found in the deciduous llanos forests typical of the drier fringes of the Amazon Basin. Weeping capuchins live in the lower reaches of these forests, and can sometimes even be seen searching for food in the deep leaf litter on the forest floor. When a predator threatens, the capuchins take refuge on high branches.

Weeping capuchins live in large groups of about 20 individuals. There is one dominant male in each troop who mates with all the female members. Other males in the troop may sneak an occasional mating, but this is rare. A female usually gives birth to a single young, which clings to its mother's fur with its hands and feet soon after being born. She nurses the youngster for several months.

These monkeys use their dextrous hands to manipulate a wide range of foods. Weeping capuchins appear to use a certain species of millipede to repel unwanted biting insects. They squash the millipedes against their skin, releasing a toxin from the crushed bodies that keeps insects away.

Mantled howler monkey

Alouatta palliata

One of the few primate species to live as far north as Mexico, this species also lives along the eastern side of Central America and in northern Colombia and Ecuador. Mantled howler monkeys live in both lowland rainforests and upland montane forests. They eat mainly leaves and fruit, preferring young leaves that have lower levels of indigestible tannins in them. In the dry season, they supplement their diet with flowers. Fruits are more common in the wet season. The monkeys move slowly through the forest; their energies are devoted to consuming large amounts of food.

Mantled howler monkeys live in groups of 10–20 individuals. There are generally three or four females for every male in the group. These males tend to be at least 6 years old. Younger males live alone or in small groups that contain no females. As in other howler monkey species, the males make loud, persistent calls, which can be heard for up to 3km (1.86 miles). Females initiate mating by wiggling their tongue at a male. He responds in the same way and mating follows soon afterwards.

Mantled howler monkeys have yellow or brown saddle-shaped patches on their back, and long hairs along their flanks. Both sexes possess a beard, with the males having longer facial hair. The males also have a conspicuous white scrotum.

Distribution: Southern Mexico, Central America, northern Colombia and Ecuador.
Habitat: Forests.
Food: Leaves, fruits and flowers.
Size: 38–58cm (15–23in); 3–9kg (6.5–19.75lb).
Maturity: 3 years.
Breeding: 1 young produced every 2 years.
Life span: 12–25 years.
Status: Common.

MARMOSETS AND TAMARINS

Marmosets and tamarins are small, lightweight, swift-moving monkeys that live in South and Central America. Marmosets are among the smallest of all primates. They do not look like other monkeys, having short arms and legs similar to those of small tree-living mammals such as squirrels. Furthermore, they have claws on their fingertips, whereas other monkeys have fingernails.

Pygmy marmoset

Cebuella pygmaea

Distribution: Upper Amazon Basin.
Habitat: Rainforest.
Food: Fruit, buds, insects and sap.
Size: 11–15cm (4.5–6in); 100–140g (3.5–5oz).
Maturity: 1.5–2 years.
Breeding: 1–3 young born throughout the year.
Life span: 10 years.
Status: Common.

Pygmy marmosets are the smallest monkeys in the world. They live in the low plants that grow beneath tall trees in tropical forests. They clamber among the thick vegetation in search of food throughout the day, being most active in the cooler hours at the beginning and end of each day.

Pygmy marmosets eat fruit, flower buds and insects, but their preferred food is the sweet, sticky sap from certain trees. Their lower canine teeth are specially shaped for gouging holes in tree bark, causing the sap to leak out from the wood beneath. A tree used by a group of pygmy marmosets will be covered in wounds where the animals have repeatedly bitten through the bark.

Like all monkeys, pygmy marmosets live in complex societies. They live in family groups, with two parents and eight or nine offspring. Families sleep together, huddled on branches. Breeding pairs may mate at any time, but most produce small litters – usually twins – in December or June.

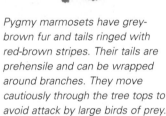

Pygmy marmosets have grey-brown fur and tails ringed with red-brown stripes. Their tails are prehensile and can be wrapped around branches. They move cautiously through the tree tops to avoid attack by large birds of prey.

Golden lion tamarin

Leontopithecus rosalia

The golden lion tamarin lives in the forests along Brazil's south-eastern coast. These forests are similar to the rainforests in the north-west of the Amazon Basin, but the trees in the coastal forests are not as tall. The tamarins live in an incredibly dense and humid environment, where leaves block out much of the sunlight, and where vines and other climbing plants fill the spaces under the crowns of trees.

Golden lion tamarins live in groups of about eight. Each group has a single breeding pair. The other members of the group help to rear the young. All group members share food and bond together by grooming each other's fur. The males groom the females more often than the females do the males. The tamarins are diurnal, sleeping throughout the night and often having a nap at midday. They eat fruit, flowers and various small animals, as well as nectar. Golden lion tamarins use their hands to collect and manipulate food. For example, they use their long fingers to extract insects from under bark.

The golden lion tamarin is named after the golden mane around its small head, which gives it the appearance of a tiny lion. The back is covered in long, silky fur which varies from pale gold to a rich reddish gold. Unlike many primates, this monkey has claws instead of fingernails. It moves through the trees by walking, running and leaping from branch to branch.

Distribution: South-east Brazil.
Habitat: Tropical forest.
Food: Insects, snails, lizards, eggs and fruit.
Size: 34–40cm (14–16in); 630–710g (22–25oz).
Maturity: 1.5–2 years.
Breeding: 2 litters of twins born in September and March.
Life span: 15 years.
Status: Endangered.

Cotton-top tamarin

Saguinus oedipus

Cotton-top tamarins have an unusual breeding system. They live in groups of up to 20 adults, but only one pair breeds. The other adults in the group act as helpers. Most of the helpers are younger individuals. Their assistance reduces the infant mortality of this species to levels lower than those of all mammals, apart from humans. Although they appear to lose out by not breeding from an early age, the helpers gain valuable experience by assisting the older breeding pair. When the helpers come to breed themselves, they are likely to be more successful. The helpers form small subgroups that move in and out of the breeding pair's home range. The home range is marked using scent.

About half of the diet of these tamarins is made up of insects. The rest comprises fruits and the sweet gums that exude from tree trunks. Nature reserves have been set up to conserve the species.

Cotton-top tamarins have a crest of white hair that runs from the forehead to the nape of the neck. The rump and inner thighs are red-orange. These coloured surfaces may be used to flash signals to other tamarins through dense foliage.

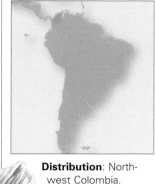

Distribution: North-west Colombia.
Habitat: Tropical rainforest.
Food: Insects.
Size: 19–21cm (7.5–8.25in); 260–380g (9.25–13.5oz).
Maturity: 1.5–2 years.
Breeding: 2 litters of twins born at all times of the year.
Life span: 15 years.
Status: Endangered.

Saddlebacked tamarin (*Saguinus fuscicollis*): 19–30cm (7.5–12in); 260–380g (9.25–13.5oz) This species occurs in Panama, Bolivia, Brazil, Colombia and Peru. Saddlebacks are most often seen near the edge of the rainforest, where the canopy is less developed and where there is more undergrowth. They have a black-and-white pattern on their faces, and a red-brown coat. Saddleback groups contain a single adult female and two adult males. The female mates with both males and they all share the task of rearing the young. Older offspring help to care for the youngest litter. Saddlebacks eat insects and fruits, and lick tree gums and sap to obtain minerals.

Black-faced lion tamarin (*Leontopithecus caissara*): 30.5cm (12in); 600g (21.25oz) Discovered in 1990, this critically endangered species lives in about 17,000 hectares (42,000 acres) of forest in south-eastern Brazil. The face, mane and tail have black hair, while the hair on the rest of the body is deep gold. These diurnal monkeys move in groups of up to 10 animals with a dominant monogamous breeding pair. They eat mainly fruit and some invertebrates.

Golden-rumped lion tamarin (*Leontopithecus chrysopygus*): 20–33cm (8–14in); 300–700g (10.5–24.75oz) The golden-rumped lion tamarin is another critically endangered species, with under 1,000 surviving in two small pockets of forest in Brazil. Long, black hair covers most of the body, but the thighs, buttocks and tail are golden. These tamarins live in family groups that forage by day. Like most tamarins, they eat insects and fruits.

Emperor tamarin

Saguinus imperator

Emperor tamarins are found in the forests of south-eastern Peru, north-western Bolivia, and vast sweeps of northern Brazil. Many of the forests within this range are regularly flooded, and the tamarins most commonly occur in forests with dry ground. They inhabit all levels of the forest, foraging by day. Being relatively small monkeys, they are able to reach food at the end of the flimsiest of branches, beyond the reach of larger species.

As in other tamarin species, the male washes the young after birth, and he helps to carry them around until they are about two months old.

Emperor tamarins are more widely distributed than most tamarins, which tend to live in small pockets of forest. Consequently, this species is one of the few that is not currently threatened with extinction.

Distribution: Northern Brazil, south-eastern Peru and north-western Bolivia
Habitat: Tropical rainforest.
Food: Fruits, insects and sap.
Size: 22–26.5cm (8.5–10.5in); 300–400g (10.5–14oz).
Maturity: 16–20 months.
Breeding: Up to 2 litters of twins, produced at any time of year.
Life span: 15 years.
Status: Lower.

The emperor tamarin is one of the largest of the tamarins, although most lion tamarins are larger. Emperor tamarins have a crown of silver and brown hair, and a long white moustache that reaches the chest.

White-tufted-ear marmoset

Callithrix jacchus

White-tufted-ear marmosets live on the edges of tropical forests in north-eastern Brazil. The species is also known as the common marmoset. However, the destruction of their forest habitat means that they are less common than they once were.

These marmosets are diurnal and live in small troops of up to 12 monkeys. Within each troop a female teams up with two or more males to form a breeding group. The female mates with all of these males. All the breeding males help the female to carry the young and find food for them. It is thought that the babies need multiple "fathers" to help them survive, because the babies are too heavy for just the mother to carry. The other members of the troop are the offspring of the adults, and these also help to raise the young. Only one female in each troop breeds at a given time.

White-tufted-ear marmosets feed mainly on tree sap and other exudates (such as gums and resins). Exudates are such an abundant resource that the marmosets can live in relatively high-density populations. Insects are another important food, and the diet also includes fruits, nectar, flowers, spiders, and sometimes birds' eggs, lizards and frogs. In addition, these marmosets have learned to exploit the food potential of plantations that grow near the forest edge.

Distribution: Eastern Brazil.
Habitat: Edge of forests.
Food: Sap, nectar, insects, spiders, fruit and flowers.
Size: 12–15cm (4.75–6in); 300–360g (10.5–12.75oz).
Maturity: 2 years.
Breeding: Twins born at all times of the year.
Life span: 10 years.
Status: Lower risk.

This marmoset is easily recognized by the white tufts on its ears and the white patch on the otherwise brown forehead. It also has stripes on its back and tail. In common with most marmosets, the tail is a little longer than the body.

Goeldi's monkey

Callimico goeldii

Goeldi's monkey is unique among marmosets and tamarins, having six molar teeth on either side of its jaws (other marmosets have four). A cape of long hair hangs from the neck and shoulders. There are pale rings near the base of the tail and buff markings on the back of the neck. Juveniles lack the rings and the mane, and often the neck markings.

This rare, unusual monkey of northern South America forms a separate group within the marmoset and tamarin family. It lives in a range of forest habitats, preferring areas with a broken canopy where light filters through to the forest floor so that undergrowth can grow. This species is also often found in bamboo glades. It spends most of its time at low levels in the forest, less than 5m (16.5ft) above the ground. However, it will climb higher into the trees to reach ripe fruit.

Goeldi's monkeys live in troops that travel together in search of food. A troop typically covers about 2km (1.24 miles) per day, moving in a roughly circular pattern within their territory, which may cover up to 80 hectares (720 acres). These monkeys sleep together as well, sheltering in a hollow tree or in dense undergrowth. They break up their daytime feeding trips with about three rest periods, during which they sunbathe and groom each other to remove parasites from their fur. Grooming also helps to strengthen social ties within the group. There is little contact between different troops.

Goeldi's monkeys make their way through the forest by climbing trees and then leaping forward. Their diet consists mainly of fruits and insects, but they will occasionally jump down to the ground to catch small vertebrate prey.

Distribution: Southern Colombia, eastern Ecuador, eastern Peru, northern Bolivia and western Brazil.
Habitat: Broken forest with undergrowth, bamboo glades.
Food: In the wet season the diet consists of fruits, insects and small vertebrates such as frogs and snakes; in the dry season they eat fungi.
Size: 21–31cm (8.5–12in); 390–860g (13.75–30.25oz).
Maturity: 14 months.
Breeding: Single offspring produced each time, but females sometimes breed twice per year.
Life span: 10 years.
Status: Vulnerable.

Silvery marmoset

Callithrix argentata

Distribution: Eastern Brazil.
Habitat: Rainforest.
Food: Tree gum and sap. plus fruits, leaves and insects
Size: 22cm (8.5in); 300–400g (11–14oz).
Maturity: 2 years.
Breeding: Twins born twice each year.
Life span: 10 years.
Status: Lower risk.

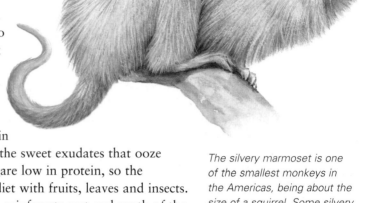

Silky marmosets have an unique jaw shape that ends in a sharp tip, and shorter canines than other marmosets and New World monkeys. This is believed to be an adaptation to feeding on exudates (gums, resins and sap) from trees. With canines and incisors of the same length, the silvery marmoset can gouge holes in tree trunks. It then laps up the sweet exudates that ooze from these holes. Exudates are low in protein, so the marmoset supplements its diet with fruits, leaves and insects.

Silvery marmosets live in rainforests east and south of the Amazon Delta. They are active by day, and rarely descend from the tree tops. They rest in hollow trees or thick tangles of vines. Like other marmosets, they have claws rather than nails, which they use to grip tree trunks while climbing.

The silvery marmoset is one of the smallest monkeys in the Americas, being about the size of a squirrel. Some silvery marmosets are brown rather than silver. These monkeys have hairless ears and faces, and their alternative name is bare-eared marmosets.

Geoffroy's tamarin (*Saguinus geoffroyi*): 20–29cm (8–11.5); 350–500g (12.25–17.6oz)
Geoffroy's tamarin is found in south-eastern Costa Rica, Panama and northern Colombia. This small monkey lives in shrubs and tall grasses, and may even be seen in areas of forest that have burnt down. It has brown and black fur with a white triangular patch on its head. The neck and tail are a dark red-brown. This species lives in groups of up to 20 individuals. It practices a polyandrous mating system, in which each female mates with two or more males. The males will help to carry the young despite being uncertain of their paternity. The group uses scent to mark its territory. Although females are dominant in the group, males are more aggressive toward members of other groups who enter the territory. This species eats insects and fruits as well as lizards, flowers and nectar. Due to habitat destruction, this species is endangered.

Black-mantled tamarin (*Saguinus nigricollis*): 22cm (8.5in); 475g (16.75oz)
The black-mantled tamarin is found east of the Andes, from Ecuador to southern Colombia and south to Peru and Brazil. It lives in primary and secondary rainforest. Secondary rainforest grows where primary rainforest has been damaged in some way. It is considerably more dense, with shorter trees but more undergrowth. This species has black fur from the head to midway down the back, after which the fur becomes red. The black-mantled tamarin's diet mainly comprises insects, particularly grasshoppers and crickets. These monkeys also eat fruits, seeds, nectar and tree gums.

Black-pencilled marmoset

Callithrix penicillata

Black-pencilled marmosets are found in the coastal region of Brazil and relatively far inland. They live high up in rainforest trees, and are seldom seen far below the upper canopy. This species is usually found in gallery forest, which grows in narrow strips beside rivers and which is characterized by frequent flooding.

This species forms monogamous pairs that often live with their young. They breed twice a year, and the older offspring assist their parents in raising their younger siblings. Black-pencilled marmosets mark their territory with aromatic secretions produced by glands on their chests and near the anus. This is primarily to deter other species of monkey from feeding in the area. Group members alert each other to danger, using specific cries to warn against different types of predator.

Distribution: Brazil.
Habitat: Gallery forest.
Food: Tree sap.
Size: 22.5–28cm (9–11in); 450g (16oz).
Maturity: 18 months.
Breeding: Twins produced twice a year.
Life span: 15 years.
Status: Unknown.

The black-pencilled marmoset has large black tufts behind its ears. The long tail is ringed with black and grey. The tail is used to help the monkey balance as it moves around in the tree tops.

HOOFED ANIMALS

Hoofed animals walk on the tips of their toes. Their hooves are made from the same material as fingernails and claws – keratin. Walking on tiptoes makes their legs very long, and most hoofed animals are fast runners because of this. Hoofed mammals belong to two groups: Perissodactyla *includes horses, zebras, rhinoceroses and tapirs, while* Artiodactyla *includes pigs, sheep, antelope, deer and cattle.*

Brazilian tapir

Tapirus terrestris

Brazilian tapirs, also known as South American tapirs, spend the day in forests of dense vegetation. At night they emerge into more open country, where they browse on vegetation. They prefer to spend part of the night in water or mud, and are surprisingly agile swimmers given their size. When on land, they walk with their snouts close to the ground. Each night, a tapir will follow one of several well-trodden trails to a favourite watering hole.

Tapirs spend most of their lives alone. They are fairly aggressive towards one another at chance meetings. They alert each other to their presence by giving shrill whistling sounds and marking the ground with their urine. Brazilian tapirs breed all year round, but most mate during the rainy season, which means that their young are born just before the rains begin in the following year.

Tapirs have rounded bodies that are wider at the back than at the front. This helps them charge through thick vegetation when in danger. They have short hairs on their bodies and narrow manes on their necks. Their noses are long and flexible. Young tapirs have red fur patterned with yellow and white stripes and spots.

Distribution: From Colombia and Venezuela southward to northern Argentina.
Habitat: Woodland or dense grassy habitats near water.
Food: Water plants, fruit, buds.
Size: 1.8–2.5m (6–8.25ft); 180–320kg (396–704lb). Height at shoulder 75–120cm (29.5–47in).
Maturity: 3–4 years.
Breeding: 1 or 2 young born at start of rainy season.
Life span: 35 years.
Status: Lower risk.

Collared peccary

Pecari tajacu

Collared peccaries are not directly related to pigs and wild boars. Pigs are native to Europe, Asia and Africa, and were introduced to the Americas by humans. Peccaries do resemble pigs, though, having similar blunt snouts for rooting out tubers and other foods, however peccaries have longer, more slender legs than pigs. Peccaries also eat snakes and small invertebrates. Like many pigs, they appear to be immune to rattlesnake bites.

This species ranges from the south-western United States to northern Argentina. It inhabits grassland and scrubland in the north of its range, but is equally at home in tropical rainforests further south. In many areas, these animals have come to live alongside humans, eating rubbish and food stores. Local people call the collared peccary the javelina because of its small, sharp tusks, which resemble the tips of a spear.

Collared peccaries get their name from the curve of pale hairs that starts behind the neck and runs under the chin to the other side, thus forming a collar. The tusks in the upper and lower jaw fit together snugly and sharpen each other as the jaw is opened and closed.

Distribution: South-western US to northern Argentina.
Habitat: Tropical rainforest and grassland.
Food: Roots, bulbs, fungi, fruits, eggs, carrion, small animals.
Size: 0.75–1m (2.5–3.25ft); 14–30kg (31–66lb). Height at shoulder 44–50cm (17.25–19.75in).
Maturity: 11 months.
Breeding: 1–3 young born at all times of year.
Life span: 8–10 years.
Status: Common.

Guanaco

Lama guanicoe

Guanacos have long limbs and necks for reaching food in trees and shrubs. They have brown, woolly fur on their upper bodies and necks, while their undersides have white hair.

Guanacos are considered the wild relatives of domestic llamas and alpacas. They are distant cousins of the camels of Africa and Asia. Like camels, guanacos have adapted to living in dry areas, although their preferred habitat – alpine grassland – is not as hot as the habitats of most camels. Like their domestic relatives, guanacos are fast runners. They have more haemoglobin (oxygen-carrying pigment) in their red blood cells than any other mammal. This allows them to survive at altitude. Guanacos mainly graze on grass, but they also pluck leaves from shrubs. They live in herds of about 15 individuals. Each herd is controlled by one adult male. Once a young guanaco reaches adulthood, it is chased away by the dominant male.

Distribution: Southern Peru to Argentina and Chile.
Habitat: Dry, open areas.
Food: Grass.
Size: 1.2–2.5m (4–8.25ft); 100–120kg (220–264lb). Height at shoulder 0.9–1.3m (3–4.25ft).
Maturity: Females 2 years; males 4 years.
Breeding: Single young born in spring.
Life span: 28 years.
Status: Vulnerable.

Llama (*Lama glama*): 1–2m (3.25–6.5ft); 130–155kg (290–340lb). Height at shoulder 0.9–1.3m (3–4.25ft) Llamas are widely distributed along the length of the Andes Mountains, from Ecuador to Chile and Argentina. However, all these animals are kept by people – there are no wild llamas. Llamas appear to be domestic breeds of the guanaco. Llamas are the most common members of the *Lama* genus, which also includes guanacos and alpacas, another domestic breed. Llamas can produce fertile offspring with these other animals, so they are probably all the same species. Llamas exhibit the behaviour of wild guanacos. Males defend a harem of about six females in a small territory. The young, or crias, can walk after their first hour of life. Young males are driven off by their fathers when they mature at about two years old.

Baird's tapir (*Tapirus bairdii*): 180–250cm (71–98in); 150–300kg (330–660lbs). Height at shoulder 75–120cm (29.5–47in)
This species has a range to the north of the more common Brazilian tapir, occurring from southern Mexico to northern Colombia and Ecuador. Baird's tapirs live in wetland habitats such as swamps and along the banks of streams. These nocturnal animals spend most of their time on solid ground, but take to the water to escape unwanted attention. The barrel-shaped body and short legs make them well-suited to running through thick undergrowth. Baird's tapirs forage with their long, flexible snout close to the ground to sniff out food such as twigs, shoots, leaves, fruits and seeds. Edible objects are picked up by the snout and transferred to the mouth.

Vicuña

Vicugna vicugna

Vicuñas are related to guanacos and camels. They live on high-altitude grasslands in the Andes Mountains of Peru, Bolivia, Argentina and Chile. Vicuñas are seldom found below about 3,500m (11,500ft). At this height, the conditions are cold and dry, so vicuñas never stray far from a source of running water.

The vicuña has teeth more like those of rodents than other hoofed mammals. The lower incisors grow throughout the animal's lifetime. The teeth are constantly being worn away by the tough alpine grasses that make up its diet. Vicuñas are ruminants, which means that they digest their plant food with the help of bacteria in the stomach, and they chew half-digested food, or cud, to help with the digestion process. They are especially adapted to living at high altitude, having a large heart and specialized blood cells.

Distribution: Andes Mountains, from southern Peru and western Bolivia to north-western Argentina and northern Chile.
Habitat: Alpine grasslands.
Food: Grass.
Size: 1.25–1.9m (4–6.25ft); 36–65kg (79–143lb). Height at shoulder, 0.7–1.1m (2.25–3.5ft).
Maturity: 2 years.
Breeding: Single calf born during February or March.
Life span: 15 years.
Status: Vulnerable.

The tawny-coated vicuña is the smallest member of the camel family. It is just a quarter of the weight of the guanaco but has a similar body form, with a long, slender neck and thin legs.

Muskox

Ovibos moschatus

Although muskoxen look like large hairy cattle or bison, they are in fact relatives of goats and sheep. These animals live on the windswept tundra within the Arctic Circle. This habitat forms in places that are too cold and dry for trees to grow. There is only enough water to sustain grasses and other hardy plants.

Both sexes of this species have large, hooked horns. Male muskox are larger than females, because they must fight other males to win and defend a harem of females. They butt each other with their horns in contests of strength. During the mating season, the bulls produce a strong, musky odour. Muskoxen live in herds, usually of 15–20 animals but occasionally up to 100 strong. When predators threaten, the herd crowds together, often in a circle or semi-circle, with the calves in the middle. This formation provides a highly effective defence, since adversaries are faced with a wall of horns and risk being gored if they attack.

The muskox's body is covered in long fur, except the area between lips and nostrils. The fur not only keeps the animal warm, but also protects it against the vast numbers of biting insects that swarm across the tundra during the short summer.

Distribution: Arctic of Canada and Greenland.
Habitat: Tundra.
Food: Grass, moss and sedge.
Size: 1.9–2.3m (6.25–7.5ft); 200–410kg (440–900lb). Height at shoulder 1.2–1.5m (4–5ft).
Maturity: 2–3 years.
Breeding: 1 young produced every 1–2 years in spring.
Life span: 18 years.
Status: Common, although extinct in Alaska.

American bison

Bison bison

Although rare, the American bison has been saved from extinction. Once, vast herds of over a million bison grazed the vast prairies of western North America, often making migrations of several thousand kilometres to winter feeding grounds in the south. They were almost wiped out by hunters during the 19th century, when the grasslands were cleared to make way for agriculture. Bison were also widely killed for their skin and meat. Originally, bison also occurred extensively in mountain areas, and also in open forest and woodland.

These large grazing animals have well-developed senses of smell and hearing. They can run at up to 60kmh (37mph) and are also able to swim well, sometimes crossing rivers as wide as 1km (0.6 mile). Bison may often be seen rubbing their shoulders and rumps against boulders and tree trunks, and they enjoy taking mud and dust baths. This behaviour scratches off fly larvae and other parasites that live on their hides.

While bison may occasionally gather in herds of several hundred, they generally move around in small bands made up of a number of females and their offspring, including young bulls. Mature bulls either live alone or move in separate groups from the cows. During the mating season, in late summer, the males join the females. They fight for the females by ramming each other head-on. After mating, a bull guards his mate for several days to prevent other rival males from mating with her.

Distribution: Patches of western Canada and central United States.
Habitat: Prairie and woodland.
Food: Grass.
Size: 2.1–3.5m (7–11.5ft); 350–1000kg (770–2200lb). Height at shoulder 1.5–2m (5–6.5ft).
Maturity: 1–2 years.
Breeding: Single young born in spring every 1 or 2 years.
Life span: 40 years.
Status: Lower risk.

Male bison are larger than the females of the species. Both sexes have sharp, curved horns, which stick out from the shaggy, brown hair on their heads.

Mountain goat

Oreamnos americanus

As their name suggests, these goats live on the sides of steep mountains. They prefer broken, rocky slopes to meadows, and they have strong, sturdy legs and hooves to allow them to negotiate such difficult terrain. Mountain goats are native to the mountains of western North America, from southern Alaska to Montana and Idaho. However, they have also been introduced to mountainous regions further south in the United States.

Mountain goats are grazers, feeding on whatever grows in their precipitous habitats – mainly grasses and similar plants. In winter, when snow covers the higher slopes, mountain goats climb down to lowland feeding grounds. As the snows melt in spring, the goats return to the higher altitudes to feed on the new plant growth. In winter, mountain goats gather in large herds, but these break up in summer into smaller groups. During the breeding season, the males fight to form a hierarchy. They do not butt each other head on, like other goats, but stand side by side and jab each other with their short horns.

Distribution: From southern Alaska to Idaho.
Habitat: Steep, rocky slopes.
Food: Grass, mosses, twigs and lichens.
Size: 1.25–1.8m (4–6ft); 46–136kg (100–300lb). Height 0.9–1.2m (3–4ft).
Maturity: 2.5 years.
Breeding: 1–3 kids born in May or June.
Life span: 15 years.
Status: Common.

Mountain goats have stout legs with large, oval hooves. The soles of the hooves are very elastic, which helps them to grip surfaces as they climb up rocky slopes.

Dall's sheep (*Ovis dalli*): 1.3–1.8m (4.25–6ft); 46–113kg (100–250lb). Height at shoulder 1m (3.25ft)
This sheep is also called the thinhorn. Compared to its close relative, the bighorn sheep, the horns of this species are much smaller and so thin that they may be near transparent. The horns have growth rings that can be counted to show the animal's age. In the mating season, males fight by clashing horns in a test of strength. The range of Dall's sheep encompasses mountain regions in western Canada and Alaska. Dall's sheep can survive at higher altitudes than other American sheep and goats, and since alpine conditions are in many ways very similar to Arctic ones, this species is also found further north than others.

White-lipped peccary (*Tayassu pecari*): 95–135cm (37.5–53in); 27–40kg (60–88lb). Height at shoulder 50–60cm (19.7–23.6in)
White-lipped peccaries live in a similar range to collared peccaries, although they are much smaller. They may form herds of up to 100 individuals as they look for food in the forest.

Chacoan peccary (*Catagonus wagneri*): 93–106cm (36.5–42in); 29–49kg (64–108lb). Height at shoulder 50–70cm (19.7–27.5in)
This South American peccary is named after the chaco – the dry thorn and shrubland region that lies mainly in Paraguay. The peccary mainly eats cacti, and it has specialized kidneys for dealing with the high acid content of these plants. It supplements its mineral consumption by visiting salt licks formed by ant nests.

Bighorn sheep

Ovis canadensis

Bighorn sheep are the most common wild sheep in North America. They are excellent climbers and are often found on rocky outcrops or high cliffs. They seek refuge in steep areas from cougars and other predators that are not agile enough to keep up with their sure-footed prey.

Flocks of bighorns can contain up to 100 individuals. They head up to high meadows in summer, then retreat to the valleys when the winter snows come. Male bighorns tend to live in separate groups from the ewes and lambs. The rams have hierarchies based on the size of their horns. Fights are ritualized, with the adversaries butting their horns together. Ewes prefer to mate with rams with large horns and refuse the courtship of others.

Bighorns are named after the males' massive spiral horns, which may be up to 1.1m (3.5ft) long. The females have smaller, less curved horns.

Distribution: South-western Canada to northern Mexico.
Habitat: Alpine meadows and rocky cliffs.
Food: Grass and sedge.
Size: 1.2–1.8m (4–6ft); 50–125kg (110–275lb). Height at shoulder 0.8–1.1m (2.5–3.5ft).
Maturity: 3 years.
Breeding: 1–3 young born in spring.
Life span: 20 years.
Status: Lower risk.

Moose

Alces alces

Moose are the largest deer in the world. They live in the cold conifer forests that cover northern mountains and lowlands. As well as being found in North America, moose live across northern Europe and Siberia, where they are known as elk.

Moose plod through the forests and marshes, browsing on a wide range of leaves, mosses and lichens. They often feed in the shallows of streams and rivers, nibbling on aquatic vegetation. These large deer have even been seen diving underwater to uproot water plants. In summer, they are most active at dawn and dusk. In winter, they are active throughout the day. They paw the snow to reveal buried plants and twigs.

Although moose may gather together to feed, they spend most of the year alone. In the autumn mating season, males fight each other for females. Pregnant females find secluded sites where they can give birth, with thick vegetation to hide the new-born calves. The moose calves are able to stand and walk within two days. They can also swim by the time they are a week old, which is an important survival skill, since taking to water is a good way of escaping some predators. At five weeks they can outrun slower animals such as bears. Mothers will defend their calves aggressively. The calves become independent when they are about a year old.

Distribution: Alaska, Canada, northern United States, Siberia and northern Europe. Introduced to New Zealand.
Habitat: Marsh and woodland.
Food: Leaves, twigs, moss and water plants.
Size: 2.4–3.1m (8–10.25ft); 200–825kg (440–1815lb). Height at shoulder 1.4–2.3m (4.5–7.5ft).
Maturity: 1 year.
Breeding: 1–3 young born in spring.
Life span: 27 years.
Status: Common.

Male moose are almost twice the size of females. The males sport huge antlers – nearly 2m (6.5ft) across – and have flaps of skin hanging below their chins, called dewlaps. In fights over females, male moose clash violently, sometimes goring each other with their antlers.

White-tailed deer

Odocoileus virginianus

White-tailed deer, or Virginia deer as they are called in the United States, prefer areas with tall grasses or shrubs to hide in during the day. When the deer spot predators, they raise their white tails to expose the white patches on their rumps. This serves as a visual warning to other deer that danger is near. If pursued, the deer bound away, reaching 60kmh (37mph).

White-tailed deer live in matriarchies, with each small group being controlled by a single adult female, which is the mother of the rest of the group. The adult males live alone or in small bachelor herds. In the autumn mating season, males mark plants with scent produced by glands on their faces, and urinate in depressions scraped into the ground. The males fight with their antlers – rut – for the right to court females.

White-tailed deer have brown fur on their upper parts and white undersides. The white fur extends under the tail, which gives the species its name. The males shed their antlers in midwinter and grow new ones in spring.

Distribution: North, Central and South America from southern Canada to Brazil.
Habitat: Shrublands and open woodland.
Food: Grass, shrubs, twigs, mushrooms, lichens and nuts.
Size: 0.8–2.1m (2.5–7ft); 50–200kg (110–484lb). Height at shoulder 0.8–1m (2.5–3.25ft).
Maturity: 1 year.
Breeding: 1–4 young produced during summer.
Life span: 10 years.
Status: Common.

Pronghorn

Antilocapra americana

Despite appearances, pronghorns are not true deer. They are the sole members of a separate group of hoofed animals called the *Antilocapridae*. Unlike true deer, pronghorns do not have antlers, but have horns like antelope, although they are forked like those of a deer.

Pronghorns are the fastest land mammals in the Americas. They have been recorded racing along at 72kmh (45mph).

In late autumn, pronghorns gather into large herds of 1,000 or more. They spend the winter in these herds and split into smaller single-sex groups when spring arrives. In October, older males compete for small territories, which they use to attract groups of females. Once females have entered a territory, the resident male will not allow other males near them.

Pronghorns get their name from the prongs sticking out halfway up their backward-curving horns. Male pronghorns are slightly larger than the females. The males also have black masks on their faces.

Distribution: Southern Canada to northern Mexico.
Habitat: Grassland and desert.
Food: Grass, leaves and cacti.
Size: 1–1.5m (3.25–5ft); 36–70kg (79–154lb). Height at shoulder 0.8–1m (2.5–3.25ft).
Maturity: Females 18 months; males 3 years.
Breeding: 1–3 young born in spring.
Life span: 10 years.
Status: Common.

Red brocket deer (*Mazama americana*): 72–140cm (28.5–55in); 8–25kg (17–55lb). Height at shoulder 67–76cm (26.4–29.9in)
Red brocket deer range from eastern Mexico to northern Argentina. They have whorls of hair on their faces and stout bodies covered in reddish-brown hair. The males have simple, spike-like antlers. Red brockets live in woodland and dense forest. They may be active both day and night, feeding on grasses, vines and the new shoots of plants. These shy deer tend to freeze when they spot danger, blending into the thick vegetation.

Pampas deer (*Ozotoceros bezoarticus*): 1.1–1.4m (3.5–4.5ft); 25–40kg (55–88lb). Height at shoulder 70–75cm (27.5–29.5in)
This species lives on open grasslands – or pampas – in the south-eastern part of South America. It has a dark red or brown coat. Males have forked antlers and glands on their hooves that produce a strong scent. Pampas deer graze on young grass shoots throughout the day. In late summer and autumn the males fight for access to females, and most births occur in the spring.

Huemul (*Hippocamelus antisensis*): 1.4–1.65m (4.5–5.5ft); 45–65kg (99–143lb). Height at shoulder 69–77cm (27–33in)
Huemuls live in the rugged hill country high in the Andes of Peru, Chile, Bolivia and Argentina. They have coarse coats and black Y-shaped face markings. Huemuls spend the summer grazing on grasses and sedges in high alpine meadows. In winter, they climb down to lower altitudes. Mating takes place in the dry winter season, and fawns are born at the end of the rains.

Southern pudu

Pudu pudu

Southern pudus live in the wet forests on the slopes of southern Andes Mountains. They are the smallest of all deer, being only a little bigger than maras – the long-legged rodents that live in the same region.

Pudus are mainly nocturnal in their behaviour, although they are sometimes spotted feeding during the day. They move through the dense forest slowly, picking off the ripest fruits and most succulent leaves and buds. They try not to draw attention to themselves and stay well hidden as much as possible. If attacked, they run away in zigzag paths and often seek refuge in the branches of trees.

Pudus live alone, patrolling small territories and only occasionally encountering other members of their species. Being so small, pudus can reach maturity much more quickly than other species of deer. They are ready to reproduce at just six months of age. Births take place in the spring, and the year's fawns are ready to take part in the breeding activity that occurs during autumn.

Southern pudus have grey and brown fur. They have short, thick legs and the males have small spikes for antlers.

Distribution: Southern Chile to south-western Argentina.
Habitat: Humid forest.
Food: Tree and shrub leaves, vines, bark, fruit and flowers.
Size: 60–85cm (23.5–33.5in); 5–14kg (11–30.75lb). Height at shoulder 25–43cm (10–17in).
Maturity: 6 months.
Breeding: Single young born in spring.
Life span: 10 years.
Status: Vulnerable.

Marsh deer

Blastocerus dichotomus

The marsh deer is the largest deer in South America. It has wide feet with an elastic layer of skin between the hooves. This makes the foot webbed, and prevents the heavy deer from sinking into mud and other soft ground. The long, coarse coat is a reddish-brown in summer, turning to a darker brown in winter. There are white rings around the eyes.

The marsh deer lives in the grasslands that exist along the southern fringe of the Amazon Basin. This habitat begins in southern Peru and Brazil and extends into northern Argentina. The deer once lived in Uruguay, but it is now thought to be extinct there.

Marsh deer browse on a range of plants that grow in waterlogged environments. They inhabit the small areas of swamp and bog that exist all year around. However, many of the grasslands in their range become flooded in the wet season, enabling the deer to disperse over a wider area. They are most active in the half-light of dawn and dusk, although they are sometimes also seen feeding during the day and at night.

Marsh deer generally live alone during floods, but form small groups of about five deer when they gather around water sources in dry periods. Males occupy a home range that covers those of several females. The males rut in October and November to establish their dominance. The ranking established by the rut is maintained throughout the year.

Distribution: South America, from southern Peru and Brazil to Paraguay and northern Argentina. Now presumed extinct in Uruguay.
Habitat: Marshy areas in grasslands.
Food: Grass, leaves and aquatic plants.
Size: 1.5–2m (5–6.5ft); 89–125kg (195–275lb). Height at shoulder 1–1.2m (3.25–4ft).
Maturity: 2 years.
Breeding: Single fawn produced in summer; gestation is about 9 months.
Life span: 10 years.
Status: Vulnerable.

Mule deer

Odocoileus hemionus

Mule deer are common in the western half of North America. They range from central Mexico all the way to the edge of the Arctic tundra in northern Canada. They occupy all habitats between these points, including desert areas in Nevada, California and Arizona, and around the Great Salt Lake. The deer range eastward to Saskatchewan in the north and Texas in the south. There are also small, isolated populations further east in Iowa and Missouri.

Mule deer are most active at dawn and dusk. They feed mainly on vegetation, plus some fungi and lichens, and they can live almost anywhere where there is sufficient plant growth. Their diet of plant food is relatively poor in nutrients, so it is vital that the deer extract the most from it. To do this, the mule deer ruminate. This involves using stomach bacteria to digest the food for them, and chewing regurgitated food, or cud, to break down as much of the plant fibre as possible.

Each mule deer has a unique set of markings made up of lines along the tail and pale patches on the rump and throat. These patterns stay the same throughout the deer's life. Female mule deer live in small social groups made up of an adult female and a number of her offspring. Males are either solitary or gather in small groups of unrelated individuals.

Distribution: Western North America, from northern Canada to central Mexico.
Habitat: Desert, forest and grassland.
Food: Leaves, twigs, grass, moss, fungi and lichen
Size: 1.25–1.7m (4–5.5ft); 43–150kg (95–330lb). Height at shoulder 0.8–1.1m (2.5–3.5ft).
Maturity: 3–4 years.
Breeding: 1–2 fawns born in June or July; gestation is 195–212 days.
Life span: 15 years.
Status: Common.

Caribou

Rangifer tarandus

The caribou, also known as the reindeer in Europe and Asia, is the only deer species in which both males and females possess antlers. American caribou have mainly brown coats with darker legs, while European and Asian animals are more grey.

Caribou herds are organized into hierarchies based on the size of the animals' bodies and antlers. Most herds make seasonal migrations in pursuit of food. Northern populations often make round trips of more than 5,000km (3,000 miles). During the migration, herds congregate into masses up to half a million strong. Caribou have been domesticated for 3,000 years, and there are huge numbers in northern Siberia.

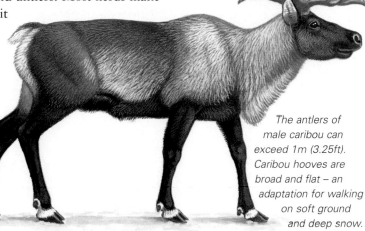

The antlers of male caribou can exceed 1m (3.25ft). Caribou hooves are broad and flat – an adaptation for walking on soft ground and deep snow.

Distribution: Alaska, Canada, northern USA, Greenland, Scandinavia, Siberia, Mongolia, and north-eastern China.
Habitat: Arctic tundra, boreal forests, mountainous habitats.
Food: Plant material (leaves and twigs; especially new growth in spring) and lichens.
Size: 1.2–2.2m (4–7.25ft); 60–318kg (130–700lb). Height at shoulder 0.8–1.2m (2.5–4ft).
Maturity: 1.5–3.5 years.
Breeding: 1 fawn per year.
Life span: 15 years.
Status: Common.

Grey brocket deer (*Mazama gouazoupira*): 85–105cm (33.5–41.5in); 17kg (37.5lb). Height at shoulder 30–60cm (12–24in)
Grey brocket deer, or brown brockets, range from southern Central America to northern Argentina and Uruguay. They occupy dry, open habitats such as chaco thorn scrub and savannahs. These deer are slightly smaller than red brocket deer, which are found in the same region but occupy more heavily forested habitats. Grey brocket deer eat fruits in the wet season, but make do with leaves and twigs during the dry season. When water is hard to come by, they feed on cacti and other succulent plants that store water in their flesh. The deer also dig up roots used by plants to store water and nutrients. Male grey brocket deer have small antlers, little more than 10cm (4in) spikes. They breed all year round, and males only need to renew their antlers every couple of years.

Fallow deer; introduced (*Dama dama*): Size: 1.3–1.7m (4.25–5.5ft); 40–100kg (88–220lb). Height at shoulder 75–100cm (27.75–39in)
Originally native to the Mediterranean and Middle East, this deer has since been introduced to other continents, including the Americas. Fallow deer are easily identified by their somewhat flattened antlers and spotted summer coats. In some places fallow deer live alone, but in others they form small herds of up to 30 individuals. Breeding behaviour is variable, and may depend on the distribution of food. Males try to attract females with dance-like rituals and bellowing – a rut. Alternatively, they may monopolize females by defending good feeding areas from rival males.

Wapiti

Cervus elaphus

In North America, wapiti are also called elk. Confusingly, in Europe and Asia the name elk is used to describe moose. It is now widely accepted that wapiti are actually an American subspecies of red deer, another large species found in northern Europe and Asia.

Only male wapiti have antlers, which reach up to 1.7m (5.5ft) across, and a shaggy mane around the neck. The males use their antlers during the rut, which takes place in autumn. They fight to establish which males will control the harems of females. Their antlers fall off in winter and regrow in time for the next year's contests.

Wapiti resemble Old World red deer in many ways, although their coat is more brown, and becomes paler in summer.

Distribution: Canada to New Mexico, as well as northern Africa, Asia and Europe.
Habitat: Alpine grasslands, forest edges.
Food: Grass, sedge, forbs, twigs and bark.
Size: 1.6–2.6m (5.25–8.5ft); 75–450kg (165–990lb). Height at shoulder 1.3–1.5m (4.25–5ft).
Maturity: 2 years.
Breeding: 1 fawn born in autumn.
Life span: 20 years.
Status: Common.

SEALS AND RELATIVES

Seals, sea lions and walruses are pinnipeds – they belong to the Pinnipedia *order of mammals (pinniped means "fin footed"). They are descended from carnivorous, terrestrial ancestors. However, it seems that seals may be only distantly related to sea lions and walruses, despite their similar appearances. Like other sea mammals, pinnipeds have a layer of blubber under their skin, which keeps them warm in cold water.*

Californian sea lion

Zalophus californianus

Californian sea lions spend the year moving up and down the Pacific coast of North America. In autumn and winter, most males move north to feed off the coast of British Columbia. The females and young stray less far from the breeding grounds, and probably head south at this time.

The sea lions are seldom far from the shore at any time of the year. They generally go on foraging trips at night, although they are often active during the day as well. Each trip can last for several hours.

During the summer breeding season, the sea lions congregate on flat beaches in the central area of their range. Most choose sandy habitats, but will use open, rocky areas if necessary. The males arrive first and fight each other for control of small territories on the beaches and in the water. They can only hold their territories for a few weeks before having to swim away and feed.

Californian sea lions have less heavyset bodies than most sea lions because they live in warmer waters. They are fast swimmers, reaching speeds of 40kmh (25mph).

Distribution: Pacific coast of North America and Galápagos Islands.
Habitat: Ocean islands and coastline.
Food: Fish, squid and seabirds.
Size: 1.5–2.5m (5–8.25ft); 200–400kg (440–880lb).
Maturity: Females 6 years; males 9 years.
Breeding: Single pup born each year.
Life span: 20 years.
Status: Vulnerable.

South American sea lion

Otaria flavescens or *byronia*

South American sea lions do not travel very far from their breeding sites during the non-breeding season, although they may spend long periods out at sea. These sea lions sometimes feed in groups, especially when they are hunting shoals of fish or squid.

The breeding season begins at the start of the southern summer. Adults arrive on beaches or flat areas of rock at the beginning of December. Males arrive a few weeks before the females, and defend small patches of the beach. The females give birth to the young they have been carrying since the previous year. After nursing their pups for a few weeks, the females become receptive to mating again. As the number of females increases, males stop controlling territories and begin to defend groups of females. Unsuccessful males without harems of their own gang together on the fringes of the beaches and charge through the females to mate with them.

Male South American sea lions have dark brown bodies with brown manes on their heads and necks. The females are less heavyset and have paler bodies and no manes.

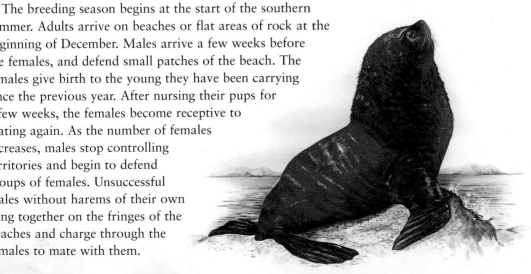

Distribution: South Pacific and Atlantic waters off the South American coast from northern Peru to Brazil.
Habitat: Coastal waters and beaches.
Food: Fish, squid and crustaceans.
Size: 1.8–2.5m (6–8.25ft); 150–350kg (330–770lb).
Maturity: Females 4 years; males 6 years.
Breeding: Single pup born in January.
Life span: 20 years.
Status: Vulnerable

Walrus

Odobenus rosmarus

Walruses live among the ice floes of the Arctic Ocean. These huge sea mammals are well known for their long tusks, which they use to stab opponents during fights. Walruses also use their tusks to "haul out", or pull themselves on to floating ice, and sometimes hook themselves to floes so that they can sleep while still in the water.

Walruses use their whiskered snouts to root out prey and blast away sediment with jets of air squirted from the mouth. They tackle shelled prey by holding them in their lips and sucking out the soft bodies.

Walruses live in large herds, sometimes of many thousands. In winter they feed in areas of thin sea ice, avoiding thick, unbroken ice, which they cannot break through from beneath. In summer, when the ice recedes, they spend more time on land.

Walruses have long tusks growing out of the upper jaw. Males, which are twice the size of females, also have longer tusks. Their bodies are reddish-brown and sparsely covered in coarse hairs. Males have two air pouches inside the neck, which they use to amplify their mating calls.

Distribution: Coast of Arctic Ocean.
Habitat: Pack ice.
Food: Worms, shellfish and fish.
Size: 2.25–3.5m (7.5–11.5ft); 400–1,700kg (880–3,740lb).
Maturity: Females 6 years; males 10 years.
Breeding: Single young born once per year.
Life span: 40 years.
Status: Vulnerable.

Hawaiian monk seal (*Monachus schauinslandi*): 2.1–2.3m (7–7.5ft); 170–250kg (375–450lb)
This endangered seal lives around small islands in the north-western region of Hawaii and other remote Pacific islands. Hawaiian monk seals hunt flatfish, lobsters, eels, and octopuses. Outside of the breeding season, these seals live alone. The females give birth on sandy beaches in areas controlled by the largest males. They then mate with the male in that area. The offspring from these matings are born the next year.

Bearded seal (*Erignathus barbatus*): 2.4m (8ft); 215–360kg (475–790lb)
This large species is found along the Alaskan coast and the edge of the Arctic sea ice, and occasionally as far south as Japan and Scotland. Bearded seals have long white whiskers that stand out against their dark fur. They live in shallow water, feeding on fish, crabs and shrimps.

West Indian monk seal (*Monachus tropicalis*): 2.2–2.4m (7.25–8ft); 170kg (375lb)
This species was declared extinct in 1996, the last confirmed sighting being in 1952. The West Indian monk seal once ranged throughout the Caribbean. It was thought to spend much of its time underwater, so it is possible that a small population still survives but is either rarely seen or is mistaken for another species.

Hooded seal

Cystophora cristata

Hooded seals rarely approach land, preferring to spend their whole lives among the ice floes in the cold Arctic Ocean. Apart from during the breeding season, hooded seals live alone. They dive down to depths of more than 180m (590ft) to feed on shoaling fish and bottom-living creatures.

When the breeding season arrives in spring, the seals congregate on wide ice floes. The females take up widely spaced positions on the ice, preparing to give birth to the young conceived the year before. Meanwhile, males compete for access to small groups of females. The victors stay near the females as they nurse their new-born calves, chasing away any intruders while inflating their nasal balloons.

Hooded seal pups are suckled for only four days – the shortest time of any mammal – after which the mothers abandon them.

Distribution: Waters around Greenland.
Habitat: Drifting ice floes.
Food: Octopus, squid, shrimp, mussels and fish.
Size: 2–2.7m (6.5–9ft); 145–300kg (320–660lb).
Maturity: Females 3 years; males 5 years.
Breeding: Single pup born in March.
Life span: 30 years.
Status: Common.

Hooded seals are so named because the males possess elastic sacs, or hoods, on the tops of their heads. The hoods are connected to their noses and can be inflated with air to amplify their calls while sparring with rival males. Female seals also have hoods, but their hoods are not inflatable like those of the males.

Steller's sea lion

Eumetopias jubatus

Steller's sea lions live along the coasts of the northern Pacific Ocean, from Japan to California. They prefer cold coastal water, where they feed on fish, squid and octopus. Between hunts, they rest on rocky shores. Adult males are about twice as large as females. Apart from their size, the main difference between the sexes is that males have huge necks, which are made even chunkier by their manes.

Sexually mature sea lions, including pregnant females, gather at breeding grounds in May. Each male defends an area of shore in the hope of encouraging females to give birth there. Fights between males can be extremely fierce, with the sea lions battering their huge bodies against each other and biting their opponent. The strongest bull is the one with the largest harem of females.

After the pups are born (the result of matings the previous year), he will mate with all the females in his territory. The male is not able to feed during the breeding season, because he is always guarding his harem. This fact, combined with the many injuries that males suffer during fights, means that males usually have considerably shorter lifespans than females.

Steller's sea lions are the largest sea lions. Adult males have a distinctive mane that makes them look larger and more impressive, and also provides protection from bites during fights over mates.

Distribution: Northern Pacific coasts of Canada and the United States to San Miguel Island, California.
Habitat: Rocky shores.
Food: Fish, octopus, squid, bivalve molluscs and crustaceans, occasionally young fur seals, ringed seals and sea otters.
Size: 2.3–2.8m (7.5–9.25); 263–1000kg (580–2204lb).
Maturity: 3–7 years.
Breeding: Single pup born in summer, usually between late May and early June.
Life span: 20 years.
Status: Endangered.

South American fur seal

Arctocephalus australis

This species of fur seal is found on both the Atlantic and Pacific coasts of South America. Its range extends as far north as the rocky shores of Peru on the western side, and to Brazil in the east. It prefers steep shorelines, where boulders provide plenty of shade from the hot sun.

South American fur seals feed on a range of fish, from anchovies to mackerel. They are known to swim up to 200km (125 miles) from the coast to find shoals on which to prey. In shallow waters, mainly near to land, these seals will also feed on crustaceans and bottom-living molluscs, including octopus and shellfish. South American fur seals are themselves preyed on by great white sharks and orcas out at sea, as well as by South American sea lions nearer the shore.

Mating takes place in spring. Large bulls adopt territories along the coast before females arrive to give birth. After the pups are born, a bull mates with all the females in his territory. He drives other males away with threatening displays and calls.

Male South American fur seals are much larger than the females. Once they reach adulthood, the males have black fur and a golden mane. The females and younger males are greyer. The pups are dark grey or black when born.

Distribution: Pacific and Atlantic coasts of South America, from southern Peru in the west round to southern Brazil in the east
Habitat: Rocky shores and islands.
Food: Fish, cephalopods, crustaceans, bivalve molluscs, and gastropods.
Size: 1.4–1.9m (4.5–6.25ft); 30–200kg (66–440lb).
Maturity: 3–7 years.
Breeding: Single pup born in summer, usually in November or December.
Life span: 30 years.
Status: Lower risk.

Northern elephant seal (*Mirounga angustirostris*): 3–5m (9.75–16.5ft); 0.6–2.3 tonnes (1,320–5,500lb)
Slightly larger than their southern counterparts, these elephant seals range from the Gulf of Alaska to Baja California. Each year a northern elephant seal will swim about 21,000km (13,000 miles). They migrate north in summer to feed in waters exposed by melting ice. The sexes follow different routes: males move to the far north, beyond the Aleutians, while females head further west into the northern Pacific. The seals come on to land to breed in winter, and again in August to moult their summer coat. They prefer sandy and rocky shores. Males are much larger than females, because they need to compete for access to mates.

Galápagos fur seal (*Arctocephalus galapagoensis*): 1.3–1.5m (4.25–5ft); 30–70kg (66–155lb)
This vulnerable species is found only around the Galápagos Islands off the coast of Ecuador. Galápagos fur seals stay close to the islands, and never dive below about 30m (100ft). They spend over a quarter of each day on land – more than any other eared seal (fur seal or sea lion). Their diet consists mainly of fish and squid.

Grey seal (*Halichoerus grypus*): 1.8–3m (6–10ft); 150–300kg (330–661lb)
Grey seals live along the coast of Canada's maritime provinces, from Labrador to Nova Scotia. They also range from Iceland to the coast of northern Europe, and into the Baltic Sea. Grey seals eat a range of fish, shellfish and crabs.

Northern fur seal

Callorhinus ursinus

This is the only fur seal in the northern hemisphere. Its well-documented migration takes it from the Bering Sea between Alaska and Siberia, where it spends the summer, to its winter destination of the northern Pacific. Populations are spread down the coasts of the Pacific, reaching Japan to the west and the extreme south of California to the east.

Northern fur seals prefer cold water and spend a lot of time far out at sea. Most of their breeding grounds are on islands in the northern Pacific. As with most seal species, the male northern fur seals arrive at the breeding grounds first and occupy a territory on the shore. The largest bulls take the best locations, usually in the middle of the beach. Females arriving to give birth move into the territory of a male. They seem to choose according to the location of the territory and the number of other females it contains, rather than by the bull's size.

Male northern fur seals are much larger than females, being up to six times heavier and about 50 per cent longer. While the females tend to be grey, the males' fur is red and black.

Distribution: Coasts of northern Pacific Ocean.
Habitat: Rocky beaches.
Food: Fish and squid.
Size: 1.4–2.1m (4.5–7ft); 50–275kg (110–605lb).
Maturity: 3–6 years.
Breeding: Single pup born in summer.
Life span: 25.
Status: Vulnerable.

Southern elephant seal

Mirounga leonina

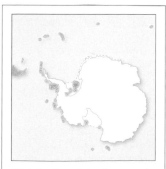

Distribution: Islands around Antarctica.
Habitat: Beaches, dunes and rocky shores.
Food: Squid, fish and crabs.
Size: 2.6–4.5m (8.5–14.75ft); 400–4,000kg (880–8,880lb).
Maturity: 5 years.
Breeding: 1 pup born in early summer.
Life span: 25 years.
Status: Common.

Elephant seals live in the waters around Antarctica and come ashore on the region's islands. They are seen as far north as South Georgia in the South Atlantic. Elephant seals feed on fish and squid.

Like northern elephant seals, these huge seals gather on flat beaches to breed in spring. The males arrive first to stake out their territories, and may stay on the beaches for the next two months without feeding. Pregnant females arrive at the breeding ground a few weeks later. A male will try to mate with females as they move up the beach into his territory, even though they have not yet given birth. Mating does occur after the young are born, and during this time a male will battle to keep rivals away from his harem. However, when males are occupied in fighting, females may move between harems. On a small beach, all the females may be controlled by a single bull, called a beach master.

Southern elephant seals are the largest animals in the pinniped group, which includes seals, sea lions and walruses. The males, which are up to five times the size of the females, have inflatable, trunk-like noses, with which they amplify their bellowing calls. They do not seem to have any natural predators.

Common seal

Phoca vitulina

The common seal's coloration is variable, but it generally consists of a grey or brownish-grey background speckled with darker spots. From a distance, the head of a common seal poking above the waves can closely resemble that of a human. As a result, these seals are sometimes mistaken for swimmers in trouble. This species is also known as the harbour seal, since it is often seen in estuaries and sheltered waters near human habitation.

The common seal is found along the northern coasts of North America, Europe and Asia, having a very similar range to that of the grey seal. The common seal has a dog-like face, with a more rounded snout than the Roman-style "nose" that typifies the grey seal. It is difficult to make accurate estimates of the size of the common seal population, because this species lives in small, widely distributed groups, and is highly mobile.

Common seals have large, sensitive eyes with specialized retinas, which allow them to see well underwater. However, sometimes the water is too murky for seals to hunt by sight, so they use their long, touch-sensitive whiskers to feel for prey in the gloom. Young seals eat shrimps and bottom-dwelling crustaceans. Older individuals take herring, salmon, anchovies, cod and other fish, as well as octopus. They can dive for up to 10 minutes but average dives last for three minutes.

Distribution: Temperate, subarctic and Arctic coastal areas of the North Atlantic and North Pacific oceans.
Habitat: Sheltered coastal waters.
Food: Fish, cephalopods and crustaceans.
Size: 1.2–2m (4–6.5ft); 45–130kg (99–287lb).
Maturity: Females 2 years; males 5 years.
Breeding: Single pup produced every year.
Life span: 26–32 years.
Status: Common.

Leopard seal

Hydrurga leptonyx

These predatory seals live all around the Antarctic, where they rest on the pack ice that covers the ocean in winter. Leopard seals are also found on most subantarctic islands, and occasionally further north in the warmer (but still very cold) waters around Tierra del Fuego, Cape Horn and the coast of southern Argentina.

Leopard seals feed on krill, which they filter from the water using their large cheek teeth, and cephalopods. They are also one of the few seal species in which warm-blooded animals make up a significant part of the diet. Penguins and other seals, including crabeaters and fur seals, are actively hunted, and many crabeaters and fur seals carry scars from attacks by leopard seals. Adult penguins are caught in the water, but penguin chicks are snatched on the ice. This species has been known to scavenge the carrion of whales and other seals.

Unlike most other seals, which propel themselves through the water with side-to-side strokes of the hind limbs, leopard seals swim by paddling with their large foreflippers. Apart from during the breeding season, these seals are primarily solitary, although they are seldom far from others of their own species. Leopard seals sometimes congregate in loose groups according to age and maturity. Breeding occurs in summer, apparently in the water, shortly after the birth of that year's pups. The young are born on the shores of the many small islands that surround Antarctica, and also at certain places on the coasts of southern South America and southern Africa. Leopard seal pups are weaned at about four weeks of age. The males take no part in the care of the young.

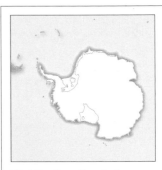

Distribution: Coast of Antarctica.
Habitat: Ice and land.
Food: Krill and some other seals and penguins.
Size: 2.4–3.4m (8–11.25ft); 200–590kg (440–1,300lb).
Maturity: 4 years.
Breeding: Single pup born in summer.
Life span: 25 years.
Status: Lower risk.

Leopard seals have large, sleek bodies, almost reptile-like heads and long canine teeth. Males are generally smaller than females. The coloration is dark grey to near-black on the back, pale on the sides and silver below, with variable amounts of grey spotting.

Crabeater seal

Lobodon carcinophagus

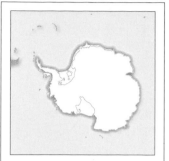

Distribution: Antarctica and surrounding landmasses.
Habitat: Pack ice.
Food: Krill.
Size: 2–2.4m (6.5–8ft); 200–300kg (440–660lb).
Maturity: 4 years.
Breeding: Single pup born in spring.
Life span: 25 years.
Status: Common.

Despite its name, the this seal never eats crabs, preferring krill instead. It feeds by swimming open-mouthed through a school of krill, sucking in the small animals from a distance of about 1m (3.25ft). Crabeater seals also eat small fish, which they swallow whole. These seals are capable of diving up to 430m (1,400ft), but the majority of dives are in the first 30m (100ft) or so of water, where they obtain most of their food.

Crabeaters are generally solitary creatures, but sometimes gather in large herds of more than 1,000 individuals. They congregate mainly on the pack ice around Antarctica, although some crabeater herds can be seen on the shores of the extreme tip of South America and other landmasses close to the Southern Ocean.

Pregnant females give birth on the ice in spring. Mating occurs after the pups are weaned at four weeks old.

The fur of the crabeater seal changes from dark brown to blonde during the course of the year. The winter coat is dark when it grows in autumn, but becomes paler from then on. The pale fur gives the species its alternative common name – the white Antarctic seal.

Ribbon seal (*Phoca fasciata*): 1.6m (5.25ft); 70–95kg (155–209lb)
The ribbon seal is found off the coasts of the northern Pacific. The largest populations occur in the Bering Sea, between Alaska and Siberia. Ribbon seals rarely come to land. They raise their pups on the ice floes that extend southward in winter. In summer, they feed voraciously to prepare for the next winter on the ice. This species gets its name from its four ribbon-like stripes. One encircles the neck, another wraps around the body, and the remaining two ring the foreflippers.

Ringed seal (*Phoca hispida*): 1.4–1.5m (4.5–5ft); 65–95kg (143–210lb)
Ringed seals are the most common seal inside the Arctic Circle. They spend the winter on and under the thick ice floes that form on the Arctic Ocean. When under the floes, they breathe via air holes that they maintain in the ice. During the long, sunless Arctic winter, ringed seals hunt in the darkness for Arctic cod, using their sensitive whiskers to detect currents caused by these slow-moving fish. In spring, the seals gather in groups on the ice. Females give birth to pups in April, and mating takes place about a month later.

Weddell seal (*Leptonychotes weddelli*): 2.5–3.3m (8.25–10.75ft); 400–450kg (880–990lb)
This species lives around Antarctica. It is named after the Weddell Sea, a large bay in the Atlantic coast of Antarctica. Weddell seals are most often found occupying ice floes. They feed at night, hunting for squid and fish, and will even attack prey as large as the Antarctic toothfish, which grows to about 50kg (110lb).

Harp seal

Phoca groenlandica

Harp seals are extremely social animals, congregating in huge numbers to give birth on ice floes in areas along the Arctic coastline.

Their sociability has led ultimately to their decline. The pups have soft, thick fur that is much sought after in some parts of the world. When the pups are gathered in large numbers, they make easy targets for hunters, who club them to death. Extensive hunting by humans reduced the total harp seal population from around 10 million individuals to 2 million by the early 1980s. Once their plight was understood, hunting pressure was reduced and the population is now gradually recovering. It will take a long time for harp seal numbers to reach their previous levels, because this species has a low rate of reproduction. Producing just one pup a year means that the population grows very slowly.

When feeding, adult harp seals may dive to depths of 200m (655ft) in search of herring and cod, which make up the bulk of this species' diet.

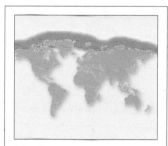

Distribution: Arctic Ocean.
Habitat: Open sea for most of the year.
Food: Crustaceans and fish.
Size: 1.7–1.9m (5.5–6.25ft); 120–130kg (265–287lb).
Maturity: 5 years.
Breeding: 1 pup born every year.
Life span: 16–30 years.
Status: Vulnerable.

The luxuriant fur of harp seal pups keeps them warm as they grow up on the Arctic icepack. The pups are weaned after 10–12 days and abandoned by their mothers.

DOLPHINS AND PORPOISES

Dolphins are small members of the mammal order Cetacea, which also includes the whales. Most dolphins live in the ocean, but a few species are found in the fresh water of large river systems. Porpoises are similar to dolphins, but tend to be smaller and have rounded snouts, rather than long beaks like dolphins. All but one species of porpoise inhabit shallow coastal waters, rather than the open ocean.

Amazon river dolphin

Inia geoffrensis

Distribution: Amazon and Orinoco River Basins.
Habitat: Dark, slow-moving river water.
Food: Small fish.
Size: 1.7–3m (5.5–9.75ft); 60–120kg (132–265lb).
Maturity: Unknown.
Breeding: Single calf born between April and September.
Life span: 30 years.
Status: Vulnerable.

Amazon river dolphins live in the wide rivers of the Amazon Basin. During the rainy season, they move into flooded areas of forest and up swollen streams into lakes. They may become isolated in pools when waters recede, but most are able to survive by eating the river fish that are trapped with them.

Dolphins live in small groups. They are thought to defend the areas around them and will stay in an area as long as there is enough food. They breathe at least once a minute, through the nostrils on the top of their head. They dive down to the bottom of rivers to search for food, using their bristled snout to root through mud and weeds.

Like other dolphins, Amazon river dolphins may use echolocation to find their way in the murky river waters. They sometimes feed in the same areas as giant otters. It may be that the hunting behaviour of otters drives fish out of the shallows towards the dolphins.

When young, Amazon river dolphins have metallic blue and grey upper bodies with silvery bellies. As they age, the dolphins' upper bodies gradually turn pinkish. Their long snouts are covered with sensitive bristles.

Vaquita

Phocoena sinus

Most vaquitas have dark grey or black upper bodies, with paler undersides. Like other porpoises, the vaquita has a blunt face. Its triangular dorsal fin is reminiscent of a shark's. Vaquitas live in pods of up to five animals.

Vaquitas live in the upper area of the Gulf of California, near the mouth of the Colorado River. No other marine mammal has such a small range, and consequently vaquitas are extremely rare and may become extinct.

Vaquitas used to be able to swim up into the mouth of the Colorado. However, in recent years so much water has been removed from the river for irrigation and for supplying cities that the Colorado is little more than a trickle where it reaches the ocean. This has probably changed the composition of the Gulf waters, too. The vaquita population was also affected by the fishing industry in the Gulf. Fishermen drowned many vaquitas in their nets by accident, and their activities have also reduced the amount of fish available for the porpoises to eat.

Biologists know little about the lives of these porpoises. Vaquitas probably spend most of their time alone, locating their prey close to the sea floor using echolocation. Births probably take place all year round.

Distribution: Gulf of California in the eastern Pacific.
Habitat: Coastal waters and mouth of the Colorado River.
Food: Fish and squid.
Size: 1.2–2m (4–6.5ft); 45–60kg (99–132lb).
Maturity: Unknown.
Breeding: Probably 1 calf.
Life span: Unknown.
Status: Critically endangered.

Risso's dolphin

Grampus griseus

Risso's dolphins live in small groups, called pods or schools, containing about ten individuals. The pods move to warm tropical waters in winter, and head toward the poles in summer. The dolphins are often seen leaping out of the water as the pod members play with one another.

Risso's dolphins feed in deep water. They dive down to catch fast-swimming squid and fish. Like other dolphins, they probably use echolocation to locate their prey in the dark depths. They produce clicking noises that bounce off objects in the water. The dolphins can hear each other's clicks and echoes, and groups may work together to track down shoals of fish or squid. In areas where there is plenty of food, dolphin pods congregate so that thousands of the leaping mammals may be seen together.

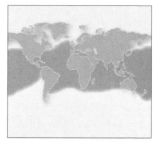

Distribution: All tropical and temperate seas.
Habitat: Deep ocean water.
Food: Fish and squid.
Size: 3.6–4m (11.75–13ft); 400–450kg (880–990lb).
Maturity: Unknown.
Breeding: Single young born once per year.
Life span: 30 years.
Status: Common.

Risso's dolphins have very blunt faces, lacking the beaks of typical dolphins. They have dark grey bodies, which are often scarred by attacks from other dolphins and large squid. Older dolphins may have so many scars that their bodies look almost white.

Short-beaked saddleback dolphin

(*Delphinus delphis*): 1.5–2.4m (5–8ft); 70–110kg (154–242lb)
Often called the common dolphin, this species is one of the smallest dolphins. It is common in European waters, but it also swims in coastal areas of the Atlantic and Pacific oceans, including along the shores of the Americas, where it is most often seen in the Gulf of Mexico. Common dolphins prefer to swim in warmer water near the surface. They have many small, curved teeth, with which they snatch herrings and other small, slippery fish. Common dolphins live in small family groups, or pods. Sometimes many pods join together to form vast clans up to 100,000 strong. Most of the time these dolphins swim at about 8kmh (5mph), but their top speed is around 46kmh (29mph).

Commerson's dolphin

(*Cephalorhynchus commersoni*): 1.4m (4.5ft); 50–85kg (110–187lb)
There are two populations of this dolphin, one in the Indian Ocean, and a larger population along South America's Atlantic coast, from the Straits of Magellan to Rio Negro province in central Argentina. Commerson's dolphins generally live in small pods of about three individuals. Pods may herd together to form temporary assemblies of over 100 dolphins, probably for breeding or feeding purposes. This species eats shrimp, fish, squid and invertebrates that live on the seabed.

Spectacled porpoise

Australophocaena dioptrica

Spectacled porpoises are rarely seen because they spend most of their time far from land. Most often they are spotted when they stray into coastal waters, especially along the Atlantic coast of South America, from Uruguay to Cape Horn and the Falkland Islands. These porpoises are also seen around New Zealand in the south Pacific, and around the Kerguelen Islands in the far south of the Indian Ocean.

Spectacled porpoises dive down into deep water to catch large fish and squid. They tend to feed in cold-water areas, such as in the currents that travel up from the Antarctic. Like most porpoises, they have fewer teeth than dolphins, but each tooth is large and chisel-shaped. This allows the porpoise to catch larger fish than dolphins. In shallower waters, the spectacled porpoise also eats crabs, lobsters and other crustaceans. It is sometimes preyed on by orcas (killer whales).

Spectacled porpoises are mainly solitary, and do not travel in large groups, although two or three individuals are occasionally seen together.

Distribution: South Atlantic, Pacific, and Indian oceans.
Habitat: Deep ocean.
Food: Fish, squid, and crustaceans.
Size: 1.8–2m (6–6.5ft); 55–115kg (121–253lb).
Maturity: About 5 years.
Breeding: Single young born in spring.
Life span: 20 years.
Status: Data deficient.

The back of this porpoise is black, while the underside and most of the face is white, except for the black around the eyes, which makes the animal look as though it is wearing spectacles – hence its name.

Franciscana

Pontoporia blainvillei

This species of river dolphin is also called the La Plata dolphin, after the Rio de la Plata (River Plate), the wide mouth of several rivers that forms the border between Argentina and Uruguay. As river dolphins, franciscanas can survive perfectly well in the fresh river water, although the tides regularly mix it with salt water. The dolphins do not enter any other rivers, but are found along the Atlantic coast as far north as central Brazil and as far south as the Valdez peninsula in Patagonia, southern Argentina.

Known as "white ghosts" by fisherman, franciscanas feed in murky waters churned up by coastal currents and tides. They have long, slender beaks that curve slightly downward. Without being able to see, they probe the bottom with their snouts, feeding on bottom-dwelling fish. Like all dolphins, franciscanas also orientate themselves using echolocation.

These smooth-swimming dolphins rarely roll or splash, and show little of themselves when they surface. On hot days they have been seen "sunbathing" on the sand in the shallows. If danger threatens, franciscanas will remain motionless near the water's surface.

Franciscanas belong to the river dolphin family. In general, river dolphins look unlike ocean-dwelling dolphins, having smaller fins, many pointed teeth and very long snouts. However, franciscanas may spend their whole lives out at sea, and as a result they look more like oceanic dolphins (although their snout, in relation to body size, is the longest of any dolphin species). The franciscana's body is greyish on top, which sometimes lightens during winter and with also age – in fact, some older dolphins are predominantly white.

Distribution: Mouth of the River Plate and coast of South America.
Habitat: Brackish and salt water.
Food: Fish.
Size: 1.3–1.75m (4.25–5.75ft); 20–61kg (44–134lb).
Maturity: 3 years.
Breeding: Single young born every two years.
Life span: 16 years.
Status: Data deficient.

Tucuxi

Sotalia fluviatilis

While franciscanas are river dolphins that are at home in sea water, tucuxis are the opposite – oceanic dolphins that have evolved to live in fresh water as well as in the ocean. Some tucuxis never swim in the sea. They live thousands of miles from the ocean in the headwaters of the Amazon River that flow down the foothills of the Andes in Peru and Colombia. Conversely, some tucuxis spend their whole lives at sea, ranging from the Caribbean coast of Mexico to Argentinian waters. Research suggests that this dolphin exists in two subspecies. Marine tucuxis are larger than riverine tucuxis. They also have a more bluish coloration, to help them blend in with the deep, clear waters of coastal regions.

Tucuxis feed mainly on fish and shrimps. They usually hunt in small groups of two to seven dolphins, although larger groups of up to 20 in fresh water and 50 in the ocean are sometimes seen. The dolphins swim and breathe in synchrony so that they can all attack at the same time when they spot a shoal of fish or other supply of food. Tucuxis sometimes swim upside-down to trap fish against the surface of the water. In fact, individuals often have bare patches on their dorsal fin, where it has been scraped on the river bottom or seabed while swimming inverted.

Tucuxis are energetic swimmers and often leap out of the water, but they are quite timid and tend to keep away from boats.

Distribution: Amazon River system, and Atlantic coastline of Central and South America.
Habitat: Fresh and salt water.
Food: Fish.
Size: 1.4–1.9m (4.5–6.25ft); 40–53kg (88–117lb).
Maturity: 3 years.
Breeding: Single young born in summer every two years.
Life span: Unknown.
Status: Data deficient.

Tucuxis are also known as grey dolphins, although their underside is a pale pink. They are small dolphins, especially those that live in the headwaters of rivers. The forehead (melon) is quite rounded, and the longish beak contains 140 teeth.

White-beaked dolphin

Lagenorhynchus albirostris

Distribution: Ranges widely throughout the North Atlantic and Arctic Oceans.
Habitat: Coastal waters.
Food: Medium-sized fish, squid and crustaceans form the bulk of the diet.
Size: 2.3–2.8m (7.5–9.25ft); 180–200kg (397–441lb).
Maturity: Unknown.
Breeding: 1 calf born every year.
Life span: Unknown.
Status: Common.

Dolphins are notoriously difficult animals to study because they are very wide-ranging. Consequently, little is known about the habits of this remarkable group compared to most land-living mammals. Like most cetaceans, white-beaked dolphins live in groups known as pods, or schools, which have very complex social structures. Pods are usually made up of 2–20 individuals, but occasionally many pods will come together to form large aggregations containing in excess of 1,000 individuals.

White-beaked dolphins are famed for a behaviour known as breaching, when they leap clear of the water, somersault and splash back down through the waves. They frequently swim alongside small boats and have also been observed playing games underwater, such as chasing seaweed. White-beaked dolphins undertake annual migrations, moving between temperate and subpolar waters as they track and feed on their favoured prey of mackerel and herring.

The white-beaked dolphin's counter-shaded coloration, with a darker upper side and pale belly, helps to camouflage it from both above and below.

Black dolphin (*Cephalorhynchus eutropia*): 1.6m (5.25ft); 50kg (110lb)
This small dolphin lives off the coast of Chile. Mineral-rich currents from Antarctica make the continental shelf here a fertile feeding ground for black dolphins, which feed on fish and sea-floor animals. To help them get at their prey, the dolphins have a relatively flat snout, more like that of a porpoise than the beak-like snout of other dolphins. Black dolphins live in small schools and communicate with clicks. Similar noises are used to locate prey by echolocation.

Hourglass dolphin (*Lagenorhynchus cruciger*): 1.6m (5.25ft); 83–100kg (183–220lb)
Hourglass dolphins are found in the colder waters of the southern hemisphere. These shy animals live in small groups and travel huge distances in their lifetime. In general, hourglass dolphins keep to the waters around Antarctica, but they occasionally follow cold-water currents moving north, such as the Humboldt Current that flows along the coast of Chile.

Short-finned pilot whale (*Globicephala macrorhynchus*): 6m (19.75ft); 2.1 tonnes (4,630lb)
Sometimes classed as a separate group of toothed whales, pilot whales (and the closely related orcas) are more usually grouped with the dolphins. This species lives in all tropical waters and is often seen in certain bays and other coastal waters that are used as breeding grounds. The name pilot whale refers to the way that pods of these animals – which number up to 20 whales – follow a single individual, or pilot.

Atlantic white-sided dolphin

Lagenorhynchus acutus

Atlantic white-sided dolphins are seldom found near shore. They prefer to swim far out to sea in the clear water on the edge of the continental shelf, where the sea floor plunges to the great depths of the mid-ocean. They can dive to about 270m (900ft), and usually hunt at about 40m (130ft) below the surface. These fast, acrobatic swimmers come to the surface for breath every 15–20 seconds.

These dolphins prefer shoaling prey such as herrings, shrimps and even certain squid. They plunge into the shoal, snapping up food with their long snout as they pass through. Like many oceanic dolphins, this species is social, living in small family groups of about six individuals. Although Atlantic white-sided dolphins are rare, they are also reported to mass together far out to sea in clans more than 1,000 strong. Atlantic white-sided dolphins are nomadic – that is, they follow no distinct seasonal migration routes, but simply move throughout their range in search of food.

Distribution: Southern Greenland to Massachusetts.
Habitat: Cold, open water.
Food: Shrimp and small fish.
Size: 3m (9.75ft); 180–250kg (397–550lb).
Maturity: 12 years.
Breeding: 1 calf born every 2–3 years.
Life span: 40 years.
Status: Common.

Female Atlantic white-sided dolphins are considerably smaller than the males of the species. These dolphins have a dark grey or black back, pale flanks and a white or cream underside.

Bottlenosed dolphin

Tursiops truncatus

This is one of the most common and familiar dolphin species. It is found worldwide but often appears along the Atlantic coast of North America, from Cape Hatteras in North Carolina to Argentina, and along the Pacific up to northern California.

Bottlenosed dolphins live in shallow water close to land, and they are generally spotted breaching in large bays. They often enter lagoons and the mouths of large rivers. They do not appear to migrate, but rather make a lifelong journey that may take them to all parts of the world. Since they prefer warmer waters, they tend to move between the Atlantic and Pacific oceans via the Indian ocean.

Bottlenosed dolphins travel at about 20kmh (12mph) and are rarely seen travelling alone. They hunt as a team, corralling shoals of fish and shrimps by circling around them and taking turns to dive through the shoal to snatch mouthfuls of food. These dolphins are known to herd fish on to mudflats and then slide up the shore to seize their prey. Bottlenosed dolphins will also follow shrimp boats to feed off the discarded scraps. Individuals consume around 7kg (15.4lb) per day.

The bottlenosed is the largest of the beaked dolphins, which are oceanic dolphins with short, stout snouts. Males are much larger than females. This species shows a high degree of intelligence.

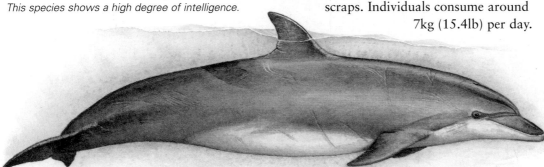

Distribution: Tropical and temperate coastal waters worldwide; both Pacific and Atlantic coasts of the Americas, and around Hawaii.
Habitat: Warm shallow water and cooler, deeper waters.
Food: Fish, squid, shrimp and eels.
Size: 1.75–4m (5.7–13ft); 150–400kg (330–880lb).
Maturity: 5–12 years.
Breeding: Breeding times vary with location. Single calf born every 2–3 years; gestation is about 12 months.
Life span: 40 years.
Status: Unknown.

Pacific white-sided dolphin

Lagenorhynchus obliquidens

The Pacific white-sided dolphin is found mainly in deep coastal waters, rarely straying more than 160 km (100 miles) from land. It ranges around the northern Pacific Rim, where a narrow continental shelf and steep continental slope create the deep water conditions preferred by this species. The Pacific white-sided dolphin is found from the waters around Hokkaido, the northern island of Japan, and along the Kuril and Aleutian islands to Alaska. It also occurs along the North American west coast as far south as Baja California, Mexico. This friendly, inquisitive species will ride the bow and stern waves of boats, and investigate motionless vessels.

Pacific white-sided dolphins live in small family groups, or pods, of 10–20 individuals. A pod contains a single dominant male who mates with the mature females in the pod. Other males in the pod are unlikely to mate. Several pods often group together, and dolphins probably move between pods during these congregations. Pod members hunt for fish together, with each adult consuming about 9kg (20lb) of fish per day. In British Columbia, pods have been observed seeking out and harassing orcas that feed on local fish shoals.

These large dolphins have a torpedo-shaped body that allows them to cut through water easily. The body has distinct counter-shading, with black on the upper surface and white below. When swimming with their dorsal fin breaking the water's surface, they look like sharks.

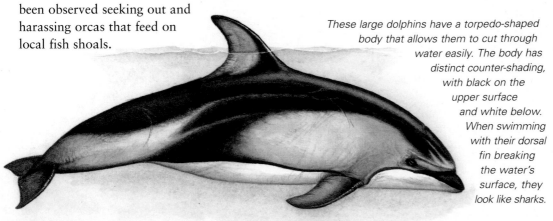

Distribution: Continental waters of northern Pacific Ocean; in North America, from the Aleutians Islands and Alaska south to Baja California, Mexico.
Habitat: Deep offshore water.
Food: Fish, squid and octopus.
Size: 1.5–3.1m (5–10ft); 82–124kg (181–273lb).
Maturity: 6–8 years.
Breeding: Single young born in late summer; gestation is 10–12 months.
Life span: 35 years.
Status: Common.

Atlantic spotted dolphin

Stenella frontalis

The Atlantic spotted dolphin is found all around the warmer parts of the Atlantic Ocean. Along the North American coast, the species occurs in the waters off Florida and in the Gulf of Mexico. The dolphin rarely moves more than 350km (220 miles) from the coast, and it spends most of its time in shallow water over sand banks, including those in the Bahamas.

Spotted dolphins are very social animals. They live in pods that range in size from just a few individuals to groups of several thousand that mass far out to sea. Within large pods, dolphins of different sexes and stages of maturity are often segregated. The dolphins communicate using high-pitched whistles, clicks, cackles and cries, which are within the range of human hearing. Each individual dolphin has its own unique identifying call.

Adults of this species have a spotted pattern. These spots are not present at birth, but appear after weaning. The number of spots increases with age.

Spotted dolphins feed on eels, herrings and other small fish. They often track shoals of prey, swimming above them just below the surface before diving down to attack as a group.

Distribution: Warm Atlantic waters.
Habitat: Shallow water above continental shelf.
Food: Fish.
Size: 1.6–2.3m (5.25–7.5ft); 90–110kg (198–242lb).
Maturity: 9 years.
Breeding: 1 calf born in summer every 2–3 years.
Life span: 35 years.
Status: Lower risk.

Southern right whale dolphin (*Lissodelphis peronii*): 1.8–2.3m (6–7.5ft); 60kg (132lb)
This species lives in the southern hemisphere. It is found around the edge of the Southern Ocean surrounding Antarctica. It also swims further north along the cold-water currents that flow from the polar region. The northern limit of the dolphin's range is in the subtropical zones where these cold currents meet warmer water heading south – for example, off the coasts of Chile and Peru, along which the Humboldt Current flows. Like the right whale, this dolphin species is largely black, with white patches on the belly and under the mouth, and it lacks a dorsal fin. The southern right whale dolphin also has a very slender body – unlike its giant namesake, which is known for its enormous girth.

Striped dolphin (*Stenella coeruleoalba*): 2.1m (7ft); 90kg (198lb)
Striped dolphins are found in the world's warm seas, including the Caribbean and Gulf of Mexico. They keep to areas where the water temperature is above 20°C (68°F), and they are just as at home in open water as they are in the shallows near the coast. They get their name from the blue stripe that runs along the entire length of the body. There are also black stripes running down to the flippers. Being inshore dolphins, they eat a range of foods, from free-swimming fish to bottom dwelling crabs and octopuses. Striped dolphins are very active swimmers. They also perform an unusual manoeuvre called roto-tailing, in which they leap out of the water in a high arc and spin around their tail.

Spinner dolphin

Stenella longirostris

Spinner dolphins are truly oceanic animals. They roam through all the world's oceans, mainly staying in the warmer regions. They seldom come close to land and are only really seen from ships or around remote islands. Perhaps the best place to see spinner dolphins is from the deck of a fishing ship in the Pacific tuna fisheries off the west coast of South America.

Spinners often track large shoals of yellowfin and skipjack tuna, swimming at the surface several meters above the fish. Tuna fishermen keep an eye out for groups of spinners (and similar dolphins) to lead them to the tuna. As a result, spinner dolphins are often caught and drowned in nets intended for tuna.

Spinners live in pods of about 20 dolphins, but are also reported to gather together in groups of more than 1,000 from time to time. Members of a pod are organized into a dominance hierarchy.

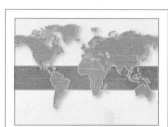

Distribution: Tropical waters worldwide.
Habitat: Open water.
Food: Fish and squid.
Size: 1.8–2.1m (6–7ft); 55–75kg (121–165lb).
Maturity: 10 years.
Breeding: 1 calf born every 2–3 years.
Life span: 35 years.
Status: Lower risk.

These dolphins are famous for leaping put of the water and spinning their body round in mid-air. Spinner dolphins that live near to land are slightly different from those that spend their time in deep ocean waters. Biologists have detected at least four subspecies, which have varying coloration and differently shaped dorsal fins.

TOOTHED WHALES

Within the Cetacea *order (which includes whales, dolphins and porpoises), there are 23 species of toothed whale. These cetaceans are hunting whales, and they include the world's largest predator, the sperm whale. Toothed whales live in family groups called pods. They hunt for food using echolocation – a sonar system that is focused through a fatty mass called the melon, which is located at the front of the head.*

Sperm whale

Physeter macrocephalus

Sperm whales are supremely well adapted to life in the deep oceans. These are the largest hunting predators in the world, with teeth up to 20cm (8in) long and the largest brains of any mammal, weighing over 9kg (20lb). They prefer areas of ocean with cold upwellings at least 1,000m (3,300ft) deep, where squid – their favourite food – are most abundant.

Sperm whales can dive to incredible depths to hunt, occasionally journeying up to 2.5km (1.6 miles) beneath the surface. They are social animals, and they live in groups of between 20 and 40 females, juveniles and young. Sperm whales have been hunted for their oil since the mid-18th century, and after serious population declines between the 1950s and 1980s, this species is now protected.

The box-like head of the sperm whale contains the spermaceti organ, which is filled with the fine oil so valued by whalers. The purpose of this organ is unclear: it may function as a lens, focusing the sounds that the whale uses to detect its prey, or it may help the whale to control its buoyancy during dives.

Distribution: Ranges throughout oceans and seas worldwide.
Habitat: Deep oceans.
Food: Mostly squid, including giant deep-sea squid, but also some fish and sharks.
Size: 12–20m (40–65ft); 12–70 tonnes (26,500–155,000lb).
Maturity: Females 7–13 years; males 25 years.
Breeding: 1 calf born every 5–7 years.
Life span: 77 years.
Status: Vulnerable.

Narwhal

Monodon monoceros

Distribution: Parts of the Arctic Ocean near Greenland and the Barents Sea. The range is patchy.
Habitat: Coastal Arctic waters.
Food: Cuttlefish, fish, crustaceans and squid.
Size: 4–5.5m (13–18ft); 800–1,600kg (1,750–3,500lb).
Maturity: Females 5–8 years; males 11–13 years.
Breeding: Single calf born every 2–3 years.
Life span: 50 years.
Status: Common.

The male narwhal's tusk is in fact a greatly elongated front tooth that spirals as it grows from a hole in the whale's lips. Females may possess a short tusk, too. The name narwhal means "corpse whale" in Old Norse, perhaps referring to the deathly hue of their white-blotched, bluish-grey skin.

Some people believe that the bizarre appearance of the narwhal first gave rise to the legend of the unicorn. The function of the male's long tusk is not fully understood. It may be used as a hunting implement, or as a tool to break up ice and create breathing holes for the whales. However, the most favoured explanation is that the males use their tusks to joust with each other, fighting over access to females during the breeding season.

The narwhal's swollen forehead is known as its melon – a feature shared with dolphins and other toothed whales. The melon serves to focus the ultrasonic clicks that narwhals and other small cetaceans use to navigate and find their food. As in a sophisticated sonar system, the narwhals listen for the high-frequency echoes that rebound off nearby objects. So sensitive is this method of orientation that narwhals can not only distinguish between food and non-food items, but they can also tell the size of an object, how far away it is and how fast it is moving.

Orca

Orcinus orca

Orcas have black upper bodies and white undersides, with grey patches behind their dorsal fins and white patches above their eyes. They are highly social, travelling and hunting together in pods.

Distribution: Throughout the world's oceans.
Habitat: Coastal waters.
Food: Seals, dolphins, fish, squid, penguins, crustaceans.
Size: 8.5–9.8m (28–32.25ft); 5.5–9 tonnes (12,000–19,800lb).
Maturity: Females 6 years; males 12 years.
Breeding: Single young born generally in autumn every 3–4 years.
Life span: 60–90 years.
Status: Lower risk.

Also known as killer whales, orcas are expert hunters, armed with up to 50 large, pointed teeth. Although orcas have been detected 1km (0.6 mile) below the surface, they prefer to hunt in shallow coastal waters.

Orcas typically live in pods of five or six individuals. Generally each pod is run by a large male, although larger groups have several adult males. Females and their young may split off into subgroups. Like other toothed whales and dolphins, orcas produce click sounds that are used for echolocation. The whales also communicate with each other using high-pitched screams and whistles. Orcas have several hunting techniques. They break pack ice from beneath, knocking their prey into the water, or they may rush into shallow water to grab prey from the shore. It is reported that they may crash on to the shore to drive prey into the surf where other members of the pod pick them off. Orcas breed throughout the year, although most mate in the early summer and give birth in the autumn of the following year.

Southern bottlenose whale (*Hyperoodon planifrons*): 6.5–8m (21–26ft); 6–8 tonnes (13,000–17,500lb)
This species is one of the beaked whales – toothed whales that are like dolphins and pilot whales in many ways, except that they are larger. Bottlenosed whales, as their name suggests, resemble bottlenosed dolphins. Most beaked whales have a bulbous forehead, but bottlenose whales have a flatter head, like oceanic dolphins. However, in common with almost all other beaked whales, this species has only two obvious teeth. These are tusk-like, and in old males they stick out at the front of the mouth. The teeth are used in fights, and older beaked whales bear numerous long scars along their backs caused by bites. The southern bottlenose whale lives in the cold waters of the Southern Hemisphere. It is often found around Cape Horn and the Falkland Islands. This species feeds on squid and fish.

Pygmy beaked whale (*Mesoplodon peruvianus*): 3.4 m (11ft); weight unknown
Although a member of the beaked whale family, this cetacean is only a little larger than its dolphin cousins. It is a very rare species and is only found in the warm waters off northern Peru. Pygmy beaked whales are deep-sea hunters that feed on squid and fish. This is one of the latest mammal species to be described. It was only discovered in 1991, and is thought to be the smallest beaked whale. No live member of this species has ever been formally identified, and everything we know about it comes from studying dead specimens.

Beluga

Delphinapterus leucas

Beluga means white in Russian, so these whales are sometimes called white whales. Belugas are also nicknamed sea canaries, because they call to each other with high-pitched trills.

Belugas live in the far north, where daylight is very brief or non-existent much of the year. Some beluga pods, or schools, spend all their time in one area of ocean, such as the Gulf of St Lawrence; others are always on the move. The pods are ruled by large males, and all pods spend their winters away from areas of thick ice. In summer, they enter river estuaries and shallow bays.

Belugas navigate using a well-developed sonar system, which is thought to be controlled by the melon – the large sensory organ on top of the head.

Most calves are born during late summer, and their mothers mate again a year or two later during early summer.

Distribution: Arctic to gulfs of Alaska and St Lawrence.
Habitat: Deep coastal waters and mouths of large rivers.
Food: Fish, squid, octopus, crabs and snails.
Size: 3.4–4.6m (11.25–15.25ft); 1.3–1.5 tonnes (2,850–3,300lb).
Maturity: Females 5 years; males 8 years.
Breeding: Single calf born every 2–3 years.
Life span: 25 years.
Status: Vulnerable.

Adult beluga whales are almost completely white, helping them to hide among ice floes. Younger whales begin life with dark bodies, which gradually become yellow and brown before fading to white.

OTHER WHALES

The largest members of the Cetacea order are called baleen whales. There are about a dozen species of baleen whale, including humpbacks, right whales and the mighty blue whale. Instead of teeth, these whales have baleen plates – long slats of keratin that form a thick curtain which hangs down from the upper jaw. This keratin curtain sieves krill, plankton and other small food items from sea water.

Northern right whale

Eubalaena glacialis

These large, slow-swimming whales are often found on the surface, so they were considered just "right" for hunting by whalers – hence the species' common name. The mouth yielded an excellent supply of baleen (whalebone) and the blubber produced a large quantity of oil. The hunting was so relentless that only a few hundred are left in the northern hemisphere.

Each winter, northern right whales migrate from cold northern waters to warmer areas in the south, where the females give birth. In the Atlantic, the whales move from the waters off Nova Scotia and Labrador to Florida. Pacific whales summer in the Bering Sea off Alaska, before heading to wintering grounds on the western coast of Russia.

The huge head of this giant grey whale makes up about one-third of the overall body size. The mouth is one of the widest in the animal kingdom.

Distribution: Atlantic coastal waters of North America.
Habitat: Shallow coastal water.
Food: Krill and other zooplankton.
Size: 17m (56ft); 55 tonnes (120,000lb).
Maturity: 10 years.
Breeding: 1 calf born every 3–4 years.
Life span: 60 years.
Status: Critically endangered.

Humpback whale

Megaptera novaeangliae

Humpbacks spend their summers feeding far from shore, in the cold waters near the poles. They feed by taking in huge mouthfuls of sea water. Their baleen plates then strain out any fish or krill from the water. Pairs of humpbacks also corral shoals of fish by blowing curtains of bubbles around them. The fish will not swim through the bubbles, so they crowd together. The whales then rush up from beneath into the mass of fish with their mouths wide open.

As winter approaches, the whales stop feeding and head to warmer, shallow waters near coasts or groups of islands. For example, populations of humpbacks spend the winter near Baja California and the Hawaiian islands. During the winter the whales do not feed; instead they concentrate on reproduction. The males produce songs that they repeat for days on end. The songs probably attract receptive females that are not caring for calves that year, and also help to keep rival males away from each other. Pregnant females stay feeding for longer than the other whales, and arrive in the wintering grounds just in time to give birth.

Humpback whales are so-called because of the dorsal fin (on the back), which may be swelled into a hump by deposits of fat. Humpbacks have the longest pectoral (arm) fins of any whale species, measuring about one-third of their body length.

Distribution: All oceans.
Habitat: Deep ocean water.
Food: Small fish and krill.
Size: 12.5–15m (41–49.5ft); 30 tonnes (66,000lb).
Maturity: 4–5 years.
Breeding: Single young born every 2 years.
Life span: 70 years.
Status: Vulnerable.

Grey whale

Eschrichtius robustus

Grey whales spend their lives on the move. In autumn they swim from Arctic waters down the western coast of North America, mating on the way, to spend the winter in bays along the coast of Mexico. The young that were conceived during the previous year are born in these bays in late January and February, and soon after, the whales set off to spend the summer in the food-rich waters of the Arctic.

A similar migration takes place down the eastern coast of Asia, but these whales are relatively few in number. Grey whales spend a good deal of time playing in shallow water during the winter. They leap out of the water and may become stranded for a few hours as they wait for the tide to rise. While on the move they "spyhop", protruding their heads above the surface so that they can look around.

Grey whales are baleen whales that feed on the seabed. They drive their heads through the sediment to stir up prey. They then suck in the disturbed water and strain the animals from it. Most feeding takes place in the summer, and whales may fast for the remaining six months of the year.

Distribution: Northern Pacific Rim.
Habitat: Shallow coastal water.
Food: Amphipods (small crustaceans).
Size: 13–15m (43–49.5ft); 20–37 tonnes (44,000–82,000lb).
Maturity: Females 17 years; males 19 years.
Breeding: Single young born every 2 years.
Life span: 70 years.
Status: Endangered

Grey whales do not have dorsal fins, but a series of small humps along their backs. They are often covered in white barnacles.

Bowhead whale (*Balaena mysticetus*): 11–13m (36–42.5ft); 50–60 tonnes (110,000–130,000lb)
Bowhead whales live in the Arctic Ocean. They have huge curved jaws with more baleen plates than any other whale. Adults have black bodies with pale patches on their lower jaws. Bowheads live among ice floes. They feed on tiny floating crustaceans, such as krill and copepods. They can eat 1.8 tonnes (4,000lb) in one day.

Blue whale (*Balaenoptera musculus*): 25–30m (82–100ft); 100–160 tonnes (220,000–350,000lb)
The blue whale is the largest animal to have ever existed. It has a blue-grey body, with spots along its back and a pale pleated throat. Blue whales live alone, travelling between subtropical waters and those near the poles. The populations of the northern and southern hemispheres never meet. They eat krill – tiny floating crustaceans – and can gulp down 6 tonnes (13,000lb) of them in a single day. Their pleated throats distend to four times their normal size as the whales take in mouthfuls of krill-laden water.

West Indian manatee

Trichechus manatus

Despite their appearance, manatees are not cetaceans. Neither are they related to seals (pinnipeds). These marine mammals belong to the *Sirenia* order, as do the dugongs – similar animals from South-east Asia. Sirenians evolved to live in water separately from whales and seals. In fact, they are believed to be more closely related to elephants than other sea mammals. Like elephants, they are vegetarian, not carnivorous.

Manatees live in both salt and fresh water, although they spend more time in fresh-water habitats. They rarely stray far from land, and may travel considerable distances up rivers to sources of warm water during winter.

Manatees feed both during the day and at night. They use their dextrous lips to pluck leaves from water hyacinths, sea grasses and other aquatic plants. Although they do not actively seek them out, the manatees also eat the invertebrates, such as water snails and insect larvae, that live on these plants. The single young is born after about a year's gestation.

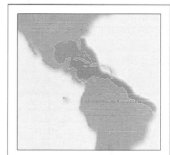

Distribution: Coast of Florida to Brazil.
Habitat: Estuaries and shallow coastal water.
Food: Water plants and aquatic invertebrates.
Size: 2.5–4.5m (8.25–14.75ft); 500kg (1,100lb).
Maturity: 8–10 years.
Breeding: Single young born every 2–3 years.
Life span: 30 years.
Status: Vulnerable.

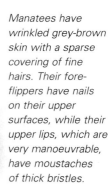

Manatees have wrinkled grey-brown skin with a sparse covering of fine hairs. Their fore-flippers have nails on their upper surfaces, while their upper lips, which are very manoeuvrable, have moustaches of thick bristles.

GLOSSARY

Aestivation A period of dormancy during hot and dry weather. Most aestivators are amphibians, which need to avoid dry periods.

Alimentary canal The digestive tract, including the stomach and intestines.

Alpha female/male The only breeding female or male in a pack of wolves or similar social group.

Amphibian A vertebrate that spends part of its life on land and part in water, and that needs water to breed. Salamanders, frogs, toads, newts and caecilians are amphibians.

Anatomy The study of how bodies are constructed.

Anus The rear opening to the alimentary canal, through which faeces leave the body.

Arthropod An invertebrate with a jointed body case. Arthropods include insects, spiders, crustaceans and centipedes.

Asexual reproduction Reproduction that does not require mating between members of the opposite sex.

Autotroph An organism that makes its own food. Plants are autotrophs.

Bacterium (pl. bacteria) A microscopic, single-celled organism. Many bacteria are parasitic or cause disease.

Baleen Horny plates in the mouth of some whales that strain food from seawater.

Biome A large area with a distinctive climate and community of wildlife.

Blubber A layer of fat found under the skin of many aquatic mammals that live in cold environments. Blubber provides insulation, helping the animal to retain body heat.

Caecilian A worm-like amphibian.

Canine A member of the dog family; or a long, pointed tooth.

Carnassial A special cheek tooth found in members of the *Carnivora* mammal group. Carnassials are used to slice up meat.

Polar bears

Carnivore An animal that eats mainly meat; more specifically, a member of the *Carnivora* order of mammals.

Cartilage A tough, gristly substance found in the skeletons of vertebrates.

Cell One of the tiny units from which all living things are made.

Chaparral An area containing many dense evergreen shrubs. Most American chaparral is in the Great Basin area.

Chordate An animal with a rigid sheath around the main nerve cord along its back. Most chordates are vertebrates, in which this cord runs through the backbone.

Circadian A lifestyle with a daily rhythm.

Cloaca A rear opening of a reptile or bird, through which both eggs and faeces pass.

Crepuscular Active at dawn or dusk, or both.

Crustacean An arthropod with a calcareous (calcium carbonate-containing) shell and pincers on the first pair of legs. Crustaceans include crabs, krill and woodlice.

Deep South Part of the US that borders the Gulf of Mexico, especially Louisiana, Mississippi, Alabama and Georgia.

DNA (deoxyribonucleic acid) A molecule in cells that contains instructions (genes) to form offspring when organisms reproduce.

Dorsal Relating to the back.

Echolocation A technique whereby some animals can orientate themselves or find prey in darkness or murky water by emitting high-pitched sounds and listening for the echoes that bounce off objects.

Ectothermic Describing an animal that controls its body temperature with external heat sources. Invertebrates, amphibians and reptiles are ectothermic (or "cold-blooded"). Mammals and birds are endothermic (or "warm-blooded"). They control their body temperature using internal energy sources.

Egg The female reproductive cell; or the earliest stage of development for reptiles, amphibians, birds and many other animals.

Embryo A young animal developing in an egg or a womb.

Epiphytes Plants that grow on other plants.

Evolution The process by which living things gradually adapt in order to become better suited to their environment.

Extinction When all the individuals in a species die out, so that none is left.

Fauna The animal life in an area. Flora is the plant life in the same area.

Foetus A baby mammal in the womb, more developed than an embryo.

Follicle The source of a hair or hairs.

Fossil The remains or imprint of a once-living organism preserved in rock.

Fungi A group of organisms that includes mushrooms, toadstools and yeasts.

Gastrolith A stone swallowed by a reptile that is used to grind up food in the stomach.

Gene A section of DNA that carries the coded instructions for a particular trait in a living organism.

Genetics The study of heredity and variation.

Genus The second smallest division in taxonomy.

Gestation The period between mating and giving birth in mammals.

Gill An organ used to extract oxygen from water.

Gland A structure inside or outside the body that secretes a chemical substance.

Gran Chaco A lowland area of South America, covering parts of Paraguay, Bolivia and Argentina.

Great Basin An arid plateau that runs from Idaho and Wyoming through the south-western US to northern Mexico.

Gonad A sex organ that produces sex cells.

Southern Pacific rattlesnake

Ground squirrel

American bison

Habitat The external environment in which animals and other organisms live.

Herbivore An animal that eats mainly plants.

Heterotroph An organism that eats other living things. Animals are heterotrophs.

Hibernation A period of dormancy that enables animals to survive cold weather. A hibernating animal's body temperature, heart rate and breathing slow right down.

Incisor A chisel-like tooth at the front of some mammals' jaws.

Insect A member of a large group of arthropods. Insects include beetles, ants, butterflies and grasshoppers.

Invertebrate An animal without a backbone, such as an insect, crustacean, mollusc, worm, jellyfish, sponge or starfish.

Kingdom The initial and largest taxonomic division. There are five kingdoms: animals, plants, fungi, protists and monerans.

Larva An immature stage in an animal's life cycle. Larvae differ greatly from adults.

Mammal A vertebrate animal with hair on its body, which feeds its young on milk.

Marsupial One of a group of mammals whose young are born early and complete their development in their mother's pouch.

Metamorphosis When a young animal takes on the bodyform of an adult.

Midwest Part of the central US south of the Great Lakes and around the upper watershed of the Mississippi River.

Migration A seasonal journey undertaken to find better weather, food or a mate, or to reach a favourable site for raising offspring.

Mollusc An invertebrate group including snails, squid and clams. Many molluscs have a chalky shell; all have a large muscular foot, which may be divided into tentacles.

Monotreme One of a small group of egg-laying mammals.

Mutation A variation in the genetic code. Mutations occur naturally, and may be harmful, beneficial or have no effect at all.

Natural selection The process by which organisms that are poorly adapted to their surroundings are weeded out. Only the most suitable to breed pass on their genes to the next generation. Over time, natural selection helps to bring about evolution.

Organ A part of an animal's body with a specific function, e.g. the heart.

Organism A living thing, e.g. a plant, animal or fungus.

Oviparous Describing an egg-laying animal.

Oviviparous Describing an animal that incubates its eggs inside its body. The young develop in the egg and hatch out inside the female before being born.

Pacific North-west A mountainous, rainy coastal region of North America that includes northern California, Oregon, Washington and British Columbia.

Pampas A grassland that grows in temperate regions of South America.

Parasite An animal that lives on or inside another animal, feeding on its food or flesh.

Parthenogenesis Asexual reproduction in which all the members of a species are female and do not need to mate to produce young.

Permafrost The permanently frozen ground beneath the topsoil in cold biomes.

Photosynthesis The process by which plants turn carbon dioxide and water into glucose, using the energy in sunlight.

Phylum The second largest taxonomic division after kingdom.

Pinniped An aquatic carnivorous mammal with limbs modified as flippers. Seals, sea lions and walruses are pinnipeds.

Placenta A blood-rich organ that develops within the womb of a pregnant female mammal to nourish the unborn young.

Plankton Microscopic plants (phytoplankton) and animals (zooplankton) that float near the surface of oceans and lakes, and which provide food for many larger animals.

Green anole

Grizzly bear

Plantigrade When an animal walks on the soles of its feet. Digitigrade animals such as cats walk on the flats of their fingers and toes; ungulagrades such as hoofed animals walk on the tips of their toes.

Population The number of individuals in a species or in a geographically distinct group.

Prairie A grassland in North America.

Protein A complex chemical made up of chains of smaller units.

Protist A single-celled organism.

Reptile One of a group of scaly-skinned vertebrate animals, most of which breed by laying eggs. Reptiles include lizards, snakes, crocodiles, turtles and tuataras.

Retina The light-sensitive layer at the back of the eye.

Rodent One of a group of mammals with long front teeth called incisors. Rodents include rats and mice.

Savannah A grassland or open woodland.

Scavenger An animal that feeds on decaying organic matter.

Sexual reproduction Reproduction that requires members of the opposite sex to mate with each other.

Species A particular kind of organism. Members of a species can interbreed to produce more of the same kind.

Spinal cord The main nerve in the body of vertebrates, which runs inside the backbone.

Steppe A grassland in eastern Europe or Asia.

Symbiosis A mutually beneficial relationship between two different types of organism.

Taxonomy The classification of organisms.

Territory An area that an animal uses for feeding or breeding.

Tundra Treeless lowlands of the far north.

Venom A cocktail of poisons made by a variety of animals to defend themselves.

Vertebrate An animal with a backbone.

Viviparous Describing an animal that gives birth to its young.

INDEX

PICTURE ACKNOWLEDGEMENTS
The publisher would like to thank the following for granting permission to use their photographs in this book. Key: l=left, r=right, t=top, m=middle, b=bottom.
NHPA: 12bl, 19b, 20tr, 20b, 21b, 22t, 22b, 23tl, 23tm, 24t, 24b, 25t, 27t, 27br, 30t, 30bl, 30br, 31t, 31b, 32t, 34t, 34b, 35tl, 36l, 37b, 38t, 38b, 39tl, 39tr, 40t, 41t, 41b, 43tl, 43tm, 43tr, 43bm, 43br, 62b.
Tim Ellerby: 39b, 41m.

Illustration credits as follows:
Jim Channell: 56–7, 160–1, 168–73, 207—11, 222–3, 234–7, 239b, 240–1, 246t.
Julius Csotonyi: 242–4.
Anthony Duke: all maps.
John Francis: 102t, 103b, 116b, 117, 120–1, 125b, 131t, 159t, 212, 213t, 214–15, 220t.
Stuart Jackson-Carter: 15t, 15b, 44–61 (habitats), 66–9, 78–81, 84–5, 90–1, 100–1, 102b, 103t, 108–11, 116t, 136–7, 140–1, 144–9, 154–5, 158, 159b, 174–5, 202, 206, 224t, 225t, 226b, 227b, 228–9, 232–3, 238, 239t, 245, 246b, 247.
Paul Jones: 82–3, 86–9, 104–7, 112–13, 150–1, 156–7, 162–3, 166–7, 198–9, 224b, 225b, 226t, 227t.
Martin Knowelden: 94–9, 114–15, 118–19, 122, 123t, 124, 125t, 126–7, 132t, 138–9.
Stephen Lings: 92–3, 180–95, 200–1, 203–5.
Richard Orr: 142–3, 152–3, 176–9, 213b, 216–19, 230–1.
Mike Saunders: 123b, 128–9, 131b, 132b, 133–5.
Sarah Smith: 164–5, 196–7.
Ildikó Szegszárdy: 220b, 221.